Opening up
Exodus

DAVID C. SEARLE

DayOne

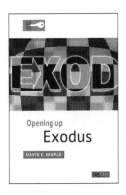

Opening up
Exodus

DAVID C. SEARLE

A quite excellent book! David Searle has provided rich theological insights, alongside detailed contextual research. When necessary, his exegesis of the text is specific, underlining the importance of the text's tenses. The rigorous explanation and application of God's truth for God's Church in all the chapters, is delivered in a very accessible style. He is a gifted wordsmith and thus, his illustrations, quotations and biographical references are stimulating and stirring. This resource, with its teasing and testing study and discussion questions, will be very useful for many preachers, students and home groups. Highly recommended!

Martin Allan, MA, BD MTh, former chairman of the Crieff Fellowship

David Searle has done it again! That is, he has produced a resource for the church that is both learned and insightful, clear and accessible. Ministers and members alike—on their own or in groups—will find it a wonderful companion for their exploration of the life and work of Moses, as recorded in Exodus.

Dr Martin Fair

One of the most affirming things for any new Christian is coming to understand that the Christian faith has a hinterland in Old Testament scripture. In *Opening Up Exodus*, David takes all of us deeper into that understanding, offering profound teaching combined with helpful application and personal insight, drawn from decades of the study of the Scriptures. Warmly recommended!

Jim Turrent, Lead Pastor, Central Baptist, Dundee

In *Opening Up Exodus*, David Searle has provided the reader with a thorough exposition of the Biblical text with helpful questions for further reading and reflection. It is warmly recommended, both for individual study as well as for small groups.

Dr Brian R Talbot, Minister, Broughty Ferry Baptist Church, Dundee.

I am delighted to recommend this book by David Searle, with its most instructive study of the life of Moses in Exodus. The background to each passage is explained simply and clearly, disguising the enormous amount of preparatory work on the text and in the commentaries which made it possible. Often, knowing that background will help our understanding of the passage in a new way. The book is also deeply challenging at a personal level. Any who think an Old Testament book will not be relevant for today need to think again. Increasingly we see what God is like and are called to follow in the footsteps of his Son, our Saviour. David brings decades of reading and study, as well as a wisdom honed by years of pastoral experience. I commend it to everyone who wants to 'go deeper' into God's Word.

Professor A.T.B McGowan, Founder and First Principal of the Highland Theological College, Presently President of Rutherford Centre for Reformed Theology, Scotland

David Searle takes us to Moses, quite possibly the greatest human being who ever lived, but never fails to lead us on to the greater Moses, Jesus Christ, in whom our humanity itself finds its fulfilment. Those who are familiar with the author will immediately recognize his scholar's mind and pastor's heart. Those who are encountering this master teacher for the first time, are in for a treat!

Christoph Ebbinghaus, Minister of Hamilton Road Presbyterian Church, N. Ireland

In *Opening Up Exodus*, David Searle's warm, conversational and insightful style quickly draws the reader into Moses' life. The wealth of anecdotal, illustrative material, drawn from a lifetime of experience and study, helps apply the text to everyday life. With the prophetic insight of a pastor and preacher, David encourages and challenges the reader to draw closer to God in their own Christian walk and think through both simple and complex theological truths. The 'For further study' sections help the reader do this within the wider sweep of scripture and the 'To think about and discuss' questions are ideal for both personal and group reflection.

Keith Field, lay preacher and Oversight Team member at Cranleigh Baptist Church, Surrey, with responsibility for Small Groups, Worship, and Safeguarding. Retired teacher of Religious Education.

Can anything new be written about Moses? David Searle manages it by a unique blend of scholarly, but easily read, elucidation of the text to bring imaginative insights into the events that shaped a great leader and lead to perceptive links with our own times which challenge our lack-lustre discipleship. Who could be better equipped to provide such insights than David Searle, a man who has given inspiring and innovative leadership throughout his life. A book to be studied individually, or in a group context, by all who want to know better The Bible and the God of The Bible.

Ann Ballentine

One of David Searle's primary gifts to the church is his ability in taking the 'then and there' to the 'here and now', so that we can learn what God is saying to us in his Word today. In *Opening Up Exodus*, he does just that in a clear and concise exposition of the story of Moses in the book of Exodus. It is classic Searle. Two things stand out. Firstly, while it is popular today to seek to find the gospel in the Old Testament, instead here, the book of Exodus is seen to be the gospel, as the great themes of God's sovereignty, providence and redemptive intent which find their fulfilment in the coming of Jesus, are unveiled at the heart of the story of Moses. Secondly, this book is not by a writer who preaches, but rather a preacher who writes out of years of extensive reading and decades of pastoral experience. In an easy, flowing style, the author draws on these, using quotations and illustrations that add colour and earth his exposition in the lives of his reader. This is a gem.

Dr Trevor W. J. Morrow, Former Moderator of the Presbyterian Church in Ireland and Minister Emeritus of Lucan Presbyterian Church.

Copyright © 2023 by DayOne Publications
First published in Great Britain in 2023

British Library Cataloguing in Publication Data

A record for this book is available from the British Library

ISBN: 978-1-84625-744-5

Printed by 4edge Limited

DayOne, Ryelands Road, Leominster, HR6 8NZ
Email: sales@dayone.co.uk
Website: www.dayone.co.uk

For Joy and Edna, both of whom have
faithfully 'laboured side by side with
me in the gospel', though in very
different roles.

List of Bible abbreviations

THE OLD TESTAMENT		1 Chr.	1 Chronicles	Ezek.	Ezekiel
Gen.	Genesis	2 Chr.	2 Chronicles	Dan.	Daniel
Exod.	Exodus	Ezra	Ezra	Hosea	Hosea
Lev.	Leviticus	Neh.	Nehemiah	Joel	Joel
Num.	Numbers	Esth.	Esther	Amos	Amos
Deut.	Deuteronomy	Job	Job	Obad.	Obadiah
Josh.	Joshua	Ps.	Psalms	Jonah	Jonah
Judg.	Judges	Prov.	Proverbs	Micah	Micah
Ruth	Ruth	Eccles.	Ecclesiastes	Nahum	Nahum
1 Sam.	1 Samuel	S.of S.	Song of	Hab.	Habakkuk
2 Sam.	2 Samuel		Solomon	Zeph.	Zephaniah
1 Kings	1 Kings	Isa.	Isaiah	Hag.	Haggai
2 Kings	2 Kings	Jer.	Jeremiah	Zech.	Zechariah
		Lam.	Lamentations	Mal.	Malachi

THE NEW TESTAMENT		Eph.	Ephesians	James	James
Matt.	Matthew	Phil.	Philippians	1 Peter	1 Peter
Mark	Mark	Col.	Colossians	2 Peter	2 Peter
Luke	Luke	1 Thes.	1 Thessalonians	1 John	1 John
John	John	2 Thes.	2 Thessalonians	2 John	2 John
Acts	Acts	1 Tim.	1 Timothy	3 John	3 John
Rom.	Romans	2 Tim.	2 Timothy	Jude	Jude
1 Cor.	1 Corinthians	Titus	Titus	Rev.	Revelation
2 Cor.	2 Corinthians	Philem.	Philemon		
Gal.	Galatians	Heb.	Hebrews		

Contents

Lord, how can man preach thy eternal word?
He is a brittle crazy glass;
Yet in thy temple thou dost him afford
This glorious and transcendent place,
To be a window, through thy grace.

George Herbert,
from 'The Windows'[1]

Moses: Messenger and Mediator

Guidance from Exodus in living the Christian Life

Foreword

Ever since the publication of *Joseph: His Arms Were Made Strong*,[1] I had felt that a sequel on Moses ought to be written. My desire to undertake this was not least because the book of Exodus has for decades been near the top of my favourite Old Testament books. As well as the story of Moses being one of the Bible's richest accounts of God's dealings with someone who, like Elijah, had 'a nature like ours' (James 5:17)—or, as the King James translation has it, 'a man subject to like passions as we are'—he was nonetheless chosen to be God's instrument, not only to deliver his enslaved people, but also to be the mediator of the Old Covenant.

In the two Appendices, which form the conclusion to this book, I have attempted to show something of the significance of the Mosaic Covenant, delivered three millennia ago, for our understanding of the New Covenant inaugurated by Jesus Christ and sealed in his blood. For, the book of Exodus undoubtedly has a dynamic relevance and importance for the church today. My prayer is that readers will find the contemporary applications I have sought to bring from this inspired book have much to teach us, no matter to which Christian denomination of the church of God we belong.

I want to express my belated appreciation to my friend

of nearly sixty years, the late Ian Barter, who checked for me the first ten chapters of this book. Ian never told me that he was suffering from a terminal illness and, when I asked for his help, he simply said he would be absolutely delighted to check the scripts; he had not expected that at the age of eighty-six there was still something he could do for the Lord. It was his wife, Gillian, who finally let me know he was no longer able to continue, but that he had been so pleased he had been able to check those ten chapters over the previous ten weeks. He went to be with the Lord just three weeks later.

I had come to know Joy Alexander while ministering in Hamilton Road Presbyterian Church in Bangor, Northern Ireland. Joy willingly took up the baton and with immense proficiency and precision completed the task that Ian had begun. Joy's competence in English grammar is quite formidable! I am grateful to both of these dear friends for their patience and forbearance with me, as there was no shortage of typos that needed to be identified and corrected.

I should also add my thanks to my former three congregations who first heard the book of *Exodus* and the story of Moses being expounded: Newhills Parish Church near Aberdeen, Larbert Old Church in Stirlingshire, and Hamilton Road Church in Northern Ireland. It has been on the foundations of those expositions that the final form of this book has been built.

Finally, last but by no means least, my thanks must go to Lorna, my longsuffering wife of sixty-two years. Throughout the many decades of my ministry, she has always been my severest critic, my closest soulmate and my greatest encourager. She has ever put her own interests and needs second to my labours in the gospel, fully aware that God and his Son's Kingdom had to come first. But she would never suggest that she had been neglected—only that she had always sought to be my willing partner in the Lord's service.

I must acknowledge the courteous and efficient help of Helen Clark, my editor, and all the staff at Day One who have published this book. I am indebted to them.

David Searle

Stonefall Lodge, Grange, Errol, 2023

Other books by David C. Searle:

Be Strong in the Lord (1995)

And then there were nine—The Ten Commandments (2000)

Commentary on Psalms Calvin abridged (2009)

Joseph: His Arms Were Made Strong (2012)

The Way to True Peace and Rest (Sermons on Isaiah 38 by Robert Bruce [trans & ed.]) (2017)

Preaching without Fear or Favour (28 sermons on Hebrew 11 by Robert Bruce [trans & ed.]) (2018)

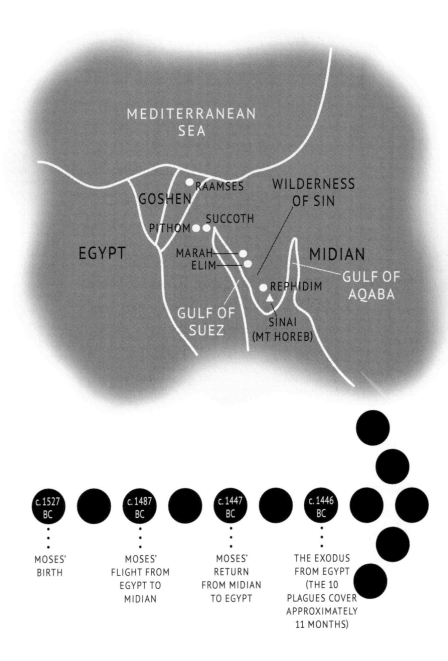

Overview

At times, our Bibles can be like the two parables Jesus told regarding the Kingdom of God: The Hidden Treasure and The Pearl of Great Value (Matthew 13:44–46). As a child, after reading the book, *Treasure Island* (R.L. Stevenson), I loved to think of someone on a deserted island coming across an abandoned chest full of precious things! After over sixty years in the Christian ministry, I have never stopped opening that metaphorical treasure chest and finding there, jewel after jewel that reveal the divine riches. Researching the Book of Exodus in general, and the life of Moses in particular, has been part of that experience. The Word has admonished, rebuked, chastened, instructed, guided, enlightened, and delighted me. To change the figure of speech, I have been like someone on the banks of a great lake, but as yet have done no more than wade in up to my ankles; I have not yet plunged very far into its deep warm, healing waters.

Before mentioning a few of the salient themes unfolded in these pages, note carefully that we must never neglect the vital part that Exodus has in that ongoing, gradual self-revelation of God to his people. We often miss the clue given to us by Luke when he records that, on the Mount of Transfiguration, the conversation

Jesus had with Moses and Elijah, 'who appeared in glory', was about 'the *exodus* (ESV 'departure') which he was shortly to accomplish at Jerusalem' (9:31). There is much we could meditate on from that single jewel in Scripture's treasure chest!

The first obvious theme is God's choice, preparation and constantly developing relationship with Moses: the baby's preservation in a flimsy basket of woven reeds; his education 'in all the wisdom of the Egyptians' (Acts 7:22); his vain attempt to do God's work in his own way; his forty years caring for sheep; his thorough knowledge of the Sinai wilderness of clay; the meaning of the divine name, 'yhwh' (known by the patriarchs but not fully understood, Exodus 3:13–15); his training in his youth which enabled him to record the ceremonial worship and the minute details of the Tent of Meeting;[1] his humility in accepting the wise counsel of Jethro; his realization of the necessity and power of prayer (Exodus 17:9–13), and perhaps most important of all his passionate zeal and jealousy for God's glory.

Another of the important themes of the history of Moses is the inexplicable love of God for the pestilent children of Israel.[2] As the account of their redemption from slavery progresses and their witnessing of miracle after miracle, still they complain, grumble, rebel and ultimately turn to idolatry, mimicking the pagan wickedness of the surrounding nations. Their ingratitude and forgetfulness of the divine deliverances and provisions for them would be completely unbelievable—if, that is, we did not know our own wayward hearts and infidelities. Our sympathies go to their leader and pastor, whose own brother virtually betrayed him while he was closeted with God on Sinai.[3] Of course, what emerges from these trials is Moses' utter dependence on God (Exodus 32:12–16).

The final great theme that cannot be omitted from this brief introduction is the unfolding revelation of salvation, against the awesome backdrop of the burning holiness of the righteous God. In the two Appendices, added to this book, I have endeavoured (inadequately, I know) to show the relevance of this for New Testament believers. We are wrong to consign to the 'out of date' section of our personal libraries the accounts of the ceremonial ritual given in Exodus (and in far greater detail in the rest of the Pentateuch). This came home to me afresh as I studied Psalm 73, where the writer confessed that he struggled with ethical daily issues which challenged his faith on every side. It was only when he 'went into the sanctuary of God' (v. 17) that he found the answers he was looking for. I think we can take it as 'a given' that the sanctuary would have been where the Scriptures were kept and, at that stage in the nation's history, it would have been mainly to the Books of Moses he would have turned—there were no New

Testament Scriptures then! But there, he uncovered the secrets and mysteries of the divine judgements and infinite grace.

If readers derive only a quarter of the pleasure and edification from this book that has been my experience, then my labour will not have been in vain.

1 The Israelites oppressed

Exodus 1

As we look out across our turbulent world, beset as it is by so many troubles—bitter hostilities, economic woes, recurrent pandemics and, above all, constantly increasing persecution of Christians—we may wonder where it is all leading. What kind of future will there be for our children and grandchildren? This first chapter of Exodus reminds us that God is always in complete control. He knows the end from the beginning. In his perfect time, all will be made plain.

A question that we often hear is, 'What has the Book of Exodus got to do with me, living as I am in the 21st century?' Or maybe the question is, 'Why ever did God allow his people to suffer so much, as this chapter says they did?' Of course, that leads on to another more relevant question for us today: 'Why does God permit some people to meet with tragedy in their lives?' Because, after all, do we not read in the newspapers of undeserved sorrow blighting the lives of families? A young mother's untimely death, leaving behind four children and a broken-hearted husband, or an innocent little girl being struck down with some incurable illness.

We watch the news bulletins with towns and cities being torn apart, or famine bringing desolation to whole tribes, and we see the harrowing clips of starving children and the dead carcasses of cattle lying on the sun-baked ground. The camera zooms in to a sick child lying limp in its mother's arms, with the flies crawling round its listless eyes. No wonder we ask, 'Why this sorrow and heartache in so many places across this benighted world? Why does God allow it to happen?'

> We find that the book of Exodus opens with the story of a nation being oppressed, persecuted and even subjected to attempted genocide.

So, returning to the first question, 'What has the Book of Exodus got to do with me?', we find that the book of Exodus opens with the story of a nation being oppressed, persecuted and even subjected to attempted genocide. For, the Pharaoh's aims were to annihilate this race of tinkers who were growing fast and whose prosperity seemed to be posing a threat to the stability of his throne. History tells us that a previous slave race, the Hyksos, had overthrown an earlier dynasty and had ruled a large part of Egypt for many decades.[1] Perhaps this had something to do with Pharaoh's concern over the growth in numbers of the Hebrews.

As we study this book of Exodus, we will realize something of great importance: we are dealing with the story of the Church of God. However contemptible these people were, however perverse, however wayward, they were nonetheless the Church. Not because they had chosen to be believers in the one God, but because God had chosen them. As we go through this book, we may well say, 'How odd of God to choose the Jews!' But perhaps we will also say, 'How strange that God should set his love on me.'

> Amazing love! How can it be,
>
> that Thou, my God, shouldst die for me?
>
> Charles Wesley (1707–1788)

A complacent church

At the end of the book of Genesis, we learn that old Jacob had been at last reunited with Joseph—the son he had assumed to be dead for more than twenty years. But Joseph, sold as a slave by his jealous and wicked brothers, had become Viceroy of Egypt and, during the seven years of famine, brought his entire family—seventy persons all together, comprising his eleven brothers with their wives and children—to live in the most fertile area of Egypt, the land of Goshen, which was situated along the Nile delta and so was well irrigated.

The little clan of seventy had settled down with their herds and flocks, and after the comparative hardship of living as nomads in Canaan, must have found life in this rich area of Egypt very pleasant indeed. And so, the years passed. Joseph's nephews and nieces married and had families, who in turn grew up and married and had families. The once small clan steadily increased. We are told the day came when Joseph and his brothers had all died, and none remained of the original generation that had travelled down from Canaan during the famine. But the clan kept growing and prospering. They had more than just herds now. Some were gardeners; some went into business and bought and sold cloth and clothing; others farmed. So, they became rich and numerous, and everywhere you might go in Goshen, you would meet members of the Israel clan.

We can offer a few reasons why they increased so rapidly. One was that they were of a unique stock. In choosing their forefather Abraham, God's choice had been of a man of great strength, of high intelligence and indomitable spirit. So, although the sophisticated and cultured Egyptians looked down their noses at these tinker people with their cows and goats and sheep, these people were in fact a highly intelligent, and vigorous people.

Another reason why they grew and prospered was they had had a privileged place in Egyptian society, given to them by the Pharaoh in gratitude for Joseph's service. All Egyptian peasants had to engage in forced labour for the Pharaoh, six months of every year. The Egyptian peasant sowed his crops in November when Nile flooded and irrigated his fields; he then reaped the harvest in April; from May through to October, he slaved under the taskmaster's lash, building pyramids and temples and cities for the mighty sovereigns of Egypt. But the Israelites so far had escaped that servitude. Life had been easy, so they had flourished.

Yet another reason why they prospered so much was that God's hand was on them. God had promised to Jacob, on his way down to Egypt to meet Joseph, that in Egypt his family would become a great nation (Genesis 46:2–4). And so, God was blessing the Israelite clan.

There is a further point we have to notice that is implicit in this first chapter of Exodus. It has been a feature of this nation for thousands of years; indeed, it is a phenomenon of Israel. It is clear from the chapter that these descendants of Abraham did not lose their own distinctive identity. They remained obviously and predominantly Israelites. They could have intermarried with the Egyptians, for they were not the only people living in this area of Goshen—they had Egyptian neighbours. We would have expected a blending of nationalities until, gradually over a hundred years or more, the Israelites would have become indistinguishable from others. But that never happened. It has never happened since then either. Thus, here in Exodus 1, they stood out as a people apart, separate, with their own customs, their own religion, their own identity.

However, something else is also evident. While they kept their own identity, they lost the vision God had given to Abraham, renewed both to Isaac and Jacob. We read about it in Hebrews 11. They had been called to be a pilgrim people, to be strangers on the earth, aliens, foreigners, not belonging to this world, but distinct and apart, because they were looking for another land, another city, 'whose designer and builder is God' (Hebrews 11:9–10, 22–26). But that promise they had lost. They had settled down and, though keeping their special identity, they lost the vision God had given them.

Now, their story is the story of the Church of God. These things are recorded for our instruction. God has called his Church to be a special, distinctive people. We are to be in the world, but not of the world. We are to be apart because we belong to God. God has chosen his Church to be a light in the world, to be salt in society. And we can only be light and salt if we, like the Israelites in Egypt, remain distinct and separate. That is clear. We must be different in all sorts of ways. It might be a very good exercise for each one of us to ask ourselves, 'How ought my home and family be different from my neighbours, who do not profess to be Christians?' How different in our attitudes, our lifestyle, our language, our thinking—for that is what we are called to be?

However, the danger is that we should succeed in being different, keeping ourselves 'separate' in a manner of speaking, and yet become complacent, comfortable, settled. It is all too possible for us to lose the vision God has given to his people—that we are strangers in this world, aliens—and to forget that we do not belong here at all, and disregard that our citizenship is in heaven.

> The danger is that we should succeed in being different and yet become complacent, comfortable, settled.

It is all a question really of our affections. You see, it is comparatively easy to remain different. Hindus, Sikhs and Muslims do that. Go to any European city or town and immediately you will recognize the Hindu, Sikh or Muslim by their distinctive dress or hairstyle. In our own country, a good number of the older Muslim and Hindi women have never even learned English, although they have lived among us for decades. Anyone can remain apart and keep themselves distinctive in the way that God asks followers of Christ to do. Nevertheless, what is far more difficult is not to fall in love with this world but stay in love with our Lord. That is the hard thing. We cannot serve God and mammon.

This was exactly where those Israelites living in Egypt began to slip. They fell in love with this material world. They lost the vision, that they were called to be pilgrims, travellers, just passing through. And they gave their hearts to their gardens, their houses, their fields, their bank balances. They remained a distinctive church—the people of God. But they became a complacent people of God—a complacent church.

A persecuted church

It is the old story. Because God does not react immediately, we think we are getting away with our wrong attitudes, and he does not mind that we have lost our love for him. We think he is not bothering too much as long as we maintain our distinctiveness. And I have no doubt that the Israelites thought like that. Because they were prospering, they assumed all was well. They may even have regularly thanked God on the Sabbath day for his many blessings.

But God was not going to let his Church drown in a sea of materialism and affluence. He knew what he would do. And so, in verse 8 we read, 'Now there arose a new king over Egypt, who did not know Joseph.' Elsewhere in the Bible, in Acts 7:18, it says, 'there arose over Egypt another king', using a word meaning 'another of a different dynasty'—'this Pharaoh could well have been one of the early kings of Dynasty XIX'.[2] That small scrap of information is of great interest to the scholars but we should simply notice that a dynasty favourable to the Israelites had been overthrown, and a new dynasty of Pharaohs had established itself—and this new dynasty knew nothing about the background of this tribe of people living in Goshen with special privileges.

It is possible that the new dynasty was from a minority group within Egypt, in which case the Pharaoh would have been afraid that if there was an attempted coup to overthrow him, the Israelite clan would ally itself with the faction that rebelled against him. Perhaps he wanted to suppress the Hebrews because they occupied the ground of the Nile Delta, and the Delta held the key to a naval attack on Egypt; should such a sea-assault occur, the Israelites could well be in a position to side with the potential attacker.

Whether or not that influenced the new dynasty, it seems that the Israelites lost their privileged position in Egypt and began to be treated in the same way as the Egyptian peasants, obliged to undertake slave labour six months in the year. The implication in verse 12 tells us the Israelites did not lose heart or succumb to despair, the way the Egyptian peasants did. They did not become resigned to their fate, but rather, with that indomitable spirit that faces hardship refusing to bow their spirits to slavery, they thrived even more. The sacred record states that, 'The Egyptians were in dread of the people.' That phrase could also be translated: 'They came to loathe the people.' However harshly they were treated, they refused to be broken. They were tough, resilient, determined.

> God is the most consummate expert when it comes to the efficiency of his working.

Why, then, did God allow these decades of suffering and hardship? God is the most consummate expert when it comes to the efficiency of his working. We can only see a small part of his plan, but the little we can see amazes us.

Firstly, it was not yet time for these people to return to Canaan. God was waiting to give the Canaanites every just opportunity to repent.[3] When Joshua led the people back a generation later, they were to bring judgement on the Canaanites. But first, in justice and righteousness, these people must be warned and warned and warned before God would lift his hand against them.

Secondly, the Israelites had to reap what their forefathers had sown. Ten of Jacob's sons had acted wickedly and we can never escape the consequences of persistent sin. Even when our sins are forgiven, the effects of our sin can live on to the third and fourth generation. That these people were in Goshen at all was the fruit of sin. It was a bitter fruit they now had to eat.

Thirdly, God was also training them and disciplining them. He did not want them to become complacent and so earthly minded they would be of no use to him. Therefore, it pleased the Lord to impose upon them the six months' forced labour every year. In this way, he was stirring them up and reminding them constantly that Goshen was not their home. Joseph had told them before he died that, one day, God would take them back to Canaan and had instructed them to take his remains with them when God at last fulfilled his promise (Genesis 50:25). Indeed, they knew that Joseph's bones were preserved and with them. Had they forgotten all about that? Now God was reminding them.

Persecution of the Church always has been used by God to purify and refine his people. I wonder if many of us do not recognize sufficiently the signs of the times all around us. I know that there are many causes of the troubles in our land and beyond. Some of us do recognize that, through the turmoil in our society, we are reaping the fruits of what has been sown in an earlier generation. The Christian faith is increasingly under attack. I do not doubt that there is an element of the demonic in the increasing discrimination against the

Christian church. And is this not at least one element in this steadily increasing pressure? God is saying, 'To your knees! Not just to cry out for the anti-Christian tide to turn, but to seek my face, hear my voice and listen to what I am saying to you!'

Nevertheless, I also wonder just how much listening and learning some of us have done. I suspect that some in our churches are as heedless and self-righteous and complacent as ever. What do you think? Have we seen God's hand and heard his voice, in this subtle, increasing discrimination against believers? When the Church is persecuted, God has not lost control. He is still sovereign and he still holds the reins of history in his hands. That is true in our land today as it was true in Egypt over 3000 years ago.

A martyr church

The little vignette about the two midwives is interesting, because it tells us several things. It tells us, for example, that there were other small ethnic groups in Egypt as well as the Israelites. Note carefully that these two midwives are called 'Hebrew midwives' (1:15), and in the early books of the Bible, the word, 'Hebrew', does not necessarily refer to the Israelites. It refers to other Semitic nomads as well. At this stage in biblical history, it is a general term. Later on, the other Semitic groups become distinguished and the term, 'Hebrew', is used only for the Israelites. But, at this stage, it is much wider in meaning. When we are told in verse 21 that the two midwives were given families, literally, 'became houses', it could well mean that they were incorporated into the Israelite nation and accepted as members of Israel, because of their kindness to the Jacob clan.

What was their kindness, for which God showed them kindness in return? It was that they refused to carry out Pharaoh's order to kill the male children the moment they were born. They 'feared God'. And so, God was kind to the midwives. It was an appalling order, anyway. Furthermore, their reaction to Pharaoh's instructions and God's clear approval of their reaction says something to us about abortion. All Pharaoh was asking them to do was to abort, but at the last possible moment, and then to claim the children were stillborn. It would only have needed a few seconds' pressure on the throats of the newly born baby boys.

If that sounds shocking, it is most probably a less painful and dangerous process than modern abortion. And if we are shocked that Pharaoh should have suggested such a scheme, let us remember that several million babies have been incinerated in the hospitals of our land during the past fifty years. Indeed, abortion is so easy in our land that women travel from elsewhere in Europe to have it done here. And, although Parliament recently has made slight amendments to the abortion laws, we all know that, for various reasons, a liberally minded doctor can ignore those guidelines—indeed it is common knowledge that thousands of times every month they are ignored. So, if the truth were known, abortion has simply become another form of birth control.

Not to be defeated by the midwives' failure to abort the birth of baby boys, Pharaoh issued his infamous edict that any Egyptian could throw into the Nile an Israelite baby boy who was newly born. Now we have to understand this in an Egyptian context. The Nile was worshipped as a god. We will think about that when we come to the ten plagues. To the Egyptian mind, the Nile was the giver of life, controlled and presided over by the Pharaoh. They had never seen the blue mountains from which the Nile flowed, and from which it had its source. Neither had they seen, nor did they know, the true source of life and goodness and bounty. And so, with the classical blindness of the human heart, they worshipped the creation, rather than the Creator. Thus, this appalling command had a religious intention and motive in that these baby Israelite boys were being offered as sacrifices to the god of the Nile. It was blatant genocide, but with a religious excuse.

I have no doubt that various brutal dictators have similarly rationalized their genocidal acts. A contemporary example would be the Islamic fundamentalists known as ISIS. They have seen their wholesale slaughter as purging their territory of infidels. By executing or shooting or blasting them with tank shells, they have seen themselves as promoting purity of faith in their caliphate. Nor can we forget that Hitler's gas chambers and mass genocide of the Jews were also perpetrated in the name of a high ideal—his Aryan race and its purity. And the genocide during the Spanish inquisition was the same: purify the church and serve God by putting to death all those who have rebelled against the teaching of the mother church. Therefore, the scenario in Exodus 1 was no unique situation. It was a brutality as old as man and one that continues to this day.

This brings us back to Pharaoh's genocidal order. How different today are men's hearts from his, and from the hearts of the people of Egypt? What are our attitudes when

> How different today are men's hearts from Pharaoh's, and from the hearts of the people of Egypt?

we hear of murderous fanatics being 'taken down' by drones, operated several thousand miles away by some technician? I suspect that, if the real truth were known and our motives and prejudices were laid out before the all-knowing scrutiny of Almighty God, we would see there is not such a big difference as we might at first believe—even in the hearts of those who call themselves Christians.

And so, the Old Testament Church of God faced extinction. For, Pharaoh's policy was to annihilate this alien race, to stop them growing and controlling more and more of the economy and commerce and wealth of the land. He wanted to rid himself of them forever. But they were God's people. Contemptible and unattractive as they may have been, God planned to use them to give his commandments to the world; to show his holiness, glory and power; then, in the fulness of time, through them to give his Son. And that, actually, was precisely why Satan put it into Pharaoh's heart to give this order that Egyptians would serve the best interests of their land and their religion by throwing all new-born Israelite boys to the god of the Nile.

The Church of God is still under attack from Satan. Make no mistake about that. It is a struggle to the death. By complacency, by persecution, by death—in these and in countless other ways—the assault is on. It came at last to be focused on a carpenter from Nazareth, in whom Satan recognized the greatest threat ever posed to his power over the hearts and lives of men and women. Therefore, he had him betrayed and crucified. But from his death flowed life and grace and love. And so, Satan was defeated as he always must ultimately be.

Do we sometimes wonder what God is doing in our

lives? Do some of us at times wonder if we have made some awful mistake, or sinned some shameful sin, and now God is visiting us in his anger? Are we sometimes afraid of that? Learn from this chapter that there is, in our lives, a conflict, just as there is in this world. But, contrary to all appearances, God remains in full control.

> For nothing falls unknown to him,
> or care or joy or sorrow;
> and he whose mercy ruled the past
> will be our stay tomorrow.
>
> Ambrose N. Blatchford (1842–1924)

For further study ▶

FOR FURTHER STUDY

1. Read carefully again the Sermon on the Mount (Matthew 5–7) to explore further how followers of Christ ought to be seen to have a completely different culture from that which is practised by an unbelieving, largely atheistic or agnostic society.

2. Follow through the sad story of the constant backsliding of the people of God as recorded, for example, in Judges chapters 2, 3 and 4.

3. Search for passages in the Old Testament (OT) that could well reflect godly memories of Pharaoh's affliction of the people of Israel, e.g., as in Psalm 94:1–7. How should such memories of persecution of the Church of God in the Christian era shape our preaching and our praying?

4. To what extent is genocide inspired by religion exercised in the world today? It might be worthwhile to study the Bishop of Truro's report of persecution of Christians, commissioned in 2019 by Jeremy Hunt when he was Foreign Secretary. (See website: Bishop of Truro's independent review of FCDO support for persecuted Christians.)

5. The midwives. Shiphrah and Puah were 'economical with the truth', as we say. Yet God blessed them. Are there occasions when 'truth' ought to be withheld, as when Corrie Ten Boom concealed Jews from the Nazis — recounted in her book, *The Hiding Place*.[4]

TO THINK ABOUT AND DISCUSS

1. Read Genesis 15:12–16 where several important issues are set out there for us.

- Firstly, God knew beforehand that persecution would arise during Israel's years in Egypt. Reflect on the historical fact that God has often permitted his people to be unjustly afflicted, and that, as Tertullian wrote in the 2nd century: 'The blood of the martyrs has been the seed of the church,'[5] implying martyrdom has brought countless others to trust in Christ.

- Secondly, part of God's purposes was that the godless, cruel Egyptian regime would be judged in a way that would become widely known across the Middle East (e.g., Josh. 2:8–11). Reflect on the patience of God in giving generations of evil-doers multiple opportunities to turn to him in repentance (Rom. 1:28–32).
- Thirdly, because Canaanite society was infinitely corrupt, God's purpose was to use his people's ultimate return of the Promised Land to the patriarchs to bring judgement upon them. How faithful ought believers to be so that on the final day we will not be guilty of having failed to act as watchmen, warning of the coming judgement (Ezek. 33:1–7).

2. How ought believers to react to persecution in ways that will be glorifying to God and a testimony to Christ's saving grace?

3. God has called out his church to be 'a chosen race, a royal priesthood, a holy nation, a people for his own possession' (1 Peter 2:9). In what ways ought believers to be evidently distinctive so that we faithfully fulfil his purposes for us to shine as lights in a world of spiritual darkness?

2 Baby in a basket

Exodus 2:1–10

One of the great truths in our Bible which is too often neglected is the providence of God. We may give mental assent to divine providence, but, in the midst of life's trials and suffering, the Lord's control of every event may be forgotten and offer little or no substance to our thinking. The account of Moses' birth, preservation and upbringing ought to strengthen and direct our prayers as we look to God to work out his purposes for our lives and his glory.

Here is a riddle for you, a life full of startling contrasts. Many have said that he was unquestionably the greatest man who lived before Christ.

He was the child of a slave, but the son of a queen;

he was born in a hut, but he lived in a palace;

he inherited poverty, but enjoyed fabulous wealth;

he was a keeper of sheep, but he led a great army;

he was the meekest man on earth, but he was the mightiest
of warriors;

he lived in the desert, but was educated in a royal court;

he had the faith of a little child, but he had the finest
wisdom the world could offer;

he wandered in the wilderness, but he was brought up in
the city;

he endured the hardships of godliness, but was tempted by
the pleasure of sin;

he had a speech impediment, but he talked face to face
with God;

he carried a shepherd's staff, but had the power of God in
his hand;

he was an outlaw and fugitive, but was an ambassador of
heaven;

he was the giver of the Law, but also the mediator of grace;

he died alone on Mount Moab, but appeared with Christ on
Mount Tabor;

no one attended his funeral, but it was God who laid him to
rest.

No prizes for guessing who he was: his name was Moses, and it is the birth and childhood of this truly remarkable person that we read about in Exodus 2:1–10.

Moses' parents

When a mother holds her newborn baby in her arms, something happens almost immediately. The psychologists call it 'bonding'. A powerful human relationship, perhaps the most powerful of all human relationships, usually develops within a few minutes, and remains steadfast as long as those two persons are alive; indeed, even when one of them passes on, that deep relationship lives on. And so, as this woman took in her arms her third child, and nursed him and fed him, there took place the bonding between mother and son.

It would be foolish to deny it was a mother's love for her baby that was a key factor in her desire to preserve his life from Pharaoh's genocidal edict. Of course, his mother and father loved him; they loved him with all their hearts. They dreaded the prospect of an Egyptian discovering that another Israelite baby had been born, and seizing him and throwing him into the River Nile, as Pharaoh had commanded. But there were two other reasons, as well as parental love, which began to motivate Amram and Jochebed. Hebrews 11 and Acts 7 tell us. One was that he was a beautiful child. Three times we are told that (Exodus 2:2; Acts 7:20; Hebrews 11:23). Quite how to understand this, I am not sure. But since this couple already had a daughter, Miriam, and a son, Aaron, we are to appreciate that they were neither naive nor over-imaginative, thinking their little boy was the most wonderful, perfect, darling, delightful, little boy in the whole world! Most mothers think that!

No, we are to understand that there was something

quite different, quite unusual, quite unique, about this baby boy. In Acts 7:20, Stephen adds that this baby was 'beautiful in God's sight', and his parents grasped something of that within the first few days of his life. He was apparently not only exceptionally beautiful, but also exceptionally intelligent and well-formed. With this additional incentive that he was 'no ordinary child', his parents resolved even more to hide him and to preserve him from the fate of the baby boys all around them.

But there was a further reason why these parents were resolved to preserve their child from Pharaoh's evil edict. As well as a mother's love, and the parent's recognition that he was an exceptional child, there was also their faith. By faith Moses' parents hid him for three months after he was born, 'because they saw that the child was beautiful, and they were not afraid of the king's edict' (Hebrews 11:23). And their faith places these two parents in that great procession that marches through the verses of Hebrews 11, who trusted God, despised the world and, in obedience to God, looked heavenwards.

I imagine that most Israelite women who were pregnant stayed indoors for several months, to try and hide from everyone the fact that they were expecting a baby. And then, when the baby was born, if it was a boy, they would have attempted to hide him. But babies are not easily hidden. They cry when they are hungry—

some of them even scream their heads off—and in the flimsy shacks in which these people lived, it would have been almost impossible to conceal the presence of a little child. Perhaps there were even reprisals taken against parents who did attempt to hide their baby boys; perhaps they were beaten, or imprisoned, or executed. That may be implied when we are told in Hebrews 11 that Amram and Jochebed were not afraid to withstand the King's edict.

And so, we have from Moses' parents a shining example for every parent today, given to us in a vivid contrast: they acted towards their baby in faith, not in fear. I believe we are to understand their faith was strong, unalloyed and firm, so that neither parent was on tenterhooks all the time, hovering over the child in case he should suddenly start to cry. Their pulse rate remained normal; their home was relaxed, even though they guarded a precious, if dangerous, secret; their faces were calm. And the baby will have relaxed and cooed and smiled in his mother's arms.

> We have from Moses' parents a shining example for every parent today: they acted towards their baby in faith, not in fear.

This statement about Moses' parents hiding him in faith, without fear, has been adapted as the title of a series of sermons on the Christian home. The book was called *Bringing up children in faith, not fear.*[1] The theme of the book was that fear in parents' hearts makes them restrict their children, and causes them to build barriers around them, weighing them down with do's and don'ts and prohibitions—don't go there, don't do this, don't do that. Whereas, when both parents' hearts are full of faith, the home will be relaxed, and the child will grow up in a secure and happy environment.

That is not to say parents who are full of faith in God for their children, having a serene confidence that God has his loving hand firmly upon their children's lives, will not discipline, train and teach their children. It certainly does not mean being soft and indulgent, thinking the little darlings can do no wrong. That kind of attitude (and some parents have it) is not faith! It is folly—plain stupidity! But parents are to learn to distinguish between fear and faith. That is the challenge of this couple and their little boy. The challenge to all Christian parents is this: What is the prevailing emotion in your hearts as you cope with the pressures and demands of bringing up your children today? Are you motivated in all your attitudes towards your children by anxiety—fearing they will let the family down by behaving foolishly? Or are you motivated by faith because you believe you have given your children to God and they belong to him?

Pharaoh's daughter

Egyptian princesses had great power and enjoyed considerable privileges, so the Egyptologists tell us. They had their own households, servants, incomes and could act quite independently. My own view is that Amram and Jochebed knew that, and when Jochebed made the little basket out of papyrus, her bold and daring plan was deliberately to place her beautiful child where she knew Pharaoh's daughter went to bathe. I do not think there was a series of miraculous coincidences or that she placed her child among the reeds at the side of the river in sheer desperation, not knowing what to do next with him. I believe (and this is only my own view) she intended Pharaoh's daughter to find him, and that, although she was acting in faith, she was also using her imagination, skill and cleverness.

But saying that does not in any way take away from the hand of God in all that happened. Rather, it shows up Amram and Jochebed's faith even more clearly, for they acted with astounding boldness and vision—not in blind despair, wildly hoping for the best; they were not clutching at straws, as we say. Nor does faith ever preclude using the natural means which in divine providence are available to us. Therefore, while Miriam waited and from a safe distance watched the precious bundle lying in the frail basket at the water's edge among the reeds, her parents were at home crying out to God to work a miracle, save their child, and bring him under the protection of Pharaoh's own daughter.

As they prayed and held on to God in faith, the royal retinue swept down to the riverbank for the Princess to bathe, as was her custom. Her slave girls and ladies-in-waiting arrived at their accustomed place. Probably there were paving stones there, and steps down into the water. There, strategically placed among the reeds, the basket was floating with a lid protecting its contents from the heat of the sun and concealing what was inside. And so, curious as any one of us, the princess ordered the basket to be brought. When the lid was removed and the sunlight streamed on to the three-month-old baby—possibly the first sunlight that had ever shone into his eyes—he began to cry. The princess's heart was immediately touched, and she took into her arms this beautiful little boy to nurse and soothe him. Then, on cue, the little slave girl appeared, curtsied and offered to find a wet nurse, who would breast-feed the child. And Jochebed was brought, charged with caring for her own little boy and paid for doing so. If ever faith was rewarded, it was that mother's faith! What praise and thanksgiving, probably with tears of gratitude, ascended to God that night in their home!

Now I am sure we are to see two very distinct phases in this little boy's life. We are to see him first of all in the care of his own mother until the age of about four years, when children in those days were weaned. So Jochebed had four years to teach her son that he was an Israelite, a member of the slave people, and not an Egyptian. She had just four years to lay the foundation of his faith in God, the God of his father and mother, and their forefathers.

I wonder how many of our children would remain faithful to God all their days on the basis of our Christian nurture of them in their first four years. I understand some psychologists believe that children learn as much in their first four years as they learn from the age of four to fourteen. I suspect that many parents leave the Christian nurture of their children to some Sunday School teacher (it could well be helpful that they attend a Sunday School). But children will not learn about God in approximately thirty sessions of fifteen minutes each year. I have gathered evidence that many Sunday Schools are not particularly beneficial to children at all. The Christian faith can too easily be trivialized by incompetent teachers, who reduce the foundational doctrines to badly told stories. When children discover that Santa Claus is largely a fable, they unconsciously may assume that many of the other stories are fables as well, so that by the age of nine or ten they have already rejected the so-called 'teaching' they have been given.

May I just say that I am not discounting all Sunday

School teachers, for there are some whose godly, gracious characters leave an indelible impression upon children's lives. But I have observed that it is more the godly, loving character of the teacher than the actual lessons taught that has the greatest effect.

On the other hand, children are with their parents the majority of the time for those vital first four or five years. The task belongs to the parents and to no one else. It is their high calling and priceless privilege to teach them the truths and duties of the Christian faith and, by prayer, precept and example, to bring them up to be true disciples of the Lord. My guess is that most homes neglect terribly that God-given task and put in only a tiny fraction of the training and teaching that could be given. Moses was with his mother about four years.

> It is the parents' high calling and priceless privilege to teach their children the truths and duties of the Christian faith.

Yet, later in his life with all Egypt at his feet, he chose to suffer with a slave people, because he learned in those first four years to know he was one of the people of God. We must all think carefully about that!

The second distinct phase in this boy's life was his training in his foster mother's palace. The book of Acts tells us he was educated in all the wisdom of Egypt (Acts 7:22). He learned to write, to read, and to know the philosophy and thinking of his day; he learned other languages; he learned to handle a chariot and the military arts and strategies of Egypt, the world's superpower of his day. He was no ordinary child, as his parents rightly saw at his birth, and so he became an expert in his grasp of the culture and learning of ancient Egypt. Why? Because the Lord God was preparing him to undertake a unique task: to lead a rabble of slaves across the Sinai desert and back to the land God had given to Abraham and Isaac and Jacob. Furthermore, he would record the complex laws and rituals for the moral, religious and civil life of God's people. That was why God placed him for thirty-five years in the Egyptian court: to learn from Egyptian scholars every known discipline and skill of that era of history.

What do you think? Are these ten verses merely a little story from the distant past, of the kind that toddlers like to hear? Has this boy's upbringing by a pagan princess anything to say to you and me in our 21st century? I am convinced that here we have one of the most dramatic pictures in the whole Bible of the sovereignty of God. We are intended to see the divine genius at work; how brilliantly and with what masterly skill, God preserved this young man, from the time he saved him from death by drowning, and throughout those four decades of his preparation for his calling to fulfil a crucial stage of God's salvific will for his church. For our part, we are called to trust in God, and to realize that everything truly does work together for good for those who love God and are called in his purposes.

My wife and I brought back from Egypt a genuine papyrus with Egyptian paintings on it. As often as I look at that papyrus I think of Pharaoh's daughter, proud, stately, with her slaves, unwittingly performing the will of God for this boy, though she neither knew God nor believed in him. Thus, she was the instrument of his mighty purposes for our salvation. And yet, you and I are often anxious about trivial things. We plan for the future and are concerned lest our plans do not work out. But Almighty God could choose and use a pagan princess to do just exactly as he wanted. No wonder the Saviour said, 'Why do you worry ... look at the birds of the air ... the lilies of the field... consider them ... and have faith in God' (Matthew 6:26–34).

The boy Moses

Think of Moses at age six, sitting in a magnificent palace with his foster mother, waited on by slaves who lavished on him all he needed. 'Mother,' he says. 'Yes, my son?' she asks. 'Mother, why am I called Moses? That means "drawn out". Why couldn't you have called me by the name of a warrior or athlete?' 'Because, my son, I found you in a basket in the waters of the great Nile, and I drew you out of the water. You were a gift from the Great River to me, my son.' And the little boy would reflect on that. He was taken out of the water of the Nile, into which, he knew, slave children were daily thrown.

We may be sure that he had the best schooling, the best teachers, the best sports instructors, indeed, the best of everything. We know that he was free to travel about the land and was given royal honour as a son of Pharaoh's household. Therefore, he must have seen his own people toiling under their taskmasters. Do you think he would have kept in touch with his mother and father, and with his brother and sister? The evidence suggests that he did, because we find, a few chapters later, the two brothers meeting, knowing each other and greeting one another with deep affection and emotion. Yes, he kept in touch.

As he grew older, into his teens and adolescence, the story was bound to have unfolded itself in his mind: who he was, who his own people were, how he was where he was, and, most important of all, where he really belonged. And here is the most amazing point: the Scripture makes it so clear that he never gave his heart to the riches, culture and sinful ways of Egypt (Hebrews 11: 25–26). Remarkably, he kept himself pure, although, like Joseph before him, he was alone in the middle of a pagan society. There was no prayer group to attend, no Bible Study or services of worship to keep his faith burning. Surrounded by every temptation that could ever be presented to a young man, he pursued with all his might and main what was good, wholesome and worthy, turning his back on all that was unworthy, unclean and evil. It is the most amazing story.

However, amazing as it is, this also has to be the story of each one of us. Because there is a pattern—a tapestry woven in heaven—for each of our lives. And God calls us to give ourselves entirely to him, to love him and to do his will. We are to turn our backs on what we know to be wrong, and rather to love what we know to be of God.

> We are to turn our backs on what we know to be wrong, and rather to love what we know to be of God.

What a slender thread it was, just one single slender thread. A young man, growing up in the bosom of the hated Egyptians, while his people suffered and were beaten, and their new-born sons thrown to the crocodiles. These slave people cried out to God. They sought his face. They thought he had turned away from them and could no longer hear their prayers. They told each other the stories of their forefathers and how God had spoken to them. And they wondered why he no longer came and spoke to them anymore, and why he left them to suffer. Meanwhile, God's purposes wove with that single slender thread, as Moses grew into a man.

God had not forgotten. He never forgets his promises

and covenant. He hears the faintest cry. And he moves in a mysterious way his wonders to perform.

I wonder if we realize that there is a single, slender thread that runs right through the lives of all God's people. That apparently fragile thread passes through the tangles that we cannot unravel; it passes through the heartaches that we think will break us; it passes through the nights when darkness seems to hide the Saviour's face; it passes through our troubles, our anxious thoughts, even through our doubts and fears and failings. It is the slender thread of the will of God, his purpose for our lives, his mighty love. Oh, that we might trust him, and keep close to him! For that slender thread joins other threads, is interwoven with them until it becomes a scarlet cord that leads at last to Calvary, Easter, and finally the Father's house and to God himself.

FOR FURTHER STUDY

1. Reflect on the experiences of Manaoh in Judges 13 and also on God's call to Jeremiah (Jer. 1:4-10). Finally, follow through David's prayer in Psalm 139 to verses 13-16. How could we incorporate the teaching of divine providence into our praying, planning, and serving?

2. Regarding the sons of Sceva (Acts 19:13-17), F.F. Bruce comments, 'when they tried to use [the name of Jesus], like an unfamiliar weapon wrongly handled it exploded in their hands'.[2] Stott comments, 'the efficacy of the name is not mechanical, nor can it be used second-hand.'[3] 'What guidelines could be given to distinguish between trying with our own methods and abilities to "help God out" or by acting as Jochebed, Moses' mother, did?'

3. Research into the Egyptian education Moses would have received as a prince of Egypt in languages, law, population management, leadership, etc. It might well enlarge our appreciation of God's providential preparation of Moses. (See web: *Ancient Egyptian Education*.)

TO THINK ABOUT AND DISCUSS

1. As you discuss 'bringing up children in faith, not fear', reflect on how parents might unintentionally be negative in their attitudes. How can we be essentially positive in today's world with the immense pressures of social media and the genuine harm it can inflict on young minds. What control ought parents to exercise over smart phones and do we often give them to children too soon?

2. What part can parents justifiably expect their local congregation to teach their children? On the other hand, is it common for parents to fall short in providing a secure, loving and biblical home for their children, training them in the Scriptures? (Exod. 13:14; Deut. 6:4-7; 20-25; Prov. 22:6.)

3. Though Moses' father, Amram, is not mentioned in Jochebed's preparation of the basket and her strategic positioning of Miriam (2:4), we may safely assume the entire strategy was planned jointly. Do believing parents always fully agree in wisely guiding the upbringing of their children, or can there be parental disagreement the children are aware of, which they can be quick to exploit in order to get their own way? Discuss any ways you could avoid the latter from happening.

3 Trying but failing

Exodus 2:11–22

In Chapter 2, the underlying emphasis was clearly on divine providence. Now, however, the foundational theme is learning to carry the cross. Finding himself in God's school, Moses had to learn humility and that God's thoughts are not our thoughts, nor are his ways the same as our ways (Isa. 55:8).

You know the kind of film that men love and women cannot stand? Some tough veteran major, who has a brilliant record of outstanding military service, is summoned to the War Office for an interview with the chiefs of staff and the Minister for War. He is politely told to sit down, and then, for an hour, is given a detailed briefing on some hazardous situation and almost certain death and disaster facing hundreds of innocent citizens, unless someone can reach them and effect a rescue operation. Being a soldier of experience and maturity, the major comments that the poor fellow chosen for this operation has about a one in twenty chance of survival, and he begins to detail the odds against any task force, and to warn the chiefs of staff against sending anyone on such a foolhardy operation.

Then comes the double-barrelled shock blast. 'One vital piece of information, Major, that, so far, we have withheld. Unless this operation is successfully completed, the whole tide of war on the eastern front could turn against the allies. And you, Major, have been selected to lead the operation. We want you to prepare what will be needed and to set out in three days' time.'

It is a well-worn introduction to the traditional war film, or to one of Alistair MacLean's novels. But—and I hope you are not too surprised—it is also the introduction to the account of how God commissioned Moses with the Mission: 'Go to Egypt and set my people free!'

I remember as a small boy being away for the day on our annual Sunday School picnic. We had gone to a public park within a former stately home's estate, and I distinctly recall that it was a most exciting place with a lake complete with paddle boats, the old-fashioned swing boats, and many other attractions which children love. I am referring to the days during the Second World War, when there was far less for children than there are today—nothing like the entertainments and places of interest to visit we have now.

One feature of this park was a maze. It was made out of ten-foot-high hedges, and it was quite the most exciting part of the park. We spent a long time in the maze, and somehow, though I could only have been about six years old, I mastered its layout. But my lasting memory of that day was an elderly gentleman with an elderly lady. They both had very white hair and one of them used a cane walking stick. They told me they were in the middle of the maze and could not get out. Could I help them? I gladly obliged, and in less than a minute I had led them to the exit. The old gentleman gave me sixpence. I thought I was the richest boy in the world. That sixpence bought me an ice-cream, a lemonade and half an hour in a small paddle boat with my sister.

As I think of that elderly couple and how agitated they were that they could not find their way out of the maze, I think of so many of us for whom life has become a kind of complicated maze. We try the path to the right, then the next to the left; we take one turning after another, always hoping to get clear of the high hedges and narrow pathways which seem to lead us round and round and back to where we started. But as the weeks and months pass, we sometimes despair of ever reaching those wide, rolling open spaces of God's beautiful Kingdom. And we would do almost anything to get clear of the tangled paths that hedge us in. Let us see if we can find a way out as we continue with the story of Moses.

Phase one: Trying alone

The zoom lens of camera No. 1 is focusing on one person: this extraordinary child who is being brought up as the son of Pharaoh's daughter. But we must not forget the wider scene, because camera No. 2 will keep on taking us back to the people of God who had grown far too comfortable in the fertile land of Goshen and had almost forgotten that they did not belong there. And camera No. 2 is still filming this tribe of peasants, who have now been toiling as slaves and are crying out under the burden of building great cities for the Egyptian tyrant.

> The New Testament makes the point very clearly that Moses went through a crisis in his own life.

The New Testament (NT) makes the point very clearly that Moses went through a crisis in his own life. Gradually it dawned on him that he had to choose between the wealth, luxury and power of Egypt on the one hand, or the hardship, shame and poverty of his own slave people on the other hand. It could not be both. And Phase One is about that choice he had to make.

Josephus, the Jewish historian,[1] tells us that Moses had become a military man of great ability. He had led an Egyptian army into Ethiopia, then called Nubia, and had captured the capital and brought the whole country into subjection to Egypt—so making a great name for himself. But the Bible passes over that, though Stephen may have hinted at this in his comments on Moses: 'he was mighty in words and deeds' (Acts 7:22). But the crunch time had to come. Right before Moses' eyes his own flesh and blood, his father, mother, brother, sister, cousins and his entire people were suffering terribly. Whose side was he on? His daily life in the Egyptian court was constantly surrounded by idolatry and pagan practices which he knew were repugnant to the people of God. Whose side was he on? It was high time for him to come to a decision, either to turn his back on God's people, or to turn his back on the Egyptian world.

I know that over 3000 years separate you and me from this man Moses. But the deep choices of life have not changed all that much. And there are many of us who are trying to do what for years Moses tried to do—be part of this world that hates God, and at the same time belong to the Lord's people. Of course, we have to live in this world. That is obvious. However, we know the score, do we not? We know that there is a level of friendship with this world—a belonging to it with its materialism and low standards—which is incompatible with belonging to the people of God. But we dither, and we try to have one foot on one side, and the other foot on the other side. Then we wonder why things do not work out for us, and why we are so uncomfortable, and uneasy.

So, the time came when Moses made his choice. It had to be all or nothing: he chose to give his heart to the people of God, and so he turned his back on worldly power and wealth and influence. He would serve God alone. He would offer himself wholly to God. He would bear the reproach and shame of being an Israelite and cease to act as if he were an Egyptian of royal blood.

Now it seems that his intention was to lead a revolt of the Israelites and break off their yoke of slavery. The New Testament commentary on this phase of his life tells us he saw clearly that God was calling him to set the people free. And we can see him putting his shoulders back, perhaps remembering his (alleged) victorious campaign to Nubia commanding a great army and returning home a hero. So, he must draw up plans and begin by reconnoitring the territory. He must gather some intelligence about the situation. If he was going to serve God and rescue the slaves, he would have to work out a plan.

Thus, we find him visiting Goshen and the building sites where the treasure city for Pharaoh was being built by sweating, groaning slaves. NIV translates: 'he went out to where his own people were and watched them at their hard labour' (2:11). The word 'watched' means 'with deep emotion he looked at them in their distress'. He was moved to see their suffering. And so, his first blow for freedom was struck when he killed the Egyptian taskmaster who had been beating an Israelite. But it was not much of a blow for freedom. See the way verse 12 emphasizes how pathetic and secretive the murder really was. He glanced this way and that way and, seeing no one, he hid the Egyptian's body in the sand. The next day, still working on his plans, he discovered that the Israelites did not want him; worse still, word about the murder had spread, and Pharaoh himself would soon be plotting to kill Moses. And so began his flight from Egypt, not by a four-by-four over the desert, but on foot, across the barren wastes to hide from Pharaoh. He had failed and failed badly!

Calvin[2] excuses Moses' murder of the Egyptian taskmaster, on the grounds that it was a judicial act, since God had appointed him to be a deliverer. But unquestionably, there is another way to understand this incident. I suspect Calvin could well agree that Moses was trying to do God's work but not in God's way. He was operating in his own strength, using his own abilities and his own human strategy. The events that occurred forty years later make it clear God does not operate in the way that Moses sought to do before he was obliged to go into banishment.

We can find it hard to learn to do God's work in God's way. For some time, a friend passed on to me an American magazine for ministers called *Leadership*. And then I subscribed to the magazine myself. A great deal of the material in this magazine was about using modern business methods to run the church. It had articles about goal setting, monitoring the work, motivating the pastoral team, and so on; and it drew from a wide knowledge of these skills in the world of business and commerce.

Without doubt we can learn a great deal from the business world, for many churches and Christian societies are sloppy and inept in their management of the Lord's work and money. However, there is a massive problem with all of that. It is the same problem that Moses had. It can all be done—the planning, organising, and motivating—in mere human strength. Nonetheless, if we are not doing the work in God's way, then it does not matter

> If we are not doing the work in God's way, we are going to end up failures like Moses, making fools of ourselves.

how many prayer meetings we have, or how much expertise we apply, or how hard we work, we are going to end up failures like Moses, making fools of ourselves.

What is it we are trying to do for God? All of us who profess to be Christians will have some calling from the Lord and so must be trying to do something for him. Even if it is to be a good parent or a good mentor to difficult and frustrating teenagers, God has given us all something to do. But whatever it is he has entrusted to us we cannot do it in our own strength. For, if we are not relying wholly upon the Lord, we will try to do it our way. And God's ways are not our ways, his thoughts are not our thoughts (Isaiah 55:8). Without him, we will fail. There is nothing surer than that. And not only will we fail, but we could even bring his work into disrepute. Certainly, however flourishing the work may seem to be outwardly, we will have achieved nothing of eternal value. We will be of the same ilk as the church in Laodicea: the Lord of the church was sick of her (Revelation 3: 14–22)!

Phase two: Living alone

Usually in the films they meet in a cafe, or a hotel foyer. He is on his own at a table, and she is on her own at another table. Their eyes meet and, as they leave, they accidentally bump into each other, and he ends up carrying her suitcase. In the Bible, they meet at a well, whether it was Abraham's servant and Rebekah, or Jacob and Rachel, or the Lord Jesus and the woman of Samaria. So it was with Moses and the girl he was to marry, Zipporah (her name, incidentally, means 'twitterer', the sound of a small bird in a bush). The handsome man in Egyptian dress, with his glinting sword in his strong hand, defends the girls against rough, uncouth men. He is invited to stay with her father Jethro, and ultimately marries her.

Having fled from the court and from his native land

of Egypt, he ended up as a shepherd, working for his father-in-law. He was, in effect, hiding from Pharaoh and his hit squads who were out to kill him. I suppose it is possible that the occasional military detachment of Egyptian horsemen went past as Moses, now dressed as a Bedouin, wandered along leading a flock of sheep. But his disguise was good enough and he was never recognized.

Let us use our imagination for a moment. Think of his mother, Jochebed, and his father, Amram. By faith they had hidden him for three months, not fearing the king's edict. How do you think they felt now that the apple of their eye, their son Moses, whom they were convinced God had chosen, had run away to a distant land and disappeared from the scene altogether? It is a good guess that, at the time of his flight, he sent a message home saying that he was running for his life from Pharaoh's wrath. Indeed, it would have been common knowledge that Pharaoh was resolved to kill him. So how would Moses' parents have felt? Would their faith, and their prayers, all have evaporated? What do you think? Would their hopes and longings all have been smashed to smithereens in just forty-eight hours? Everything up in smoke. Ruined. The years of training, those years of waiting for Moses to become the leader to set them free, now all wasted through one ill-advised act.

A young man called Augustine,[3] who lived in North

Africa, was breaking his godly mother's heart. Every day she prayed for him with tears. Writing some years later, he tells us that with her tears she soaked the earth against which she pressed her face in prayer. She knew he wanted to leave Carthage and go to Rome. And all night she prayed God would stop him going to such a den of iniquity as the capital of the empire. But he deliberately deceived her, getting up in the middle of the night to board a ship, and when she woke in the morning, the ship was far out to sea. She went frantic with distress and despair and cried out to God asking why he had not answered her prayers that her son should be kept at home where he could hear the truth and become a Christian. But Augustine was to become a Christian in Milan after he had moved from Rome, a disillusioned young man. God had far more daring and important plans for his life than his mother Monica had.

I heard first-hand from a very well-known person[4]—someone who has written bestselling Christian books—about a member of her family. Away back in the 1950s, before public morals in this country had taken the massive fall we have seen in the last three or four decades, this person's sister shocked her family by going off to tour Europe by motorcycle with a young man to whom she was not even married. The family were ashamed and affronted. Worse still, she came back pregnant and, to spare the family embarrassment, she stowed away with the young man on a cargo ship going to Australia. She had a baby four days after arriving in Australia and, a couple of years later, married the father; but then she proceeded to divorce him. More shame and distress to the family. She ended up marrying again, this time in Malawi. But while in Malawi, the Lord met her, and she fell in love with Jesus Christ and her life was totally changed.

I know that some of us are concerned about our children. We have prayed for them, tried our best to train them, done all we could for them, for we had great hopes for them. And then, off they went into some far-off country, and the reports we now receive are little better than those that Monica received regarding Augustine or that the family, I have just referred to, received of their daughter who was so rebellious. So, we wonder what has gone wrong. Why has God not answered our prayers? We forget that he works in his way, not our way.

As Moses wandered across the desert wastes, leading his sheep from scraggy grass to scraggy grass, it appears he never thought that one day he would be leading his people over this same inhospitable territory. But the point was that he was now in another school, quite different to the universities of Egypt. He was now in the course's module on *Humility*; and the first lesson was that in his own strength alone he could achieve absolutely nothing. He called his first son *Gershom*, a name which is a pun, meaning both 'alien' and 'expelled'. That he should have given his first son such a name clearly tells us that he saw himself expelled and an alien far from home.

Are there any readers who are deeply concerned for their children, some of whom may now be in a distant place? Do you constantly wonder each day how they really are, not just the snatches of news gathered from emails, postcards or brief telephone calls? What exactly are they doing? Did you once genuinely give them to God at their baptism, or at a dedication service? Then you must hold on in faith that in that distant country God's hand must still be in control. He has not forgotten—how could he ever forget them? Like Monica, mother of Augustine, soak the earth with your tears as you pray. But do not expect God to answer in exactly the way you think he should.

> Do not expect God to answer in exactly the way you think he should.

Of course, it is quite possible that some readers of this book have been put into God's *School of Humility*. He wants you to learn the hard way this painful lesson, that without him you can do nothing. Until we have learned that lesson, nothing of eternal spiritual value will happen. Not a thing! Nor is God in the kind of hurry that we are often. He can, and he will wait until we have learned the power is his, the glory also is his, and therefore the method must be his.

Phase three: Feeling alone

Verse 23 states: 'During those many days, the king of Egypt died.' We are to understand several things from this small detail. Firstly, of course, that as long as that particular Pharaoh was alive, Moses was pinned down. But there is also the implication that the Israelite slaves hoped the burden of slavery might be eased when this particular Pharaoh died. The king who initiated the genocide had been an evil man. He was the despot who had made their forced labour increasingly heavy. Now that, at last, he had died, perhaps their lot would begin to improve a little. Something like the Scots in the 17th century hoping that Charles II would be more amenable to the Reformed Kirk than his father had been towards them, when, in fact, he turned out to be even worse and thousands of covenanters were executed. It had been 'out of the frying pan into the fire', as the proverb says.

Likewise with the Hebrew slaves, it did not turn out as they had hoped. The beatings, cruelty and oppression continued unabated. And for the first time we are told the people began to look to God and to pray: 'Their cry for rescue from slavery came up to God' (2:23b). That is not to say that here and there, men and women of faith such as Moses' parents had not been crying out to God for years. Rather, it means that until this point there had not been a widespread turning to God by his people.

Yet, there seemed to be no answer. They cried, they wept, they held prayer meetings, and they did away with practices they knew were offensive to God. But still there was no answer. And so, they felt profoundly alone. God had forgotten them, or he must have turned his back on them.

Have you ever felt like that? Have you felt abandoned and alone, your prayers unheeded, your cries to God unnoticed? I must confess that at times I have. During my ministry in Northern Ireland, I spoke with a man who was vicious about what he regarded as the impotence of God. He spoke ferociously to me saying, 'I have been an angry person for quite some time!' My presence in his home seemed to anger him even more, probably because I was a minister and I reminded him of the God he hated. 'Twenty-two years!' he shouted. 'For twenty-two years we've been being killed by the terrorists. What kind of a God allows people to suffer and be bombed? You people (he meant Christians) have prayed, but no answer has come. And it's Roman Catholics who are doing the killing. That's religion for you!'

There were many in my congregation who had suffered the loss of loved ones, or their businesses; whole communities had been adversely affected, and they could certainly have identified with that man. They

> God's ways are not our ways. His thoughts are not our thoughts. When will we learn that?

could also have identified with the Hebrew slaves who saw no sign of any answer to the great volume of prayer rising from the flimsy peasant huts night by night. Meanwhile, a lonely man was wandering after sheep in the wilderness of a distant land. God's ways are not our ways. His thoughts are not our thoughts. When will we learn that?

With a touch of anthropomorphism,[5] the account continues. 'And God heard their groaning, and God remembered his covenant with Abraham, with Isaac, and with Jacob ... and God knew' (2:24–25). The verb 'he knew' is full of meaning; the NIV translates it as, 'So God looked on the Israelites and *was concerned* about them.' God had a purpose, and that purpose had been expressed in a covenantal promise to Abraham, Isaac and Jacob. He intended—he had never intended otherwise—to honour his promise and fulfil his purpose, because it was not just this tribe of herdsmen and shepherds, despised by the Egyptians, who were involved; it was his own Son, who was to be given to the world through this fledgling nation. *Law* and *grace* were to be given through them and, in the fullness of time, the Redeemer and Saviour himself.

Yes, over three thousand years separate these people

from us today. But God's promises still stand. His covenant still stands—only now it is the new covenant in the blood of Christ. And that covenant in Jesus' blood cannot be broken. God remembers it. How could he ever forget it? He has fulfilled it and will continue to fulfil it in his people's lives today.

Are you trying to serve him alone? Or are you living alone and feeling alone, in spite of all your prayers? Are you in a maze, seemingly lost, going round and round, but always ending up at the same place, back to where you started? We have only one hope, and it is God's promise to us, his covenant sealed in the Saviour's blood. As the old hymn has it:

His oath, His covenant and blood,
support me in the whelming flood;
when all around my soul gives way,
He then is all my hope and stay!
On Christ the solid rock I stand,
All other ground is sinking sand.

Edward Mote (1797–1874)

Conclusion

Every one of us faces a challenge. None of us can be called to follow Christ without being challenged: challenged to accept the cross being laid upon him; challenged to obey God, do his will and reach out to others for his sake. And, if we have grasped the content of the job description that Moses was given, we will see that all he was being asked to do was to have faith in God in order to carry the cross being laid upon him. Only through faith could he do that. He must believe God with a faith that obeyed! That was all! Hard enough, but the enabling would be given. And when you and I can trust our God; accept his Word; believe his promises; have the firm assurance that he is strong enough, powerful enough and faithful to fulfil what he has promised; then is the time to lift up our hearts, because the Lord has now come to us in his love, grace and truth!

FOR FURTHER STUDY

1. Although Scripture neither explicitly sanctions nor condemns Moses' murder of the Egyptian taskmaster, consider how God can overrule human actions in that Moses' behaviour led to his forty years as a desert nomad, as God had planned.

2. Contrast Moses' ill-advised course of action with Esther, who called on all her people to hold a fast on her behalf, as she took her life in her hands by appearing before king Ahasuerus without his explicit invitation (Esth. 4:12–17).

3. The same verb used of Moses standing up to the bullying shepherds and 'saving' the shepherdesses (2:17) is also used in Exodus of God 'saving' his people (14:30). Does this suggest that Moses had a profound godly concern for justice and, if so, does it reflect something of his parents' earliest teaching while they cared for him as a young child at the request of Pharaoh's daughter?

4. To what extent might Moses' concern for justice suggest that, although the image of God in women and men has been seriously marred by the Fall, nevertheless that image has not been completely obliterated? See John 1:4–5.

TO THINK ABOUT AND DISCUSS

1. 'By faith Moses, when he was grown up, refused to be called the son of Pharaoh's daughter, choosing rather to be mistreated with the people of God than to enjoy the fleeting pleasures of sin' (Heb. 11:24–25). When you deliberately turned your back on the world's values, did obedience at first seem obvious for anyone who would follow Jesus? But were you ever tempted later to envy those who indulge in 'the fleeting pleasure of sin'?

2. Are there still ways in which we try to do God's work without considering if we are doing it in his way? Can you think of contemporary examples of this?

3. Consider the concept of humility. We easily acknowledge that Moses had to learn complete humility, but do we sometimes refuse to undertake some work for the Lord using 'humility' as an excuse for our unwillingness to obey?

4. Helen Roseveare's sister shocked and grieved the family when she went off to tour Europe on the back of her boyfriend's motorcycle and then stowed away on a cargo vessel bound for Australia. For years the family prayed for her before she came to know Christ. How faithful are we in praying for the 'prodigal sons' in our families, and does the point ever come when we assume God is not going to answer? (1 Sam. 12:23)

4 The burning bush

Exodus 3:1-8

The entire Bible is unquestionably concerned with God's self-revelation to men and women of his nature, purposes, and redeeming grace. The book of Genesis ('Beginnings') is a prime example of this, mainly through men such as Enoch and Noah, and then of course, the three patriarchs and Joseph. Exodus 3 takes up where the Genesis narrative left off (Genesis 50:24–26); now the ongoing self-disclosure of the Lord God continues apace as God speaks to Moses through the flames of the burning bush.

A few fortunate people seem to be able to get the balance of their lives just right. I meet such people occasionally. I saw once a survey in a magazine regarding those who were bored because they had not enough to do, and those who were stressed because they were too busy.

I wonder if you are in either of these two groups. The aim of the survey was to help readers find out if they had their balance of living just right—whether they were bored, kicking their heels, without enough to occupy themselves? Or, on the other hand, were they over committed, wondering what to give up, yet not wanting to give anything up? Reading this survey, my impression was that many of us are busy people, often far too busy.

About the same time as I came across the survey, I read in a national newspaper of a young woman of the yuppie generation. How is this for busyness? 'I am taking seven modules at university this year. I am pushing on with my career during vacations. I am taking singing lessons plus ballet lessons every week. I keep up with my five closest friends. I steal time for Michael Jackson and Thomas Hardy. I am doing voluntary work in the evenings to help deal with kids who are abusing drugs. And, oh yes, I keep three horses, three cats, two birds and my dog Rover.' The magazine with the survey had concluded that being 'too busy' meant you did not want to miss anything!

My guess is that Moses for many years had been too busy. He had had a full programme, something like that girl. But now, he was no longer too busy. He had time to catch his breath and was living at a very different pace. At last, he was ready to listen to what God had to say to him.

Now, in what I am about to write, I am addressing one

particular person—myself! If you are not interested you could skip this chapter and move on to the next one. However, for my part, I found that being in the ministry could lead to my being ridiculously busy. So, over the years I have had to ask myself why this should be so. Has it been the pressure of my work? Or was it that too easily I gave in to people's demands which I knew I could never satisfy? Or did I think that what I *was* would be decided by what I *did*? Had I fallen for the foolish error of thinking I would be measured by my activity, rather than by what I am as a person?

'What's wrong with being busy?' asks someone. 'Far better to be busy than to be idling and doing nothing. Far better to be always on the go, rather than vegetating.' But

> While Moses was busy, active and always on the go, it would seem he was not ready to hear God speaking to him.

you see, while Moses was busy, active and always on the go, it would seem he was not ready to hear God speaking to him. I suspect that many busy people often find it difficult to take time to be alone with God. The busier we are, the lower down in our priorities will prayer become. And if prayer is meeting with God, and listening to him, then busy people are not going to do much praying; they are not going to make time to meet with God and listen for his voice. For ministers of the Word, surely that is bad news. It is bad news for their congregations too. For when the preacher comes to bring them God's Word, he will be jaded and will be serving up 'cold kale', as we say,[1] from months back.

What is my excuse for not taking time either to meditate on his Word and for prayer, and being still and quiet before the Lord? Is it that I am too busy? Then the message for me from this passage of Scripture is that God cannot use me until I learn to cease from frenetic activity and spend time alone with my God!

Knowing ourselves

Do you remember those days a long time ago, when we stood and tried to hide from mother what we had been doing? But mother had a kind of sixth sense. She could read our minds, and she sensed and knew straight away when we were 'up to something', as she used to say. It was very uncomfortable when she began to cross-question us, and it became clear that we had been rumbled and found out.

As the bush burned and continued burning, Moses understandably wanted to try and find out the reason why it did not burn itself to ashes. This was something exceptional, something most unusual. Common enough for a desert bush to burst into flames, but normally it was reduced to dust in a couple of minutes. Why was this bush burning on and on? As he came near, he heard his name being called. Had he taken on a false name in the land of Midian to hide his identity? My guess is that he had. But the voice, calling so clearly and distinctly, was using his real name that forever reminded him of his miraculous deliverance at birth. His heart must have begun to beat faster. Who knew him? Who had discovered him away out here in the wilderness? Who knew his true identity?

When we have time to listen, and when God speaks, then we begin to have that most uncomfortable experience of being found out—when we have hidden from our real selves for years, concealed behind our busyness and activity. We have worn a mask and put on an act. We have played the part. But now, alone with God, there begins this embarrassing experience of having to face ourselves. For if mother had a kind of sixth sense when we were young, God has a far greater sixth sense, and we cannot ever hide anything from him. Our mask and pose both melt away, and we are what we are—nothing more and nothing less.

The thing about meeting with God is that there is only one way to do it, and that is through humility. Go through the Bible and try to find out how many times the word 'achievement' occurs. Or even a list of achievements. There is almost (not quite, but almost) total silence on the subject of achievement. Instead of qualifications and talents being listed, we find the Bible saying that

God has chosen the weak things of the world, the lowly people, the despised and poor people, to accomplish his gracious purposes (See 1 Corinthians 1:26–29). We do not find him choosing those with impressive CVs. Certainly, there are many biblical characters of that ilk, but they are passed over. Nor does he necessarily choose those with lots of talents and abilities to offer, but he often selects those who appear to have nothing going for them at all.[2]

> When you and I come face to face with God, all our achievements somehow melt away and vanish and become as nothing.

The odd thing is that when you and I come face to face with God, all our achievements somehow melt away and vanish and become as nothing. Paul called his impressive list of attainments 'rubbish' (Philippians 3:8). And in the presence of the Almighty, we discover that we are poor, foolish and feeble.

In Moses' day, taking off one's shoes was a sign of profound respect. Thus, he took off his shoes and hid his face. What a difference from the proud prince who had drawn his sword and launched his one-man campaign to free the slaves. Then he was a royal prince, a trained military man, with an impressive list of achievements, which history records for us, but the Bible passes over.[3] Which is the man God can use? Not the proud prince of Egypt, with his learning and grasp of languages and military strategy, but the Bedouin shepherd, with his shoes slipped off, and his face covered as he bows to the ground before God.

The fire of the burning bush symbolizes, among other things, the holiness of God—for God's holiness burns with an inextinguishable flame. Today many behave as if God has become senile. But God is certainly not in the early stages of Alzheimer's Disease, having mislaid his thoughts about his moral laws and his Ten Commandments. Those commandments, every one of them, burn on and on, for they express the holiness of a God who is 'a consuming fire' (Hebrews 12:29). And humility, which forgets all our assumed talents, lays to one side all our puny achievements, for profound humility is the only appropriate response to God.

It was, I believe, Bernard of Clairvaux, the hymn-writer, who said that comparison is the first step into pride. We look sideways at other people and compare ourselves with them, the way the Pharisee did as he stood and prayed with himself in the Temple: 'God, I thank you that I am not like other men' (Luke 18:11). But God now has Moses in the place where he cannot compare himself to anyone else. He is alone with God. A mighty work is at last going to be done, because God is going to reveal himself to Moses, and this man is going to humble himself before God as he has never done before.

Knowing ourselves! Have we time for God to show us ourselves as we really are? Or are we too taken up with ourselves and what we can offer to God? I cannot find a single man or woman in the Bible who came and offered his or her talents to God. You may find one. If you do, let me know; I would be interested to learn about such a person. But, so far in my reading of Scripture, I have yet to come across anyone who was accepted by God on account of his achievements.

It is when we take off our shoes, so to speak, and hide our faces as we bow before the Lord, that we are at last ready for him to speak to us.

Knowing our God

We all have lots of ideas about prayer. Some of them have an element of truth in them. For example, we say that prayer is sending a quick text message to God, urgently asking for his help in an emergency. There is certainly something in that, for we read of Nehemiah being struck with fear as King Artaxerxes challenged him about standing in his royal presence with a sad countenance. Who would want to deny that, in such a crucial moment, Nehemiah's yearnings were not directed heavenwards (Nehemiah 2:2)?[4] Or else we say that prayer is bringing our requests to God, and of course that also is very true.

However, the danger with oft-repeated requests is that they can become a kind of shopping list which we run down, almost forgetting to whom it is we are praying. Prayer is not visiting some kind of spiritual supermarket, where we select certain items, put them in the trolley, and leave without ever meeting the manager.

However, when we study the great prayers of the Bible, we find another element in them entirely, which so often is missing from our own prayers. Let me put it like this. I am told that when a mother is carrying a child in her womb, the heart pulse of the mother penetrates the whole environment of the foetus. And during the months of pregnancy, the unborn child actually registers its mother's emotions: her anger, fears, love, peace, excitement and so on. Doctors believe they have evidence that our personalities are actually being formed during our time in the womb so, by that heartbeat, we are being fashioned into what we are going to become.

Now do you see what is happening here as Moses hides his face and bows before God? God is speaking and Moses is not just listening; he is receiving the message of the heart-pulse of God. 'I have surely seen the affliction of my people ... [I] have heard their cry ... I know their sufferings ... I have come down to deliver them ...' (3:7–8). Moses' mind and emotions and will are being touched and influenced by the presence of God and by his words. He is learning to know his God.

If you wondered why I was not very enthusiastic about describing prayer as texting or emailing a list of requests (although both may well be genuine prayers), it was because it is all too easy to send messages to God that have nothing to do with his purposes and will. Indeed, I suspect much of the problem with my prayers, and perhaps with yours, is that they are not sufficiently founded upon, and grounded in, the real character and nature of God. And we do not know God very well because we are too busy, too taken up with filling our days with endless activity. Do not think I am accusing anyone other than myself. I really mean it when I say that, as I write, I am talking to myself.

That is why it is so important for me to spend time with God's Word. For it is there, in the best of books, that I am going to meet with God, in both the Old and New Testaments, but supremely in the life and work of the Lord Jesus Christ. The only prayer-life which will be effective in God's hands will be a prayer-life which flows from a truer and deeper grasp of the heart and mind of God as I find it revealed in Jesus Christ.

Knowing the will of God

In the past, many thought Christians explained what we could not understand in our natural world by saying,

'That's done by God's power.' But as science pushed further back the boundaries of knowledge, so the need for God as 'the God of the gaps in our knowledge' was pushed further and further back. But it was quite wrong to say, 'Those aspects that we now understand and can explain with science, we no longer need to attribute them to the power of God; it is only those aspects of creation that we still can't explain that we attribute to God's amazing work'[5] 'That was a completely wrong approach. All the universe, along with all its secrets, belongs to God. The fact that some miracles of this universe have been understood and explained does not make them any less the work of God.

> The fact that some miracles of this universe have been understood and explained does not make them any less the work of God.

Now, I wonder if it has occurred to us that we have made the same mistake with prayer. One hundred years ago, child mortality was very high in our land. The chances of your children reaching the age of five were much lower then, than they are now. So, a mother prayed fervently for her children that they would not contract smallpox or diphtheria or scarlet fever. She prayed that her children would be kept safe and would live.

However, today in the west we no longer pray about that because child mortality is now very low in our society. Medical science has taken away the need for that prayer. Pension schemes and the welfare state (for all the criticism it receives), along with our wonderful doctors and nurses and public services, have actually eliminated the need for many of the prayers people prayed a hundred years ago. So, as a result, people pray far less. That is a simple fact.

But that kind of prayer was not what Moses was going to be engaging in. The Lord God was speaking to him and sharing with him his will, plan and concerns for his chosen people. This man's heart was being set on fire and, for all the protests that would shortly come from him, his heart would be set on fire by the will and purpose of God. No advance in technology, or medical science, or social services, or improved security will ever take away the need for this kind of prayer. Because those who clearly see, understand and know the will of God, will pray even more earnestly than before.

As well as much prayer disappearing because conditions have improved, much prayer has also disappeared because customs have changed. Aristocratic families, for example, knew exactly what to do with their sons. The eldest son inherited the family estate. The second son entered the army or politics. The third son entered the church to be a gentleman parson. And if there was a daughter who could not be married off, she was put into a convent. Prayers were then offered through traditions and customs. That was the way it was done in Victorian times and right through the Edwardian period until disillusionment crept in through the Great War of 1914–18. In the stately homes of our land, the gentry saw prayer as a good thing for the servants. So, each day, and especially on Sunday, the servants were obliged to pray, or at least to go through the motions as the master of the house prayed or led them in procession to the local parish church. It kept the servants in their place. Prayer was good for them.

Customs change, and with these changes those prayers have disappeared. But when a fire has been kindled and burns on and on in a person's heart, prayer will not disappear, because God has spoken and God has shown himself and his will. Now, in those prayers will be objectives and goals that are the revealed will of God.

Thus, we come back to where we began: being too busy. Too busy really to pray. Too busy to be alone with God to listen to him. Too busy to learn his mind and heart. Instead, we are taken up with what we are doing, our talents, our plans, and with what we might offer to him. We have never hidden our faces and bowed low before the flame of his burning presence and heard what he wants to say to us.

The burning bush, with its logo *nec tamen consumebatur* ('nor was it consumed') is the motto of the Kirk in Scotland. In the Presbyterian Church in Ireland, it is, *ardens sed virens* ('burning yet living'). The living fire of God burning on and on and on. Perhaps the author of the Letter to the Hebrews had this in mind when he said of God that he was 'a consuming fire'.

I wonder just how much you and I know about the purposes of God—about the desires of our holy God who has not changed since Moses' day or since Jesus' day; who still hates sin; who still loves the sinner; who still commands men and women everywhere to repent.

Think about your praying—about your prayers last night, or this morning. Are they prayers which could disappear with the progress of technology, or with a change in customs? Or are they prayers which come from the flame of God's holy love?

May our hearts all be set on fire for the God who calls our names to share with us his own desires and purposes for our lives, for his church and for those perishing in this fallen world.

FOR FURTHER STUDY

1. In his massive work, the *Institutes of the Christian Religion,* Calvin states as the title of Book I, Chapter 1, 'The knowledge of God and that of ourselves are connected. How they are interrelated.' His first section of this first Chapter has the heading: 'Without knowledge of self, there is no knowledge of God.' Then his second section continues with the heading: 'Without knowledge of God there is no knowledge of self.' The third and final section of Chapter 1 has the heading: 'Man before God's majesty.'[6] Explore Calvin's line of thought on knowing ourselves to see if it is confirmed by Scripture.

2. In 1 Timothy 2:1, is the apostle indulging in a tautologous statement, repeating four words which basically mean the same thing: 'First of all, then, I urge that supplications, prayers, intercessions, and thanksgivings be made for all people ...'? Can you find in Scripture meaningful examples of these four ways of addressing God?

3. Reflect on Paul's commission given to him by God: Acts 26:14–18. Are there any biographies you have read of those whom God has called and graciously used which might be worth re-reading and studying in the light of Exodus 3:1–6?

TO THINK ABOUT AND DISCUSS

1. How difficult do you find it to make quality time each day to spend with the Lord and your open Bible? Discuss the time of day you find most helpful, and whether you have a private devotional corner in your home which you reserve for your 'quiet time' with God, away from the distractions of your phone, laptop and tablet?

2. 'Comparison (of ourselves with others) is the first step to pride.'[7] What practical lessons can we learn from the parable of the Pharisee and tax collector (Luke 18:9–14)? Discuss the implications of a humility that

considers others 'better' (or 'more significant') than ourselves and how such humility can be achieved (Phil. 2:3, 5–11).

3. 'God uses our likeness to Jesus more than all our talents' (Robert Murray McCheyne).[8] How might Paul's prayer in Ephesians 3:14–19—if we make it our prayer also—work through the Holy Spirit to bring about some measure of 'likeness to Jesus' in our lives?

5 God's call to Moses

Exodus 3:1-17

This important passage in Exodus unfolds timeless principles: firstly, regarding the nature of God and his self-revelation in the divine name; secondly, his compassion for his chosen people; thirdly, the spiritual condition of the kind of person he chooses to use; fourthly, the faith needed to grasp the complete veracity of his covenantal pledges; and finally, the implied promise of One to come who is the same yesterday, today and forever.

During my years in the ministry, especially in the 1960s and 70s when the standard of church public address systems was not nearly as good as it is nowadays, members of the congregation with hearing impairments often heard only bits and pieces of the sermon because the preacher kept turning his face away from the microphone. It was a complaint often made. We would all acknowledge that it must have been very annoying for those with hearing impairments who came to church, expecting the Kirk's sound system would keep them in the loop (so to speak) but were not able to follow either the conduct of the service or the preacher's sermon because those taking part waggled their heads about. Fortunately, that complaint is seldom made today, thanks to greatly improved technology.

However, when it comes to God speaking to us, things are a little more complicated. For a start, we too often break off in the middle of a conversation with God, and so fail to stay long enough to hear what he is saying to us. That can be the first problem in his communication with many of us. But then, even if we do listen for long enough to hear what he has to say, too often we do not like what we hear or, worse still, we do not want to hear what he is saying.

> We too often break off in the middle of a conversation with God, and so fail to stay long enough to hear what he is saying to us.

The main theme of Exodus 3:1–17 is 'God's Call to Moses'. This call of God occupies nearly two whole chapters of this book but, in this chapter, we must consider further what we have already learned about the conversation between God and this man, as recorded in Exodus 3.

When my family and I lived in a rural parish, where I was minister of a country church for ten years, we had a very large, walled garden of some half an acre. It was, I might say, a most fruitful garden. Not only did we grow all our own potatoes and vegetables, but we also had fruit—apples, plums, damsons, gooseberries, blackcurrants, raspberries and strawberries. In those days, few people had freezers, so we bottled most of the fruit. In addition to all that, I kept six hives of bees, and most years we harvested up to 200 pounds of honey.

Off the manse hallway and under the stairs was a large walk-in cupboard with shelves on three sides. It was my delight to show visitors inside that cupboard, especially at the end of autumn when it was full. The shelves would be stocked with provisions for the winter. There would have been maybe 200–300 pounds of soft fruit in preserving jars, standing in neat rows, and approximately another 200 pounds of clear, clover honey—all home produce. Throughout the winter months, my wife simply had to go to the cupboard under the stairs and there was a seemingly endless supply of fruit and honey. It was like living in the Promised Land.

In some ways, Exodus 3 is like that cupboard. Therefore, for the second time we turn to the story of Moses and the burning bush. We could return repeatedly to this passage of Scripture, for here is an inexhaustible supply of spiritual fruit and honey for our delight and nourishment. Of course, the whole Bible is like that, a vast store of good things for hungry hearts and lives.

There are three questions that arise from this chapter: 'What is this?', 'Who am I?' and 'Who are you?'

The first question: What is this?

There will always be a doubter, for there are still plenty of 'doubting Thomases', both outside and inside the church. Some have doubted the story of this bush that burned and burned but was never consumed. Others have suggested it was a desert bush in full and brilliant flower, with the evening light of a red, setting sun catching it with ruddy rays, giving the impression that it was on fire. If you or I were lost, and tramping in the Sinai Desert, I would be the first to offer an explanation like that. But Moses had been forty years in these hot, sandy wastes. There was no way a desert Bedouin of his experience was going to make a mistake like that. And so, his curiosity raised the question in his mind, 'What is this?' He does not put it in quite those words but that, in effect, is what he is asking when he says, 'I will turn aside to see this great sight, why the bush is not burned' (v. 3).

Some readers may know how Presbyterians across the world today understand the significance of our emblem of the burning bush: the burning bush stands for the life of God falling upon an otherwise lifeless thing and causing it to become the medium of God's presence. We understand that the bush, dry, arid and scorched by the desert sun, symbolizes the church; and we take the meaning of the fire to be the power and presence of the Holy Spirit, giving life to the Lord's people—a life that burns on and on.

Be that as it may, we can be absolutely certain that Moses had no such thoughts. And so, we have to come to this account and ask with him the question: 'What is this?' I mean, what did it mean for Moses? What was the significance of this phenomenon for this Bedouin shepherd? We cannot impose our post-resurrection theology onto this story. We must try and understand this event in its most basic and primary meaning.

It is not a hard question to answer. My own guess is that if we asked a group of 21st century believers to write down the meaning of the burning bush for Moses and the significance of what God said to him from the bush, we would have over ninety per cent agreement. It was simply the instrument of God's call to this man to leave his sheep and his comfortable, settled life, in order to make the arduous journey back to Egypt to challenge Pharaoh to give the Hebrew slaves their freedom. Surely most of us recognize that. God was calling Moses to serve him, and I think it is worthwhile just to notice again the simple elements of that call to leave everything and follow God.

The first element in this call was that God called the man by his name: 'Moses! Moses!' God knew him. God had come to him deliberately. It was not a chance meeting, an accidental encounter. James Barrie and Robert Louis Stevenson met accidentally. One busy shopping day the two young writers bumped into each other in Princes Street, Edinburgh. Barrie is reported as having said, 'I beg your pardon, I do apologize!' R. L. Stevenson replied, 'Entirely my fault, please forgive me!' A conversation followed. And so it was that the author of *Peter Pan* and the author of *Kidnapped* and *Treasure Island* met, entirely by accident. But not so this meeting. God deliberately came to this man and called him by his name.

We are, at this point, at the heart of the Bible's message. God coming and calling our names. We often get this the wrong way round. We think that we go looking for God. I once heard a minister telling his congregation how that past week a young man, after his father's funeral, had asked to speak to this minister, and with tears had said, 'I want to get right with God.' We might truthfully say, 'Clearly that young man was seeking God.' But there will have been far more to it than that. Our Bibles would say to us that it was God himself who was seeking that young man and calling him by name—the way in the Gospels we read of Jesus calling people to follow him.

An example could be the call of Philip. John records in his Gospel: 'The next day, Jesus decided to go to Galilee. He found Philip and said to him, "Follow me."' (John 1:43). Then we read: 'Philip found Nathaniel and said to him, "We have found him of whom Moses in the Law and also the prophets wrote, Jesus of Nazareth, the son of Joseph."' (John 1:45). Philip claimed he had found Jesus, but John explicitly states that Jesus first found Philip. Similarly, day after day, week after week, year after year, God still calls. Have you heard him? Has he been calling you?

> Day after day, week after week, year after year, God still calls.

A second element in this call is humility. The command came to Moses to remove his sandals. Why should that instruction have been given? The slave went barefooted. In many lands today, the custom is still to remove shoes when someone enters a church or Mosque or Temple. But people have forgotten why. It is to show utter humility before God. It is the same as bowing in prayer. When we bow our heads to pray, we almost take it for granted we should do so. But why bow? To show humility before the Lord. A humility that implies submission, because in God's presence, none of us can boast. None of us can hold up our heads unashamed. We are all but dust and ashes before the living God. We are sinners before the holy God. In biblical times, men and women who worshipped bowed low, so low that their foreheads touched the ground. That was why, immediately before the Lord's ascension, we read: 'They came up and took hold of his feet and worshipped him' (Matthew 28:9).

God then speaks and tells Moses that he is the God of his fathers and, hearing this, Moses was afraid. Fear: that is the third element in this call. Fear of God. Moses hid his face because of this holy fear. May I ask if you, reader, have ever hidden your face for fear of the Lord? Have you ever known his presence so strongly, so clearly, that you have been filled with reverent fear, and have bowed low and hidden your face? When did you last know such a holy awe before the living God?

When God speaks to us, he calls our name. And we will know when that happens, because we will bow in utter humility, and hide our faces before the radiance of his presence.

The second question: 'Who am I?'

This is a question I have heard many times. I have heard it from those who were members of the congregations where I have ministered. In my pastoral work, often I have approached someone to explain that there was a task in the church that needed a worker. 'We are looking for someone,' I have said, 'to undertake this particular work. It's not an easy job, but would you be willing to take it on?' That is when I have heard this question: 'But who am I?' And the reaction too often has been, 'Me? Not me! Who am I to take on that work?'

I am quite sure that Moses was well aware of the dire situation in Egypt. I would even suggest that often he had prayed about it. I cannot accept that, during his years as a shepherd, he had forgotten the Lord or the miraculous way in which his own life had been spared. He knew exactly why he had been forced to become a refugee. I suspect he had carried on his heart, for those long years of exile, the burden of the wretched circumstances of his own people with whom he had chosen to identify. As the apostle tells us: '[He had] refused to be called the son of Pharaoh's daughter, choosing rather to be mistreated with the people of God than to enjoy the fleeting pleasures of sin' (Hebrews 11:24–25).

The words of Psalm 90[1] which are attributed to Moses in the title, record prayers he offered in his lonely wilderness days:

Make us glad for as many days as you have afflicted us,
and for as many years as we have seen evil.
Let your work be shown to your servants,
and your glorious power to their children (vv. 15–16).

Nevertheless, we find Moses saying, 'Who am I that I should go to Pharaoh and bring the children of Israel out of Egypt?' (3:11). God had told Moses about those wretched slaves—about their suffering, their cries because of their brutal taskmasters, and their pain and hurt and God said something which might appear to be paradoxical: '*I have come down* to deliver them ... Come, I will send you ... [to] bring my people ... out of Egypt' (3:8,10). Moses feels his knees knocking, his hands trembling, his body beginning to break out into goose pimples, and so he says, 'Who am I?' It is as if he is saying, 'Not me, Lord. I'm just a humble shepherd. Me? No, not me! A great idea to rescue the Hebrew people. They deserve to be rescued. I'm so glad, O God, that you are going to do that. I am filled with joy. That's wonderful. I am all behind that plan. I have been yearning and praying for that for years. It has my one hundred per cent support, as long as you don't send me!'

He may even have argued that his advanced years made it impossible for him to undertake such a task. He was nearing the four-score mark, so surely a younger man was needed for such an onerous assignment. In Psalm 90, from which I have just quoted, he says,

> For all our days pass away under your wrath;
>> we bring our years to an end like a sigh.
> The years of our life are seventy,
>> Or by reason of strength eighty;
> yet their span is but toil and trouble;
>> they are soon gone and we fly away (vv. 9–10).

Nevertheless, God offers Moses two supports. The

first is his own presence: 'I will be with you' (v. 12). The second was a sign that this was a real call from God: he would one day return to this very place to worship God. For this was the place where the law would be given, and the covenant sealed between the Lord and his people.

Now both of these promises—the Lord's own presence and the assurance that Moses would return to this very place to worship God along with the freed slaves— demanded faith. A faith, we will discover in chapter 4, that came hard to Moses. God, as we shall see, had to encourage and nurture his feeble faith until he was at last willing to obey this call.

For you and me today, there are certain lessons from Moses' question, 'Who am I?' One is that God uses weak, trembling people to do his work: '*I have come down* to rescue these slaves from Egypt ... Come, I will send you ... [to] bring my people ... out of Egypt.' God's time had come. God's plan and purpose was to bring this vast rabble of slaves across the Sinai desert and into the land of Canaan. But Moses had to do it—fearful, inadequate, unwilling Moses. 'I am sending *you*, so now, go!'

> God uses weak, trembling people to do his work.

We cannot begin to rehearse the needs in our world today. Nor can we begin to try and give even a hazy sketch of Almighty God's eternal purposes and plans.

But we all know without any fear of contradiction that there is desperate, urgent, crying need across the nations. We know too that God has plans to do a great deal about those needs. The point is that he has chosen ordinary believers, one after another. Has he chosen you, and is he calling your name? If he is, then I pray you feel both humility and fear. There was a time, we must remember, when Moses knew neither humility nor fear. And what a mess he made. But he came through a course in God's own training school, a course lasting four decades of shepherding. And it was on account of the lessons he had learned that, in humility and in fear, he asked, 'But who am I? Not me! Surely, not me!'

Consider the two promises: 'I will be with you,' and 'You will come back safely and worship me here.' God is solving the paradox of those earlier words: '*I have come down* to rescue the slaves ... so now, go. *I am sending you* to rescue them.' The solution is, '"We" will go together, you and I, side by side and hand in hand.' In effect, the Lord is saying, 'You will never be alone.' Consider the prisoners of conscience, languishing in stinking jails on account of their faith in Jesus Christ. Do you think they are alone? Do you think John Bunyan was ever alone in prison as he wrote his great book, *The Pilgrim's Progress*? Or Samuel Rutherford in his tiny, cold prison cell in Aberdeen, which he called 'Christ's palace'?[2] Then why do we hesitate and dither? Why are we afraid, and unsure of ourselves, and ask, 'But who am I?'

The third question: Who are you?

Was Moses wrong to request God to reveal his name? Certainly not! He needed to know more about the One who was calling him and commanding him to return to Egypt. He needed to have a message both for the slaves, and for Pharaoh. Thus, his argument: 'Suppose I go and say to the Israelites, "The God of your fathers has sent me," and they ask me, "What is his name?" then what shall I tell them?' That question was reasonable, and, I believe, permissible. And so, God disclosed to Moses the great name: 'I AM WHO I AM' (or I WILL BE WHO I WILL BE) (v.14).

When students read philosophy at university, one branch they study is called Metaphysics, which is the science of being and knowing. Descartes, the French philosopher, is perhaps the best-known exponent of metaphysics. He asked the question, 'How do I know that I am not dreaming? How do I know that everything going on around me is real? How do I know that all the people I meet and talk with are not just figments of my imagination?' He came up with the answer that the only thing of which he could be sure was that he himself existed. And he worked that out by saying, 'I think, therefore, I exist'—*Cogito ergo sum*.[3]

However, when God said to Moses, I AM WHO I AM (or I WILL BE WHO I WILL BE), he was not introducing Moses to metaphysics. This was not some philosophical statement about the being or existence of a deity. God was saying, 'You will learn who I am and what I am in the events that will unfold. I will be known by what will happen through my presence and my power working for you.' This great name of God, I AM, is the expression of God's dynamic involvement in the lives of his people. '*I have seen* the misery of my people ... *I have heard* their crying out because of their slave drivers, *I am concerned* about their suffering. So, *I have come down* to rescue them.' Those are the words of the great I am.

> This great name of God, I AM, is the expression of God's dynamic involvement in the lives of his people.

This name remains definitive for us today: *Emmanuel, I am the bread of life; I am the Good Shepherd; I am the door; I am the vine; Before Abraham was, I am.* We see how the Lord Jesus took these very words *I am* on his lips, using this name given to Moses by God—'The LORD, the God of your fathers, the God of Abraham, the God of Isaac and the God of Jacob' (3:15), and applying it to himself. That was one reason why Jesus so shocked the religious people of his day. The formula, 'I am', was regarded by the Jew as sacred. It was blasphemy to take those words on your lips. They were preserved for God alone. But Jesus repeatedly took them on his lips. And when he said, 'Before Abraham was, "I am",' you may remember how furious the Jews were and how they picked up stones to throw at him for such blasphemy (John 8:58–59).

As we consider the birth of the Saviour in that cave with its cattle trough; as we think of his labour at a carpenter's bench with chisel and hammer and saw; as we recall his ministry of teaching and healing; and as we come to his passion and death; then on to Easter morning and his resurrection; and then to his ascension to God's right hand and the pouring out of the Holy Spirit at Pentecost, we have exactly the meaning of I AM WHO I AM (or I WILL BE WHO I WILL BE). For God is dynamic, moving, present, a living Being. He is not a God away out there, watching the events of our lives with vague disinterest. He is a God who is active, concerned, involved, present and eternally contemporary.

The problem with many of us who 'believe' is that there seems to be a veil over our faces and over our understanding. We hardly sense God's presence and hardly notice what he is doing. Our minds are dull and slow and sluggish. Dimly we see, and darkly we understand. What do you think God is doing today in our land? Do we think God is idle, opting out, baffled, perplexed? What are our thoughts on God's purposes and plans for his church and people in my homeland of Scotland and the country where you live? The answer is still 'I AM WHO I AM. My purposes are ripening.' With inexorable, relentless timekeeping, God's work is moving forward.

But can we see it? Are we in touch? This applies to each individual believer. What about our lives? What is God doing in them? Are we even aware that he is working? Do we realize he has a great deal of work to do on us, in us, with us and through us? Or are we much the same as poor Moses, stuttering and stammering and saying, 'Great Lord, this is what I have yearned and prayed for all these years. I am so pleased to hear what you are about to do, as long as it is not me that you are calling!'

Three questions:

- Firstly, 'What is this?' Answer: 'God's Call! So go now, I am sending you!'
- Secondly, 'Who am I, Lord?' Answer: 'I will be with you and bring you back. You and I will go together!'
- Thirdly, 'Who are You?' Answer: 'Jesus Christ, the same yesterday, today and forever.'

FOR FURTHER STUDY

1. In Exodus 3:2, we read that Moses had brought his flocks to the vicinity of Mount Horeb (Sinai).[4] God's promise was to bring Moses and the delivered slaves to this same mountain (3:12). Follow through the many references in Scripture to Horeb (Sinai) to see it as a symbol (in the New Testament, allegorical) of both the old and new covenants: Exod. 19:1–3, 11–25; Deut. 4:9–14; Judg. 5:5; 1 Kings 19:8–18; Acts 7:30, 38; Gal. 4:21–31; Heb. 12:18–29.

2. From 2:4 onwards we find the name LORD (Yahweh) used constantly throughout Genesis. However, it was not until God spoke to Moses from the burning bush that the meaning of LORD was disclosed. Search out the other names used of God in Genesis and from their meanings follow through the ongoing process of the self-revelation of the divine character through the titles given: 14:18–'God Most High' (El Elyon); 16:13–'God Who Sees' (El Roi); 17:1–'God Almighty' (El Shaddai); 21:33–'God everlasting' (El Olam); 22:14 (KJV, ASV)–'The LORD Provides' (Jehovah Jireh). You might also want to include 28:13,–'The LORD, the God of Abraham'(compare with Matt. 22:31–32).

TO THINK ABOUT AND DISCUSS

1. What Bible passages have taught you most about God's nature: (a) his sorrow over our sinfulness, (b) his call to us to surrender ourselves to him, (c) the assurance of his steadfast, unchangeable love?

2. Would it be too embarrassing to share with others some Word of God brought to you which you neither wanted to hear nor obey? Gideon felt unequal to a great challenge that came to him, but God gave him a sign that he would be with him (Judg. 6:11–16; 36–40). Have you ever been challenged to undertake some service for Christ, but you have been too afraid to take it on? Did God reassure you, and if so, how?

3. Read again John 8:56–59 and then see how many other 'I AM' sayings of Jesus you can find in John's Gospel. See John 6:35; 8:12; 10:7; 10:11; 11:25; 14:6; 15:1–11. Discuss how each of them applies to us today in the light of Hebrews 13:8.

6 The three signs

Exodus 4:1–9

It surely must amaze us that a man who was to become a type of our matchless Messenger and Mediator, the Lord Jesus himself, should have been so full of excuses to the extent that ultimately God became angry with him! Nevertheless, the Scripture passage we consider in this chapter shows how God condescends to give every encouragement to his unwilling, reluctant, chosen servant, backed up by the three signs, which ought to have left him without excuse.

There is a well-known issue of someone who is looked up to as a spiritual leader, admired and even adulated on all sides, but the reality is that this person, being ordinary flesh and blood, has feet of clay, and is just the same as the rest of us—full of faults, doubts and fears. I am sure most readers will have come across this problem before. It is a tension we have to live with in the Christian faith.

On the one hand, we want our elders and ministers to be people of good character, those we can look up to with respect; on the other hand, we have to recognize that we are all human, and therefore there was only one perfect man, our Lord and Saviour.

A Jewish historian by the name of Josephus (I mentioned him in Chapter 3), who lived in the 1st century, wrote a massive book called *The History of the Jews*. In his book, Moses, at this stage in his story, is treated very kindly. The actual facts of the case, as recorded in Exodus, are softened down, as Josephus gives Moses more than the benefit of the doubt. But the sacred record of Scripture is perfectly clear: Moses was extremely reluctant to obey God. He knew perfectly well what God was asking him to do and, frankly, he did not want to do it.

Now this story is speaking to all who profess to love and follow Christ. What often happens is that we meet some of our contemporaries who have taken early retirement, and they say, 'I can thoroughly recommend it! It's great! I have a small part-time job, and I've never been so happy in all my life.' Speaking of those who are ministers, you will know that they are never normally offered early retirement. However, with each passing year, the church authorities are closing down or else linking together very small congregations. Previously life could have been less hectic in such a location, and there a pastor could be completely on top of his work, and have time left over for study and recreation and—most important of all—for that most neglected factor in every busy person's life, the family.

As I see it, in this passage in Exodus 4, Moses is being called to give up the quiet shepherd's life, where he was content and happy in the love of his wife and children; he is being asked to surrender all that and to enter into a calling that is going to stretch him to the limit (even at times beyond his limit), and demand all his strength, energy and time, so that ultimately he will be on the verge of a breakdown, suffering from burnout and exhaustion. And, frankly, it is tempting to assume that he preferred the quiet life.

I do not know about you, reader, but I can readily empathize with Moses' reluctance. Why not choose a simple, peaceful life, with wife and children close at hand? Why not stay in a job he had come to enjoy and could easily cope with? Why break up his home, and go off to be immersed in toil, tiredness and trouble? Why? After all, he was now eighty years of age, and it was time to take things more easily.

> Man of faith that Moses was, nevertheless, like all of us he had feet of clay.

Man of faith that Moses was, nevertheless, like all of us he had feet of clay. We must never forget that. His heart yearned and longed for a pleasant, leisurely future. And who in such a situation is without sin and can throw a single stone at Moses?

We must never think of a call from God in romantic, rosy terms. God's call invariably summons us to engage in a spiritual battle, a battle with our own wills. We will find we have to engage in a struggle with the desire for an easier way forward! But the Lord's call will always lead to a spiritual conflict that will never be easy, and could well bring much heartache, pain and toil!

The sign of the shepherd's staff

As they travel by coach from Jerusalem to Jericho, visitors to Israel will usually catch sight of Bedouin shepherds along the rolling hills on either side of the winding road. They will notice the slow, gentle pace of a shepherd's life in that part of the world. I do not mean that shepherding is easy, for sheep need tending, guarding and leading. Rather, I am implying that the conditions in which the shepherds live are very different to the noisy, crowded streets of Jerusalem. The contrast could hardly be greater.

The visitors on their coach will quickly realize that the shepherd's lifestyle has hardly changed over 3000 years. For yes, the Bedouin shepherd will be carrying the age-long symbol of the shepherd's craft: the crook or staff. In our reading, we see that Moses has his staff—his crook—in his hand. The Lord says to him, 'What is that in your hand?' He replies, 'A staff.' And God tells him to put it down (4:2–3a).

That was a hard thing to ask him to do, for the staff symbolized his whole way of life. 'Throw it down. Let it fall to the ground. Give it up. Yield it up at my command,' God is saying.

Now we have to notice at this point the paradox of the Christian's obedience to God. Because, up to this point (and well beyond this point), Moses has been arguing with God. He has offered excuse after excuse as to why he should not leave his pleasant, comfortable life, and take on the impossible assignment of freeing the slaves from Egypt. But Moses' reluctance and unwillingness has at its root a dilemma.

His dilemma is that he believes God. He is, after all, a man of faith. He knows that it is God who is speaking to him. He believes God when he says he has heard the prayers of the Hebrew slaves, that he is concerned for them and the time has come to deliver them from their bondage. What God says, Moses believes. It is precisely because he believes God that his reluctance is in turmoil. There is a battle going on in his will. Had he not believed God, there would have been no battle. If he did not believe, he could have just walked away and forgotten the whole episode of the burning bush. But because he believes, he is caught on the horns of a dilemma: his own way, which he wants, and God's way, which he does not want.

Therefore, when God commands him to lay down his shepherd's staff, he obeys, albeit reluctantly. Spare a thought for Moses. Consider what it cost him to throw that staff to the ground. Torn as he was, there alone with God, to say his unwilling 'yes' in this symbolic way of letting go of the thing he wanted most: a comfortable, safe and easy life to which he had submitted and grown to accept.

There is, however, more to the rod lying on the ground than that. For as the rod becomes a snake, and then a rod again when Moses takes it up by the tail, God is saying something else. It is that the pride, pomp and power of Egypt are going to be challenged by the contemptible and despised shepherd people, and by their God. Without doubt, Moses was a realist. He could picture himself perfectly clearly, dressed as a Bedouin shepherd with staff in hand, standing in the royal palace before the mighty Pharaoh seated on his throne, his features concealed by his golden mask. Moses knew the Egyptian king would be surrounded by his learned men and his works of beautiful art, along with the

> The pride, pomp and power of Egypt are going to be challenged by the contemptible and despised shepherd people, and by their God.

commander of Egypt's great military force. And Moses could see the sheer absurdity of such a situation; he knew how utterly ridiculous it was that he was being called to go and confront Pharaoh.

In today's terms it would be similar to sending a farm servant from some little croft in the Outer Hebrides to Downing Street to say to the Prime Minister, 'Establish the population of North and South Uist, along with Benbecula, as an independent state, its own government, currency and its own official language to be the Gaelic! Do that right now.' There stands the Hebridean ploughman, in his boots and dungarees, bonnet in hand, in the reception chamber of 10 Downing Street. At least the British Prime Minister would have been unlikely to do anything other than show our highland crofter out. 'Hamish, laddie, there's the door. My office manager will see you out!' with an icy smile that said, 'and don't come back and waste my time'.

By contrast, Moses knew that he could lose his freedom at best and his head at worst, going to Pharaoh as a Bedouin, representing a ragged race of shepherd slaves, despised tinker-cowhands. And so, the sign of the rod was full of meaning. This simple staff, symbol of the contemptible slave race, would become a sign of the awesome deadly threat to Pharaoh's might, as Moses obeyed God and stood before the Egyptian magnate.

You and I have a problem today with our churches:

we have gained some degree of respectability. We are still a force to be reckoned with (a diminishing force, I admit!). We have hundreds of fine buildings, well-kept, well-supported, and well thought of. We might think that is good. And I suppose, up to a point, it is a good thing. But it is not the way God has chosen to work. God, *because* he is God, prefers to work through what is low, contemptible and despised in the eyes of the world. He prefers that way because, when the odds against us are too great, the task is clearly impossible, our hearts faint and we are ready to give up, then his power shines all the more radiantly, and his glory is not shaded by our purely human achievements.

Throw down the staff in your hand. Give up what you hold dear: the rod that supports you, the crook that sustains you. Give it up, and when you have given it up and let go of it, see what I will do, and how my power will confound the mighty.

The hand made leprous

The second sign was that Moses' hand should first become white with leprosy, and then be restored again to normality. Now, I am going to do some guessing. I think there is a deeper significance here for Moses and for the slave people who were to witness this sign. Moses, for many years, has been away from Egypt. Remember the position he had when he lived there.

He was a royal prince, an adopted son of Pharaoh's daughter. He had power and influence, as we have seen. But suddenly, he had been forced to flee for his life. And he had been in hiding, like a desert rat, all these forty years. His power and influence had been snatched from him, and the truth was—though at the moment he is not wanting to admit it—he has become an outcast, thrown on the scrapheap, doing nothing useful or fruitful either for God or for his people.

He had been given, you remember, the very best education. We saw how the New Testament tells us he was skilled in all sorts of learning and languages and military training. And all that was being wasted as he lived the simple, slow life of a Bedouin shepherd, doing nothing for God as he watched the occasional caravan of camels passing in the distance. He had become a metaphorical leper: ineffective; achieving nothing; cut off from his people; cut off from the world. And now, as suddenly as it had happened, the leprosy is healed and his hand is restored. He is being called back to a useful, fruitful life.

One writer[1] suggests that the slaves in Egypt would certainly remember Moses—how could they have forgotten one of their number who had been rescued from the Nile by Pharaoh's daughter and brought up within the Egyptian court! But they would also remember the total hash he had made of trying to stand up for them against the Egyptian might, and how he had run away like the fugitive he had become. He needed a new authority and the leprous hand was a demonstration not only to himself, but to his people, that God was restoring him.[2] This call of God would shine forth like a resurrection, so that he was endued with authority.

Once again, we have here a pearl of pure gospel. The Bible never excuses Moses for trying to do God's work in his own strength. It never suggests that his enforced exile all these years was anything but his own fault. But it does teach us that it was by God's grace and call that he was restored again to service.

Many of us have known what it means to be put to one side by God because of our failure. Oh yes, we may have continued to go through the motions of serving God. But the power had gone. The effectiveness had waned. We ourselves knew in our heart of hearts that we were achieving nothing for eternity. We had been disqualified by our own sin. But when that has happened, God comes and says, 'I'm going to restore you. I'm going to heal that leprosy of soul and bring you back into the centre of my will, where I can use you again. "I will restore to you the years that the swarming locust has eaten ..." (Joel 2:25)'.

Like Moses, we shrink back. Like him, many of us are reluctant. Once, in the past, we were straining to go, but no longer. And God asks us, 'Who made your hands? Who made your feet? Who made your lips and eyes and ears and mind? I the Lord, who created you, will put the wholeness and health and strength back into your body so that you can at last serve me the way I want you to serve me.'

From now on, Moses' hand would be a gentle hand, kind and firm. It would be a strong and wise hand because it had been restored by the grace and power of God. So the hand that let go of his staff—yielding his past life, giving it up—is now given a new strength and a new control by the touch of God to hold his staff for a new purpose, to achieve a work that God had planned from the beginning of time.

> Have we let go of what we hold on to, so that God can then restore us, to serve him where he has placed us, in the way he chooses?

Have we given our hands to God; have we let go of what we hold on to, so that God can then restore us, to serve him where he has placed us, in the way he chooses?

The water turned to red mud

The word, 'blood', is, I think, to be understood as referring to the red colour and sticky texture of blood. Moses is told that when he takes some of the water of the Nile and pours it on the ground, it will become polluted, undrinkable, unusable: a smelly, red, muddy mess. What is the meaning of this third sign?

We will look at this in greater detail when, in Exodus 7, we come to the Ten Plagues. But just now notice this fact: life in Egypt was totally dependent on the River Nile. Without the Nile, Egypt would become a desert waste because, by the rise and fall of the Nile each year, the land along its banks was irrigated and so rendered fruitful and fertile. The river too was used for transport, for importing goods; indeed, exporting the Egyptians' wares and produce made it a lifeline for their land.

It was, and remains to this day, the mighty natural resource on which the entire economy of the nation depended. Yet now, Moses was being given the warning that, through the arrogance and hardness of Pharaoh's heart, the entire national economy was going to come to a standstill, for human power is nothing compared to the power of the Creator God.

If the first two signs were mainly for Moses about himself and what he was being called to do, this third sign was about the judgement of God upon a cruel and despotic regime, which for too long had flagrantly ignored human rights, and had been guilty of some of the worst crimes against humanity in human history.

Conclusion

I conclude this chapter where we began with Moses' unwillingness to obey God. We saw his reluctance to take up the cross to which God was calling him, and his desire that God would do his gracious work and deliver the slaves, but not through him! He was saying, in effect, 'Do your mighty work, Lord, but choose someone else as your instrument—not me!'

There has been a clear tension in these nine verses, in that Moses is so unwilling on the one hand, but on the other hand he cleverly blames his reluctance upon the people of God—'They will not believe me or listen to my voice' (v. 1). Do you see that tension? Verse 10, where he begins to complain about his stammer, gives the final clue. However, until now he is saying, in effect, to God, 'Those slaves are a hopeless lot. They'll never believe. They will never trust you or accept that you have sent me. It's a lost cause, Lord. I know. They refused to believe me, or back me before. Remember, Lord? Things will not have improved. We're having a wonderful talk together, Lord, you and me, here in this sacred place. I'm so grateful to be with you, Lord God. But your people are utterly useless. Forget them. The Church is all but dead!'

That is what it amounts to. And I hear from my own heart, and from the lips of others, exactly the same excuses to this day. Let me say something that may surprise, even shock you. When God called me to become a minister, he never asked me to believe in the Presbyterian Church. He never asked me to think that the Presbyterian Church was a good church, or a strong church, or an admirable church. Quite the contrary! Bound up in my call to serve God was the basic truth that the Presbyterian Church, and every other church, for that matter, is flawed and full of faults and failings, and that is precisely why God called me, and why he calls anyone.

> Our faith is not in the Church. Our faith is in God.

Our faith is not in the Church. Our faith is in God. And it distresses me more than I can say when I meet people who have broken away from their denomination and formed yet another denomination. I constantly meet such people and hear the usual tale of the church's failure, impotence and faults. But the way forward is not to go and form another church, which rapidly will also have failings, flaws and faults. The way forward is to see that God loves the Church, gave his Son to be her Saviour, and wants to change her from being ineffective and faithless and inconsistent, to being effective, strong and full of faith in him.

Some people have spoken to me as if I accepted the call to their congregation where I was ministering because I thought it was a marvellous church and a wonderful congregation. Those who think like that cannot be more mistaken. When any minister is interviewed to be pastor of a congregation, its praises are sung to him by the 'search committee'. But no minister with any sense will believe a word of such commendations, any more than Moses believed he would be welcomed with open arms by his own people.

So, take the shepherd's staff, the leprous hand restored, and the water turned to mud—take these signs to heart—and understand that, come wind, come weather, God is determined to work. Therefore, resolve to bow to his will, obey his call and embrace him as he embraces you and me. For it is by obedience and submission that we enter into the life of victory and honour to his glorious Name!

For further study ▶

FOR FURTHER STUDY

1. In his Introduction to his *Commentary on the Psalms*, Calvin writes: '... although the Psalms abound with guidance on holy and righteous living, they will principally teach and train us to bear the cross, which is a genuine proof of our obedience.'[3] Select two or three Psalms (e.g., 41, 42, 43) and see if you can extract that 'training' to which Calvin refers.

2. Not many of God's servants have been given miraculous signs—as Moses was—to affirm their calling. Nevertheless, can you illustrate from Scripture examples of clear confirmation God has given to those he called to serve him?

TO THINK ABOUT AND DISCUSS

1. Sometimes obedience to God demands that we have to surrender aspects of our daily living in order to serve him as he is asking us to do. Can you think of examples of this from your own experience, or perhaps from biographies of Christian leaders you have read?

2. Undoubtedly, Moses had become a kind of outcast on account of his rash and pathetic attempt to free his people. But God is in the business of restoration: 'he restores my soul' (Ps. 23:3). See if you can find a character from the Old Testament and one from the New Testament whom God had to restore, e.g., Jonah 3 and 4; Luke 22:54–62 and John 21:15–17. Can you describe any significant occasion (s) in your own walk with God when he has had to restore you?

3. The task to which God was appointing Moses was, humanly speaking, totally impossible. Describe any challenge of which you are aware that faces a Christian congregation or leader today which also appears to be impossible. Can you think of good reasons for asking for divine confirmation before we attempt to face such challenges?

7 Good reasons for disobedience

Exodus 4:10–16

Considering that Moses became not only God's messenger and mediator and so, the Old Testament's most significant forerunner of Christ, it is nothing less than astonishing for us to read of his persistent unwillingness to obey God's call to him. Indeed, he was so stubborn that God became angry with him. Yet the Lord condescended to deal graciously with his recalcitrant servant by telling him of Aaron's impending approach and his future role as Moses' spokesman.

When I was a schoolboy, it was common for some pupil to forget his book and, as he was trying to explain why, the teacher would severely scold him, saying, 'Excuses, excuses, excuses!' Did you ever hear that?

When the Lord asks us to do something for him, how often do we make excuses? While you and I have decisions to make every day, there are times of crisis in all of our stories when we have a really important, life-changing choice to make. Too often we choose to go our own way.

Yet the truth about being a Christian is that we only really behave like Christians when we go God's way and not our own way; we only win the battle when we yield our wills to him. Those who have been called to serve God in some far-off country will know what I mean and will empathize with Moses at this point in his life.

We must not think of God's servants as ready-made saints who always want God's Word to fill their hearts. They know exactly what Moses was going through because they too have shared his experience.

> We must not think of God's servants as ready-made saints who always want God's Word to fill their hearts.

And perhaps some readers already know themselves well enough to admit that they too still have plenty of fight left in them when it comes to choosing between their way and God's way. Indeed, all of us need to be reminded that we only win the battle when we surrender, and we are only victorious when we yield to God. As long as we hold out against him, we are losers, and there is nothing more unhappy and wretched than to be defeated in a battle we know the Lord's will was that we should win.

The reason why we *should not* serve God

When it comes to you and me expressing our opinions, we always consider that we talk a lot of sense. We are not completely wrong about everything. We are usually right about some things. We have some experience of life, at least; we have noticed how things are in this world; we have our own opinions and we most definitely are right on a number of issues.

On the face of it, Moses was the perfect man to go to Egypt to free the Hebrew slaves. He was tailor-made for the job. Had he not been brought up in the Egyptian court, so that, of all his people, he alone knew Egyptian manners and etiquette? Had he not grown up speaking the Egyptian language, and been educated in the best university under the finest of Egyptian scholars? Was he not skilled in military strategy and in all the wisdom of Egypt, the world's super-power of his day? It was obvious: he was the ideal candidate for the assignment. Indeed, the only candidate!

But God had apparently forgotten something which Moses had remembered. It was that Moses had a speech impediment. Now some people are inclined to suggest that Moses did not have a speech impediment at all, but was only making excuses, trying to get out of obeying God's call. But I am inclined to believe Moses did have a serious speech impediment. For a start, God never contradicts Moses on this issue. And this is not the only time Moses raises this matter. A couple of chapters later, we find him again saying that he has faltering lips, so however could he attempt to address Pharaoh? (Exodus 6:30, NIV).

Some time ago, I spoke to a speech therapist about Moses' problem. When he says he is 'slow of speech and of tongue' (v. 10), he could well be referring to a syndrome known as 'cluttering'—a tightness in the lips and tongue which slows down the speaking process. This condition is found among those who were bilingual at an early age, and is caused by the child avoiding words in one language that cause difficulty and using the other language so as not to have to use the words he or she finds harder to pronounce. Later on, when those difficult words have to be used, the person finds a tightness in the lips and tongue, now called 'cluttering'; it is quite different to stammering. The interesting thing is that Moses' early life fits the case exactly. For, from his days as a toddler, he was learning two languages—Hebrew and Egyptian—as his time was divided between his own family and Pharaoh's daughter.

Furthermore, if parents try to force the pace with a small child, the speech may sometimes be affected and, going hand in hand with this slowness of speech, there can be temper tantrums caused by the frustration of being slow of lip and slow of tongue. Think of Moses killing the Egyptian taskmaster, and his smashing of the tablets of stone on which the Ten Commandments had been written (Exodus 2:11–12; Deuteronomy 9:16–17). Thus, the biblical evidence available to us would suggest that Moses was not making an excuse at all, but was absolutely right; he may well have had a problem with his speech.

'Oh, my Lord,' he says (notice that in verses 10 and 13, the AKJV, RSV, ESV have, '*Oh, my* Lord,' correctly translating the Hebrew which uses a particle of pleading. The NIV omits '*my*' and translates simply as 'O Lord'). 'Oh, my Lord, I am not eloquent, either in the past, or since you have spoken to your servant, but I am slow of speech [lip][1] and of tongue.'

There is an implied criticism of God here. It is as if he said, 'You have called me, Lord, and have been speaking with me now for some time, but you haven't corrected or healed my lips and tongue. I'm still having difficulty with my speech and finding it hard to express in words what I want to say. If you wanted me to go and speak to Pharaoh, why haven't you healed my speech impediment?'

So, we conclude that Moses had a genuine reason for not going to Egypt. His argument was valid, for he did have a problem. And what is more, God had not helped him or healed him. His disability remained. It was still there. Therefore, with this speech impediment, it was ridiculous to suggest he should go and act as God's spokesman before the world's most powerful monarch.

Everyone called to serve God has some excuse for declining the call. Often, as with Moses, not an excuse but a legitimate reason why God should send someone else. Some would prefer the Lord to assign them to undertake something other than the task to which he is calling them. What then of those of us who are not called to some hard vocation in a far-off land, but whose place is to live in our home country in some modest role in life? Their case is no different from that of the missionaries. Because every one of us has reasons why we should not be serving God. Let me give you some of them:

There are some in our churches who cannot serve God because they are far too busy at work. They have very responsible jobs, which oblige them to bring work home to complete in the evenings. They are under increasing pressure at work, and so God should give them an exemption and choose someone else instead.

Then there are those who do not have much education, and they consider it ridiculous that they were being asked to help with children's work. There are plenty of people in the congregation who are trained in working with children and who should undertake that task. So, they regard themselves as having every reason for refusing.

Several times during my ministry, because I wanted

to improve the pastoral care of the many housebound in the congregation, I asked if there were any church members who might like to consider adopting one of our elderly members who lived alone and make it their task to call fairly regularly and keep in touch. Of course, this was not a ministry that would suit everyone, but I learned that quite a number who heard of this need did not fancy the idea of bothering with a frail old man or woman. They argued, 'Does not that person have family? Is it not their relative's responsibility to look after them?' And so, the excuses came tumbling out. I recall one that often cropped up: not only were they naturally shy, but they were already committed most afternoons with their indoor-bowling club, as well as doing a regular 'work-out' at a fitness club in the town.

All of us have excellent reasons, valid reasons, real reasons (though some simply invent excuses), why we should not be agreeing to do something for God.

> All of us have excellent reasons, valid reasons, real reasons, why we should not be agreeing to do something for God.

There is always someone more fitted, more gifted, more suitable, to serve God than they are. There is always something that disqualifies them. It always has been so, and always will be so. Nonetheless, still God calls each of us by name and tells us that he has a plan and purpose for our lives—there is something to which he is calling us, and it is usually the very thing that we can think up a reason for not obeying. Have we recognized this is true of us all?

The reason why we *should* obey God

It is most unpleasant to see a child deliberately defying and disobeying their parents. I am sure many of us have been embarrassed and annoyed as we have witnessed some little brat 'getting away with murder', as we say. But how much more offensive, how much more unpleasant, how much more wrong, when a man or woman deliberately disobeys God, for whatever reason.

There are two aspects to this question. The first side of the coin is that some push themselves forward to serve God when he has not called them. The missionary societies tell us that they have to use a most thorough screening process before they accept anyone for service overseas. In the past, those who volunteered were sent abroad and, with more idealism than common sense, their claim to have a call from God was believed. When they arrived in some missionary area, it was soon evident that, not only had they clearly not had a call from God, but also that they were complete misfits, so at the earliest opportunity they were sent home. Some people can be very bold, impetuous and self-confident.

It is not God's call that urges them on, but their own rashness.

The other side of the coin is that when we know our own weaknesses and see that we do not have the ability to do what God is summoning us to do, we are going to fall back on God in the way we should, and his glory is going to shine out more brightly because of our human weakness. That was why Paul's physical illness was never healed. God said, 'My grace is sufficient for you, for my power is made perfect in weakness' (2 Corinthians 12:9).

Be that as it may, there is nevertheless something of a problem here in Moses' claim to have a speech impediment. Because, in Acts 7:22, Stephen states, 'Moses was instructed in all the wisdom of the Egyptians, and he was mighty in his words and deeds.' At a first glance, it might appear that Stephen was forgetting Moses' comments about his lips and tongue, or else Stephen regarded them as excuses, not genuine reasons. However, we have to be grateful for Stephen's words that Moses' speech was 'mighty', even in his younger days in Egypt, because he is pointing us to an important distinction between being a good orator and having something of weight to say. The two are not the same.

Maybe you have heard someone with 'the gift of the gab', as we sometimes say. He had a great flow of words, spoken with outstanding eloquence but, when he had finished, you asked yourself whether he actually said anything worth saying. On the other hand, you may have heard someone very plainly spoken, with no airs, graces or rhetorical flourishes, but the content of what was said was very powerful and telling. That is the distinction we have here.

God had not made a mistake at all in choosing Moses. Agreed, he had a problem, but God knew he also had a gift, which he himself had given him; he was able in his mind to assess a situation, and then to express his case in words that were powerful. Like Jonathan Edwards—the great revivalist of the 18th century—whose nose reputedly scarcely left the page of his sermons, for he was short-sighted, so there was no oratory from him, and yet, scores were converted to Christ, so powerful were his words.[2] That is the distinction to which Stephen is pointing us.

> God knew Moses better than Moses knew himself, for God had destined him since before his birth for this calling.

God knew Moses better than Moses knew himself, for God had destined him since before his birth for this calling. The fact that his rhetoric and oratory would be below par was beside the point. God needed neither rhetoric nor oratory, only obedience, so that this man could pass on words filled with weight and power, because they were the words God had given him.

Like Moses, we may ask, 'Dare I take on this work to which I believe God is calling me?' But ought we not to ask, 'Dare I fail to take it on?' I have heard this so often: 'I'd be afraid that I wouldn't manage that! I'd be frightened that I wouldn't cope!' But how I wish I had heard more often, 'It would be wrong of me not to agree to help in the Sunday School,' or, 'I'd be afraid not to sing in the choir, if that is what God is asking me to do,' or, 'I'd be disobeying the Lord if I refused to take on visiting that district, if God is asking me to visit it.'

It was quite in order for Moses to tremble and to be afraid of what lay ahead of him. That was a right and godly fear. But where Moses failed at this point, and why he caused God to be angry with him, was that he was not also sufficiently afraid of disobeying God. Should we not ask ourselves if God has ever been grieved with us because we have turned down his call to serve him in some task to which he has called us? That is what we are to fear. We are to be afraid lest God's anger should burn against us for failing to obey.

'Who has made man's mouth? Who makes him mute or deaf, or seeing, or blind? Is it not I, the LORD? Now therefore go, and I will be with your mouth and teach you what you shall speak' (4:11–12). You will deliver my message to Pharaoh in spite of all your deficiencies!

When he truly calls us, the Lord most certainly will give us all the enabling that we need to fulfil his commission, however menial it may be.

The reason why we should not doubt God

Have you ever seen a donkey that was refusing to budge? Their owner was there at their head, tugging away and trying to persuade them to start moving. When he failed, he got someone to push from behind, so there was the comic sight of one man pulling at the head, and another pushing at the rear, and the stupid animal at last had no other option than to move. Usually, it is when a donkey is being loaded into a horse box that such measures are needed.

Here is another kind of donkey—a stubborn, unwilling man. On his deathbed, when he was blessing his sons, Jacob predicted that Issachar would end up being a metaphorical donkey, bowing his shoulders in submission to the local tribes and becoming 'a servant at forced labour' (Genesis 49:14–15). Here in our Bible passage, God wants to move Moses from his peaceful, quiet, but entirely wasted life in Midian, and send him off to a foreign land where he will become a mighty instrument in God's hands. But Moses does not want to be transported off anywhere. So, firstly God pushes him from behind, as it were, and then pulls him from in front.

'How does God do that?' you may ask.

'Aaron, your brother ... is coming out to meet you, and when he sees you, he will be glad in his heart' (v. 14). So, while God pushes Moses from behind, he uses Aaron to draw him from the front, so to speak. Consequently, Moses is now under pressure to obey, both from where he is standing, and also from the very place to which he is being sent. His stubbornness is being broken down, until, ultimately, he sees he has no other option but to obey God.

We may ask why Aaron was coming to meet Moses. On the human level, probably to find him and let him know that those who were trying to kill him were now all dead. On the divine level, he was already on his way because the Spirit of God had put it into his heart to come looking for his long-lost brother. But Aaron's journey south into the Sinai desert was no coincidence. There are no coincidences for the child of God. As his servants begin to move at his command, they find door after door opens before them, and the pathway ahead becomes clear. However reluctant, unwilling and stubborn we may be, the Lord's purposes become clear, and the way stretches clearly before us. We find that there are helping hands, just when we need them, and friends to care and provide, timed precisely when we require help and provision.

Christ promised as much when he sent out seventy-two of his disciples two by two (Luke 10:1). Saul of Tarsus found the same thing in the weeks immediately after his conversion (Acts 9:19b–31). As the apostle Paul, he experienced God's providential care and provision throughout his whole tempestuous ministry.

And so, God swept away, one by one, Moses' objections: his unwillingness; his stuttering tongue; his reluctance to believe God; until Moses saw that he had no alternative but to trust God. Doubt was no longer possible. The final two chapters of the book of Acts, 27 and 28, exemplify this perfectly.

We should use some sanctified imagination and put ourselves in Moses' place as he led his flock back home to his father-in-law's encampment, and to Zipporah his wife and to his two sons. A few hours earlier, he had been a typical Bedouin shepherd, pleasing himself, bothering about no one, doing his own thing, as the days of his life slipped past without usefulness either to God or man. But now, as he makes his way back to his desert home, it is for the last time.

The staff in his hand has dramatically changed its character; it is now the rod of God. In his heart there burns a fire, kindled at the burning bush. The Word of God is in his heart, a Word that has come to him clearly and overwhelmingly. His will has been bent to God's will, and he now knows he has to begin the journey to Egypt to undertake the most formidable task any man had ever undertaken. His brother, Aaron, was already travelling along the desert road to meet him. One thinks of Martin Luther, standing before all the pomp and power of the Church and the Holy Roman Empire, saying simply, 'I can do no other, so God help me.'[3] Moses could do no other; God alone must and would help him.

All those who step out in obedience to the call of Jesus Christ know perfectly well that there are perfectly good reasons why they should not be responding. But they also know that there are even better reasons why they cannot, and dare not, disobey the One who has called them. They also know why they must never doubt God's will and provision and goodness in sending them.

> Every single person who knows the Lord has also been called to serve the Lord, in however humble or seemingly mundane a place.

What of those of us who are not called into some seemingly romantic assignment in some exotic land? For most of us must remain at our humdrum jobs, plodding along in some unspectacular role. We too must also be obedient, for every single person who knows the Lord has also been called to serve the Lord, in however humble or seemingly mundane a place. We too have our excuses why they need not obey God. All the Lord's people need to learn to tremble, lest they disobey him. Every one of us needs to know that when he calls, we dare not, we must not, doubt his Word. So may you, reader, go forward together with the staff of God in your hand, his Word in your heart, and with his presence as your assurance. 'Now go! I will help you to speak, and will teach you what to say and do in my name.'

FOR FURTHER STUDY

1. The Greek scholars tell us that when Jesus says, 'I know whom I have chosen' (John 13:18), a legitimate translation of the pronoun 'whom' would be, 'I know *the kind of man* I have chosen.' Make a list of the Lord's complete knowledge of the hearts of those whom he calls to serve him (including yourselves), even before that call is given. For example, besetting sins, frailty, stubbornness, pride, lust and so on. Consider and illustrate from Scripture the fathomless depths of his love, condescension, understanding, patience and tenderness towards all his servants.

2. Moses' 'stuttering' tongue was not a disability God was going to heal. There are various suggestions from a variety of commentators on the meaning of Paul's 'thorn in the flesh' (2 Cor. 12:7–9). How likely is it that it could have been something to do with his sight (Gal. 4:13–15; Col. 4:18)? Could a 'thorn in the flesh' ever be a moral problem such as sexual orientation?

TO THINK ABOUT AND DISCUSS

1. How probable is it that we can all have genuine reasons for being reluctant to respond to God's call to serve him in some particular way? If so, how ought we to deal with our reluctance?

2. Look up on any search engine about the cobbler William Carey and/ or the housemaid Gladys Aylward. In both of their cases it was others who thought they did not have what it took to serve God either in India (William Carey) or China (Gladys Aylward). How ought we to react to those who want to disqualify us, when we are sure God is calling us to serve him and how ought we to respond to God's voice?

3. Can you think of something you have sincerely said or done in good faith that has made God angry with you? If so, what made you wonder if God was angry with you? How do you think God responded to Jeremiah's bitter complaint (Jer. 20:7–18; but see also 31:31–34)?

8 Courtesy, confirmation and commitment

Exodus 4:18–20

When studying our Bibles, it is too easy to pass quickly over a few verses and fail to grasp the handful of metaphorical gold sovereigns contained there. The verses considered in this chapter have a message about family relationships, as well as about God's gracious confirmation when, trembling and uncertain, we obey him. They remind us too that a life of discipleship will be costly and will involve carrying the cross. It is the path the Master trod; must not the servant tread it too?

The passage from Exodus 4 that we are now to consider could well be topical for some readers. Nowadays, working people no longer have guaranteed stability, for as employment is increasingly temporary, moving home to a fresh place of work is often a necessity. In one of the congregations where I ministered some years ago, we had an annual turnover of at least ten percent in our congregation and when, ten years later, I was invited back to share in anniversary services, over fifty percent of the congregation had not been members during my ministry there. Instead of standing to preach in a building where almost every face was familiar, I found myself addressing a company of worshippers, many of whose faces I had never seen before.

No doubt there will be some readers who have been born, educated and lived all their lives in the same city, town or village. But it is equally probable that others will have had Moses' experience of having to move to a new home in an unfamiliar community and embark upon the adventure of starting a new life surrounded by relative strangers. Nonetheless, whichever category we are in, let us try to empathize with Moses, who was by our contemporary criteria now a senior citizen. For here we have the account of him packing his bags and leaving Midian for a new life and vocation in far-off Egypt. Obviously, it is a highly compressed and summarized account of his departure. But I am sure we will all find there are principles embedded here which are relevant for our lives today.

Courtesy

No one I have known who receives a call from God, goes home and, without a word to anyone, packs his bags, shuts up his shop, and disappears into the blue. That only happens when someone intentionally disappears to hide either from the police or from a criminal gang who are out to get him. But for normal citizens making a move just does not happen that way.

We have families. We have our occupations, our homes, our friends. And although some are called to move to another country where they are to serve God, it takes a long time to make the arrangements, tie up all the loose ends of their lives, and uncouple themselves from their familiar environment before they can leave for their new calling.

Now I know that life was far simpler in those days. We can be sure Moses had no mortgage. Nor did he have any property either to sell or put into the hands of an estate agent for letting. Neither did he have any visa to obtain or passport to renew. But even though life was undoubtedly simpler than today, it was not all that simple. For many years, he had been employed by his father-in-law. My guess is that he had been an excellent employee, that the flocks and herds had done well under his management and that he had become a most valued asset in Jethro's business.

Moreover, Jethro and his family would be deeply attached to Moses and his little family, for their daughter was Moses' wife, and the two boys were their grandchildren. What grandparents want to say goodbye to their grandchildren, or what parents find it easy to say goodbye to their daughter? So, matters were complicated enough for Moses. Therefore, we must not underestimate his problems in packing his bags and leaving Midian for far-off Egypt.

The compressed account of his resignation from his job, his selling off or disposing of the possessions he had gathered and his packing of the few essential items for the journey—all this is described in just a couple of sentences. But in the brief account that we are given are tucked away some important principles for you and me in our everyday lives.

Firstly, we see Moses' courtesy and respect towards his father-in-law. He goes cap in hand, as it were, and humbly asks to be released from his job, and for permission for the four of them to leave and travel back to Egypt where Moses' family were. Now straightaway we recall Jacob who failed to show that kind of courtesy, but did a moonlight flit, and left while Laban, his father-in-law, was away on business (Genesis 31:17–21). And what trouble and hostility, anger and aggro, Jacob's action caused. That was not how it was with Moses.

Consider the dilemma he was in. God had spoken to him. A fire had been kindled in his heart; the flame of the burning bush had ignited his soul. Yet he dared not share with his father-in-law the real reason for his going. He is completely silent about that. Not a word about the call of God to him to free the Hebrew slaves. 'Why?' you may ask. I suspect that he was afraid that Jethro would think him mad.

Spurgeon once wrote: 'No one knows the loneliness of a soul who has outstripped its fellows in its zeal for the Lord of hosts. It dare not reveal itself lest men count it mad; it cannot conceal itself, for a fire burns within its bones. Only before the Lord can it find rest.'[1] Moses, I believe, knew a loneliness now that he had never known all those years in the wilderness with only the sheep for company. It was the loneliness of a man with a mission and a message, which he dared not share with anyone, lest he be thought of as mad.

> Moses knew a loneliness now that he had never known all those years in the wilderness with only the sheep for company.

And yet he must do the right thing and ask Jethro's permission to go. It is significant that the Holy Spirit records for us that Jethro gladly and graciously gave his permission. 'Go in peace,' he said to his son-in-law. It is as if he said, 'We'll miss you and our daughter and the boys, but I wish you well!' That speaks volumes about Moses. It tells us that Jethro trusted and respected him. It says that over those long years, Jethro had come to admire his son-in-law, and believed that he would look after Zipporah and the two young lads. It was a testimony to Moses' life and work.

In his first letter, the apostle Peter urges believers to live in such a way as to win the respect and approval (as far as that is possible) of their neighbours and workmates. During years when the persecution of Christians was becoming increasingly common, he wrote,

'Have unity of mind, sympathy, brotherly love, a tender heart and a humble mind. Do not repay evil for evil, or reviling for reviling, but on the contrary bless, for to this you were called, that you may obtain a blessing ... Now who is there to harm you, if you are zealous for what is good?' (1 Peter 3:8–9).

Similarly, Paul wrote that we should '... lead a peaceful and quiet life, godly and dignified in every way. This is good and it is pleasing in the sight of God our Saviour' (1 Timothy 2:1–3). And again, 'If possible, so far as it depends on you, live peaceably with all' (Romans 12:14–18; 1 Thessalonians 4:11–12).

I do not believe that God calls anyone into his service whose workmates or employees say, when he or she leaves, 'Well, that's a relief to see the back of them.' But I suspect (and I am by no means the only one) that in these days of difficulty in finding employment, some turn to full-time Christian service as an easy option. Indeed, I have had both young men and women coming to speak to me about work abroad, about the ministry, or concerning some kind of church work but, after speaking with them, it has been quite evident that many of them are turning to Christian service, assuming it will be an easier ride.

Notice that when Jesus called his twelve apostles, many of them were busy working—some as fishermen, another as a tax-collector. So it was with Moses. And the courtesy Jethro showed in giving his permission to Moses to leave was, on the human side, clear testimony to his high standing and excellent reputation, both as a man and as an employee.

So, think about both the courtesy of Moses and the courtesy of Jethro in return. Think about Moses' excellent standing in his family after decades of work. Then apply that to everyday living in Scotland or England or wherever God calls men and women to serve him who are well respected in the work they are already doing/engaged in. (Although this principle holds true, we must acknowledge that it may not apply where there is unjust discrimination against those who are persecuted for the sake of Christ.)

Confirmation

We come now to verse 19: 'And the LORD said to Moses in Midian, "Go back to Egypt, for all the men who were seeking your life are dead."' There is a small problem of translation here. The AKJV and ESV versions have,

'And the LORD said to Moses …', but the NIV, which some readers may use, changes that slightly and has, 'Now the LORD *had* said to Moses …', making the verb the pluperfect tense, as if this was something God had said earlier. However, the tense should read as in the AKJV and ESV. For the meaning appears to be that it was only when Moses was taking his leave from the family, packing up the essentials for his journey and disposing of everything he would not need to take with him, that then God came again to reassure him and confirm to him the call. In other words, confirmation was added to his impending obedience to the call.

Moses already knew that Pharaoh was dead. We have that in chapter 2:23. But what about the head of Egyptian intelligence? What about the chief of police? What about the Crown Prosecutor? It was not only his former stepfather, the great Pharaoh, who was no longer living. It was all the security staff who had been ordered to track him down, and from whom he had been hiding all those years in his Bedouin disguise. Doubtless these thoughts troubled him as he prepared to leave. Therefore, God comes once again with gracious and clear confirmation. 'You're safe to go back; every single one of those who were searching for you is now dead. There is no risk at all. It's an entirely new administration.'

We have the same scenario possible today in our own country. It is called 'the statute of limitations'[2], where no one is any longer interested in pressing an outstanding case. So, I can almost hear the sigh of relief and see the face of Moses relax. I see him sleeping that night with his worried thoughts all banished. God had so kindly assured him he was taking the right course of action—the burning bush had not been a wild dream; it had not been a brainstorm. God himself had now confirmed his call with this reassurance and had taken away the fear of something his servant had been dreading and worrying about.

Now there are two points for us in this simple statement of verse 19. The first is that problems and obstacles you and I may foresee as we consider the cost of obeying God very often melt away when we actually reach them. I myself have often experienced that. We go to do what we know is right, but we are dreading the reception we expect. Yet, when the moment comes, all that we dreaded simply evaporates and we are left wondering why ever we had been so anxious and afraid. Then the Lord chides us gently and says, 'I told you to trust me; why were you afraid? Where was your faith?'

> Problems and obstacles you and I may foresee as we consider the cost of obeying God very often melt away when we actually reach them.

I wonder if some reading this know that God has called

them to do something for him, but they are dithering, hesitating, hanging back, because they can see all sorts of problems and difficulties. They are trying to cross the river before they reach it. Learn that, when we step out in obedience and reach the river, we will find a good stout bridge or else firm stepping-stones, and we will cross over without the hassle we expected. That is the first lesson for us from verse 19.

The second is quite different. It is about the vexed question of how to know God's will in some matter. You have a feeling God is calling you to do something for him. You may have a dream, even a 'vision' of some sort. You wonder, 'Is it God? Or is it merely my own vivid imagination?'

This is a most important question. It would be difficult to emphasize how important. The history of the Christian church is littered with wreckage caused by people who acted because they thought God had called them, or spoken to them, or given them a vision, when God had done no such thing. They acted from what is sometimes called 'an inner prompting'. Most dangerous! Be very, very careful!

Let me give you some examples of godly men and women who acted in response to what they thought were 'inner promptings' of the Spirit of God, but which were not from the Holy Spirit at all. Here are two from the Welsh Revival of 1904.

One very godly man believed God had told him to have all his teeth extracted so that new teeth could grow in. So, he went to his dentist and had every tooth in his head removed, in spite of the dentist advising against such reckless action. But you have guessed it; no new teeth grew in.

Another very godly, sincere, but not very wise Welsh minister believed God had told him to march down to the seashore with members of his congregation and there he would be given power to walk on the waves. So, after agonizing over this, he at last obeyed this 'inner prompting' that he was convinced came from the Holy Spirit. Wearing his cassock, white preaching bands and gown, he marched ahead of his flock. As they stood and watched, they saw the sorry spectacle of him splashing about in the water, totally unable to walk on it, but getting soaked through, until he emerged shame-faced and discredited.[3]

There are more serious examples. The Seventh Day Adventist Church was formed as a result of a 'so called' vision from God. The vision was given to a man and a woman, revealing the exact date of the Lord's return. Well, the date came and went with no cataclysmic return of Christ, but the Seventh Day Adventist Sect was left behind—yet another breakaway group from Christ's church to confuse and bewilder the enquiring public outside the church.[4]

We must be very sure and have solid, firm evidence that God has called, before we venture to begin some new thing, or respond to what we believe to be a vision. There must be a divine confirmation that a number of mature Christian friends agree is the green light from God. Not that such a confirmation makes things easier, as we will see in due course. But without it, we must not move!

Commitment

There was no airport in Midian. Moses and his family did not board a jumbo jet for Cairo. Those who have visited Israel can perhaps more easily imagine the scene. Because, as one drives through the Judean wilderness on the Jericho Road, it is common enough to see some Bedouin boy riding a donkey along a narrow hillside path. Moses' two boys must have been still very small—maybe eighteen months and four years old—for them both, and their mother, to travel on a donkey's back. Also slung over the donkey would be a couple of panniers with essential supplies of food and water, as the resting places where water and fresh food such as dates could be obtained would each be several days' walk apart. Moses would have been on foot, more supplies slung over his shoulders. And so, he set off, the halter of the little donkey in one hand, and the staff of God in the other hand.

Paul writes that he was a fool for Christ's sake (1 Corinthians 4:10; 2 Corinthians 12:11). I think Moses too, in human eyes, was a fool for Christ's sake. It was ridiculous—quite crazy. A comparatively old man, well past retiring age, setting out on foot with a young wife and two toddlers to look after, on a long and hazardous journey across the Sinai Desert towards Egypt, with the mission of setting free from the Egyptian tyrant several hundred thousand slaves.

But Moses presents us with a parable. For this little cameo of a lonely man, with his donkey and its frail burden, trotting along a sandy path to nowhere, speaks to us of the way in which God still works. The Saviour spoke of faith like a mustard seed. And a mustard seed is so small that most people cannot see it without spectacles. Jesus spoke, too, of God's kingly rule being like that seed—a speck of dust—which, when it germinates, grows into a shrub where the birds can perch.

I think we are quite wrong if we look at the church today and say, 'Yes, I get it; the tiny seed has germinated and is now fully grown into the tree. That's us. Today we're the full-grown shrub which had such an unlikely beginning.' Some people understand Christ's parable in that way. But I think that interpretation is mistaken. In human eyes, God's kingly rule will always appear contemptible and fragile. God's purposes are always seemingly insignificant in the world's eyes, as God takes some frail person and pits that unlikely man or woman against all the might of the world's opposition to his Kingdom.

> God's purposes are always seemingly insignificant in the world's eyes.

What could Gladys Aylward do in China, the world's most populous nation? Or Amy Carmichael in India, with its teeming millions? Or Mary Slessor in Nigeria, with its scattered communities and dangerous tropical climate? No more than this Bedouin shepherd could achieve, slowly making his way across the desert, leading a little donkey on which sat a woman and two small boys.

But Moses' step and stride were sure. His face was set like flint, as was the face of Jesus[5] when he also strode along a narrow path on his way to Jerusalem, knowing full well that he was going to the city where he was to be betrayed into the hands of those who hated him. The record in Exodus says nothing of Moses' simple supplies, or of the little money he carried in his belt. It speaks only of the staff of God that he carried in his hand. And I think no Egyptians, seeing him at last reaching the outskirts of the first Egyptian villages, would have had any fear, or thought that he was someone to be reckoned with. It would never have entered their heads that here was a man to watch, for such a man may overthrow the might of one of the world's most powerful empires. I doubt whether anyone he passed would have even turned to notice the dusty, elderly traveller with his shepherd's staff.

Chiselled on the monument to the Reformation in Geneva are the words in French of John Knox: 'A man with God is always in the majority.'[6]

Each follower of Christ is called to free slaves, slaves to sin (John 8:34), because the devil has far more slaves than we might sometimes think. There are tens of thousands of slaves who live in danger: old people who are slaves to fear of the final summons to die; middle-aged men and women who are slaves to possessions that will all be left behind on that final journey; young people, who ought to be hoping for happiness and fulfilment, but who are already slaves to disillusionment as they turn to drink and drugs. There are plenty of slaves in our communities. The answer is not really a mass crusade or series of rallies, though God can use such means. Rather, the answer is a little band of men and women who are not afraid to obey God and who will commit themselves to becoming fools for Christ's sake. For God's Kingdom is remarkably like a tiny seed that falls into the ground, there to germinate, and grow into a tree that bears fruit—the fruit of God's Spirit in human lives. God calls each one who knows and loves him to obey him, and, by their lives and lips, tell of Christ, that slaves might be set free.

FOR FURTHER STUDY

1. There are many references to servants of God being alone as they face daunting odds stacked against them. Search out some of these for further meditation. Suggestions could be Elijah in 1 Kings 18 and 19, or the Psalmist in Psalm 42, or the apostle in 2 Timothy 4:9–18, esp. 16–18.

2. Divine confirmation can be a very subjective experience, but God often will strengthen trembling faith, as in the account of Gideon's fear and uncertainty recounted in Judges 6:36–40 and 7:1–15. See also Lamentations 3:19–27.

TO THINK ABOUT AND DISCUSS

1. Do differences of opinion about your faith sometimes cause friction and even divisions in your family circle. What are the best ways to handle this without bringing discredit on the Lord? What guidance do these references offer? 1 Peter 3:1–4, 13–17; Romans 12:14–18; 1 Timothy 2:1–3; 1 Thessalonians 4:11–12.

2. We read, in Acts 16:6–7, that twice Paul and Silas' plans had to be cancelled. What suggestions can you make as to what these two phrases mean: 'having been forbidden by the Holy Spirit to speak the word in Asia', and 'the Spirit of Jesus did not allow them'? How might the next verses, 8 to 10, offer an explanation, not as to *how* God spoke, but rather as to *why* he spoke, causing them to cancel their plans. See also 1 Thessalonians 2:17–18.

3. In Matthew 13:31–33, faithfully recording Jesus' teaching, the evangelist links together the parable of the Mustard Seed and the woman making bread by kneading yeast into her dough. Can you find the explanation for Jesus pairing these two parables? Could it be that the second one was intended by Jesus to help us know how to understand the first one?

4. Is the cross always heavy for the disciple to carry? (Mark 8:34–38.) Can you identify two aspects of the 'cross' for David in Psalm 23:4a and 5a? How do these darker aspects of his experience of the Lord harmonise with verses 2, 3 and 5b–6?

9 Zipporah and Moses

Exodus 4:24–26

God had called. Eventually, Moses had obeyed. Now he was on his way to Egypt. But there was something not right in his relationship with God and it arose from his relationship with his wife. Therefore, God intervened. The journey could not be continued until what was wrong had been put right.

As you read the verses that we are about to consider in this chapter, your reaction may be one of surprise. You may wonder what there can be in this short passage for the Christian life in the 21st century. It is one of those parts of the Bible that few ministers ever use for a sermon. All the more reason, therefore, that we should consider these three verses. Perhaps it will challenge us to think and to ask ourselves why ever it should have been included in the Bible at all.

Moses, you remember, had been adopted by Pharaoh's

daughter and brought up as a prince of Egypt. But he had to flee for his life after killing an Egyptian taskmaster. We have seen how, decades later, when he was living in the Sinai desert as a Bedouin shepherd, God had spoken to him through the burning bush and commissioned him to return to Egypt to demand that Pharaoh set free the Hebrew slaves. Now he has set out with his wife, Zipporah, and his two sons and it was during his journey that this strange incident took place.

The implication is that his older son, Gershom, had been circumcised at eight days old, but against Zipporah's wishes. When the second boy was born, she refused to allow Moses to perform the Hebrew rite on him. Moses gave in to her. He knew that circumcision was the outward sign of the covenant God had made with Abraham, and it had been laid down that anyone who neglected this rite would be cut off from the people of God (Genesis 17:1–14, especially v. 14).

Yet, in spite of that, he had taken a weak line and allowed his rather tempestuous wife, Zipporah, to have her way. But apparently, it was on his conscience. Here he was, on his way to free the Hebrew slaves, and his own son did not have the mark on him of the people of God. So, when he fell dangerously ill at the halting place by an oasis, and was clearly near to death, he realized God was speaking to him. He told Zipporah he would die unless she performed the Hebrew rite on their second son. She was furious but cornered. So angrily she performed the rite, and Moses recovered from his illness. [1]

Before we try and tease from this seemingly bizarre story the meaning for ourselves in this 21st century, I must remind you of the significance of the Old Testament rite of circumcision for you and me living in the gospel of the New Testament.

Circumcision in the Old Testament corresponds to baptism in the New Testament and foreshadows it. Putting this the other way round, three reasons are given to us in the Bible to indicate that baptism is the successor to circumcision. The first is that both speak of life, in the sense of the new birth. Circumcision was performed on the organ of procreation and therefore spoke of new life. Baptism speaks of being buried with Christ in his death and being raised to a new life through Christ's resurrection life.

The second reason for this connection between the two ceremonies is that both speak of cleanliness—that is of forgiveness and then a new life of clean living before God. Baptism, with its symbol of water, is a cleansing ceremony; circumcision was a minor procedure that helped in personal hygiene. Remember that in those days, you were lucky to get a bath once a year, but the Jews were fastidiously clean, and this rite helped that cleanliness. [2]

The third reason to link the two ceremonies is that

both speak about the Saviour, the seed of Abraham, through whom the whole world would be blessed. So, both baptism and circumcision are signs of begetting children, for when we are baptized into Christ, we become the Father's children in the sense of being adopted into his visible family on earth.

I have reminded readers of this because it is fundamental to our understanding much of the teaching in these three verses. Circumcision under the Old Covenant corresponds to baptism in the New Covenant.

Think first of Zipporah.

I am sure that we will have some sympathy for this Bedouin woman. I know I am venturing into the realm of speculation, but I cannot help recalling that Moses ran away from Egypt a hot-tempered and impetuous man; he returned, according to our Bibles, the meekest man in all the earth (Numbers 12:3). And I am sure

> The transformation in Moses' character was due to God's own discipline in his life.

that the transformation in his character was due to God's own discipline in his life, pinning him down as a lonely shepherd for all these years, after the life of importance, rank and status he had been living in Egypt. That must have been severe discipline on him. It was 'from riches to rags', as we say. The equivalent today would be for a male member of the royal family suddenly to be catapulted from a life of wealth, luxury and constant publicity into a life as one of the poorest crofters in the Scottish Highlands—from a life of maximum exposure to the public, with a seemingly unlimited bank balance, to a life of extreme poverty and total obscurity.

Nor did Moses have the book of Proverbs to console him, where it says who the Lord loves he chastens, and the comfort of knowing that he was being dealt with in this way because he was a child of God (Proverbs 3:11–12).

However, what if part of the discipline to teach him to curb his temper and learn patience and meekness was his marriage to this Bedouin woman? There is enough in this all too brief description to support the supposition that the once proud prince, adopted son of the Egyptian royal family, now had to endure the ranting and raging of a volatile spouse. Please do not think I am being sexist. We all know that there are countless meek women who patiently endure the ranting and raving of hot-tempered men. Nevertheless, this incident suggests that Moses suffered from Zipporah's tongue on more occasions than this one here. And I believe that in God's providence he had planned it this way. It was to teach Moses loving patience, to quell his pride, to humble him. Zipporah's name in Hebrew tells us she had a great deal to say and maybe to repeat when her husband apparently had not heard![3]

Zipporah had her lessons to learn as well. What she had not yet learned was that it was not only her husband with whom she had to deal, but her husband's God as well. She must also learn that her angry protests about this Hebrew rite of circumcision were completely ridiculous. For the simple procedure at eight days old was little more severe than the piercing of her nose to wear a gold ring, or the piercing of her ears—from a purely human point of view.

But from the divine point of view, she was up against the eternal covenant of Almighty God and his saving purposes for the world, expressed in pledge by that simple sign of his eternal covenant. Rant and rave at Moses she may, until he learned infinite patience, but she could not gainsay Moses' God.

She certainly did not want to lose her husband, her protector and provider, the father of her two little boys. And so, at this lonely halting place (the word simply means a stopping place beside a source of water) in the middle of nowhere, and where it would have probably meant the death of the mother and her two boys had Moses himself died, there God had to corner her, and suppress her pride.

Now, can we see the meaning of this for ourselves? It is a difficult lesson to learn. For it is saying to us that when we rant and rave against God, he will sometimes let us use him as a kind of punching bag, to beat our fists against him, and take out our aggression on him, foolish and ignorant as we are! He puts up with that and waits and waits, until at last his time and opportunity come and he says, 'Alright, my dear, you have had your say; now do what I have been asking you to do!' And he leaves us no alternative but to obey or suffer real loss.

It is with a heavy heart that I draw this lesson. Because it takes little imagination to know or even guess how very painful and distressing it can be to be cornered by God like this. But it is not a rare occurrence. You and I can be so strong-willed, so devious, so wanting our own way, so determined we know better than God, that ultimately it can mean a real crisis before we will obey God. And he will not allow his purposes to be thwarted by our stupid pride and prejudice.

Now, I know there are questions about all this. One issue is that surely God wants an obedience that is loving and warm, not the angry, reluctant obedience that Zipporah gave. I have no doubt that the day came when Zipporah bowed in worship before her husband's God—not only she, but her father and his family too. We have that later on in the story. But just now, God would have her obedience, however unwilling, until at length she found peace and joy in a glad and triumphant obedience. Is this a word for some reader of this chapter?

Is God cornering you to win from you an unwilling obedience to him, content to wait, as your God, for your willingness one day to be from a full and grateful heart, with thanksgiving and praise?

Think now of Moses.

There are three practical lessons for us from Moses' part in this strange story.

Firstly, it is quite clear that Moses and Zipporah were strongly disagreeing over a matter of Moses' faith and the practice of his faith. Therefore, the first lesson concerns those living with a marriage partner who does not share our (Christian) faith. So, what can we learn about a couple where one is trying to obey the Lord in daily life, but the other is not interested, and even may be antagonistic over certain matters?

The New Testament is clear about this. We are taught that the Christian partner in such a marriage is to be patient, understanding, forbearing. Moreover, the Christian partner ought not to try and force his or her faith on the non-Christian partner. You have that in both 1 Corinthians 7 and 1 Peter 3. Peter goes as far as to say that the Christian partner in the marriage should not say a single word about their Christian faith. Rather, they should live a life of love, truth, patience and joy, kindness, meekness, goodness and self-control:

Likewise, wives, be subject to your own husbands, so

that even if some do not obey the word, they may be won *without a word* by the conduct of their wives—when they see your respectful and pure conduct. 3:1–2.

The hope is that the non-Christian partner will be convinced, not by any arguments, but by the quality of life being lived. That may take a long, long time. It can often be years before the unbelieving member of the marriage at last surrenders to Christ. The same, of course, applies to any member of a family where there are non-Christians. The lesson is, let your life speak, not your lips.

The second lesson here is about Moses' disobedience to God. You see, for the Christian partner in any marriage, there are some things that are not negotiable. All believers must know and accept that. There are certain aspects of our Christian faith that we cannot ignore. I think of worship on the Lord's Day, for example. Or, of bringing the children up within the Church's fellowship and teaching. We can make allowances on many sides, and lone Christian members of the family may have to make costly, difficult compromises. But we must not surrender our walk with our Lord and God. So, we will be in God's House, on the Lord's Day. We will maintain certain standards in our home.

> For the Christian partner in any marriage, there are some things that are not negotiable.

Our Bibles know all about that tension in a marriage. Paul foresaw that being faithful to God, even in a minimum of ways, could well cause the non-Christian partner to walk out (1 Corinthians 7:12–16). I have witnessed such unhappy outcomes more than once. But that would be the exception because, very soon, the unbelieving partner will see that the other partner is a better, more loving, more faithful, truer husband or wife on account of their faith.

This was where Moses failed. The rite of circumcision was non-negotiable. He compromised over something on which he ought never to have yielded.

In this connection, perhaps we ought to ask ourselves if we, as New Testament believers, treat the sacraments with the reverence and honour they deserve (for circumcision was an Old Testament sacrament). Neither baptism, nor the Lord's Supper, are negotiable. It is no use arguing that they are only outward signs of an inner reality. We all know that. We all know that baptism signifies God's cleansing and the new life his Holy Spirit brings. We all know the bread and wine speak of the body and blood of Christ. Yet these outward signs have been given to us by God through his beloved Son. And it is wrong to neglect them.

If you have trusted Christ, and he is your Saviour, why do you not come to his Table? Why neglect to receive the bread that speaks of his body, and the wine that speaks of his blood? Ponder on these three verses and ask whether you are declining both a gracious offer and a clear command from the Son of God.

The third and final lesson from this passage is very obvious. How could Moses serve God when there was this glaring omission in his life? Here he was, off to fulfil God's calling, but something in his life was wrong. There was this one matter in which he had been disobedient and neglectful. He may have thought God would overlook this one thing. But the fullness of the Holy Spirit could not come upon him until his life was right; until he had given God obedience in everything.[4]

For the Christian, every shadow, every deviation from obedience to God, matters. I am not suggesting that God looks for us to be sinless. We will never be that. But I am saying that if there is a persistent and continuing disobedience to God, we will disqualify ourselves from his service or certainly render our Christian service unfruitful. Moses knew why he was dangerously ill on this occasion. This was more than just a bad cold, or a desert fever. This was God's hand, God's voice, God's word, saying: 'You cannot serve me until you put this matter right.' An old hymn went like this:

Master, speak Thy servant heareth, waiting for Thy
    gracious Word ...

I am listening, Lord, for Thee; what hast Thou to say to me?

Master, speak, and make me ready, when Thy voice is truly
   heard,
With obedience glad and steady still to follow every word;
I am listening, Lord, for Thee; Master, speak, Oh speak to me

Frances Ridley Havergal (1836–1879)

Is the Holy Spirit carrying that lighted candle of his Word into the private, deepest vaults of your soul, to throw its flickering light onto secret sins, that must be put away before the Spirit of God can bring to you fullness of joy and flood your life with the peace and assurance that he brings? Then do not attempt to extinguish that light or close your eyes to what it reveals. May the Lord soften all our hard hearts and bend our proud wills, until we obey his Word and surrender ourselves to his loving embrace.

FOR FURTHER STUDY

1. God's love is the most all-embracing, tenderest love in the whole universe for *God is love* (1 John 4:8); follow through, however, the clear implication in this verse that the divine love is also a tough love and search for other examples in Scripture that imply this (I Sam. 3:10–14; 4:10–11; Job 1:12; 2 Kings 5:15–27; Matthew 23:37–39, etc.).[5]

2. Some define the sacraments as 'a means of grace'; others understand the sacraments as simply 'memorials'. Can both these views co-exist side by side or do you consider them mutually exclusive? (Romans 6:1–11; 1 Corinthians 10:16–17; 11:23–30.)

TO THINK ABOUT AND DISCUSS

1. In the light of 1 Peter 3:1–2, how difficult is it for a believing spouse to be subject to their partner and to witness faithfully without a word about Jesus being spoken? How ought the Christian spouse in a marriage react when actions are being taken which are clearly dishonouring to God?

2. Read 1 Corinthians 7:12–14. The word 'holy' (ESV) occurs three times in these verses (NIV has 'sanctified'). Applied to Moses' marriage, it means that though at this point his wife did not fully share his faith, nevertheless his marriage was still a holy union. How might this insight help the believing spouse in a 'mixed marriage'? (NB. In verse 12, Paul's meaning is that this is a subject on which Christ himself never made any recorded pronouncement.)

3. Could you share without any personal embarrassment an example in your own Christian life of some disobedience you persisted in until, at length, God dealt with you? If so, can you say how he dealt with you?

10 By faith, Moses ...

Exodus 4:27–31; Hebrews 11:23–27

Moses now arrives in Egypt and the elders are gathered to hear Aaron deliver his brother's message. Aaron they would have known but perhaps not many of them remembered the former prince of Egypt. However, so far it seemed that all was going well as they listened to the Lord's words and saw the signs. Indeed, they 'believed' and 'worshipped'. But how strong would their initial faith prove to be?

There are always two, if not three sides to any question. For example, those who have the role of acting as counsellor in some dispute between two people—say, an aggrieved wife and husband—will hear what the wife has to say, and then hear quite a different account from the husband. It takes a special skill and sensitivity to navigate between the two. In my own pastoral experience, there was generally some truth in what each had said, but there was almost invariably, on both sides of the argument, a great deal that had been omitted. Thus, in our consideration of Moses' life, we have tried to unravel something of what the man himself felt and why he acted as he did. But it is time in this study to take fuller account of the New Testament assessment of what was happening in Moses' life. Otherwise, our reflections will fall significantly short of the truth.

The price

In Chapter 3, we saw how Moses had realized that he had a choice to make between the luxury, wealth and power of being a prince of Egypt, or identifying himself with his own persecuted people who were slaves suffering great affliction. We noted that it had dawned on him how he had been chosen by God to take his stand in the defence of the Hebrew slaves. Was this not why he had asked himself how it was that he had the status of being the adopted son of Pharaoh's daughter? Had he not concluded it was in the providence of the living God? Therefore, it is time now to give due weight to the apostle's words in Hebrews 11:

By faith Moses, when he was grown up, refused to be called the son of Pharaoh's daughter, choosing rather to be mistreated with the people of God than to enjoy the fleeting pleasures of sin. He considered the reproach of

Christ greater wealth than the treasures of Egypt, for he was looking to the reward (vv. 24–26).

Thus, it is clear that somehow, we have to bring his impetuous action in killing the Egyptian taskmaster together with his faith, through which he had chosen to turn his back on the glittering prospects of life as a member of royalty with all the privileges and pleasures to which that would entitle him.

It cannot be denied that often, in the loneliness of the desert, Moses must have reflected on his past life in an Egyptian palace: waited on by servants; clothed in fine garments; eating the richest food; surrounded by lackeys who would help him to bathe each day; then walking in gardens with shady trees and the sweet scent of blossoms and flora. Nevertheless, as he recalled his earlier years, there would have been no regret or yearning after his past. Rather, his motivation and thoughts were steadfastly upon the promise of God to his forefather, Abraham, and renewed to Isaac and Jacob. Also, what of Joseph about whom his parents had taught him? Had he not on his deathbed assured his brothers that God would visit his people and take them from Egypt to the Land

> Moses' motivation and thoughts were steadfastly upon the promise of God to his forefather, Abraham, and renewed to Isaac and Jacob.

of Promise? And were not Joseph's mummified remains still waiting to be carried back to Canaan for final burial there? (Genesis 50:24–26.)

On the other hand, although we can be certain Moses had no regrets about his choice of being 'mistreated with the people of God', we should not neglect the tempter's oft repeated assaults upon him. Satan was just as active in those days as he is today, and doubtless he would have taunted the Bedouin shepherd as he endured the desert heat, the days of loneliness, thirst and poverty. Only in eternity, when we shall 'know fully, even as [we] have been fully known' (1 Corinthians 13:12), will we understand the lonely battles fought and won in the wastes of the wilderness during those decades the Lord's servant spent as a fugitive. But of this we can be certain, he endured with a resolution enabled and strengthened by the Spirit of God. Just as a heavenly messenger ministered to the Saviour in his hour of darkest conflict (Luke 22:43), so also the Lord's silent, unseen 'visitor' will have affirmed and confirmed Moses in his faith in God's gracious purposes. We can be certain that he would never have considered the price he had paid having been too costly.

The partnership

Our Bible passage, Exodus 4:27–31, ushers us into an entirely new phase in Moses' calling. The Lord had promised the final, firm evidence of the reality of Moses' commission, in that, after he had been brought to the point of death on account of his disobedience in failing to circumcise his younger son, and had again continued his journey towards Egypt, his brother Aaron would come to meet him. Their meeting would be the most tangible indication of the reality of the divine purposes for his life's true work. This was why he had been preserved from Pharaoh's evil edict, fostered by Pharaoh's daughter, and educated in literary skills by the most learned scholars of the ancient world. This was also why he had been subjected to those long years in the wilderness. Little did he realize at the time that his experience of desert life was just as essential to his calling as his education in Egypt's finest centres of learning, for his would be the responsibility to direct his nation's lives for many years in that same desert.

Think first about Aaron. He too needed to obey God's word: 'Go into the wilderness to meet Moses.' We can safely assume that Aaron had been on his way for some time, for we have already been told that he was on his way: 'Behold, he is coming out to meet you, and when he sees you, he will be glad in his heart' (4:14). The meeting place, 'the mountain of God', was about halfway between Midian and Goshen.

Scripture gives no hint as to how the Lord spoke to Aaron; neither do we know if he had even been aware that his younger brother was still alive. Calvin comments, Aaron 'now receives the joyful announcement, from the mouth of God, that Moses is alive.'[1] It is idle to speculate as to whether there was a prophet among the slaves, or if the message came to Aaron in a dream, or simply in a clear prompting in his heart. It is clear, however, that there was no dubiety in his mind: Moses was not only still alive and well, but he was about to embark on his journey back to Egypt, and Aaron must go and meet him. Although there is no mention of God's impending intervention in the life of his people, the older brother must have been sure that some token of God's favour was about to be bestowed upon the oppressed slaves.

The seemingly insignificant phrase, 'he met him ... and kissed him' (v. 27), encapsulates, as had been predicted (4:14), an emotional reunion after long years of separation. The brothers met and embraced with tears of joy. Much is implied in verse 28. God had left it to Moses to give Aaron the full explanation for his unexpected return to Egypt. Although Moses had said nothing to his father-in-law of God's call and the purpose of his journey, a full account was given to Aaron, so that, along with God's Word to him to travel south through the wilderness to meet his brother, the reality of God's impending intervention must have become absolutely clear. Though Moses was the younger brother, the implication is that he was to be the leader in the enterprise, and Aaron must willingly accept that reversal of the natural order of the elder leading the younger. Nonetheless, the Lord had an important role for him to fulfil as Moses' spokesman. It was to be a most significant partnership in the gospel.

As so often is seen in Scripture, God's choice frequently defies the natural order. Jacob and Esau are examples, as is the divine choice of Judah to be the pre-eminent tribe in Israel, and from whose stock Jesus Christ would be born (Genesis 49:8, 10). None of us earns priority in God's Kingdom on the grounds of our birth, family, nationality or ability. God's choice of leaders, whom he will anoint and bless, arises solely from the mystery of his gracious purposes.

Yet, that is no reason for any true follower of Christ to sit back and do nothing, for all who are true disciples of Christ have his Spirit, and the Spirit always endows believers with the gift of service according to his sovereign choice. Concerning these gifts, which are entirely for use in edifying the church and sharing the good news with others, the apostle writes in 1 Corinthians 12:11, 'All these are empowered by one and the same Spirit, who apportions to each one individually as he wills.' However, we ought not to neglect the stern warning contained in the Lord's parable of The Talents in Matthew 25:14–30, and the punishment meted out upon the servant who hid his one talent in the ground.

Each of us must humbly and faithfully use what has been entrusted to us according to the measure granted to us (See 1 Corinthians 12:21–26).

The proclamation

When they at length arrived in Goshen, 'Moses and Aaron went and gathered together all the elders of the people of Israel' (4:29). By this time, the population of the Israelites had increased enormously,

> Each of us must humbly and faithfully use what has been entrusted to us according to the measure granted to us.

and it would have been impractical, if not impossible, to call together all the people. Hence the summoning of the elders, each of whom would represent a clan or a large extended family. Now Aaron, as his brother's spokesman, rehearses to the gathering a full account of God's call to his brother, and his promise that Pharaoh would ultimately be compelled to let the whole nation depart from Egypt (3:20). One wonders if included in Aaron's account had been the warning, already given to Moses (3:19–20), that there would be a prolonged struggle with Pharaoh who would intensify the slaves' burdens. It would appear that part of the message was withheld, as is suggested by the anger of the slaves' foremen when their burdens were greatly increased (5:20–21).

So unexpected and seemingly impossible was God's message to Moses, passed on through Aaron, it was only when the signs were added to the Word that the elders then realized God had seen their affliction, heard their prayers, and so they believed the good news. This belief was signified by their bowing to the ground in worship.[2]

Two questions arise, both of which are relevant today. The first is whether the elders' 'belief' was genuine or superficial. It would appear that it was dependent upon the signs. And yet, as we have already noted, it would soon be tested and found wanting in that they angrily turned on Moses. However, we must look a little more closely at this in the next chapter.

Jesus spoke about a 'belief' that was superficial, without any genuine root. The Parable of the Sower in Mark 4:1–20 immediately springs to mind. The seed that fell onto rocky ground and quickly germinated, but then withered because it had no root, denoted those who heard the Word and immediately received it with joy, but just as quickly, when persecution came, fell away. However, perhaps a more pertinent New Testament reference is that found in John 2:23–25, where the evangelist records that 'Many believed in his name, when they saw the signs that he was doing.' But Jesus knew theirs was a superficial faith and so he did not entrust himself to these supposed 'believers', for, comments John, 'He knew all people and needed no one to bear witness about man, for he himself knew what was in man.'

A careful reading of the Gospels shows that the word 'sign' (Greek *semeion*) occurs twenty-five times, and about twenty of these speak derogatively of them. For example, a wicked and adulterous generation demands a sign (Matthew 12:38–39), or again, false Christs shall arise and produce 'signs' and lead many astray (Matthew 24:24). On the other hand, signs were at times given, not to generate faith but to confirm it, as when Jesus turned the water into wine: 'This, the first of his signs, Jesus did at Cana in Galilee, and manifested his glory. And his disciples believed in him' (John 2:11). They had already heard his call, forsaken all and followed him, having believed and obeyed.

Therefore, because the hearts of men and women have not changed over the centuries, the Hebrew elders who heard God's message through Moses and Aaron and believed, having seen the signs, did not necessarily have genuine faith. We cannot deny, however, that as events unfolded, true faith would be born and nurtured in many of them. So it is today. Every gathering of the Lord's people will have men and women whose 'belief' varies immensely. Yet, it is not the preacher's task to sort out the sheep from the goats, or the good from the bad, or the wheat from the weeds. That belongs to God, for he alone knows what is in the human heart. However, while in this life there undoubtedly will be an ongoing winnowing of wheat from chaff through the faithful preaching of his Word, the parable of the sheep and the goats warns us of a once for all final, irreversible judgement (Matthew 25:31–46).

> The parable of the sheep and the goats warns us of a once for all final, irreversible judgement.

The second question arises from the apparent absence in the message to the Hebrew elders of the coming tribulations still to be endured. Herein lies the preacher's dilemma. When Christ is lifted up and the gracious invitation is proclaimed, must it always of necessity be accompanied by the solemn warning that unbelievers can only follow the Lord if they not only repent and plead for mercy and grace, but also bend low to take up the heavy cross? For my part, during my years of sharing the unsearchable riches of Christ, I often sought to draw my hearers to the Saviour by seeking to unfold his beauty and love as fully and clearly as my limitations allowed. Nonetheless, early on in their Christian lives, I was bound to point out that 'through many tribulations we must enter the Kingdom of God' (Acts 14:22), and that it would be through those tribulations that true Christian character and maturity would be reached (Romans 5:3–5).

So, it came about that as Moses' ministry was

initiated in partnership with his older brother, they found a grateful and encouraging response, contrary to his former fears (Exodus 4:1). These were the earliest of days, and much was to follow, for it would not only be a thorny path for the Lord's people, but also for his faithful servants. All those who embark on any kind of ministry may well be granted by our wise and gracious Father some early encouragements and tokens of his promised blessing. But let us never forget that we walk in Christ's steps and, if they persecuted him, they will also persecute us. Isaac Watt's great hymn faithfully expresses this truth.

> Awake, our souls; away, our fears;
> let every trembling thought be gone;
> awake and run the heavenly race,
> and put a cheerful courage on.
>
> True, 'tis a strait and thorny road,
> and mortal spirits tire and faint;
> but they forget the mighty God
> that feeds the strength of every saint:
>
> The mighty God, whose matchless power
> is ever new and ever young,
> and firm endures, while endless years
> their everlasting circles run.

From you, the overflowing spring,
our souls shall drink a fresh supply,
while such as trust their native strength
shall melt away, and droop, and die.

Swift as an eagle cuts the air,
we'll mount aloft to your abode;
on wings of love our souls shall fly,
nor tire amidst the heavenly road.

Isaac Watts (1674–1748)

FOR FURTHER STUDY

1. The devil chose the wilderness as the place to tempt Jesus. Consider the nature of Satan's temptations of Moses alone in the wilderness: he could have reminded him of his past failures, and of the personal cost of rejecting 'the treasures of Egypt'. Bear in mind that Moses had no fellow believers to support him, no pastor, no prayer group. How would God's servants such as Elijah (1 Kings 19:10), or Jeremiah (Ch. 38) or Paul (2 Tim. 4:16–18), have stood firm without the support of other believers? In your personal experience, reflect on how you have coped in your 'wilderness experience'.

2. Continuing the theme of personal temptation, the apostle Paul wrote of standing firm against the 'cosmic powers over this present darkness, against the spiritual forces of evil *in the heavenly places*' (Eph. 6:12). This phrase, 'in the heavenly places' occurs in Ephesians five times: 1:3, 20; 2:6; 3:10 and 6:12. How can the fourth occurrence in 6:12[3] relate to the three other occurrences? (See Job 1:6–12; Psalm 55 and 56.)[4]

TO THINK ABOUT AND DISCUSS

1. Hebrews 11:24–26 emphasizes the cost to Moses but makes it clear that, like Abraham (Heb. 11:10), he was looking towards the final, eternal fulfilment of God's covenant—in our language, to heaven. Can believers today have the same incentive described as 'the blessed hope' (Titus 2:11–13) or 'a living hope' (1 Peter 1:3) or a 'hope' that causes us to yearn to live pure lives (1 John 3:1–3). How much do we live each day in the eager expectation of seeing Christ face to face? (Psalm 16:11; Daniel 7:13–14; 2 Timothy 4:8; Revelation 21:22–22:5.)

2. God's choices of his servants may go against what we consider the 'natural' order as with Moses, the younger brother of Aaron; Jacob, the younger brother of Esau (Genesis 27:19, 37); Joseph who was younger

than ten of his siblings (Genesis 37:1–3); and David, the youngest of his seven siblings (1 Samuel 16:6–13.) Do you ever have low expectations of fellow believers on account of their outward appearance, or high expectations of others, as Samuel initially had of Jesse's eldest son Eliab (1 Samuel 16:6-7)? How can we avoid such superficial assessments of others? (See Philippians 2:1–11).

3. Have you ever experienced, either in your own life or within the fellowship to which you belong, some remarkable 'sign'? If you have, share it in your group discussion. Consider Jesus' parable of the rich man and Lazarus (Luke 16:19–31). If we take seriously Abraham's reply to the rich man's request (vv. 27–31), how ought we to be praying for our unbelieving friends?

11 Three interviews

Exodus 5:1–23

If Moses had relayed to the slaves all that God had promised, including the warnings in 3:19–20 (and I think we can safely assume from 4:30 that he had), then they had only heard what they wanted to hear, namely, that God was going to deliver them. This chapter, therefore, sets the scene for what might be called 'a clash of the Titans' as a false god and the Almighty One prepare to enter the lists for the impending battle.

I am often surprised when people say that they find the Bible a dull and boring old book, without any relevance today. Certainly, in Bible times they did not have electricity, or micro-chips; there were no petrol engines or jet engines; nor were there televisions or communication satellites. But people in those days still had all the problems of human nature that we have today.

Think of Iran and its industry of lethal drones, or

the bitter war between Saudi Arabia and Yemen. Think too of Isis, which security experts tell us is secretly re-grouping and planning for future operations. Why, over the past decade, have over 400 British soldiers been killed in Afghanistan? Why were they there at all, if not to try and stave off a world-wide wave of terrorism? Think too of Russia's unprovoked attack on the Ukraine and tens of thousands of deaths as well as tens of billions of pounds' worth of destruction on both sides of this appalling conflict.

Or consider South Sudan, that newest of sovereign states established as recently as 2011. Within two years of its inception there has been civil war and, as a consequence, there are well over two million of its eleven million citizens in vast refugee camps, as well as one million of its population who are now immigrants in neighbouring states. Are these huge swathes of people in north-east Africa suffering in much the same way as the Hebrew slaves were suffering in the days of Moses?[1] Probably many of them are.

However, there was another dimension in the affliction of the slaves in Exodus 5. It was not the result of any political struggle, rather it was that the people of God were being cruelly oppressed. Therefore, Exodus chapter 5 has a special relevance for us who today are believers in the same God as they. Three interviews in this chapter are recorded for our instruction.

The first interview: Moses and Aaron with Pharaoh (vv. 1–9)

Many readers will have had the experience of going for an interview. When you enter the room and sit down, usually you want to present yourself in a good light. You want to impress those interviewing you so that you will get the job or are given a place in the course you have applied for, or whatever. With that in mind, you answer as carefully and politely as you can the questions you are asked and say what you hope the interviewers want to hear.

My understanding of Moses' and Aaron's interview with Pharaoh was that they actually stood an excellent chance of obtaining what they were asking for. The scales were all weighted very much in their favour. Let me explain why I think their chances were so good.

Firstly, archaeology has established that it was commonplace for various tribes and ethnic communities in Egypt in those days to be given time off for religious festivals. Ancient Egyptian records explain the absenteeism of slaves for a period of some days because they had been permitted to go and fulfil their religious duties. So, asking for a week or so to hold a festival to the Lord was neither an unreasonable nor uncommon request.

Secondly, if we wonder whether the three days' journey might have been a problem for Pharaoh, the answer apparently is that it would not. The various tribal gods were thought of as holding sway in their own particular areas, and the fastidious Egyptians would have understood that the Hebrews wanted to travel a 'three days' journey' (v.3), in order to reach the border of Egypt, so they could worship their God in an area uncontaminated by any other gods.

That is the significance of the *three days' journey*— it would take the Israelite slaves to Egypt's border. And there would be no fear of them then escaping. As Pharaoh implied later on (8:28; 10:24), they would be hemmed in by the desert, which was as effective a barrier as any Khyber Pass or that former dreadful Berlin Wall.

Thirdly, no suggestion was made that these slave people were asking to be set free from their slavery. They were simply asking for the customary leave of a week to hold a religious festival. The assumption was that they would return to their brick-making duties. They had no option. What tribe, with its women and children and sheep and goats, could ever venture out into the inhospitable Sinai desert? They could easily be pursued and herded back again.

So, these two men, given their audience with Pharaoh, ought to have been reasonably confident of success. Humanly speaking, there was no reason why Pharaoh should not grant their request. What was it, then, that went so badly wrong?

The sacred record tells us. Here is Pharaoh, one of the greatest ruling monarchs of his day, probably the first in a new dynasty. He has just overthrown the former dynasty,[2] won military victories and established himself as undisputed master of Egypt. He is worshipped as the child of the sun gods, and he sees the whole of Egypt as existing for his pleasure; the Nile, the peasants, the thousands of priests and the entire Egyptian aristocracy, were there to serve his every whim. He was the mighty one, before whom an entire nation cringed.[3]

This was the crucial first interview as into his presence come two men who, though they observe the proper courtesies for his royal presence, do not fawn, or bow and scrape; instead, they issue a mandate—a command—from a God he does not know. They order him to give the Hebrew slaves the customary break for a religious festival.

The problem was that the great potentate was being *commanded* by the slaves' God. Though he was asked politely, he was not pleaded with for a gracious favour, nor grovelled before with flattery or fancy speeches; he was being *ordered* by the God of a despised inferior race. This is what the Lord, the God of Israel says, 'Let my people go that they may hold a feast to me in the wilderness' (5:1). In effect,

> Pharaoh was being *ordered* by the God of a despised inferior race.

Pharoah's response was, 'Who is the Lord that I should obey his voice and let Israel go? I do not know the Lord, and moreover, I will not let Israel go' (5:2).

Pharaoh's problem was exactly the same as ours today. God comes to us and, firstly, he commands us to repent and turn to him and submit our lives to his Son. The invitation does not come first. First comes God's command to you and me. It is his command to every single person in our land. Paul concluded his address at the Areopagus with these words, 'The times of ignorance God overlooked, but now he *commands* all people everywhere to repent, because he has fixed a day on which he will judge the world in righteousness, by a man whom he has appointed ...' (Acts 17:30–31).

The Lord says, 'I am the Lord, that is my name; my glory I give to no other' (Isaiah 42:8; see also 48:11). Our problem is that we bristle with resentment at that because, like Pharaoh, we are not at all inclined to obey this God. Obeying him really means submitting our wills entirely to his control, yielding all to him. We will touch our caps to him by attending church on a Sunday morning. We will make a contribution to his church's funds. We will do a bit here and there. But when it comes to moving over from the driver's seat of our lives, and sitting instead in the passenger seat, so allowing God to take the controls, then that is different. Not that! So, without realizing it, we echo Pharaoh's words and say, 'Who is the LORD that I should obey him?'

Nothing daunted, Moses and Aaron press their case. But it gets worse: they say, 'The God of the Hebrews has met with us.' For the Egyptians, the word 'Hebrews' was a pejorative term. It was used of wandering nomads, tinkers, dirty unhygienic people (Genesis 46:34c).[4] The Egyptians were so sophisticated. 'The God of the Hebrews? What is he, compared to our gods with their mighty stone temples?' But Moses and Aaron continue: 'Please let us go a three days' journey into the wilderness that we may sacrifice to the LORD our God, lest he fall upon us with pestilence ...' (v. 3).

Now that was a clear warning: 'sacrifices' spelt atonement, covering of sin and wrongdoing. The ancients understood that. Forgiveness and mercy were to be sought, or else there might be reprisals such as some plague, or an attack from a foreign power. And any plague or attack on this tribe of slaves could also be an assault on Egypt. Clearly, it was a warning.

The Lord's commands, his calls to us to sue for mercy, and the warnings of the direst consequences of rejecting God, have the same effect on many of us today as they had on Pharaoh. We toss our heads. We turn our backs. And far from bending the knee, we make decisions which confirm us in our selfishness and pride. We can keep up our pretence of religion for long enough. It is when God begins to press us hard, and Christ begins to drive us into a corner, that we harden our hearts and find ourselves going further and further away from him.

This first interview is really the same as our first real interview with Jesus Christ, as he stands in our pathway and commands us: 'Give me your heart!' The elements we have here never change, for human nature never changes. He asks us to surrender to his imperious commands, and he warns us of judgement if we refuse him. It is all unmistakably plain. Therefore, we all must ask ourselves, 'Are we aware that God has spoken his Word to us, and that this is what he has been saying for months, perhaps even years?'

> God asks us to surrender to his imperious commands, and he warns us of judgement if we refuse him.

The second interview: Pharaoh and the foremen (vv. 10–19)

Here is a situation I guess we will all recognize. Someone at work has said or done something that has been seen as causing trouble. There has been an unholy dust-up. Tempers have frayed and offence has been taken. The repercussions are spreading wider. Or it may have been with a neighbour, perhaps even within a family. We have all seen this kind of thing. So, the 'supposed troublemaker' decides he will have to try and sort things out and, in some trepidation, approaches those he has offended to apologize and to try and make amends.

That is approximately the case before us. The enraged king of Egypt had decided to make life for the slaves even harder than before. Instead of straw for the mud bricks being provided, the slaves now had to make the same number of bricks but gather from the countryside their own straw. The effect was that the workload for the slaves was doubled. When they failed to keep up the same rate of production, they were beaten by their taskmasters. Therefore, that was why the Hebrew foremen arranged to see Pharaoh themselves face to face and tried to make amends.

I am not sure whether the interview with Pharaoh should have taken place at all. The question is whether the Hebrew foremen were right in going to see him to try and sort out this mess. Look at the details as they are recorded for us:

Firstly, the people had heard God's message from Moses and Aaron and they had believed and worshipped God (Exodus 4:29–31). But now, they are being told by their Egyptian bosses and slave drivers that it is all rubbish. We read, in Exodus 5:9, that Pharaoh told the slave drivers, 'Let heavier work be laid on the men so that they may labour at it and pay no regard to lying words.' So, what we have here is a direct challenge to God and his promises, just as we have today: 'Don't believe the Bible. Modern science has disproved all that. No one pays any attention to it nowadays.'

There is, of course, a more subtle challenge to the authority of God in our contemporary society. It has been generated by the growing number of those with religions other than Christianity. The argument is that it would be offensive to deny the various ethnic groups any validity in their beliefs; consequently, there has developed a form of 'relativism' which declares that 'truth is what a person sincerely believes'. Truth has taken on an entirely new meaning: what a person sincerely believes, for them, that is truth.

Therefore, when the foremen have their audience with Pharaoh, he does not beat about the bush. He tells them in no uncertain terms that their problem is all this foolish talk of their God and sacrifices to him. So, he dismisses them with harsh, unyielding words.

Can you see what this means? It means, quite simply, that there can be no sort of accommodation reached with those that are opposed to Christ. I am not talking about everyday life and work. You and I have to respect our employers and employees; we have to try to get along as well and righteously as we can with our neighbours and colleagues (Romans 12:18).

What I mean is that there is a spirit of the age—the spirit of the world—and with that there can be no compromise. We are back to the heart of the matter. For the heart of the matter is the matter of our hearts. And we cannot give our hearts to both the world and God. God says one thing, but the world says the opposite. And the world often, very subtly, flies directly in the face of all God says. So, to go and try to parley with the world over the issue of our souls is quite futile.

Can you understand what this means for each of us, for whom Christ is the very Word of the living God? At our work or among our circle of unbelieving friends or elsewhere, can we not see that to compromise over what the world believes and does, will take us further and further away from the promises of God, and from his grace and presence? To respond to its demands on us will alienate us from the Lord.

This is very real. It is not mere imagination. The world still echoes Pharaoh when he said that faith in God was all fairy tales—'lying words'. But those who know the Lord also know that God is very real, more real than anything else in the whole world; for this world is fleeting and transient, whereas God is eternal, enduring, unchanging. Thus, there is this ongoing battle between the same spirit that possessed Pharaoh and the Spirit of God. Indeed, it is a struggle which is secretly raging in many of our lives today. Like these poor, discouraged foremen, we are often driven to try and make it up with the spirit of the world. We ask, 'Can't we come to some amicable arrangement? Can't we be friends with you? Can't we have our God, and serve you in some way too?'

John sets out for us very plainly the impossibility of such an accommodation:

> Do not love the world or the things in the world. If anyone loves the world, the love of the Father is not in him. For all that is in the world—the desires of the flesh and the desires of the eyes and pride of life—is not from the Father but is from the world. And the world is passing away along with its desires, but whoever does the will of God abides forever. (1 John 2:15–17.)

The third interview: Moses and the Lord (vv. 20–23)

As the foremen were sent from Pharaoh's presence (probably with blows and insults), waiting for them outside the palace were Moses and Aaron, the Lord's ministers. And what a tongue-lashing these two received! Those who had been their 'converts' a few days before, worshipping and praising the Lord, are now reviling them and calling down God's judgement on them. Worse, they say that all Moses and Aaron's requests have done is to make them 'stink in the sight of Pharaoh and his servants and have put a sword in their hand to kill us'. They are very bitter! How do you think Moses felt?

Have you ever dared to be angry with God? We are

supposed to be very reverent and submissive before the Lord, are we not? But have you on some occasion been anything but reverent or submissive? Instead, you have raged and ranted and been violent in your spirit towards the Lord. You have accused God of failing to do what he promised. You might even have said to him, 'I knew this would happen. I told you so! I don't know why ever I listened to you in the first place. I must have been mad!'

As we go through the next chapters, we get a clear timescale of these events. We see that the deliverance of the slaves took about ten months to accomplish—not long really, when one considers all the generations during which they had been slaves. We discover that God's purposes were actually very complex. He was about to show the Egyptians (and all tyrants and dictators since) the enormity of the sin of brutally suppressing any ethnic group. He purposed to make his people willing to leave behind everything in Egypt and make the journey back to where they belonged. He had planned that their deliverance would be the instrument of his self-disclosure, unveiling to them his nature of holy love. He yearned to draw them to himself and win their trust. He wanted to expose the complete falsehood of Egyptian claims to Pharaoh's deity, and to lay low Egyptian arrogance. God had much to do. And he was going to do it in the space of less than one year.

But Moses, with the usual short-sightedness and myopic vision[5] we all have, could only see today and tomorrow. His 'worm's eye view' could only see the present suffering. He had lost sight of the future glory. God's promises of freedom and a mighty redemption seemed hollow and vain in the face of suffering.

Here we are, you and I, and we are in a situation not so far removed from this man as we may think. We have a landslide decline in followers of the Christian faith in our land, with gross materialism and greed, the exploitation of a whole generation which is obsessed with sex and lured into the abuse of drugs. As we see an ailing, failing, languishing church we ask, 'Is God doing anything at all?'

But our question ought to be, 'Is it that God has some severe lessons to teach his church? How long will he have to let the churches decline before we will hear what he is saying?'

I know many have personal troubles of their own. They have known both his rod laid across their shoulders in discipline, but also his staff supporting them in their weakness. Nevertheless, even if that applies to us, still we question his wisdom. Still we doubt his will. We are like Moses in that painful interview with the Lord, angry, baffled, at our wit's end, wondering if we can still believe at all.

Although Moses went and fell before God with his letter of resignation in his hand, so to speak, God spoke with him and told him to tear it up. That is the point from which the record continues in Exodus 6, as God then went on to renew his promises and to assure Moses, the tyrant would be defeated and the slaves freed. Thus, once again he renewed Moses and filled him afresh with his Spirit.

Every servant of God should be able to give this personal testimony, that they have never yet risen from their knees, even after the most painful and agonizing of encounters with the Lord, without having found his Word, his assurance, and his peace again coming afresh to them.

The application of this is for all humanity under his 'common grace'. But under his 'saving grace'[6], it is especially for many persecuted believers who are suffering throughout this broken world of ours. As we read the book of Exodus, these truths must be carried right into our hearts and lives, into our daily living and work, our homes and families. Ultimately it is the conflict between God and Satan, a conflict that is going on within us all. What we must do is weigh the cost and dire consequences of serving the devil against the cost and eternal blessings of serving God.

Nonetheless, we must not forget that the land of slavery had many advantages and pleasures (Numbers 11:5)! Yet God's call is to deliver us from tyranny and to lead us to a Land flowing with milk and honey, to a good and broad land of hills and valleys. Satan's service will destroy us at the end, but God's service will remake and renew us. God says, 'If you will serve me, then I will supply you with the finest of wheat and fully satisfy you. And I will be your God, and you, my child. For the sacrifice has been offered, the pestilence and sword have been averted. So come to me and live!'[7]

FOR FURTHER STUDY

1. 'Pharaoh's problem was the same as ours today.' The apostle speaks of unbelievers who 'live for themselves' (2 Cor. 5:15); his description of the spiritual condition of unbelievers in Ephesians 2:1–3 is almost mind-blowing. In the same epistle (5:8), he states that unbelievers are darkness (NB: *not in* darkness). What language—metaphors, analogies, illustration—could be used in contemporary preaching of the gospel to make these same chilling points effectively?

2. Do you agree that Moses, as described in 5:22–23, had temporarily lost sight of the glory of God? Gather together from the New Testament as many exhortations as you can find which exhort believers to live with heaven in full view. You could perhaps start with Jesus' final discourse to his disciples in John 13–17, before you come to the letters written to the early church.

TO THINK ABOUT AND DISCUSS

1. Discuss whether you think that, in their request to Pharaoh in Exodus 5:1, Moses and Aaron were being evasive in not admitting their ultimate intention was to leave Egypt altogether? The real crunch is in 5:2, when Pharaoh's authority was challenged by a God he does not recognize. How can we explain to non-Christian friends that, at the heart of the gospel, is the demand that a person surrenders everything to Christ's control? Ought we to adopt a much softer approach?

2. The issue of, 'What is truth?' (asked 2000 years ago by Pontius Pilate: John 18:38) is a major issue today. Discuss whether belief in 'some kind of' god is no longer as important as it once was, and if the important question today is whether there is truth in all religion. How valid is the argument that if someone believes in certain ideas, those ideas must be true for them?

3. The question of being upset with God on account of what he has asked us to do, does occur elsewhere in Scripture, as with Elijah (1 Kings 19:12–14), Jeremiah (20:15–18) and others. In 'For Further Study' above, 2 Corinthians 5:15 is cited under point 1. Look up this verse and from the previous verse (14), share what you know personally about the three motivations Paul quotes for 'no longer living for ourselves': Firstly, Christ's love; secondly, his atoning death; thirdly, our death to self. How does Paul sum this up in verse 17?

12 A renewed commission

Exodus 6:1–13

It is easy to assume that a passage such as Exodus 6:1–13 belongs to another era, in which the problems of the Lord's people have absolutely no bearing on the church's problems well over 3000 years later. How mistaken is such an assumption! The humanity of Moses, fallen as it was, more than meets its match in the humanity of God as he condescends to stoop down and raise up his discouraged servant with powerful assurances of his purposes and power.

'The LORD spoke to Moses and Aaron and gave them a charge ...' (v. 13)

What is the meaning of this word 'charge'? The word 'charge' is one of those very versatile words of our English language which are such a bane to foreigners trying to learn English. The *Oxford Dictionary* gives seven different meanings for 'charge'. The first four meanings have to do with guns and shopping—the 'charge' for an explosive, or the 'charge' for getting your boiler serviced, or the summons to court for your unpaid parking fine, and so on. But there are three other meanings given in the dictionary and they all correspond very neatly with the Hebrew word (*'uwd*) used in this verse.

Firstly, in military terms, 'charge' can mean the *signal sounded for an attack*, or the actual attack itself, as in 'the charge of the Light Brigade'. Secondly, a 'charge' can also mean a *task*, or a *commission for a task*. Thirdly, 'charge' can also be used of an *exhortation*, or *directions given*.

> Christian service is often represented in the Bible as warfare, never against people but against spiritual forces, wickedness, evil powers.

In this passage, the definition of 'charge' as, *an attack* or *the signal for an attack*, has possibilities. Christian service is often represented in the Bible as warfare, never against people—'not ... against flesh and blood' wrote Paul in Ephesians 6:12 in the passage on the gospel armour—but warfare against spiritual forces, wickedness, evil powers.

A *task*, *duty* or a *commission* are also obviously very near the mark, too. And if we combine these first and second meanings of 'charge' with the third meaning, an *exhortation* or *directions*, we are on to, fairly precisely, what it appears that God was giving to Moses and his brother Aaron. He was giving them the signal for an attack, together with their task or commission, together with an exhortation and directions for them to fulfil his divine call to them.

This flexible word, with its several meanings, encapsulates for all of us what the Lord has to say to every child in his Kingdom. He adopts us into his family in order that we should be on his side in that ongoing conflict with the world, the flesh and the devil. So let us see what relevance this charge to Moses and Aaron has for each of us today.

The need for our call to be renewed

I well remember a woman who I asked to take on a difficult job in a congregation where I was minister. She needed lots of assurance and gentle persuasion, but I was quite sure she was just the right person for this job. So, at last, she agreed to give it a try.

But, after a few months, she was ready to give up. She had faced jealousy, outright opposition, and huge obstacles. And she was now drained of all enthusiasm and strength, and almost too discouraged to go on. What she needed was a fresh 'charge' from God, and masses of encouragement and continued guidance before she was willing to continue—which she did! Indeed, she won through and the work with which the Lord had charged her, began to be fruitful for the Kingdom.

Moses found himself in just that position. We know how he had argued with God at the burning bush, and how he had brought excuse after excuse for not obeying God's call, until God had become angry with him for his faintheartedness. So, at last, reluctantly he had obeyed. And he had gone to Pharaoh to deliver God's command: 'Let my people go that they may worship me!' But Pharaoh had sent him packing with a flea in his ear, as we say, and had then increased the burden on the Hebrew slaves until they too turned against him.

The results so far had apparently been disastrous. Moses was left not only with Pharaoh's anger directed against him, but also with the bitter resentment of the very people he had come to deliver burning against him with terrible intensity. So, he had handed God his resignation, saying in effect, 'Here's my resignation, Lord. I'm through. This is ridiculous. It's impossible. You've sent me here on a wild goose chase. That's it! I have had enough. Find someone else! I want to go back home to my old job as a shepherd.'

It was at this point that God came and renewed the 'charge' and poured fresh strength into his spirit. That is what we have in Exodus 6—a re-commissioning of this man.

It would not surprise me (and it certainly would not

surprise the Lord) if after a few months of being engaged in your various tasks in your congregation, some of you began to feel like packing it all in. It has not worked out as you hoped and, therefore, it seems that the only sensible thing for you to do is to call it a day and resign. May I tell you that many, if not most, of God's servants (and I include myself) have often felt like that in their work for the Lord.

If that ever happens to you, turn to these two chapters, Exodus 5 and 6. Follow this man's story through, and listen to him as he complains to God with his bitter protests. But notice carefully how God answers him and repeats the call all over again, re-commissioning him to his service and renewing the charge he had originally given to him.

God may well have to do that for you, as he has done it so often for me—yes, not once or twice, but again and again.

How does God re-commission someone?

When a young graduate was offered an appointment in middle-management at a large factory in one of my previous parishes, he was given about six or twelve months working a few weeks in every part of the factory, in order to familiarize himself with what the company was doing. The idea behind this was that he could not be a useful member of the staff unless he first had learned about the whole process of manufacture: production as well as the handling and despatching of orders. He needed to know as much as possible about the company he was to be working for.[1]

I think that, here, God does something rather similar to that for Moses. He reminds Moses of himself. After all, Moses has been called to work for God, so he says, 'This is what I am like; this is the kind of Person you're working for; this is what I intend doing.' Let us consider quickly three points about the kind of Person God showed himself to be and the kind of work he was planning.

First of all, God asks us to look back to our roots, to our past. He tells Moses his name is *El Shaddai*, the 'All Powerful One'. Centuries later, Jewish teachers defined it as meaning 'The All Sufficient One', but the original meaning of *Shaddai* is 'power' and 'strength'. This name for God is used mainly in Genesis, but also here in Exodus 6:3—also in Job and once in Ezekiel. It was the name Abraham, Isaac and Jacob used of God, and by which God spoke to them. Clearly, therefore, God was pointing Moses to the past and to lessons he had taught the patriarchs.

Here, then, is a wonderful lesson to instruct us, to expand our thinking and encourage our hearts. For, like Moses, we need to be reminded of our past, of the first time we heard Christ's voice and of early answers to prayer. We need to recall lessons God has already taught us, but also mistakes we have made and the grace that came to heal and restore us. Too easily we can forget them. So, God has to come and say, 'What did you learn about me when such and such happened? Look back and remember!'

> We need to recall lessons God has already taught us, but also mistakes we have made and the grace that came to heal and restore us.

El Shaddai was the covenant name of God. It spoke of his covenant promises made to Abraham, Isaac and Jacob. And God wants us to remember the New Covenant in Christ's blood, that he made with us even before we were born. In other words, he wants us to come back to the cross, there to kneel, and to remember his eternal promises sealed in the death, resurrection and ascension of his beloved Son.[2]

Secondly, as well as the past, there is also the present. God also asks us to realize that he is with us in the here and now and that he knows all about us. He sees all we are going through and understands and sympathizes with us. We have that in verse 5, where God says to Moses, 'I have heard the groaning of the people of Israel, whom the Egyptians hold as slaves, and I have remembered my covenant.' He says that he knows about it all; he has not forgotten or abandoned them.

We must never let a day go past without spending time with the Lord, because the Lord is concerned with our present problems. He is able to be touched with the feelings of our weaknesses. 'We do not have a high priest who is unable to sympathize with our weaknesses, but one who in every respect has been tempted as we are, yet without sin' (Hebrews 4:15). He knows our sorrows. He shares our heartaches. He comes right alongside us in our suffering and loneliness. He is the God of today, of the here and now.

Thirdly, there is yet another aspect of the nature of God we must learn. It is his vision for the future. There are seven future verbs in verses 6–8: 'I *will* bring you out … I *will* deliver you … I *will* redeem you … I w*ill* take you to be my people … I *will* be your God … I *will* bring you into the land that I swore to give to Abraham, to Isaac and to Jacob … I *will* give it to you for a possession …'.

God must give us a vision of his purposes and promises. And he does. His Word draws back the curtain of his plans just a little, and we are given a fleeting glimpse of the heavenly glory that lies ahead. He says to us, 'This is my great purpose for my people; this is what I am planning; this is where my gracious actions are leading.'

In other words, God turns us to his Son and he asks us to see him as the eternal contemporary, as 'Jesus Christ … the same yesterday and today and forever' (Hebrews

13:8). That, in essence, is what we have here. But unless you and I encourage ourselves in God, we will grow tired, disillusioned and discouraged. However, if we keep the Lord before us—his *past* promises and covenant, his *present* grace with us beside us and before us, and his *future* purposes for us –he will constantly renew his *charge* to us and refresh us. Then, his strength and peace will encourage us in the midst of all our difficulties and struggles.

How does all this theory change my problems?

You may say, 'This is all very well when I am sitting comfortably at home or in church surrounded by friends and other Christians.' But I can imagine you saying in a few days' time when you are up against it, 'You are prescribing a long, concentrated look at God when I'm lonely, discouraged and frustrated. That's all very well for those who are not facing head-on the miserable problems that I am facing. I'm at the coal face and it's hard going. People today are no more interested in hearing the gospel than those slaves were willing to listen to Moses all those centuries ago.' In other words, you are thinking that what is offered here in this passage is cold comfort, unrelated to daily living which is completely different from what the slaves faced over 3000 years ago.

Not so. Your objection is exactly the same as that of

Moses. But give him credit for this: he did believe in God and his mighty power—of course he did!—and he did take a long, searching look at God's past, present and future promises, and he was refreshed and encouraged by all of that. Yet in spite of that, the people out there were as hard and indifferent as ever. They could not care a finger snap for his gospel. It was not that they had no need of it. Not at all! If ever a nation needed God, it was these oppressed, exploited Hebrew slaves. Nevertheless, in verse 9 we read, 'Moses spoke thus to the people of Israel, but they did not listen to Moses, because of their broken spirit and harsh slavery.'

> If ever a nation needed God, it was these oppressed, exploited Hebrew slaves.

Moreover, Moses' personal problems were still the same. Like the late King George VI (perhaps some of you have seen the film, *The King's Speech*), he still had that dreadful stuttering tongue, as he reminded God in verse 12, when he said, in effect, 'How will Pharaoh listen to me when I'm such a hopelessly poor speaker?' Can you see that apparently nothing had changed? It is vitally important for us to recognize that, because God never waves a magic wand. He never offers us a quick fix. He never says, 'Here's a chairlift, jump on and I'll give you an easy ride up this mountain.' It is so important for us to grasp that.

However, when we read on and finish the story, we find the people *were* freed from slavery. God's Word *was* fulfilled. Deliverance *was* accomplished. They *did* enter the land. And it *was* a good and broad land flowing with milk and honey. That is the point.

In other words, the answer can only be that we are entirely thrown back on God. The work is his. The strength is his. The gospel is his. The church is his. The grace is his. The convicting and converting Holy Spirit is his. It is all his. You and I are nothing more than helpless, rather pathetic little creatures on whom the Almighty God has set his loving compassion and through whom he has chosen to do his work.

This is the charge for us today and every day. It is for every child of God. It is pure gospel. I suppose if we were to ask for a New Testament verse to sum up these thirteen verses of Exodus 6, it would be the words of our Lord Jesus: 'Have faith in God' (Mark 11:22). Perhaps, like the disciples, we reply by saying, 'Lord, increase our faith.' The Lord's answer to that request was to tell them of the servant who did his menial duties as his master expected. And then Jesus simply said, 'When you have done all that you were commanded, say, "We are unworthy servants; we have only done our duty"' (Luke 17:5–10). In other words, Christ is saying to us, 'Obey me as dutiful servants. I will do the rest.'

Be assured of this: the God of Moses is our God. He has

spoken to us through his Son, Jesus Christ, and he asks us to place all our confidence in him, and in him alone. And, as we will see as the story of Moses continues, he asks us to obey him, even when he issues us with seemingly impossible commands!

FOR FURTHER STUDY

1. What other examples in Scripture can you find of God giving his servant a 'charge'?

2. Looking at the Gospels; trace the Lord's pastoral concern for those he had chosen to be apostles.

3. In Exodus 6:6, a word is used for the first time in Scripture whose meaning has been contested by theologians of differing views. It is the verb, 'redeem'—*gaal* in Hebrew; a synonym is *padah*. Both words mean, 'deliverance at a cost', or 'ransom'. Consider in what ways there must have been a cost to God in redeeming his people from Egypt.

4. What might be the significance of this encounter between God and Moses in which Aaron has no part. Does Aaron's apparent exclusion suggest loneliness for Moses or rather his unique intimacy with God? (See also Mark 5:37; 9:2; Acts 27:23–24.)

TO THINK ABOUT AND DISCUSS

1. The background against which this encounter, in Exodus 6:1–13, takes place is Moses' discouragement at the seeming ineffectiveness of his attempts to obey God's instructions. Discuss the effects of discouragement in churches today and the way in which it hinders the Lord's work.

2, If you have met with discouragement and its deadening effects, how have you dealt with it? How can the flame of faith be kept burning brightly when discouragement persistently returns and threatens to cause you to doubt your calling?

3. What do you think is revealed about the nature of God in his divine condescension of reassuring Moses by repeating his promises seven times with the words 'I will ...' (vv. 6–8)? Discuss how this insight into the heart of God corresponds with what we learn in the Gospels about the heart of Jesus.

13 The first nine plagues

Exodus 6:14–30; chapters 7–11

Pharaoh could be understood as foreshadowing the New Testament's reference to 'the prince of the power of the air', in Ephesians 2:2, with the proviso that he was already at work in Pharaoh himself, seeking to thwart the purposes and plans of God. The great principle behind the events of the nine plagues is that, in the final analysis, the Lord triumphs over Satan and his minions, even though those who seek to serve him may be driven almost to despair at the enormity of the opposition.

I wonder if nowadays young people who are Christians have to cope at school with sneers and jeers about their belief in the Bible as the Word of God. They probably do. When my own family were in their teens, the jibes and jokes from their peers about the Bible were a constant cause of harassment. The problem arose not only from their fellow pupils, but on occasion it came from teachers who ought to have known better.

What I mean is something like this. Although few would deny the Bible contains great teaching, wise counsel and an excellent ethic for living, nonetheless the supernatural element in Scripture does cause problems for many. Take for example this section of Exodus that we have reached in these studies: the plagues that fell on Egypt. Whoever is going to believe all this about the waters of the Nile turning to blood, and the frogs, gnats, flies and locusts? It appears even more absurd when the account claims the disasters that happened to the ancient Egyptians completely by-passed the Hebrew slaves. And so, the sceptics laugh these chapters out of court. They dismiss them as old wives' tales, myths, legends and folklore, never to be taken seriously in the first place. What are we to say about all this? And how are we to regard the plagues on Egypt? Moreover, do they have anything at all to say to us today? We will try to address these questions in this chapter.

The first nine plagues

Christians today are fortunate in that, over the past decades, serious biblical scholars,[1] who hold firmly to the inspiration and complete reliability of the Bible as originally given, have researched very thoroughly sections of the sacred records such as these chapters in Exodus we are about to consider. I want to draw on some of that recent research as we quickly run through the first nine plagues. I am restricting this chapter to the first nine plagues because they stand firmly together as a remarkable unity.

[i] *The First Plague* was the contamination of the River Nile (7:14–25). Moses was commanded by God to stretch out his staff over the Nile waters, so that they would be turned 'into blood' (v. 17). The fish would die, the river itself (and the irrigation canals from it) would stink, and the water would be quite undrinkable.

Every schoolboy knows[2] that the annual rising of the Nile in July, caused by the rains in the far-off southern area of its source and upper reaches, is now controlled by the great Aswan High Dam.[3] The Low Dam downstream had been completed in 1902, but it was realized that a much bigger dam would be far more effective in preventing unwanted flooding of the river in its lower reaches. Thus, the High Dam was built between 1950 and 1960. It brought immense benefit to Egypt, for now irrigation could be carefully controlled and there was the added benefit of hydroelectricity.

In Moses' day, however, there were no Aswan Dams and, when the Nile rose, the areas along its banks flooded without any human control. Mud dykes were then built to retain the flood water until the river fell and the ground, now soaked and irrigated, could be sown for crops. Then, when the young seedlings were growing in the fields along the riverbanks, the mud walls could be breached little by little in a controlled manner to irrigate the fields.

Very occasionally, perhaps once in several hundred years, the Nile could rise to far higher flood levels than usual and, when that happened, it carried with it from the basins of the Blue Nile in the far south of Egypt very fine red earth. This excessive flooding also brought bacteria and microcosms known as 'flagellates', which did two things: firstly, they poisoned the fish in the lower reaches; and secondly, they rendered the water so muddy with a deep red colour that it was undrinkable.

> The miracle of the first plague was not that this excessive flooding happened, but that it happened precisely at this time.

The miracle of the first plague was not that this excessive flooding happened, but that it happened precisely at this time; moreover, that Moses accurately predicted it. So, for about four months, the river stank and the Egyptians had to dig deep to find uncontaminated water: 'And all the Egyptians dug along the Nile for water to drink, for they could not drink the water of the Nile' (v. 24).[4]

[ii] *The Second Plague* consisted of swarms of frogs (8:1–15). Seven days after the pollution of the Nile,

Moses again sought for an audience with Pharaoh and warned him that his continued refusal to let the people go would result in a plague of frogs. Right on cue, as Aaron stretched out Moses' shepherd's staff over the Nile and its multiplicity of canals, frogs, which were in abundance in the river, swarmed out and filled the houses, bedrooms, beds, ovens and kneading bowls.

This was a virtually unheard-of event. Why did it happen? Think about it. The decomposing fish, being washed along the back waters of the river, would pollute the usual haunts of the frogs, so that they would come ashore to escape the polluted waters. Scientists have suggested that the sudden death of the frogs, together with the foul smell arising from their rapid putrefaction, all indicate that they died from a condition known as internal anthrax.

It is unlikely, though not impossible, that Moses knew anything of internal anthrax. What he did was faithfully deliver the message God gave him. Then, after Pharaoh professed to have relented, he besought God to halt the plague. Sure enough, his word came to pass; the second plague occurred, just as he had said, and then ended on the appointed day, just as he had said it would (8:6, 10–14).

[iii] *The Third Plague* was gnats that covered 'man and beasts' (8:16–19). Those who have carefully researched the plagues tell us that the abnormal state of the Nile

would create ideal breeding conditions for the gnats. Gnats were an everyday hazard of the Egyptian climate. But, this autumn, they came in vast, unprecedented numbers—a veritable plague, again, just as Moses said they would.

[iv] *The Fourth Plague* consisted in vast swarms of flies (8:20–32). The insect referred to was most probably *stomoxys calcitrans*. We sometimes call it the 'horsefly'. It bites into flesh and sucks up blood, and can make its victim quite unwell. I recall visiting a man in hospital who had been bitten just above his knee by a horsefly and his thigh had swelled to twice its normal size; in fact, he was seriously ill. The thought of hundreds of these huge flies rising from the rotting piles of stinking frogs and landing on the people and their food is quite horrible. Once again, it happened just as Moses said it would.

[v] and [vi] *The Fifth and Sixth Plagues* were the cattle disease followed by an epidemic of boils (9:1–7; 9:8–12). Note that the disease only infected the cattle in the fields, not those in their stalls. That suggests at once that they contracted anthrax brought into the fields by the infected frogs. Those in their stalls, being fed from stored food, would escape. So, the Hebrew slaves, warned by Moses to keep their cattle in their stalls, would have kept their livestock free of the disease. Yet again, Moses predicted what would happen.

The plague of boils was probably skin anthrax and would have been passed on by the horseflies, which bred in decaying vegetation, and would have become carriers of the anthrax from the infected haunts of both frogs and cattle. We are told that Pharaoh's magicians could no longer stand before him (9:11). Their bare feet, covered only partially by sandals, would have been bitten by the flies, and consequently would have developed the boils of skin anthrax. Again, God's Word through Moses forecast it all.

[vii] *The Seventh Plague* consisted of heavy hail with thunder and lightning (9:13–35). The barley and flax were ruined, but not the wheat or the spelt, which were not yet grown up (vv. 31–32). That detail enables us to date this plague as happening in early February. The fact that the hail and thunder were concentrated in Upper Egypt, but did not occur in Goshen to the south, where the Hebrews lived, fits the climatic phenomena of the whole region. A similar situation today would be like seeing in the distance the heavy snow on the northern Scottish hills that overlook the fertile plains of Perthshire, for those who live to the south of the Grampians often escape the snow altogether.

[viii] *The Eighth Plague* consisted of raiding locusts (10:1–20). The heavy precipitation in Ethiopia and the Sudan, which had led to the extraordinarily high floods of the river the previous summer, now also provided the

right conditions for a dense plague of locusts around March. The east wind would drive the locusts right up the Nile Valley: 'The LORD brought an east wind upon the land, all that day and all that night. When it was morning, the east wind had brought the locusts' (v. 13). Not a green thing remained across the land of Egypt as every plant and the fruit of every tree were consumed by the marauding swarms of these vicious insects.

[ix] *The Ninth Plague* was a thick darkness (10:21–29). The detail in verse 21, that it was 'a darkness to be felt', is important. The extraordinary and heavy flooding had carried with it masses of red dust, which had been deposited along the Nile Valley and now, had completely dried out. When a *khamsin* wind blew, it would stir up the dust and literally fill the air, making it thick and opaque. Probably the dust settled on people's faces and clothes, getting into their eyes and nostrils. The light of the sun was blotted out for three days (v. 23). The climatic conditions of Egypt suggest two things: firstly, this ninth plague would have occurred in March, shortly after the swarms of locusts; secondly, that, like the hail and thunder, the land of Goshen would not have been affected at all. Yet again, just as Moses had said.

It is significant that the nine plagues were all linked together and followed on in a natural, ecological order. It is quite remarkable. I have already hinted that earlier generations in our country were very sceptical about these four chapters. However, contemporary research has confirmed that they are in perfect keeping with the effects of the excessive inundation of the river, although this excessive flooding of the Nile happened very rarely. The construction of the Aswan Dams ensured that such destructive climatic disruption would not take place again.

One is tempted to think of the freezing of the Thames in 1683–84, when Londoners built a bonfire on the ice and roasted an ox. There is a famous painting by Thomas Wyke of a *Frost Fair* held on the frozen Thames at that time. However, there have not been such severe frosts in England for the past 250 years. The so-called 'Little Ice Age' has not recurred.

What can we learn from these first nine plagues?

The first point that strikes us is the remarkable accuracy of the Bible's account of the nine plagues. It is most unlikely that the Hebrew people living in Palestine would have known anything at all of such conditions. The consecutive nine ecological disasters could not ever have occurred in their land of Canaan. But they could (and did) occur in Egypt. Yet, how else would the Hebrews have preserved an accurate and detailed account of all this, unless they themselves had been in Egypt and had not only witnessed it all, but had kept a record of it?

Here, then, is an example of the most unexpected evidence of the historical reliability of the book of Exodus. It presents us with a surprising indication that the ancient Hebrew people were indeed slaves there and did live through the quite extraordinary events of an ecological turmoil.

> God's power is contrasted with an undeniable demonstration of the powerlessness and falseness of the gods of the Egyptians.

The second point we should note is that, in these nine plagues, we see the most astonishing demonstration of the power of God as the Creator who sustains and controls all that he has made. His power is contrasted with an undeniable demonstration of the powerlessness and falseness of the gods of the Egyptians. In this palpable conflict of the 'Titans', the God whom the slaves worshipped won hands down in every single encounter of the battle.

Let me explain what I mean. Egypt's gods were bound up with the forces of nature and it was against the forces of nature that each plague was directed. They had the sun-god, Re, whose light was blotted out by the ninth plague. There was Ha'pi, the Nile-god of the annual flooding, which usually brought fertility to the fields and crops; but this year, Ha'pi was shown to be powerless before the might of the Lord God whom the slaves worshipped. There was also Heqit, the goddess of fruitfulness, whose symbol was the frog; but the frog had only brought disease and disaster. So, the Lord God stood, at the end of the nine months from July to March, as the undisputed victor in this contest with the gods of Egypt. The score was 9–0 to the slaves' God. And that, the scholars tell us, would be how the Hebrews on the one hand, and the Egyptians on the other hand, would have seen it. The Lord's power had been made manifest.

The third lesson for us concerns the role of Moses as opposed to the role of Pharaoh. The Egyptian Pharaohs all claimed to be divine. They were held to be the special favourites of the sun-god, Re. They claimed a divine authority, and certainly they had a pseudo-divine pride. Moses, by contrast, was only a humble shepherd who had been sent by God to act as his messenger and prophet. He never claimed special powers. He was not a stuntman, doing tricks. His message was consistently, 'Thus says the LORD, the God of the Hebrews ...'.

We have to understand that Moses was faithfully preaching God's Word, week by week, month by month, not only to Pharaoh and the Egyptians, but also to his own people. And as he preached the Word, God acted. Many were deeply moved. When we carefully read through the whole account, we find the royal advisers pleading with Pharaoh to give in, to admit defeat. We find the reputation of Moses and his God increasing and growing all the time. Thus, we have in large colour pictures, as it were, an account of the human heart, and how some defy God in the face of the most compelling evidence,[5] while the hearts of others are softened so that they acknowledged it was the Lord who was at work.[6]

When we turn to the New Testament Scriptures, we find a passage in Revelation 6 not dissimilar to what we have been studying here in Exodus. There we read of plagues, spoiled crops, famines and troubles. However, in this sixth chapter of Revelation, it is not ancient Egypt experiencing these disasters, it is our world during what Scripture calls, 'the latter days': cataclysmic events, causing, not just one nation and country to reel, but the whole earth to be shaken. No world summit in Tokyo or Rio can ever take wholly effective measures to mitigate or stay the inexorable approach of cosmic or ecological disasters. For those cataclysmic events are not merely the consequences of our human greed and ignorance; ultimately, they are directed towards the coming again of Christ to reign as Lord of all. They point unerringly to the 'new heavens and a new earth in which righteousness dwells' (2 Peter 3:13).

In the final analysis, we (and by 'we' I mean 'our world') have steadily departed further and further from the righteousness that God demands of humanity. Centuries ago, Amos, another humble servant of God (in some ways similar to Moses the Bedouin shepherd)—

not a prophet or the son of a prophet but a 'herdsman and a dresser of sycamore figs' (Amos 7:14)—was called by God from following his flocks. He made a passionate appeal, which is as relevant today as it was in the 8th century before Christ: 'Let justice roll down like waters, and righteousness like an ever-flowing stream' (Amos 5:24; 7:14–15).

In our lifetime, we have had a clear demonstration of the failure of communism in the collapse of the Soviet Union, leaving behind massive problems in every area of living, not least in the world's worst pollution of rivers, seas and air. I understand pollution is so bad in some areas of the former Soviet Union that average life expectancy is as low as forty years. But is capitalism the only alternative? While a small section of this world flourishes, most starve.

> As in Moses' day, most remain obdurate, yet a few do listen and turn to the Lord.

While a few are comfortable, most suffer. While we have plenty, most have too little. Surely this should make us think deeply. Our world remains spiritually bankrupt and yet, the light of God shines out through his faithful people and his Word of grace continues to be proclaimed. As in Moses' day, most remain obdurate, yet a few do listen and turn to the Lord.

The mighty God cares for people

Linking Exodus 6 and Exodus 7 is one of those Hebrew genealogies which we usually just bypass with its list of names. The main purpose is most likely to give us Moses' family tree. But it is noteworthy, as it brings us a record of people long since forgotten, who lived and died over 3,200 years ago. Here they are, recorded in this book.[7]

We might ask what this has to do with the mighty acts of God in Exodus 7–11, far less the fearful threats to planet earth given in Revelation chapter 6? It reminds us of an all-important fact: the mighty God who controls the seasons, who nudged the earth into its orbit and who measures the infinity of space with the span of his hand, cares for and knows the most ordinary people, their names and their families. He knows our names—yours and mine. To extrapolate this further, we are assured certain names are recorded in God's book: 'But at that time your people shall be delivered, everyone whose name shall be found written in the book' (Daniel 12:1). Again, 'And if anyone's name was not found written in the book of life, he was thrown into the lake of fire' (Revelation 20:15).[8]

God is not so taken up with global warming that he has lost sight of you and me. He is not so intent on watching the destruction of his creation, when all rain forests have been destroyed and oxygen can no longer be provided to sustain life, that he has forgotten about his love for us and his life in our hearts and souls. Neither is he so concerned to monitor the erosion of the ozone layer that he no longer hears our prayers or cares for us in our sorrows. He is the God who knows each one of us and who records the names of his chosen ones in his eternal records.

Just as that little genealogy is slotted in before the record of the account of the plagues on Egypt, so is your name also recorded in the Lamb's Book of Life? In God's Book are the names of all those who hear the Saviour's voice and follow him. Changing the figure slightly, the apostle urges us to 'be all the more diligent to confirm your calling and election, ... in this way there will be richly provided for you an entrance into the eternal kingdom of our Lord and Saviour Jesus Christ' (2 Peter 1:10–11).

You may ask, 'What has this to do with Exodus chapters 7 to 10?' We are simply looking down the long corridor of many centuries and seeing that the sovereign God, the Creator and Lord of history, is also the loving Father who calls men and women to himself. He calls us to have faith in his beloved Son, so that, in the final line-up on that last Great Day, when the sheep are separated from the goats (Matthew 25:31–34), we may be on Moses' side—our names, like his, recorded in God's records.

This is the ultimate issue. It is why the awesome account of the plagues is prefaced by a list of names, reminding us, lest we forget, that this mighty God is the One who cares so much he sent his Son to call us to living faith in him. Thus, whatever the future generations of humanity may encounter on this dying planet, we may have the quiet assurance that the Creator God is our Father, his Son our Saviour, and our names are written on the palms of his hand.

For further study ▶

FOR FURTHER STUDY

1. Contrast and compare biblical events in which research has uncovered natural evidence to confirm the accounts of unusual occurrences on the one hand, and on the other hand those self-evidently miraculous occasions when there is no possible explanation, other than that God himself intervened in human affairs: e.g., the burning bush (Exod. 3:2–6); the 'angel of the Lord' in Gideon's call (Judg. 6:20–24); the sun on the dial turning back ten steps (Isa. 38:8) etc.

2. What evidence in the book of Exodus can you uncover to lead to the conclusion that Pharaoh was indeed a type or foreshadowing of Satan. To put the same question negatively, can it be shown that Pharaoh, like Satan, is an exact antitype of God himself?

TO THINK ABOUT AND DISCUSS

1. How ought we to reply when friends who do not believe the Bible accuse it of being full of myths and legends, and of course the book of Exodus is an example of this. Does research into the plagues help to provide an answer?

2. Think about the faith and courage of Moses in announcing one by one the first nine plagues. What does that say about the need for faith, courage and courtesy when we give an answer for the hope we have in Christ (1 Peter 3:15–16)?

3. By what 'secret arts' did Pharaoh's magicians replicate the first sign and the first and second plagues of Moses (7:11–12, 22; 8:6–7)? Note that by the third plague, which they could not copy, they declared 'This is the finger of God' (8:18–19).

4. Trace the progression in Pharaoh's hardening of his heart. First, read 5:2 where Pharaoh denied and defied the Lord God. Next, read 7:3 where God says he will harden Pharaoh's heart. Finally, read 7:14, 22 where it

would seem Pharaoh hardened his own heart. Who do you think was to blame for this hardness of heart?

5. How can we reconcile the paradox of what Paul writes in Romans 9:14–18 with what Peter says in 2 Peter 3:9 that God is 'not wishing that any should perish, but that all should reach repentance'? Does what Peter writes, in Acts 2:21 and 40, throw any light on this paradox?

14 The tenth plague

Exodus 10:24–29; 11:1–10; 12:7, 13

Anyone reading the Book of Exodus for the first time would realize that events were moving inexorably towards a crisis of enormous proportions. The conflict between the mighty Pharaoh and the God of the Hebrew slaves is about to reach its zenith. Moses' palpable anger against the tyrant's obduracy leaves us fearing the worst, for the final, decisive plague will be devastating in its effects across the whole nation.

From time to time, clips appear on our TV screens of Adolf Hitler, facing thousands of his *Wermacht* (defence power) in serried rows on the specially constructed, vast parade ground at Nuremberg, and declaring with frenetic ferocity his Nazi propaganda. It chills us to the bone to hear him. Some of us prefer immediately to switch to another channel. We all know the appalling lengths to which his evil ideals—the 'Final Solution'—led. It hardly bears thinking about. In Exodus 10:28, there is briefly related the fury of another despot, probably equal in wickedness to Hitler. It is the divine judgement on Pharaoh that concerns this chapter, but alongside that judgement is the preparation for the means of the redemption and deliverance of God's people.[1]

We have already seen that the first nine plagues were a kind of clash of the Titans—the God of the Hebrew slaves versus Pharaoh, who regarded himself as the god of the Egyptians. But instead of Pharaoh and his array of under-gods controlling nature's fertility, the Nile, as well as day and night and Egypt's natural seasonal cycle, had been thrown into total confusion. Moses, the spokesman for the slaves' God, had accurately predicted each disaster, time and time again. The score had been 9-0 to the Lord God of Israel.

But what of the tenth plague? It is enough to make anyone's hair stand on end. Infinitely terrible and awesome!

Moses' anger

By the time the terrible sandstorm, which had blotted out the sunlight for three days, had died down, Pharaoh was absolutely furious. No doubt the nine months of disasters had completely worn away his patience. It was going to take several days to clear away the sand from every nook and cranny, the linen chests, the food cupboards, the furniture, the cooking vessels and utensils, the plates and cups and knives and spoons. Indeed, for weeks, slaves would still be sweeping up sand and grit which had found its way into the most unlikely corners.

Nevertheless, Pharaoh still sat on his golden throne in his stately palace, his features and expression perhaps concealed behind a golden mask, similar to the one earlier Pharaohs had worn.[2] But his fury could not be concealed. 'Get away from me,' he said to Moses. 'Take care never to see my face again, for on the day you see my face you shall die' (10:28). This mighty potentate, who claimed to be a god descended from the sun-god, Re, through the sexual relationships Re was reported to have had with royal women, has at last realized that his credibility was in shatters. Three days of darkness, and him supposedly descended from the sun! These two men, Moses and Aaron, were undermining his very godhead!

But if Pharaoh was provoked to absolute fury, so was Moses! He replied:

> As you say! I will not see your face again ... Thus says the LORD: About midnight I will go out in the midst of Egypt, and every firstborn in the land of Egypt shall die, from the firstborn of Pharaoh who sits on his throne, even to the firstborn of the slave girl who is behind the hand-mill ... There shall be a

great cry throughout all the land of Egypt, such as
there has never been, nor ever will be again ... And all
these your servants shall come down to me and bow
down to me, saying, 'Get out, you and all the people
who follow you.' And after that I will go out (10:29;
11:4-8).

And then we read that Moses then went out from
Pharaoh in hot anger! (11:8b).

Moses was furious—storming out of Pharaoh's
presence in hot anger! How awful. Imagine it, a man of
God losing his temper with one of the most powerful
men on earth! Some object and
say, 'But doesn't the Bible say
that Moses was the meekest
man in all the earth (Numbers
12:3)? Why ever then did he
react like that? Would Jesus
have done that?'

> Imagine it, a man
> of God losing his
> temper with one of
> the most powerful
> men on earth!

I saw a film years ago about the American Civil War.
The Confederates had a powerful encampment in a
position virtually impossible for the Yankees to capture.
But what they did not know was that they had made their
base above a whole series of tunnels, which were mine-
workings. The moment came in the hours of darkness
when the tunnels, which had been secretly packed with
barrels of gunpowder, suddenly erupted in a series of
massive explosions. No one in the Confederate army

had known, and no warning had been given. The result was a total massacre.[3]

Not so in Egypt at this time. Warning after warning had been given, appeal after appeal, but all to no avail. Moses saw it all so clearly. Time after time God had honoured him by fulfilling his predictions. Not one word he had spoken had fallen to the ground. Surely, after all that happened over these past nine months, the Egyptians would take heed. Indeed, the record tells us that 'the man Moses was very great in the land of Egypt, in the sight of Pharaoh's servants and in the sight of the people' (11:3). Yet, after his final horrific message to Pharaoh—and yes, it was nothing less than horrific, for every family in Egypt would lose their firstborn son in one night's devastating destruction—but Pharaoh saw the death of Moses as the only answer to all that had gone wrong; 'We must kill him, then we will have peace!' was his reaction (10:28).

That is why Moses openly and deliberately displayed hot anger! Perhaps his towering rage would move some of the courtiers standing there who had heard all he said. Perhaps a few firstborn sons would be saved if they paid heed to his message, because anger sometimes works when plain words fail. A close friend in the ministry, who was generally a very quiet and gentle man, told me that the parts of his sermons his elder son remembered most clearly were when he was most vehement and tended to shout passionately. That young man later trained for the ministry and, like his father, became a most fruitful pastor and preacher.

What would Jesus do? Well, we have only to read the Gospels to find examples of his fearsome anger. Twice he cleared the temple courtyard of the cheating traders (John 2:13–17; Mark 11:15–17), who, incidentally, held licenses from the high priest permitting them to trade as long as they gave him a kick-back—not for the temple funds, oh no!—but for his own bank account. Can you imagine how awesome the anger of Jesus must have been as he turned over their tables and knocked over their pens with the animals. His whip was used on the rascals' backs, and it will have stung and left many a purple weal there too.

Then there was his horrendous prediction of the destruction of Jerusalem, as he wept over the city (Mark 13:2; Matthew 23:37–39). He could see it all so clearly: the Roman armies, the siege, the starvation, the suffering and ultimately, when the city fell, the slaughter. He, 'gentle Jesus, meek and mild', as Charles Wesley's children's hymn has it, this gentle Jesus foresaw all that and with a breaking heart warned them most solemnly with tears.

So, what would Jesus do? We are so fond of quoting John's words from his First Letter that 'God is love' (1 John 4:8). But how often these days do we hear the solemn warning that 'our God is consuming fire' (Hebrews 12:29)? Those words are also in our Bibles. Isaiah, the prophet, wrote of sinners suffering as they 'dwell with everlasting burnings' (Isaiah 33:15), and he also speaks of dwelling with 'the consuming fire' (Isaiah 33:14). Yet, he hastens to add that the eyes of the righteous will 'behold the king in his beauty' (Isaiah 33:17). Moreover, the final book in the Bible, Revelation, speaks of 'the wine of God's wrath, poured full strength into the cup of his anger' and the torment of those who turn their backs on his love and grace (Revelation 14:10).

> Although righteous anger at times is unquestionably appropriate, whenever we are angry, we can come very near to sin.

We who seek to follow Christ in our daily lives know that, at times, we have fits of temper and anger. Often our tantrums are very wrong and are due to our lack of self-control. But anger is not always wrong. Yes, love must be our greatest aim, but there are times when pure love can experience real anger. Paul, alluding to a psalm, wrote, 'Be angry, but do not sin' (Ephesians 4:26; Psalm 37:8), because, although righteous anger at times is unquestionably appropriate, whenever we are angry, we can come very near to sin.

Who would not be angry to see a child being exploited by evil men and women for sexual gratification; or to

OPENING UP EXODUS

discover a frail old woman had been beaten to death in her bed by a drug addict for the few pound in her purse, as has been reported in the national press several times in recent years. It would be wrong and even inhuman not to be angry. And in the spiritual realm there can be anger driven and stirred up by the Spirit of God. Oh, for more of that holy wrath at the right time and in the right place in churches today over certain aspects of our society!

Furthermore, there are personal and persistent sins in believers as well. Charles Wesley (1707–88), expressed it aptly in his hymn, 'Depth of mercy, can there be mercy still reserved for me?' The second verse has the memorable lines,

> I have long withstood his grace,
>
> Long provoked him to his face;
>
> Would not hearken to his calls,
>
> Grieved him by a thousand falls.

Hugh Binning, Scottish minister of Govan Parish Church from the age of twenty-two until his death in 1653 at the age of twenty-six, preached a series of twenty-eight sermons on 1 John 1:1–2:2, in which he did not spare his congregation regarding their persistent sins, especially 'respectable sins'—if there are any such sins![4] Why else did the Father hide his face from his beloved Son as he hung from the cross, bearing upon his soul the full weight of the divine wrath? Nonetheless, it stands to reason that the obvious difference between human and divine anger is that, because God cannot sin, his anger is invariably justified and wholly righteous, whereas human anger is always susceptible to sinfulness.

The final warning

You must have been in a supermarket or some other store and witnessed a small child behaving rather badly. Mother constantly tries to restrain her child but without any effect. I recently witnessed this in my bank. The threats became more and more severe. But the six-year-old girl paid not the least bit of attention. She dashed about and pulled out bank leaflets, scattering them all over the floor; she climbed on to a desk in a small private interviewing area, opening the drawers and messing with the phone there. Mother's warnings became threats which degenerated into statements that when they got home the child would be 'murdered'. But the little girl had heard such warnings many times before, knew they were empty threats, and paid not the slightest bit of attention.

Down the years, the international community has often issued all sorts of dire warnings to various brutal dictators, but they have paid about no more attention to them than that little girl did to her mother's empty threats. The so-called 'red line' set by world leaders has been boldly crossed with total impunity.

Moses gave a final warning. Behind that final warning were the first nine plagues. We have already noted that God had given him very real credibility among many of the Egyptians and even among those who served in Pharaoh's court (Exodus 8:19; 11:3). Therefore, his warnings were self-evidently to be taken with the utmost seriousness.

What about preachers of the gospel today? I have to say that we have no right to say we are giving a 'final warning'. Only God knows when each one of us will hear the gospel for the last time. It is not impossible that someone in their usual place of worship, during the week you read this chapter, will never again sit under the sound of the call of God to trust wholly in his beloved Son, and in nothing and no one else for salvation. So, what all preachers are entitled to say is (with the Psalmist in Psalm 95:7–8), 'Today, if you will hear his voice, do not harden your hearts ...'. What guarantee do any of us have that we will see the dawn of tomorrow? There are sometimes occasions when God's warnings can be very stark.

When I was minister of Larbert Parish Church[5] near Falkirk in the 1970s, I was privileged to have as my associate pastor a very wise and godly retired man who had been in the ministry for nearly 50 years. He had been Clerk of the Dumfries Presbytery for twenty-five years and was highly respected throughout the whole denomination. One Sunday he preached on John chapter 3, 'You must be born again' (v. 7), and about five times during his sermon he said, 'If this is the last time I shall ever preach in this church, my message to all of you is, "Unless you are born again of the Spirit of God you will not enter his kingdom."'

As people shook hands with him at the door they were saying, 'Oh Mr Davidson, you gave us an awful turn saying this might be your last time preaching to us. We'll have you for many years yet!' They were wrong. That night he went to bed, slept well and at daybreak he wakened up in the Lord's presence. I conducted his funeral service that week and hundreds from all over the country attended. But he was not with us; he was with Christ which is far better.

This was Moses' final warning to Pharaoh. Within three days Pharaoh would be drowned in the Red Sea. He had heard God's voice for the last time. So often faithful ministers of the Word of God must repeat the psalmist's solemn appeal, 'Today, if you will hear his voice, do not harden your hearts ...'.

The tenth plague was a judgement of retribution.

I have to bring to every reader's attention something that is very important. Although occasionally I slip into sharing my personal views as I am writing, that is not what I ought to be doing. My opinions are of no importance to you; they are my concern, not yours. No, my God-given commission is to bring you his views, his Word, his truth, however unpalatable that may be to modern minds and attitudes. I know that what I am about to write may be totally unacceptable to many people. But in preaching on this subject of the tenth plague I have to record it. Otherwise, I will be disobedient to the Word of God.

> My God-given commission is to bring you his views, his Word, his truth, however unpalatable that may be to modern minds and attitudes.

All of us, including me, shudder when we read that this final tenth plague consisted in the death of the firstborn son from every Egyptian family. We ask however the God and Father of our Lord Jesus Christ could do such a terrible deed. We hear it read from the Bible and listen in stupefied silence and latent unbelief. What right had a loving God to kill the firstborn son from every household in the land?

The answer is plain: it was naked retribution—wound for wound, blow for blow. It was an eye for an eye, a tooth for a tooth.[6] Do you think that God had not heard the cries of Hebrew baby boys as they had been thrown into the Nile by any Egyptian Tom, Dick or Harry—and indeed by Pharaoh's authority and order? (Exodus 1:22). Do you think the Lord God had not heard the screams of the Hebrew mothers as their suckling infants were torn from their breasts? Can you believe that their anguish and grief had gone unnoticed? No, the cries of those Hebrew slaves and their butchered children, had echoed round the throne of Almighty God and had been preserved in the eternal records. God had seen it all and had heard it all.

And now it was retribution—a life for a life. The judgement day had arrived for this nation.

Do you think that God did not see and hear the cries of the family of Shahbaz Bhatti, Minister for Minorities and the only Christian in Pakistan's government, who was shot on 2 March 2011 because he was trying to defend the rights of the Christian minority in Pakistan. Three months earlier, he had told the BBC that he would not shrink from seeking to repeal his country's blasphemy laws and he had predicted he would be assassinated for endeavouring to fulfil this remit of his portfolio as Minister for Minorities in the Pakistani Cabinet. Do you think God has not seen and heard of the millions of persecuted Christians in Afghanistan, Indonesia, India, Sudan, Somalia, Libya, Morocco, North Korea and other lands, so many of whom have lost their lives. The lesson of this tenth plague is that one day, righteous judgement will be seen to have been done.

But this is only part of biblical truth. We must not neglect that there was with this tenth plague a way of escape, not only for the Hebrew slaves, but the way was open for every Egyptian also. It was the blood of a lamb without blemish, which had to be sacrificed and its blood put on the doorposts and lintels of each home. The promise was, 'When I see the blood, I will pass over you' (12:13).

The Passover will be the theme of the next chapter. However, just now notice that our communion service often begins with these words from the Bible, 'Christ our Passover is sacrificed for us' (1 Corinthians 5:7, KJV)[7]. Our just and righteous punishment was laid upon our Saviour when he died on the cross. He died in our place, for our sins, failures, rebellion, selfishness, deceit and wrong doings. As the lovely paraphrase of Psalm 23 has it: 'Perverse and foolish oft I strayed, but yet in love he sought me ...' (Henry Williams Baker, 1821–77).

So, while the message of this horrendous tenth plague is one of judgement, it also one of glorious hope and forgiveness, of deliverance from the slavery of sin. It is a signpost pointing forward to Jesus Christ, the Lamb of God, who takes away the sin of the world. He is ready to be your Saviour, Redeemer and Lord and only needs us to hear his invitation, to acknowledge our need, to bow before him in faith, and surrender. It is that total surrender that many of us find the hardest act of obedience. George Matheson's poem puts it like this:

> Make me a captive, Lord, and then I shall be free;
>
> force me to render up my sword, and I shall conqueror be.
>
> I sink in life's alarms when by myself I stand;
>
> imprison me within thine arms and strong shall be my hand.
>
> George Matheson (1842–1906)

FOR FURTHER STUDY

1. The first nettle to grasp in this chapter is the subject of anger. Throughout Scripture, anger is stirred up in God's faithful servants and, alongside it, we find the divine anger which human rebellion provokes in a loving God. A helpful study of this phenomenon of our Christian faith can be found in the imprecatory Psalms, such as Psalm 109 or Psalm 139:19–22. Two useful studies can be found in C. S. Lewis' *Reflections on the Psalms,* and Calvin's *Commentary of Psalms.*[8] See also some of Calvin's comments on Psalms 7:6; 5:9-10; 28:4; 35:4-6; 40:14, etc. Spurgeon is very direct and poignant in his expositions of the imprecations and his *Treasury of David* is easily accessible online. Alistair Begg, Parkside Church, Ohio, preached a very powerful and insightful sermon on Psalm 139:19–24 on Sunday 19 February 2003; it is available on his website.

2. The second nettle to grasp is that of the stark reality of divine retribution. Consider why, in the Old Testament, retributive justice is worked out, in part at least, in the here and now (with suggested examples), whereas, in the New Testament, retribution is promised as an awesome reality in the future.

TO THINK ABOUT AND DISCUSS

1. Discuss what makes you angry and whether sometimes your anger is sinful. Also consider some examples of events and actions over which complacency would definitely be the wrong attitude, e.g., Jonah Ch. 4.

2. Read Genesis 49:1–7. Probably to the surprise of Reuben, Simeon and Levi, their aged father had not forgotten certain wickedness of which they had been guilty: Reuben of incest and Simeon and Levi of brutal cruelty. Ought Jacob to have ignored their sins, forgotten them or forgiven them? Alternatively, was he righteous in removing the headship of the family from Reuben, and the land inheritance from Simeon and Levi?

3. Do you think there is a difference between the Father's heart and Jesus' heart? Does the Father punish while the Son forgives? Or are their hearts essentially one heart? See Luke 15:20; Matthew 3:17; John 14:8, 13; 2 Corinthians 1:3; Hebrews 1:3; 1 John 4:15–16.

15 The Passover

Exodus 12

Christ, our Passover lamb has been sacrificed (1 Corinthians 5:7). Very soon the midnight hour will strike and find all those who have heeded Moses' instructions sheltering under the blood of their Passover lamb.

I t is now five minutes to midnight. The climax had almost been reached. Alas, casualties litter the pathway that God has instructed his servant to follow. But there has been a significant number of once-loyal followers of Pharaoh who are on the brink of changing their allegiance to the God of the Hebrew slaves.

As you read this book, perhaps sitting in a comfortable armchair in a pleasant living room or on a train taking you safely to your destination, many tens of thousands of people across the world have immense worries. Multiple disasters afflict our broken world: floods that render villages, towns, roads, bridges and fields desolate; the aftermath of war and terrorist attacks;

drought that leaves crops withered and useless, so that poverty-stricken peasants face certain famine for the months ahead; epidemics causing widespread disease and death. While it is true that most parts of the world remain relatively stable and affluent, we are always conscious that, whatever our immediate circumstances may be, the extreme trials and suffering experienced in some places on earth are a long way off from our particular country.

The immediate context of the Passover was the seemingly interminable suffering of a race of slaves, whose baby sons were being seized and drowned, whose backs were raw and bleeding from their taskmasters' lashes, and who had all but given up any hope of ever being rescued from their lives of misery. But surely, you may think, their situation bears little or no relevance to our lives today, nor to those who suffer through war, famine, drought or some other natural disaster.

> Whatever life throws at us, the gospel of Jesus Christ can provide us with the inner strength and endurance that we need to face life's demands.

I am not for one moment suggesting that we do not have any anxieties at all. Of course, we all do, even though in the West we live in relative peace and security. But whatever life throws at us, the gospel of Jesus Christ can provide us with the inner strength and endurance that we need to face life's demands. In Chapter 12 of the book of Exodus we have reached the Passover. This Jewish festival not only foreshadowed the Lord's Supper, but it gives us an outline of the origins of the promised Christian gospel.

No yeast

The Passover was to be eaten with bread made without yeast and accompanied by bitter herbs: 'They shall eat the flesh that night, roasted on the fire; with unleavened bread and bitter herbs they shall eat it' (v. 8). We will take each part of this statement in turn.

Firstly, why no yeast?

I remember during the war years my mother sending me to the baker to buy a little yeast from the bakery, for she fed her family on homemade bread. I recall as a boy being fascinated by the effect that small lump of yeast had on the batch of dough, turning it into a heaving, panting mass and causing it to rise as it sat on the hearth beside the open fire.

However, before the Passover night, all yeast had to be cleared out of each home and only unleavened bread (that is, bread made without any yeast) was to be eaten. So strict was this instruction, that anyone found to have yeast in his home was to be excommunicated from the people of God.

Yeast, which bubbles and heaves and completely permeates the dough—and which is used also in the fermentation of wine—on this occasion[1] stood for the all-pervasive, hidden, secret influence of evil. It symbolized sin which permeates every one of us—our minds, our wills and our passions. So, this simple detail about the Passover stands for this great principle of the gospel: the need to turn decisively from everything that is wrong, unclean and unholy. The meaning is that we must be rid of the secret, personal wrongdoing in our lives, and be renewed with holy strength. In other words, when you and I draw near to Christ in prayer, as well as to the Lord's Table, we are called on to turn away from all that we know is selfish and displeasing to God in our lives. The evil must be put away from us.

The apostle Paul states this very clearly when he says, 'assuming that you have heard about him [Christ], and were taught in him, as the truth is in Jesus, to put off your old self, which belongs to your former manner of life and is corrupt through deceitful desires, and to be renewed in the spirit of your minds …' (Ephesians 4:21–23). The verb, 'to put off', is in a Greek tense which implies a decisive, determined act of our wills. It is not something that can be done for us by anyone else. We ourselves must resolve to be rid of the leaven of the pervading influence of our past lives. Paul is not suggesting that the root of sin in us can ever be eradicated. Elsewhere he writes about the on-going struggle between the indwelling Holy Spirit in the believer and the desires of the flesh (Galatians 5:16–26). Nevertheless, you and I must daily resolve to turn our backs on what we know to be sinful.[2]

When I was a boy, the railway network ran trains all over Scotland. From my hometown in Arbroath there was a branch line to Forfar, Brechin and insignificant Angus villages such as Friockheim and Guthrie. Consequently, Arbroath had a very busy station with four platforms and a large goods yard. I used to watch the goods wagons being shunted from one siding to another, or into the great railway sheds. Today that area is waste ground and there are just two platforms, north to Aberdeen via Montrose and Stonehaven, and south to London, via Dundee and Edinburgh.

Before you and I consider approaching the Holy Table, there are most probably quite a lot of damaged goods in our lives—'wagons', so to speak, full of unwholesome 'cargo'. Therefore, we must resolve to uncouple those wagons of sin, and all that offends our holy God and separates us from him. We cannot be effective Christians unless there is a daily renewal of repentance. 'Why daily repentance?' you may ask. Because we have secret 'railway sidings' in our lives, where forbidden wagons are standing, laden with our selfishness, meanness and folly. Repentance means that every day we must renounce what is wrong, because wrong keeps creeping up on us all the time. It is like the lees lying at the bottom of the fermentation jar; when the jar is shaken the lees immediately rise and cloud the clarity of the new wine. To return to the metaphor of the railway yard, we must shunt away the evil freight into the sheds that open up on to the incinerator. That is what William Cowper (1731–1800) meant when he wrote this verse of his hymn, 'O for a closer walk with God':

The dearest idol I have known,

whate'er that idol be,

help me to tear it from thy throne,

and worship only thee.

No yeast was to be eaten with the Passover lamb. But what about the 'bitter herbs' that had to be eaten with the unleavened bread?

Bitter herbs

Here is a quotation from the Jewish Passover Service, as it has been celebrated for three thousand years with scarcely any change in its liturgy:

Wherefore is this night distinguished from all other nights? On all other nights we may eat any species of herbs, but on this night only bitter herbs ... (*and the whole family answer in unison*) 'Because we were slaves to Pharaoh in Egypt, and if the Most Holy had not brought forth our ancestors from Egypt, we had still continued in bondage.'[3]

The bitter herbs were a reminder of the bitterness of slavery. The memory of that bitter bondage had to be kept alive. This must not only be true of Jews, as to this day they still share the Passover meal with their families, but it must also be true of all Christian people that we never forget the bitterness of sin. Often, we are to remember the vinegar and gall which the dying Saviour tasted as he hung in anguish on the cross. The bitterness of his suffering and sorrow was the bitterness of our sin which took him to Calvary.

> One of the devil's highest priorities in his work of deception in this world is to conceal from men and women the ultimate poisonous pain caused by sin.

I am convinced that one of the devil's highest priorities in his work of deception in this world is to conceal from men and women the ultimate poisonous pain caused by sin. Every day, we are confronted by images of sins of various colours and kinds. We see these images on our television screens, in our newspapers and magazines, as well as in many of the advertisements, and at times we can feel their seductive power. The multitude of allurements appear to offer all that is bright, attractive and harmless. But when we tear away the disguises and see the reality behind those images, we are able to see the ravages of evil in people's lives and something of the agonizing remorse, as well as the pain and suffering it brings.

More than anything else, the devil wants to hide that from us. I think of people I have spoken with in my hometown over recent months and years. Oh, the unhappiness, misery, hurt and loss—not just financial loss, but loss of friends, family, children! Invariably it has happened because someone at some point took a turn directly away from the path of righteousness, and then another turning downward, followed by another and yet another.

I think of Rachael (not her real name), a woman in her thirties. When I first saw her fourteen years ago, she was slouching painfully down the aisle to get out of the church during a Sunday morning service. At the time I assumed she was a woman in her late fifties or early sixties. I correctly guessed that she was a heroin addict. Anyone could see that hard drugs were killing her. She was completely enveloped by the bitter effects of her addiction. Not only was her physical condition affected, but also her mental and psychological condition. She was a human wreck.

Just over four years later, our minister introduced the congregation to a very beautiful young woman who, he said, had found Christ. (I would have liked him to have said that Christ had found her.) There was absolutely no way I would ever have guessed she was the same Rachael who had dragged herself from the church four years previously. It was quite impossible to recognize her as being the same person. She had been restored to the beautiful young woman God created her to be. She was now halfway through her training in Bible College to be an evangelist to other women who were being killed by the bitterness of sin, as she herself had been until Christ found her and healed and transformed her. My wife and I became very close to her and we have kept in touch down the years since then.

There are no prizes for guessing that drug addiction goes hand-in-hand with sleeping around, and so with sexually transmitted infections (STIs). It is usually accompanied by theft and dishonesty, even violence, for drug habits are expensive to feed. Rachael's case was an extreme one, though tragically common in our land. Nevertheless, it is not only the sins of addiction and immorality that bring bitterness. Grudges, resentments, jealousy, greed, selfishness—every sin you care to name reaps the same bitter harvest!

You will understand that, when a Christian pastor is out visiting, people always do their best to present themselves to him in as good and respectable a light as possible. They imagine their pastor would be shocked to hear of very bad things. Let me tell you that, over the decades of my ministry, I have seen life in the raw. I have gone home and wept. At times I have been haunted for days by what I have heard and seen. My sleep has been disturbed by bad dreams that have arisen from the hours I have spent with various troubled people. I have even broken down as I have conducted funerals for those who could find no escape from the bitterness of their sin and had taken a lethal overdose or hung themselves from the stair banisters.

The Passover feast, eaten with bitter herbs, was observed every year, and still in all Jewish homes is a constant reminder of the bitterness of bondage. And for Christian people, the communion bread and wine carry the same message. Lest we forget, lest we forget. 'See from his head, his hands, his feet, sorrow and love flow mingled down ...'.[4] That memory is the call of divine grace to us all to turn daily, and hourly, to our Lord Jesus.

Why the sprinkled blood?

We turn now to the instruction in verse 7: 'Then they shall take some of the blood and put it on the two doorposts and the lintel of the houses in which they eat it.' So why had the lamb's blood to be daubed on the doorposts and lintels?

Nowadays, we go to the butcher for our meat. We see the various cuts all neatly set out in the display cabinet, and we choose what we want—venison, beef, lamb, pork or poultry. In Moses' day there were no butchers. The man of the house was the butcher. If you wanted a roast dinner you did the work yourself, right from the point where you began by choosing the animal to be prepared for the family meal.

But for this night of the first Passover meal, it was to be roast lamb and the blood of the newly killed lamb had to be sprinkled on the doorposts and lintels. That had to be done before midnight. After that, no one must venture out-of-doors, for the Lord[5] himself was to visit every family in Egypt. Only where the Lord saw the sprinkled blood on the doorposts and lintels would he pass-over any home. Hence the name 'Passover'.

What lessons are there here from the Passover meal, and what do we learn from the blood sprinkled on the lintels and doorposts? Further, why do our Bibles say, 'Christ, our Passover lamb, has been sacrificed' (1 Corinthians 5:7)?

The same God who visited judgement on the Egyptians also passed-over the slaves' homes bringing redemption.

Firstly, God the Judge and God the Saviour are one and the same Person. It is not really appropriate and accurate to say that God the Father is the Judge, and Jesus Christ the Saviour. The same God who visited judgement on the Egyptians also passed-over the slaves' homes bringing redemption. The God who must judge our sin, is the God who alone can forgive and save us from our sin. Three Persons but One God!

Secondly, we also learn from the sprinkled blood that the Hebrew slaves were only saved from this terrible tenth plague because a sacrifice had been offered in the place of each family. Their firstborn sons were spared because a lamb had died in their place. This is that awesome principle of retribution. As we saw in the previous chapter, God had not forgotten what had been happening for generations. The Egyptians had been culling the Hebrew children the way children are being culled today in some of the cities of South America,[6] except that it had been newly born babies that had been seized and thrown into the Nile as sacrifices to the god of their great river. God had heard their cries and seen the suffering of those Hebrew mothers whose baby boys had been torn from them. And now retribution was being visited. A life for a life.

However, anyone, not just the Hebrew slaves but Egyptians too, could offer a lamb as a substitute, and if the blood was sprinkled on the doorposts, then the atonement for sin would be accepted. The communion service that is at the very heart of our faith reminds us that Christ, our sacrifice, has been offered for us. He died in our place. When I should have been punished for my sin, the Saviour took my place. 'Christ, our Passover lamb, has been sacrificed' (1 Corinthians 5:7). He was a substitute for me so that I could be freed from sin's slavery.

Thirdly, also from the sprinkled blood, we learn there had to be individual appropriation of the sacrifice. Every home must have the sprinkled blood on its doorposts. Your neighbour's doorposts sprinkled with blood would not be sufficient for you. Neither would your mother's doorposts sprinkled with blood provide atonement for you. Your own doorway must have the marks of the sacrifice upon it.

How is it with you? I mean, has the blood of Christ been sprinkled upon the doorway of your heart? This must be intensely personal; the doors into all of our lives must each have the mark of the New Covenant in the blood of Christ. The final day will come when divine judgement will be visited on our world. It is an unchangeable law of God that sin must be punished with eternal banishment from his presence. The Bible calls this terrible punishment the 'second death' (Revelation 2:11; 20:6, 14; 21:8).

But God has provided a sacrifice to cover our sin. And every time we draw near to God in the name of Jesus we are urged to come; moreover, we are warmly welcomed and embraced in the Father's arms, because of his Son's death as the Lamb of God in our place. Supremely, we celebrate this when at his Table we partake of the bread and wine.

Surely it goes without saying that you and I must recognize our need of the Lamb of God, the great Passover Lamb, and then deliberately, by an act of our will, take shelter beneath the Cross of Christ.

> There lies beneath its shadow, but on the farther side,
>
> The darkness of an awful grave that gapes both deep and
> wide;
>
> And there between us stands the cross, two arms
> outstretched to save,
>
> A watchman set to guard the way from that eternal grave.
>
> Upon the cross of Jesus mine eye at times can see
>
> The very dying form of One who suffered there for me;
>
> And from my stricken heart with tears two wonders I confess;
>
> The wonders of redeeming love and my unworthiness.[7]

Conclusion

There we have it. Firstly, the unleavened bread—that is bread without yeast—thus speaking of repentance and rooting out from our hearts all that is unholy, untrue and impure. Then the bitter herbs, for we must never forget the bitterness of sin with its defilement and destructive effects in our lives. Thirdly,

> We must never forget the bitterness of sin with its defilement and destructive effects in our lives.

the sprinkled blood which looks forward prophetically to Christ's blood, for he is our Passover Lamb, and his blood was shed for all who believe that we might be delivered from the slavery of sin.

There is something every reader can do just now in the privacy of your own heart. Where you are sitting, you can turn to the Lord Jesus Christ, and acknowledge him as your Passover Lamb. You can ask him, by his costly atonement, to cover you from the just punishment of God the Judge. This is the provision that God himself has made for all who will reach out in faith, for God the Judge is also God the Saviour who loves us and gave his beloved Son for us.

What unfathomable depths there are in the divine plan of redemption, foreshadowed so clearly in this awesome twelfth chapter of Exodus: Christ, our Passover Lamb, is indeed sacrificed for us. Therefore, as often as we are able, it behoves every believer to keep the feast.

For further study ▶

FOR FURTHER STUDY

1. Sinless perfection was explicitly taught in the late 19th and early 20th centuries; John Wesley's only published book in his lifetime had the title, *A Plain Account of Christian Perfection*[8] and expounded the view that once the root of sin was eradicated, 'perfect love' (sinless perfection) could be a real experience. Trawl through the Scriptures to identify as many passages as you can find which explicitly state that, in this life, we remain children of the first Adam and only in the resurrection do we become completely children of the second Adam (1 Cor. 15:21–22). Start with Romans 7:15–25; Galatians 5:17–26; 1 John 1:8–10.

2. Examine the balance in Christ's preaching between retribution and saving grace.

3. In the Acts, compare and contrast the predominant offer of salvation in Christ in Peter's sermons with the warnings of retribution in Stephen's sermon (Acts 7).

4. What should the balance be today between Paul's clear gospel statement in Romans 1:16–17 and the declaration of judgement in the following verses 18–32?

TO THINK ABOUT AND DISCUSS

1. Think about the Parable of the Leaven (Matt. 13:33) to understand the effect of leaven [i.e., yeast]. Then read 1 Corinthians 5:1–8 and discuss why Paul uses this metaphor of leaven in such a shameful situation as that in the congregation in Corinth. What are the implications of this (a) in our personal lives and (b) in our congregation's life?

2. In Acts 10:9–16, Peter was given a vision which clearly meant that the Old Testament dietary regulations were entirely abolished (v. 16: the vision happened three times). Do you think using animals' blood in food would have been included in this vision? If so, why did the Council

of Jerusalem retain the regulation about food made with animals' blood (15:19–21, 28–29)?[9] Is there a 'let out' clause in verse 21 so that Black Pudding, for example, can be eaten by Christians?

3. In two of the earliest chapters in the Bible, Genesis 4:10; 9:4–6, we are given the religious significance of blood. Why do you think God declared blood to be so sacred (Leviticus 17:10–12, 14)? What could be the implications of this for the blood of Christ?

4. It is clear that the Christian doctrine of *substitutionary atonement*—that is, an innocent substitute's blood being shed to atone for the sins of someone else—was in the heart and mind of God when the Passover was commanded and enacted. Why do you think 'a lamb without blemish' made a suitable type or picture of Jesus as 'the Lamb of God who takes away the sin of the world' (John 1:29)?

16 The departure from Egypt

Exodus 12:29–50

The passage of Exodus, dealt with in this chapter, contains doctrinal teaching which may come as a mild surprise to some readers. Implicitly brought to our attention is the great theme of divine providence, followed closely by subliminal teaching on Christian generosity, which is then followed by an unexpected definition of the much over-worked and little understood doctrine of worship. Readers should always be prepared to find in God's treasure chest, not only things old, but also some things which may be quite new (Matthew 13:52).

The tenth plague, namely the death of the firstborn, marked the Israelites departure from Egypt. It was the climax of the termination of many decades (possibly covering more than three generations) of slavery, but it also marked the first stage of the momentous task for which Moses had been destined from before his birth: to lead Israel out of Egypt. God had wonderfully prepared him through his education and training as a prince of Egypt, although his spiritual preparation as a shepherd for forty years in the wilderness had been far more significant than his years in Pharaoh's daughter's palace. Having called him to his seemingly impossible assignment of procuring the exodus of the Lord's people from a land to which they did not belong, God had then sustained his servant over the past months of the consecutive ecological disasters. He had caused his servant's word to be highly honoured as plague after plague afflicted the land, with the precise accuracy predicted by Moses. Now came the culmination in Israel's departure from Egypt.

When I was in my teens, many of my peers regarded those who were following Christ as being consigned to a life of boring monotony. They wanted the so-called *thrills and spills*. They imagined that being a Christian would rob them of all the excitement of life. They could not have been more mistaken. When God calls anyone to take up the cross and follow his Son, he is going to endow each one with his own anointing, and they will discover that his demands will enable them to achieve complete fulfilment of all the abilities latent in their hearts and minds. In God's service, the character of the obedient Christian will be developed and used absolutely to the full by the Lord. I would even venture to opine that those serving Christ unreservedly will achieve more than they ever could as unbelievers, however well they might have been able to acquit and distinguish themselves in their lifetime.

We have seen how Moses' parents recognized at his birth that he was no ordinary child. Nor was that fanciful thinking. Their perception of him was inspired by the Spirit of God. Now, from this point in the Book of Exodus, we will see how this man chosen by God was going to be stretched to the limit of his immense natural abilities, probably achieving more during his life than any other mortal ever did in the world's history—other than, of course, the incarnate Son of God.

> When God works through his chosen instrument, the glory will always be seen as belonging to him alone.

However, simply to state that the Lord's servants find their potential more than fulfilled is to present only one component in the equation, and the lesser component at that. The key factor that makes sense of the equation is that, when God works through his chosen instrument, the glory will always be seen as belonging to him alone. So it is here, for we witness the awesome judgement of God on those who hated him being meted out alongside the merciful salvation that was being wrought for his chosen people who acknowledged him as their God.

The 'destroyer' (v. 23) was commissioned by God, and his passing over the Hebrews who were sheltered under the blood of unblemished lambs was also according to the divine command. Likewise, the gifts of silver, gold and lengths of linen (v. 35) were also from the hand of God according to his promise (Exodus 3:21–22).[1] As the apostle Paul would write centuries later, though in a different context, 'All this is from God'(2 Corinthians 5:18). Again, Paul eloquently brings together the human and the divine in these profound words: 'So let no one boast in men. For all things are yours, whether Paul or Apollos or Cephas or the world or life or death or the present or the future—all are yours, and you are Christ's, and Christ is God's' (1 Corinthians 3:21–23).

The blood of the Passover lamb

I have been asked many times why the Scriptures make so much of 'the blood'. I recall one very intelligent woman telling me she thought the 'obsession' (her word) in the Bible with blood was an unhelpful vestige of primitive religion and needed to be extirpated from the language and liturgies of a civilized church. When I was a student in St Andrews many decades ago, a distinguished theologian, preaching in St Salvator's Chapel, declared that the church today needed a hymnbook from which the word 'blood' had been completely removed. So why does the whole Bible use this word, always in the context of sacrifice?

The answer is not difficult to find. Far back in the earliest records of biblical history, when life began anew after the Great Flood, God had given explicit instructions to Noah in the covenant he made with him. The passage, in Genesis 9:1–10, is important and I will quote the relevant in full:

> And God blessed Noah and his sons and said to them,
> 'Be fruitful and multiply and fill the earth. 3 Every moving thing that lives shall be food for you. And as I gave you the green plants, I give you everything. 4 But you shall not eat flesh with its life, that is, its blood. 5 And for your lifeblood I will require a reckoning: from every beast I will require it and from man. From his fellow man I will require a reckoning for the life of man.'
>
> 8 Then God said to Noah and to his sons with him, 9 'Behold, I establish my covenant with you and your offspring after you, 10 and with every living creature that is with you, the birds, the livestock, and every beast of the earth with you, as many as came out of the ark; it is for every beast of the earth.'

Man (in its generic sense as 'humanity') is made in God's image, and the life of man is in his blood. That is clearly stated in verse 4 of the quotation above. Again, in verse 5, when a man's lifeblood is shed, God will require a reckoning for the life that has been taken. Implicit in these words is the sixth commandment, 'You shall not murder' (Exodus 20:13, ESV).[2] However, the main point we must notice is that the blood, whether of man or beast, stands for that creature's life, and all life belongs exclusively to God.

Pharaoh and his people had shed the lifeblood of countless slaves and their newborn sons, and the tenth plague was the divine reckoning of which the Word of God had spoken. The blood of the Passover lambs clearly meant that a substitute had yielded its life on behalf of each family. And thus, the foundational meaning was established for all the sacrifices in the Old Testament ordinances of worship. They were all prospective, looking forward to the final mighty sacrifice of 'the Lamb of God who takes away the sin of the world' (John 1:29). That his blood was shed meant that his life was poured out in death.

> The blood of the Passover lambs clearly meant that a substitute had yielded its life on behalf of each family.

Another question I have been asked on this subject is why Jehovah's Witnesses refuse to have blood transfusions, arguing that the New Testament enjoined followers of Jesus to abstain from blood (Acts

15:20). I do not want to dwell here on the subject of the discontinuities of the Old Testament ordinances of ceremonial law now that Christ has fulfilled those laws.[3] (I do not hold that the moral law defined in the Ten Commandments belongs to those ritualistic discontinuities.) There is a far simpler point to make regarding blood transfusions. When doctors give blood as a surgical procedure, a life has not been given, far less taken away: in blood transfusions life is being 'shared' not 'taken'. This same principle must apply to the implanting of body parts such as liver, heart, kidney, when someone has already died.

Calvin sums up the importance and significance of the Passover lamb's blood when he states that the whole people of God were 'preserved from destruction by the mark of blood, for the Paschal Lamb was a type of Christ, who by his death propitiated his Father, so that we should not perish'. He continues that we must understand that 'what was put before [his people] must be spiritually fulfilled ... It is from the testimony of Peter that our souls are sprinkled with the blood of Christ by the Spirit (1 Peter 1:2).'[4]

'What do you mean by this service?' (12:26)

The Hebrew word, 'abad, translated here as 'service', is first used in the Bible in Genesis 2:15, where it is correctly rendered as 'to work' (ESV, NIV): 'The LORD God took the man and put him in the garden of Eden to *work* it and keep it.' It could be more meaningfully translated here as, 'to *serve*', for, 'Even in his relationship with the soil, mankind must maintain his humility'.[5] The same word is used again in Genesis 24 when Abraham's servant met Rebekah at the well and realized that Abraham's God, to whom he had prayed (v. 42), had heard and answered his prayer: 'Then I bowed my head and *worshipped* the LORD and blessed the LORD, the God of my master Abraham, who had led me by the right way to take the daughter of my master's kinsman for his son' (v. 48). The implication is that Abraham's trusted servant, having discovered that the Lord had heard and answered his prayer, now pledges his allegiance to, and faith in, his master's God; from now on he would *serve* him alone.

This same verb occurs again in Exodus 20 at the second commandment: 'You shall not make for yourself a carved image ... You shall not bow down to them or *serve* them ...' (vv. 4, 5, ESV; NIV translates this same verb as *worship*). In my view, it is unfortunate that some modern translations opt for the same translation of the Hebrew, '*abad*, as the NIV, for it seems to me that this has weakened the meaning of '*abad* as pledging loyalty, trust, obedience and lifelong service, and allowed many sincere believers to slide into the false assumption that 'worship' means 'singing'. Worship is by no means simply singing, though self-evidently praise of God may be expressing genuine submission to him. However, often singing may be no more than an emotional response to a good tune being dominated by a noisy band.

> Often singing may be no more than an emotional response to a good tune being dominated by a noisy band.

The Greek equivalent of the Hebrew verb, 'abad, is *latreuo*. One quotation from the New Testament will make the point very clearly. In the third temptation that the devil brought to the Lord, he offered him 'all the kingdoms of the world and their glory' (Matthew 4:7). He said, 'All these I will give you, if you will fall down and *worship* me' (v. 9). Satan was definitely not asking Christ to sing him a song! Rather he was asking that Jesus should surrender his will to the devil; in other words, that the Son of God should sin the 'great transgression' (Psalm 19:13), of deserting his heavenly Father, changing sides and becoming Satan's lifelong servant.

Something of the profound commitment invariably implied in this word *serve* regarding our relationship with God is caught in the fourth verse of Isaac Watts' incomparable hymn, 'When I survey the wondrous cross.' The final two lines go like this: 'Love so amazing, so divine, demands my life, my soul, my all.'

Thus it is, that the apostle Paul constantly asserts that he *serves* God.[6]

Moses' words in Exodus 12:26, 'And when your children say to you, "What do you mean by this service?"', he unwittingly anticipates the widespread use of the term 'service' to denote a formal gathering together of the Lord's people to praise him, approach him in prayers of adoration and intercession, and to meditate on his Word and listen to its exposition. All believers should take to heart the true meaning of 'service', used to denote their gatherings together on the Lord's Day. We are to recognize that we assembly together to renew our vows and pledge anew our allegiance to the God who has redeemed us through the blood of the Paschal Lamb, for that is precisely the context of verse 26.

'Six hundred thousand men on foot' (v. 37)

A little later in the book of Exodus, we are told that the men left Egypt marching 'equipped for battle' (Exodus 13:18), for the phrase, 'on foot', is commonly used of infantry. Scholars have calculated that 'six hundred thousand men' would have constituted a column of soldiers some twenty-two miles long, marching fifteen abreast with a yard between each line. When we add on the rest of the slaves, such as the elderly, the women and children, it would mean there was a company of some two million people, without even including the unknown number of the 'mixed multitude' (v. 38). The Hebrew word used in this term, 'mixed multitude', is literally 'a swarm' and is employed in 8:21 to describe the plague of flies. This 'mixed multitude' was possibly made up of other non-Hebrew slaves as well as many Egyptians, who now regarded the God of the Hebrew slaves with fear and awe.

It has been questioned as to whether the area that had been occupied by the Israelites could have supported such a vast population. The land of Goshen covered little more than 60 square miles, and other scholars have argued that its agricultural produce could only have sustained about 20,000 souls. Also, no Egyptian chronicles have ever been discovered recording such a colossal migration from the land around this time.

Some years ago, I discussed the problem of this vast number with the late Joyce Baldwin, a well-known Old Testament scholar,[7] and she helpfully pointed out that there was strong evidence that in the earliest biblical documents, the word *'elep*, translated in English versions as 'a thousand', usually meant 'a company' or 'a clan'. She pointed out that in the later, post-exilic, biblical documents, the meaning of *'elep* had developed to be much nearer to our understanding of a 'thousand'. Alan Cole, in his commentary on Exodus, reminds us that the company that left Egypt was both 'great enough to terrify the Moabites (Numbers 22:3), yet small enough to be based on the oases around Kadesh-barnea (Deuteronomy 1:46).'[8]

I do not think we should regard these numbers as merely fictitious or simply invented to present a view of the population of the children of Israel as even greater than it was at that time. While we must always accept and honour Scripture as the inspired Word of God, we must also face up to the kind of problems which occasionally occur such as 'the six hundred thousand men on foot'. That is why I myself am inclined to respect Joyce Baldwin's vastly superior knowledge of the Hebrew language, compared to my own. In addition, there is no theological point that depends on our understanding of the Hebrew word, *'elep*. Whatever its early meaning may have been at that point in the history of the Lord's people, it is clear that we are intended to envisage a huge migration of men, women and children, followed by the 'swarm' of others. We can confidently say with the Psalmist, 'This is the LORD's doing; it is marvellous in our eyes' (Psalm 118:23).

They plundered the Egyptians.

A vivid picture is painted in verses 33–36. By the time the tenth plague struck the land, we may be quite sure that most Egyptians wanted the children of Israel to leave. We have already seen that many of them 'feared the word of the Lord among the servants of Pharaoh'

(Exodus 9:20), and at that stage there were still three plagues to come. Little wonder then that 'the Egyptians were urgent with the people to send them out of the land in haste' (v. 33).

We are now told that the people had been explicitly instructed by Moses to ask for silver, gold and linen. Why should this have been so? At the very least, it would have been fair reparation for the decades of unpaid labour as the slaves toiled under a pitiless sun, only to be rewarded with lashes across their backs if they did not work fast enough.

We learn a significant truth from the sacred record when it states that 'the Lord had given the people favour in the sight of the Egyptians, so that they let them have what they asked' (v. 36). I have already suggested that this 'plunder' was most probably the source of the gold and silver that would be required when the Tent of Meeting and its furnishings came to be fashioned.[9] God knew that such materials and provisions could be provided ahead of the time when they would be needed. But the underlying truth is that all generosity towards the Lord's people and in aid of the work of his Kingdom is dependent on his Spirit causing men and women to open their hearts and their wallets to give freely in the way the Egyptians gave.

Recently a minister confided in me that a young man, who had not yet made any profession of faith, had approached him to say that he had received a legacy from a relative and wanted to give a fairly substantial amount of it to God's work. He had lately started to attend a place worship, but his desire to give was a clear indication that the Lord had begun to work in his life. Sure enough, after a few months, he approached the minister and asked for baptism as he now wanted to make a public profession of his new-born faith.

In 2 Corinthians 9 the apostle writes eloquently of the grace of generosity, saying that God loves the cheerful giver. Those who sow sparingly will reap sparingly, whereas those who sow bountifully will also reap bountifully. The Lord's work in his people's hearts will never cause them to give reluctantly; rather, when he touches our wills we will give generously, at times even recklessly. Let no one give hoping that they will be rewarded in return; the Spirit of God never inspires mercenary bargaining with God. On the other hand, the Lord promises that grace will abound for the cheerful giver.

> Let no one give hoping that they will be rewarded in return; the Spirit of God never inspires mercenary bargaining with God.

Not often have I heard good explanations of the enigmatic parable Jesus told in Luke 16 of the dishonest manager. You may remember that he 'cooked the books', as we say, in order to provide for his own future when his employer made him redundant. We are surprised when Christ then states that the sons of this world are more shrewd in dealing with their own generation than the sons of light. We wonder how ever a true follower of Christ could learn from such blatant misuse of funds that had been entrusted to the villain.

The punch line of the parable, however, is in verses 9–13. There Jesus tells us that we have to use 'unrighteous wealth' to make friends for the Kingdom, so that when our 'unrighteous wealth' fails, as it assuredly will, we will not enter our heavenly home empty-handed. What did the Lord mean by 'unrighteous wealth'? Wealth is morally neutral. The problem is not with wealth itself, but with the relationship we form with it. In this verse the word 'righteous' (including its opposite 'unrighteous') refers to a relationship. Jesus calls wealth unrighteous because those who form a wrong relationship with their wealth will find themselves deceived. They will look to their wealth for happiness, security and protection. But wealth cannot permanently deliver any of these, even though it seems to promise to do so.

For Christians, forming a wrong relationship with such wealth as God has entrusted to them means that their confidence is diverted from their Lord and Master, and becomes focused instead on what he has given them. This amounts to worshipping the gifts rather than the Giver; they are not using his bounty towards them to further the work of his Kingdom. Whereas those who use what is entrusted to them to further Christ's work are laying up treasure in heaven. This is the whole application of the parable. The dishonest manager took what had been entrusted to him to steward and used it to provide for his own future. That is precisely where so many of the 'sons of light' were failing, according to Jesus. They were not providing for those who would be blessed and reached by their faithful use of God's bounty to them, in order to bring them as 'sheaves' at the final harvest.[10]

The full explanation of the parable is given in Luke 16:10-13. In effect, the Lord is teaching us that those who are faithful in very little (in stewarding material blessings), will also be faithful in much (that is, in spiritual growth), whereas those who are dishonest in a very little (in material things), will also be dishonest in much (that is, in spiritual things). We may paraphrase the next stage of the Lord's teaching in verse 12 as, 'There can be no real spiritual growth, far less maturity, for those whose relationship with their wealth is unrighteous. For, we cannot serve God and money (v. 13).

My reference to Luke 16 is not a diversion from Exodus 12:33-36. It becomes plain as the history unravels that the children of Israel became unfaithful and idolatrous over their relationship with the wealth which the Egyptians had lavished upon them as they had departed from Egypt. Moses had disappeared into the mists of Mount Sinai, and he was now assumed to be 'missing', possibly dead. We read how, in his absence, they took their gold ear rings, and Aaron (of all people!) fashioned the golden calf. Then the people declared, 'These are your gods, O Israel, who brought you up out of the land of Egypt.' They were imitating the practices of surrounding pagan tribes (Exodus 32:1–4).

Today, although we would not expect such blatant idolatry from professing believers, nevertheless, how often those who ought to know better choose to go with the general flow of society. Thus, when God seems for a time to hide his face (just as in the incident of the golden calf, Moses appeared to have disappeared in the mists of Mount Sinai), too easily we can stray from steadfast trust in the Lord's eternal faithfulness. Too few of us continue to say with Job, 'Though he slay me, I will hope in him' (Job 13:15, compare with Job 1:21). Consequently, in our troubles our hope for the best outcome becomes subtly focused on our material

> When God seems for a time to hide his face, too easily we can stray from steadfast trust in the Lord's eternal faithfulness.

resources, as we turn from the Giver to his gifts. The very jewellery that had been given through the Egyptian's divinely inspired generosity, in order to provide for the fashioning of the symbols of the divine redemption in the Holy Place and Holy of Holies, were abused in rash infidelity.

May it be our daily prayer that we will never receive the grace of God in vain, but will be kept daily in his redeeming love, vouchsafed to us through Christ our Passover Lamb, who has been sacrificed for us, and now reigns as Lord of all, having poured out his Spirit upon us and is seated at the Father's right hand. So may all glory be given to the Father, the Son and the Holy Spirit both now and for ever.

For further study ▶

FOR FURTHER STUDY

1. The full text of the Westminster Confession of Faith (WCF) is easily accessible on the internet under https://www.ligonier.org/. Chapter 5 is 'Concerning Providence'; paragraph 3 states: 'God uses ordinary means to work out his providence day by day. But, as he pleases, he may work without, beyond or contrary to these means.' Try to follow up from Scripture his 'work without, beyond or contrary to these [ordinary] means.' Also, research some 'ordinary means' he uses providentially.

2. Chapter 5 of WCF under paragraph 5 states: 'In the fulness of his wisdom, righteousness and grace, God often allows his own children to be tempted in various ways and for a time to pursue the corruption of their own hearts. God does this to chastise them … so that they may be humbled.' Look up the full statement. Can you agree with and support paragraph 5 by reviewing in Scripture the lives of a few of those whom God used greatly to fulfil his redemptive purposes?

3. In his commentary on *The Pentateuch*, Calvin subsumes all the regulations of ceremonial worship together with rules of conduct into ten sections which correspond with the ten commandments. What explanation might you give as to why he places the Passover under the first commandment.

4. Search the Scriptures to find out how Paul came to refer to himself as Christ's *doulos* (lit. slave): e.g., Gal. 1:10; Phil.1:1; Titus 1:1. To what extent do you think he was identifying with Jesus as in Phil. 2:7? What might be the relationship of the title, *doulos,* to 'worship', i.e., 'abad?

TO THINK ABOUT AND DISCUSS

1. Think about your own Christian life from its conscious beginning up to the here and now. Are you able, looking back, to see God's providence in your life, and if so, in what ways has he secretly worked to guide and keep you?

2. Work out a personal audit of how you spent your income: how much on absolute necessities and how much on yourself—day outings, holidays, meals out, membership of clubs or gyms or bowling clubs or whatever. Then compare your expenditure with what you give to the Lord's work, both through your local church, and also through agencies such as Tear Fund, OM, Bible Society and so on. How much is your budget guided and controlled by the Holy Spirit?

3. Can you find any evidence in the Bible that 'worship' consists purely of singing? Why do you think that the word, 'worship', has a metaphorical 'Siamese twin' in the phrase, 'bow down'? (Genesis 24:26; Exodus 20:5; Psalm 95:6; Matthew 28:9; by implication, Matthew 4:9.)[11]

4. Make a list of Christian hymns which explicitly speak of total surrender and submission of our wills and hearts to God, e.g., 'All to Jesus I surrender'; 'Take my life and let it be'; 'Jesus, Master, whose I am'. Do you think that very few of these 'surrender' hymns are used in Church Services today? If so, why might that be? Could it be because the word, 'worship', has been misunderstood and undervalued?

17 The feast of unleavened bread

Exodus 13:1–16

Our heavenly Father knows far better than we do how easy it is for congregations, and the families which constitute them, to grow lukewarm and, by losing their first love, ceasing to have that vital, attractive communal life that will draw others towards the Saviour. Therefore, the Lord prepared means to enable his people to stay close to him.

Some years ago, when Lorna and I were on holiday, we attended a well-known parish church in Edinburgh. The building stood in the heart of a parish of some 13,000 people—the only other place of worship being a small evangelical church which met in what was little better than a wooden hut. On paper, the congregation of this church we attended numbered nearly 1700 communicants. But the attendance that Sunday morning (and the summer holiday season had not yet begun), could not have been more than a hundred. There were no children or young people present, and the average age must have been well into the sixties, possibly higher. Certainly, we were by far the youngest couple there, and at that time we were in our late fifties.

Later on in our holiday, we spent a few days in our hometown of Arbroath. Fifty years ago, when we were children, there were eleven parish churches there, each self-supporting and with its own minister. Though the town has grown considerably in size over the past several decades, there are now only two churches, each being linked to very small congregations well outside the town in the Angus countryside.

Today, we are well into the third decade of the 21st century and many are asking, 'Where have the churches gone wrong?' We are bound to ponder that question and wonder how it is that erstwhile flourishing congregations lose their vitality and strength, and begin to slide downward into weakness, ineffectiveness and ultimately oblivion. I am going to suggest that we have at least part of the answer to this question in Exodus 13 verses 1–16.

The key phrase on which the problem turns is in verse 5: 'a land flowing with milk and honey'. The point would appear to be that, historically down the generations, the great enemy of the Church is neither persecution, nor opposition, nor lack of funds, but prosperity! For when affluence abounds and we have plenty of this world's goods and life becomes deceptively easy, then our hearts can turn away from God. It is a 'catch-22' dilemma, for when Christians live according to their faith, are conscientious, hardworking, reliable and honest, they generally prosper. And it is the very prosperity which comes as a reward for the Christian ethic of life and work that can so easily bring our churches problems.

> It is the very prosperity which comes as a reward for the Christian ethic of life and work that can so easily bring our churches problems.

The snare, mysteriously built into the Christian faith, is that God gave his people 'a land flowing with milk and honey'. Along with the prosperity, which can be the reward of faithful Christian living, a spiritual lethargy can gradually overtake us, and consequently the things of God can be neglected. For if the father and mother grow cool in their faith, the chances are that their children will have only a nominal faith, and then the grandchildren will have little or no interest in the Lord at all. The passing of three successive generations is all that it takes.

The teaching in Exodus 13 contains three safeguards against this hazard that has faced every generation of God's people. As we study the book of Exodus, we have seen that the deliverance from slavery in Egypt was taking place. And the Lord knew perfectly well that in the decades and generations ahead grave dangers would loom large. And so, he gave three instructions whereby the faith of his people could be guarded and preserved. They were firstly, the Feast of Unleavened Bread; secondly, the instruction of children; and thirdly, the redemption of the firstborn.

In passing, we should notice that the month of 'Abib' (it approximates to our March/April) was to be the first calendar month of the Jewish year. This had already been stated in chapter 12, verse 2. It was not to be the first month of their annual calendar for seasonal reasons in that 'Abib' ushered in the spring, but because it was in this month God had delivered them from slavery. It appears that the announcement (along with the ordinance of the consecration of the firstborn in 13:1–2, not fully explained until vv. 11–16) was made as the people were about to begin their journey towards the eastern borders of Egypt: 'Remember this day in which you came out from Egypt...' (v. 3).

There may have been two reasons why Moses sent this message around the entire company of slaves— presumably through the elders as in 3:16—as they were on the point of setting out. Firstly, so that they would journey in the right frame of mind: their deliverance had been by the 'strong hand' of God, and so they must travel in reverent gratitude towards him. Secondly, after years of suffering under the ruthless cruelty of Pharaoh's taskmasters, they should now set their hopes on a secure future ahead of them in the land of their forefathers, for the ordinances being given to them were to encourage them to believe that God would go with them and fulfil his promise.

We come then to the first safeguard that God gave his people.

The feast of unleavened bread

It was very simple. For seven days in succession before all future annual celebrations of the Passover, they were to have a holiday—'no work shall be done on those days' (Exodus 12:16)—and they were to eat no bread made with yeast. All yeast was to be cleared out of their houses. And these days of holiday prior to the Passover were to be called 'The Feast of Unleavened Bread' (Exodus 12:17). What did this mean? Several points may help to elucidate it.

Firstly, it meant that they had been delivered from slavery. The bread without yeast was to be called 'the bread of affliction' (Deuteronomy 16:3). It was reminding them, negatively, of the bad old days, when they were slaves; but positively, of their deliverance by God.

It also meant that for seven whole days they had to

remember their redemption—not just the one night when they would celebrate the Passover, but for a whole week prior to its observance. The change of diet was something no one could ignore. The entire family pattern of eating in every home changed as all yeast was banned for the week, and the bread used at every meal was significantly different.

Furthermore, it was a festival. That meant it was a time of joy and family reunions, a time of coming together and relaxing. All ordinary work stopped, and only essential work of food preparation was done (Exodus 12:16). It was a week everyone was going to enjoy. Our children would have said, 'Goody, goody, no school this week!' They would have asked, 'Is Granny coming on Friday, and Uncle Tom and Auntie Elizabeth as well? Great!' (Because Uncle Tom was a favourite with the children, and Aunt Elizabeth always brought delicious baking with her.) Yes, it was a celebration to be enjoyed, but remember it culminated in the Feast of the Passover Lamb.

Now for ourselves today, living on the nearside of the cross, we can sum up the great principles of the Old Testament Feast of Unleavened Bread in three words: family, assurance, and celebration. And a celebration of this nature was the first safeguard against a failing and faltering church.

At the centre of a strong congregation will be a

strong family; a family that sticks together and makes time to be together; a family that lives in the firm conviction of God's love in the Lord Jesus; and a family able to celebrate and rejoice and have the happiest of times together. That is the kind of family this Feast of Unleavened Bread was creating.

We are thinking about *parents* with real faith and about *homes* in which spending time with the children is a priority. We are also thinking about *marriages* that are stable and loving and about *families* that worship together. For such families, having fun, laughter, relaxation and friendship together is the most natural thing in all the world, and all this in a context of a living faith in God as Father, Saviour, Friend.

To some readers this might appear to be the most unlikely defence of the life of the Church of God. But be assured that it is fundamental to the life of a strong and healthy congregation. You may wonder why this should be so. The answer is that the rot sets in when parents are woolly about their faith, are not quite sure whether God is really God, or are uncertain as to whether Christ is really the living Saviour. Where there is that doubt and hesitation in parents when it comes to setting the family's course through the hazardous seas of today's society, with its treacherous moral currents and dark waters concealing hidden rocks, there is no clear and safe passage being chartered. Consequently, very soon, the boat either begins to take in water, or strikes jagged reefs.

We all know the problems: undesirable places the children's friends frequent; activities their friends are allowed to engage in; the money their friends have to spend. What pressures there are today on families going through the teenage years! But God's provision here is that the family that *prays* together and *plays* together also *stays* together. This is the family that will withstand the storm and this is the family that is the kernel of the Church of God.

God's provision here is that the family that *prays* together and *plays* together also *stays* together.

Those who are parents ought to be working to create for their children what Edith Schaeffer has called *a museum of memories*.[1] I know we have certain celebrations built into our culture, such as Christmas, Easter, summer holidays and birthdays. But if you are a parent (or grandparent), why not work at creating your own family culture of celebrations, such as special things you do at certain times, or favourite places you go to stay at other times, or occasions when you deliberately take the family to entirely new places. In that way, parents can build up for the family a museum of memories which they will look back on with pleasure and affection.

As I study the Old Testament, I come across something

that increasingly surprises me. I find that the people of God were those who knew how to celebrate. True, their festivals were religious festivals. But they were holidays, times of fun and laughter and family reunions. The Jews' celebrations were creating memories of the pleasure and security of family love.

Is there not a need for Christian parents consciously to work at this—for mothers and fathers deliberately to plan family events designed to build a museum of memories? It must begin from the children's earliest days—outings, little treats that have something of the ritual about them so that the children can look forward to them. Yet this is impossible, unless plenty of time is invested in the family.

That was something of what the Feast of Unleavened Bread achieved: a family time of relaxation, and all in the context of praise and worship. There is, however, a further aspect of the preservation of faith among the Lord's people, for the instruction of children is a second safeguard of the Church of God.

The instruction of children

This has already been laid down in chapter 12 (v. 26) where the Passover itself is more fully described. However, we have it again here in chapter 13 verse 8: 'You shall tell your son on that day, "It is because of what the Lord did for me when I came out of Egypt".' It is the explicit injunction that parents must teach their children of their faith in their God. Let me outline for you something about family life in the early days of the people of God.

There were no formal schools for children in Old Testament days. Both sons and daughters stayed at home with their mother during their early years, when she taught them all she knew; that was an important stage of learning. However, at the age of eight years, the boys went to work with their fathers, and from their fathers each son learned, not only his trade, but also his nation's history and with it his father's faith.

A father may have worked with leather; or maybe he was a carpenter and worked with timber; or he might have been a tailor and worked with cloth. Many men were farmers who worked the land. But whatever the trade might have been, the boy joined his father who taught him how to earn his living. And alongside that, he taught him about God and also the story of God's people. The father's teaching was supplemented by the boy attending the village council meetings and, on the Sabbath, accompanying his father to public worship, where they would hear the priest reading from and expounding the Scriptures.

Therefore, in both chapters, Exodus 12 and 13, we have it laid down that each father must teach his son these things and, by the same token, each mother must teach her daughter. What is the relevance of this for us today?

The first point I have to make may surprise you. It is the question of whether Sunday Schools, as they are today, were ever the intention of those who first started that excellent movement. For, the first Sunday Schools were never intended for the children of believing parents; they were for street children— for boys and girls whose parents never went near a church. They were formed as part of the evangelical churches' response to the urgent needs of their day. But instead, they have become somewhere for children from Christian homes to go to, usually as an alternative to attending the whole church service.[2] We have flipped over Sunday Schools, turned them upside down, as it were, and allowed them to develop into something for which they were never intended.

> The first Sunday Schools were never intended for the children of believing parents.

The inadvertent and unfortunate result of this is that many parents think that the Christian training of their children is being done for them in their congregation's Sunday School. And that, of course, is a tragic fallacy. Effective Christian nurture can never be done in that way.

Consider this simple fact. The teaching and learning

time in any one year offered by a Sunday School is an absolute maximum of forty hours per annum, though often significantly less. Whereas, deducting time for sleeping and day school, a child will spend thousands of hours in a year with one or other parent or both. In other words, the mother and father have over one hundred times more opportunity for influence upon their children than a Sunday School teacher can ever have!

Whether parents realize this or not, and whether they like it or not, they are teaching their children all about their own Christian faith every hour they spend with them. They may be teaching them to criticize the minister or the singing in church. They may be teaching them to poke fun at some of the people who attend church, or to belittle some of the deacons or elders. They may even be teaching them to have a long lie in bed on a Sunday morning, and only bother with church occasionally, just to keep up appearances. It is remarkable how many disturbing lessons parents may be teaching their children.

If we could somehow gather together all the thoroughly negative lessons some parents have consistently been teaching their children about the faith and weigh them against the teaching faithfully given in Sunday School for those few (perhaps less than) forty hours in any year, we would be driven to our knees to cry out to God for a miracle. Indeed, it would need something bordering on the miraculous, because God would have to overturn the colossal weight of anti-Christian lessons by the slenderest weight of the little that is done on a Sunday morning. The odds would be about the same as a mouse taking on a horse. For remember, our Sunday School teachers have a mere forty hours against the parental thousands of hours!

Do you see what this means? It means that, however excellent a Sunday School may be, however well its work is done, however committed are its staff, nothing can ever be an adequate substitute for the Christian teaching at home of the children by parents. The Bible does not have it wrong charging *fathers* with the teaching of their sons, and *mothers* with the teaching of their daughters. That is the biblical and wise method of Christian nurture.

This is part of the reason as to why congregations become frail and sick, when parents make the massive mistake of thinking they can leave the godly nurture of their children entirely to the church. Yes, of course the church has a vital role. Of course it does. But the church's role was never intended to, nor ever can, replace the role of parents.

Over my five decades and more of Christian ministry, I have watched this carefully. I have observed homes and families where parents apparently give no clear Christian guidance, and I have seen whole congregations going down and disintegrating like a very slow-motion film of Hiroshima being struck by the atomic bomb. In vain, I have repeatedly petitioned the leaders of the denomination to which I belong, to prepare materials to guide parents in training their children in the Christian faith. I know that some parents are already attempting to fulfil this godly responsibility. But for every family who do, there must be more than fifty who do little or nothing—even worse, who teach, without realizing it, lessons that are entirely negative and can only have the effect of turning their children away from God.

Parental training of children in the faith was the second safeguard for the life of the Church of God laid down in the Bible passage we are studying. This brings us to the third safeguard God gave his people.

The redemption of the firstborn

There was a third safeguard that God gave as an antidote against the eroding influences of faith in the believers' pilgrimage through the wilderness of this world. For, all around every generation of his people's lives, there are ungodly pressures seeking to undermine the Lord's work of grace and goodness among his people. This third bulwark was through the law regarding the redemption of the firstborn son in every Hebrew family.

Each firstborn boy had to be redeemed (v. 2). That means, a price had to be paid as the cost of the child's life. The law extended to animals as well. Firstborn animals were to be sacrificed or else redeemed—that is, bought back from death with a price. A donkey, being an unclean animal, could not be sacrificed but only redeemed (v. 13). I understand that today, in orthodox Jewish families, a ransom is still paid to God for the life of every firstborn son.

It is easy to see why this had to be. It was to remind the people of their redemption from Egypt and the tenth plague, when their firstborn sons were redeemed by the blood of the Passover Lamb. And so, in dramatic, vivid terms, that deliverance was to be re-enacted in their daily lives. Every firstborn son must be redeemed and the ransom paid to God.[3] Every firstborn lamb or goat or calf must be redeemed, or else given to God as a sacrifice. In a mainly agricultural society, hardly a month would go past without each family and village being reminded of that night of their deliverance from slavery.

There are no prizes for guessing how this applies to Christians today. The direct successor to this strange and unexpected law is the memorial in bread and wine that speaks to every believer of the price that was paid for our redemption from slavery to sin. It was the Lord himself who asserted that those who commit sin are slaves to sin, and that only he, God's Son, could set us free (John 8:34–36).

How often ought believers to take the opportunity

to come to the Lord's Table? The traditional practice of the Presbyterian Church in Scotland has sadly been to celebrate communion only twice or four times each year. We need more frequent, informal communion services so that we can look back more often and be reminded afresh of the cost of grace. However, we do not only look back to that awesome event at Calvary during communion for, as we partake of the bread and wine at communion, also by grace we receive Christ spiritually and feed from him as we look forward to the final marriage supper in heaven (Revelation 19:6–9):

'As often as you eat this bread and drink the cup, you proclaim the Lord's death until he comes' (1 Corinthians 11:26).

> Communion is God's divinely appointed ordinance, and it is disobedience for us to neglect it.

While it is true that we do not need to partake of bread and wine in a communion service to remember the cost to God of his love in giving us his Son as the Saviour who cleanses and forgives us sinners. Nevertheless, communion is his divinely appointed ordinance, and it is disobedience for us to neglect it. For whenever God's people meet together at the Table, we do so in the Saviour's name and he, who still bears the marks of the cross on his resurrection body (John 20:27; Revelation 5:6), is there among us.

Perhaps some who are reading this chapter know that their faith often grows cold. They honestly long to have a warm, burning faith and know Christ's nearer presence every day. But that experience does not seem to come naturally. Let me assure you that the way to feed the flame of living faith is to come often to Calvary and there to bow before the Redeemer; we all need to be reminded that it was our sin that drove the nails into his hands and feet, it was our pride and selfishness that forced the thorny crown on to his brow. So, we must often remember the Lord and nourish our souls on his Word.

Three ways to keep a church strong. Three safeguards God has given to his people:

- Family life that is strong in faith and celebrates with the joy and laughter of innocent fun.
- Parents who teach their children the Lord's ways and truths.
- And a Church where there are constant reminders of the redeeming work of the Lord Jesus.

Here is a simple prayer. 'Gracious Father, there is so much in your Word that we can easily overlook and fail to appreciate. Open our eyes to see, unstop our ears to hear, enable our hearts to understand, and bend our proud wills to obey you; all for your glory. Amen.'

FOR FURTHER STUDY

1. What further examples are there in Scripture of family celebrations with joy, perhaps even with the exhortation to rejoice? E.g., Numbers 10:10; Psalm 42:4; Nahum 1:15.

2. What provision could congregations make both to encourage and to enable parents to instruct their children in the Christian faith through the various stages of childhood? What is your congregation's history of facilitating family worship?

3. What is the relationship between knowing God as *Father* (Rom. 8:15; Gal. 4:6), Jesus as *Brother* (Heb. 2:11–12, 17), and the Church as *Mother* (Gal. 4:26)? If we take each one of these three relationships as a metaphorical 'leg', how well can someone balance on one 'leg', or someone else on two 'legs', though God's purpose is that we should all stand firm on all three 'legs'?

4. How can pastoral ministry empower believers to appropriate for themselves a firm stance?

TO THINK ABOUT AND DISCUSS

1. Have you any experience of a congregation where provision was made, perhaps by a specially prepared leaflet for each Sunday's sermon, to enable children to enjoy listening for the main points of their pastor's sermon and then write them down or illustrate them in some simple way? What benefits might there be in such a scheme, and would it be preferable to a creche/playgroup with games, videos or other means of occupying children?

2. What suggestions could you offer that might help parents to create a 'museum of memories'?

3. Do you think it is possible for some worshippers to have saving faith, but not yet to have assurance of faith?

4. Ought participation in communion to be only a 'confirming' ordinance for those who already have assurance of faith, or could it also be a 'converting' ordinance, either for those who as yet do not have assurance, or for others who may still be seeking the Lord?

18 The desert road

Exodus 13:17–20

Here is an interesting quotation: 'God can lead us when we are not even aware of being led.'[1] However, the wonderful thing about the *Desert Road* for the Lord's people in the trackless wilderness was that his presence was known and seen. Clear guidance, such as the pillars of cloud and fire, is an amazing blessing, though as we read on, we find it was too often taken for granted. Yet not always is there the blessing of such firm assurance. Nonetheless, looking back, believers can invariably say with Abraham's servant, 'As for me, being on the way, the LORD led me...' (Genesis 24:27, NKJV).

I magine a few friends going on a really long hike. Five young lads are planning the route and have the map spread out on the table. One puts a finger on the map and says, 'This is where we'll start from.' They find the place they want to get to, a location about ten miles away; then they look for a suitable route. There are two possibilities. The easiest route is fairly direct. A second route leads over a mountain range and would be much longer.

As they discuss which route to take, one of the lads says: 'Let's take tents and let's go this way,' and he traces a path in the Cheviots which goes to the south, through a deep gorge and then up and over several mountains; the path leads far up into barren areas, following a slow curve round to the east, and then a long, slow haul back north.

'You can't be serious,' the others say. 'That would use up all our holiday. We only want to go from here to there—12 miles; you're suggesting we do 120 miles. You must be crazy; look at the provisions we'd have to carry. The idea was a one-day hike, not a two-week trek!' But he answers thoughtfully, 'I think we should take my route. It would do us all the world of good.' The rest of the group shake their heads in disagreement.

Why God chose the long route

'God led the people around by the way of the wilderness'—the desert road (v. 18). If you look at a Bible atlas, you will see that there were several possible routes from Egypt to Canaan. It is not possible to trace it accurately today because, over the past 2000 years, the coastline has considerably altered. But, studying a map of the Near East, you will still be able to see the obvious two routes: one much shorter and the other far longer.

The shorter route from Egypt to Canaan: due east, bearing slightly north. With flocks and herds and children, it would be about four weeks' hiking. However, trace the route they actually took, and you will see it was like the crazy route that young fellow suggested—their entire two weeks' holiday spent trekking instead of one day of hiking.

God led his people by a far longer route that took a year, instead of one that would have taken a month.

So, God led his people by a far longer route that took a year, instead of one that would have taken a month. Why?

The text tells us: 'Lest the people change their minds when they see war and return to Egypt' (v. 17), and archaeology confirms it. The Egyptian state was always prepared for an attack across its eastern border. So, at each crossing point they maintained armed outposts; border guards were dug in with strong fortifications. They kept careful records of every single traveller entering or leaving Egypt, and some of these records survive to this very day.

Therefore, instead of taking the obvious, direct route home to Canaan, Moses led them due south, and told them why: it was to avoid armed conflict and the need to break through the powerful border defences. This way, there would be no border guards and therefore, no trouble. A much longer way round, but a quieter way. He knew it; it was the way by which he himself had returned to Egypt.

Moses' explanation appears to have satisfied the people. They went along with him, marching in ranks. They were not a rabble but an orderly and disciplined company. 'And the people of Israel went up out of the land of Egypt equipped for battle' (lit. 'marching in ranks', v. 18). For, God's people ought always to be orderly, controlled and disciplined—never an undisciplined rabble.[2]

Perhaps you are wondering, 'Now why should God take these people deep into the wilderness, by a route that was going to take a year, when they could have been home and dry in Canaan within a month? Surely the God who would soon take them over the Red Sea on dry land could easily have got them past the Egyptian border guards. God could have laid on a sandstorm—some diversionary tactic—to distract the guards. How odd of God to lead them by such a roundabout route.'

That is an excellent question. It is good because there were other reasons. The answer emerges as we read on in Exodus. We find that God had many lessons to teach these people. He needed them in the wilderness to make with them his Covenant and, with it, his Law and the Ten

Commandments. Also, he planned to form them into a nation and commonwealth. But most of all, he wanted to prove them, to humble them, and to test them (as we read in Deuteronomy chapter 8).

Roundabout routes God still chooses today

We are not thinking now of climbing in the Cheviots or the Grampians. We are thinking of our lives and of that journey all believers are on to 'the city that has foundations, whose designer and builder is God' (Hebrews 11:10), because this is something that God at times does in the lives of us all. He sometimes chooses to lead us by the most unexpected and roundabout route.

It may be that, for many years, we have followed an obvious and straight path. I will explain what I mean. You finished school and then went ahead and did your training to be a tradesman, a civil servant, a teacher or a secretary—or whatever. Then, perhaps after a wait, the right position came up. After this, you started your own first home. All went much as you had hoped and expected.

Perhaps there was the usual struggle to get established. Looking back, you realize that did not do you any harm. You are none the worse today for those early years when the going was hard and you were strapped for cash. But your journey was mainly straightforward.

The route went from A to B, and then to C and on to D, much as you had anticipated.

Yet, some readers may see it differently. As you look back and recall certain past events in your life, you are puzzled. Because the journey of life for you seemed at certain points to have been quite illogical. It was not by your choice. You had no other option than to take a route you would never have chosen. You did not want to go that way. But somehow there was no alternative, and it turned out to be a desert road.

Perhaps illness in the family brought not only worry and heartache, but it obliged you to alter completely your plans. Or you were made redundant, lost your job and were left wondering where to turn. Maybe a member of your family acted foolishly and landed you into a difficult situation and you were at a loss how to handle the consequences of their irresponsibility. Or else plans you had carefully and prayerfully made, fell through and you found yourself with broken pieces to pick up.

Travelling on the desert road

In case you think I am being a bit free in my interpretation of this passage, let me remind you that there are plenty of examples of this desert road elsewhere in the Bible. Think of Joseph: his

> Think of Joseph: his desert road led into slavery and then into prison.

desert road led into slavery and then into prison, though he was innocent of a false and scandalous accusation. Or think of Elijah: he spent long months living on the breadline beside the Cherith Brook, fed only by ravens, and then in Zarephath, in the home of a widow. Or think of Jeremiah: for thirty years a mighty preacher but with no congregation. Or think of the Lord Jesus: he took the twelve away with him into the north, far from the towns and villages with their crying need. Or think of Paul: after his conversion, he disappeared into Arabia for three years.[3]

These and many others, travelled along the desert road.

This desert road is one God sometimes asks us to take. It is a most unexpected route. At the time we feel that it is an unnecessary diversion and, as we travel it, we protest and point out to God that there is a much better way of doing things. 'Why don't you heal me, Lord? You are the great Physician.' Or, 'Why don't you send your Spirit and change my son, my daughter? You easily could do that, Lord.' Or, 'Why didn't you get me that job, Lord? You know I could have done it well and would have given it my very best and more.' Or, 'Why didn't you leave me where I was? I was happy and fulfilled there.'

But there we are, on the desert road, heading in what seems to be the wrong direction altogether. Is that you? Does your life seem like a wasteland, without colour or joy? Does it seem as if an endless road lies ahead of you, stretching into a meaningless future?

The secret purposes of God

The Bible passage makes two further points, both of which are important in thinking about this desert road.

The first is that the people knew perfectly well they were supposed to be travelling towards Canaan. The place in Egypt where Joseph's remains had been kept had become a kind of shrine, where the promise of their return home had been kept alive (v. 19). Many years earlier, on his death bed, Joseph had told them that God would come one day to take them home to Canaan, and when that happened, they had to take his mummified remains with them to bury beside his ancestors in the family burial cave in Shechem (Genesis 50:24–25). Therefore, there was no fooling the people. They knew perfectly well they were supposed to be heading for Canaan. And yet they were travelling away from Canaan along this desert road.

But there was also a second reason why the people accepted that unwelcome road south by east, as well as Moses' explanation that they were avoiding the powerful Egyptian border guards. It was that they had the assurance of the presence of God with them. By day, there was a pillar of cloud leading them, and by night, a pillar of fire. Many suggestions have been made as to what the cloud and fire were. Perhaps a column of smoke rose each morning from the sacrificial altar and yet, unlike any normal cloud of smoke, it did not drift away, but stayed with them, guiding them on their journey. Whereas at night, the pillar of fire may have arisen from the flame of the evening sacrifice but, like the burning bush that Moses saw, was not extinguished until dawn came and it was replaced by the pillar of smoke.

Whatever explanation may be offered for the pillars of fire and smoke, John Calvin is surely right when he says that what we have here is a sacramental way of speaking of the Lord's presence, leading and guiding the people.[4] In other words, we are to understand that the people knew, beyond all shadow of doubt, that God was with them. He was there, his presence was real. And it was that tangible evidence that gave them the firm conviction which supported them along the desert road. God himself was leading them along the way.

Ahead lay many trials. God would humble them and uncover to them what was in their hearts. He would reveal his own character and bring to them the burning holiness of his standards in the Ten Commandments. He would give them a pattern for their community life as a nation, and for their worship as his people. Looking back, we can see why God took them by the desert road. Hindsight is always easier than trying to anticipate the future, is it not?

So, what can we say about the Lord's people today who are being led along a desert road? If that is where you are just now, there are three things you must know. The first is that you must be sure of your destination. We do not have the mummified remains of Joseph with us, as a reminder of the Promised Land. Rather, we have a living Saviour, the Redeemer who died and rose again. We have the Lord's own word, 'I am going to prepare a place for you; I will come again and take you to myself, that where I am, there you may be also' (John 14:3).

Are you sure of your destination? As the map of your life is spread out, can you put your finger on it and say, 'This is where I am just now, and this is where I am heading. I am in the City of Destruction, and I am on my way to the Celestial City.'[5] From earth to heaven; from weakness to power; from bodies of dishonour to glorious bodies, for we shall be changed; from time to eternity. For the Christian, the destination is very clear. Is it clear for you?

The second thing we must know is that God is with us and just as real as that pillar of cloud by day, and fire by night. What a comfort that must have been. It made the desert road, the right road. Without it, the desert road would have been discouraging and pointless. But with the sign of God's presence going before, all was well.

You may ask, 'How does his presence come to us?' The presence of God is known and felt through the ministry in our lives of the Holy Spirit, who brings a peace and assurance that is utterly real. What are the words with which our Services conclude each Lord's Day? 'The grace of the Lord Jesus Christ, the love of God, and the fellowship and communion of the Holy Spirit, the Comforter and Counsellor, be with you all.' God's presence is known by the fellowship and communion of the Spirit of God. You and I must have that assurance. Without it, the desert road is unthinkable. So, have you that firm, quiet conviction? Ask God to bring it to you, and his promise is that those who seek shall find and to those who ask it will be given.[6]

The third thing we must know is that God's way is best. God has a secret and hidden purpose in leading us along this mysterious desert road. He has lessons to teach us. He has a work to do in our lives. That is why he has planned this long, apparently illogical, roundabout way. He wants us to learn much about ourselves; but, more important, he wants us to learn much more about himself.[7]

> God wants us to learn much about ourselves; but, more important, he wants us to learn much more about himself.

So, he takes us along the desert road, as a lover takes his girl along a quiet country road to delight in her company, and so that together they will come to know each other better. The Lord also wants us to come to know him far better, and the lonely desert road is the ideal place for that to happen—away from distractions and our busy routine to a place where we will be with him, to listen and to learn of him. Your journey. The journey of us all.

'So, God led the people around by the desert road' (v. 18, NIV). Is God just now taking you down an unexpected path? You have wondered why. You may even have been angry with him and demanded that he should lead you back on to the safe and familiar path you were on before. I confess I have at times been angry at pathways God has chosen for me. On occasion it has taken me months, even years, to accept his will, so you are not alone.

We need have no fear.

As the years slip past and we look back, we see and understand a little more. Just now 'we see through a glass darkly'.[8] One day, however, when we see the Lord 'face to face', then the beauty and purpose of that providential pattern of our lives will become gloriously clear as we are able to survey the whole intricate tapestry from start to finish. Then we will 'bless the hand that guided, and the heart that planned, where glory, glory dwelleth in Immanuel's land'.[9]

So, keep close to the pillar of cloud by day, and to the pillar of fire by night—I mean, keep close to Christ himself and, in spite of all the difficulties you may experience, the journey will have a glorious end.

FOR FURTHER STUDY

1. In this chapter, there was mention of several biblical characters who were led along the desert road. Firstly, suggest possible reasons why the Lord guided each of them in this way. Secondly, see if you can find any other characters in Scripture who were similarly directed by God and also suggest why.

2. Considering the pillars of smoke and fire in 13:21–22, can you find in Scripture other equivalent manifestations of the tangible presence of God, such as that in Genesis 15:17.

3. Outside biblical examples, have you read or heard of remarkable experiences of God's servants who experienced completely unexpected assurances of the Lord's presence?

TO THINK ABOUT AND DISCUSS

1. In 1 Corinthians 10:1–5 there is a most solemn warning. After confirming the presence of the pre-incarnate Son of God with the people of Israel in the wilderness – 'the Rock was Christ' – the apostle then points out that, even though they had been physically very near to God, their hearts remained hard, and they were 'overthrown in the wilderness'. In the same chapter, in verse 12, Paul issues a most solemn warning. Discuss how necessary that warning is to Christians today.

2. If you have experienced anything of the 'desert road', and if you feel able to share that experience with others, say what God taught you by leading you in that way.

3. In the Introduction of her autobiography,[10] Dr Rhiannon Lloyd writes, 'These stories [i.e., her 'story'] show how God can lead us when we are not even aware of being led.' Looking back over the past years, can you see God has been leading you when you were not aware of it? If so, if you are able to, can you share your experience with others?

4. In this chapter, the question is asked, 'How does his presence come to us?' Are there tangible ways in which you have known the Lord's presence? Do you feel his presence 24/7? If at times the Lord hides his face from you, do you know why? (Psalm 27:9; 102:2, etc.).

19 Crossing the Red Sea

Exodus 14

As we ponder the challenge to Moses' faith, hemmed in by the sea ahead and by Pharaoh's chariots behind, let us remember that he had no idea as to how the Lord was going to deliver his people in this seemingly impossible dilemma. What other recourse in his lonely anguish had he other than to cry out to God?

Published over 50 years ago was the book, *The Road Less Travelled* by M. Scott Peck.[1] It begins with these words:

Life is difficult. This is a great truth, one of the greatest truths. It is a great truth because ... once we truly know that life is difficult—once we truly understand and accept it—the fact that life is difficult no longer matters.

The Israelites had known that life was difficult. For generations, they had been slaves suffering under the taskmasters' lashes. But now, through a series of the most amazing acts of God, forecast and coordinated by divine appointment through Moses, they were at last free of Egypt, and marching to the Promised Land. Problems all ended ...? Perhaps many of them thought so for a few days, as the whole immense caravan of women, men, children and animals slowly progressed towards the Egyptian border at the Red Sea.

Is this what you think—that it is possible to leave all our problems behind? I have occasionally heard irresponsible preachers urging their hearers to come to Christ who, they have insisted, can and will solve all their problems. I have yet to find anywhere in the Bible where such a promise is made!

> We must never forget that Christ's call to us is always that we must deny ourselves and take up the cross and follow him.

As we consider Exodus chapter 14, we will see whether Scott Peck is near the truth when he wrote 'Life is difficult'. We need to ask how true this is for our daily lives, as well as for our work and witness for Christ, for we must never forget that his call to us is always that we must deny ourselves and take up the cross and follow him (Mark 8:34).

Looking back

The first few verses of the chapter are important because they are clearly saying that God deliberately instructed

Moses to lead the people into a *cul-de-sac*. Behind them would stretch the desert, but in front of them lay the Sea of Reeds, or the Red Sea. To anyone who knew that region, it was the wrong route to take if the intention was to cross the border and leave Egypt behind.

However, in front of them was the column of cloud, that sacramental sign of God's presence. And so, the vast company stepped out defiantly, leaving their slavery behind. But alas, when they looked back, they saw a cloud of dust in the distance, and as they listened, they heard the thunder of six hundred horses' hoofs and the rattling of six hundred chariots, drawing ever nearer. Understandably they were terrified.

Problems. Difficulties. Who said that life would be easy when we are being guided by God? That is not what my Bible teaches me. For plainly, God had intentionally led them into this terrible situation.

I would like to share with you certain problems I myself have had in the past. I was in my seventh year of ministry in my third congregation in Ireland. It was a large congregation of well over 2000 members. I had found the first three years extremely stressful, so colossal was the challenge of the task of pastoring such a large flock. However, the elders had been very supportive and so together, over the next five years, we had built up a pastoral team of nine staff. We had spent the equivalent today of about £6 million on the church building and ancillary halls. The needs of the congregation were being met and the opportunities for outreach to the community were constantly increasing.

Then, out of the blue, I received a call to return to Scotland to take up an appointment as Director of a bankrupt theological study and training centre in Edinburgh. It was in debt and one of the Trustees confidentially admitted to me that they would be unable to guarantee my salary for even two years. Moreover, the salary I was being offered was sixty per cent lower than the one I was receiving at that time in Ireland. Worse still, out of that much lower salary, I would have to pay either rent or a mortgage as there was no accommodation available to act as a manse.

I can honestly say that the drop in income was never an issue. But re-launching that theological study centre seemed to me to be like trying to get airborne an impossibly heavy four-engine Lancaster aeroplane that had crash-landed in a deep bog, having smashed its undercarriage. Yet I knew, beyond any shadow of a doubt, that God had called me to this new assignment. I never once doubted it. His word to me to leave my congregation and move to Edinburgh could not have been clearer.

Nevertheless, I did not want to go and, when I was installed in my new position, I hated it for the first two years. I was really angry with God. Every day for months

I complained bitterly to him: 'Why God, why? You had placed me as minister in an encouraging congregation that was growing all the time. Why have you taken me from a land of plenty and put me into this arid, desolate wilderness?'

So, who said life was going to be easy? The Bible never says that. There are always problems confronting us. Yes, life can be very difficult!

But, back to those fleeing Israelites, who were now hearing the thunder of a pursuing army and, seeing the desert dust rising from the Egyptian host, realized they would be overtaken within a few hours.

The last phrase of verse 8 says, 'the people of Israel were going out defiantly'. Is there a suggestion there of an element of arrogance in their attitude? The verse seems to suggest they were presumptuous, headstrong and over bold. Certainly, like me in my rebellious spirit towards God when he moved me to Edinburgh, they lacked both prayerful humility and a meek submission to the divine purposes.

When they looked back, all they saw was the Egyptian army pursuing them. Had they looked back further with prayerfulness, they would have recalled the amazing events of the past ten months which had demonstrated God's power working on their behalf. They would have remembered how the gods of Egypt had been routed and defeated by the God of Abraham, Isaac and Jacob. And they would have acknowledged that God had always been in full control and had never once let them down. But, looking back now, all they saw were horsemen and chariots pursuing them.

All of us can be daunted as we face our problems and, for some of the Lord's people, scarcely a year goes past without some difficulty closing up on them from behind. There is always some cunning scheme of the devil snapping at our heels like a ferocious dog, threatening to tear us from the Father's care.

> There is always some cunning scheme of the devil snapping at our heels like a ferocious dog, threatening to tear us from the Father's care.

Into what state of mind do we unintentionally slide? Have we become self-satisfied? When we look back and see the threat and begin to tremble and cry, have we fallen out of step with Christ? Or, on the other hand, do we look back and recall the Father's constant love and the ways he has provided and guided in the past? In what frame of mind do we look back?

Looking forward

I remember a hike in the country many years ago with a group of about forty young people. We were crossing a meadow on a beautiful summer's day when, from apparently nowhere, a herd of about fifty bullocks began to follow us. The curiosity of cattle can often be aroused by laughing, chattering teenagers. So it was with these beasts.[2] Seeing them following us, we began to hurry, but so did they, until they closed in on us in a semi-circle. When they were only a few yards from us, just like in the westerns, they prepared for a stampede, tossing their heads and snorting.

In those circumstances, we did not look back too long. Instead, we looked forwards. Forwards to the nearest way out of the field, which happened to be a very strong, barbed-wire fence. My job was to try and get twenty hysterical girls and twenty trembling boys over that fence as quickly as possible. Being a gentlemanly kind of fellow (I am speaking sarcastically!), I was last over, and it was the fastest I ever jumped a fence, for I actually felt the bullocks' breath on my neck as I cleared the barbed wire without a scratch or torn trousers!

What, then, did the Israelites see as they looked forwards? Not a mere barbed-wire fence. Rather a stretch of sea, probably at this point about one or two miles wide. Trapped! Hemmed in completely! Disaster! That is the reality of what they saw as they looked forwards.

Even worse, they saw Moses as the one who had led them forward to this complete impasse. They saw *him* as setting the route and they blamed *him* for bringing them to this impossible dead end. And so, not only did they curse him, but, in verses 11–12, we read they reneged on God and swore they would have preferred to have died in Egypt than to be in this appalling situation. Indeed, they openly admitted the fickleness of their sinful hearts, saying, 'Is this not what we said to you in Egypt, "Leave us alone that we may serve the Egyptians"'?

So, what do you and I see as we look forward? What are we saying to ourselves, or even to our God? Are we saying we wish we had never come this far along the path of faith and service? Are we going back on our promises to the Lord, and revealing what faithless people deep down we really are? And are we looking round for someone to blame?

'Then what ought the Israelites to have seen?' someone may ask. 'Surely we can't blame them when all that lay ahead was an expanse of water?' But was there not something else ahead of them as well as the waters of the Sea of Reeds? Was there not also a pillar of cloud, that sacramental symbol of the Spirit of God, guiding them forwards? Nevertheless, is it not true that our human reaction is often similar to that of these people—we see only the immensity of the problems, and we forget the Spirit of God and fail to acknowledge the presence of the risen Christ with us?

Looking forward. What do you see as you look forward at this stage of your Christian life? We all have our problems, for, remember, life is difficult and we are carrying the cross that Christ has laid upon us. There is no such thing as a worthwhile life that does not have such challenges to our faith and endurance. So, what do you see as you look forward? A barrier you cannot possibly overcome? Or do you see that pillar of cloud, God's Spirit, leading the way?

I know his words were written in a very different context,[3] but John Henry Newman's verse expresses well the darkness that sometimes envelops the Christian:

Lead, kindly Light, amid the encircling gloom, Lead thou me on;

the night is dark, and I am far from home, Lead thou me on.

Keep thou my feet, I do not ask to see

the distant scene—one step enough for me.[4]

Looking upward

Read this chapter again and think carefully about the implication in verse 15, where we find the Lord asking Moses why he was crying out to him—presumably in desperation for the situation was indeed desperate. Yes, the implied message is that, as the people turned on him so viciously, he himself turned on the Lord and cried out for help. However, it is possible that there is another way to understand his reaction. It is that, in faith, when the people protested so ferociously, he at once pointed them upwards: 'Fear not, stand firm, and see the salvation of the LORD which he will work for you today' (v. 13). Nevertheless, either as he was calling on them to 'Stand firm,' or immediately after, he cried out to the Lord for deliverance.

It may seem paradoxical that this man should appear ambivalent when, on the one hand he spoke with courageous and daring faith into a seemingly impossible situation, yet, on the other hand, in his heart he was crying out to God for a miracle. Yet this is true in the experience of every true servant of God. Calvin expressed it well when, commenting on the almost incredible scenario of a man (Jacob) wrestling with an angel (God himself) and prevailing, he says that the Lord fights against us with his left hand, but supports us in the fight with his right hand.[5] I think, here, Moses experienced that same conflict of faith, as he declared the people would see the salvation of God, while in his heart he was crying out to God for mercy. Thus, at God's command, he stood on the seashore, raised his shepherd's staff towards the water and called upon God to save them from their enemies.

Three further incidental points may be in order regarding the story at this point, because modern scepticism has been fuelled by a misreading of this chapter.

Firstly, sometimes in Sunday Schools, Moses has been foolishly and inaccurately portrayed as a magician with a magic stick that could make the sea go back. But, as children grow up, they discover there are no such things as magic sticks which make seas divide in half.

Secondly, some Bible story books have shown illustrations of the people marching along with a high wall of water on either side of them, as if held in by colossal panels of glass. But the text does not imply that. When we read of 'the waters being a wall to them on their right hand and on their left' (v. 22), the meaning is that the waters formed a barrier so that Pharaoh's chariots could not overtake them to outflank them.

My third comment is that it was neither Moses' staff nor his command that divided the Red Sea; it was the breath of God. All through the night (v. 20), over a twelve-hour period, 'the LORD drove the sea back by a strong east wind' (v. 21).

Now for those who are interested, there are records of a similar parting of the Red Sea occurring on other occasions through the waters

> It was neither Moses' staff nor his command that divided the Red Sea; it was the breath of God.

being driven back by strong winds. A good library might be willing to borrow for you the *Journal of the Royal Geographical Society of Egypt* (it is in French), Vol. XXI, August 1946; the relevant pages are 231–2, where the account is given of the waters of the Bitter Lakes—that is the most northerly part of the Red Sea, just below the present site of the entrance to the Suez Canal[6]—being parted by gale winds. In other words, as so often in the Scriptures, the miracle lay in God's perfect timing, for this event happened that very night, as the Egyptian armies were poised to overtake, surround the people, turn them round and march them back into slavery.

For my part, the most remarkable element in this epochal, miraculous event was that the cloud, which had been leading them onwards, is here revealed as being 'the angel of God' (v. 19). So, it was the divine presence that moved between the host of the people of Israel and the Egyptian army, and became darkness to the latter but light to the former.[7]

That night, few, if any, came to Moses to complain; all they could do to survive was to wrap their cloaks about them and cover their faces from sand and salt spray, as the wind howled and blew past them like a tornado. When dawn broke, the way forward was clear, and they marched across on dry land—dry enough, but still too soft for heavy chariot wheels. Because, when the Egyptians tried to follow, the wheels of their chariots sank up to the axles in the mud.

Do not be too hard on those Israelite people rejoicing (see Exodus Ch. 15), as, once they were all across, the strong wind dropped, and the sea waters flowed back over their enemies. Rather, tremble that sin must, as a divine necessity, be judged. Be certain that all who defy him, whether it be the suicide bomber with his explosive-belt concealed under his anorak, or the criminal in his pin-striped suit in a chauffeur-driven car, or very ordinary sinners who have deliberately kept God out of their lives year in and year out, persisting in turning their back on the Saviour, be assured and tremble that God must judge all who defy him. Fear God! 'Oh how I fear thee, living God, with deepest, tenderest fears!'[8]

Look upward! We all worry about the problems that seem to pursue us. And we worry too that we cannot possibly cope with the problems in front of us. How often we all forget to look up to remember what God has done in the past and how he is now ahead of us leading the way. How quickly we panic!

God's Word in this chapter brings us at least three clear instructions. Firstly, to be humble in heart and mind before the Lord, and not to live proudly or defiantly, but to walk with him in meekness and lowliness. Secondly, as we face our next problem, we must remember God's faithfulness in the past, and acknowledge that Christ himself is going ahead of us. Therefore, we must look upwards to him in faith. Thirdly, we must always joyfully acknowledge his gracious favour, and so give our Saviour all the praise and all the glory, as he delivers us and leads us safely on towards the Land of Promise, elsewhere called 'the city that has foundations, whose designer and builder is God' (Hebrews 11:10).

For further study ▶

FOR FURTHER STUDY

1. In his Introduction to the *Psalms*, Calvin writes, 'The Psalms will principally teach and train us to bear the cross,' which is 'a genuine proof of our obedience.'[9] Bearing in mind the earlier quotation from the same theologian in the Introduction to this chapter, see if you can find further biblical evidence of this kind of personal conflict in the Lord's godly servants.

2. Consider and try to appraise the value of the suggestion of a three-directional look in times of profound spiritual trials: the backward look at past blessings; the forward look at 'the angel of God who was going before the host of Israel' (v. 19); and the upward look in verse 14, 'The LORD will fight for you, and you have only to be silent.' Is this past/present/future structure merely a homiletical device or is it an underlying biblical principle; if the latter, can you find other examples in Scripture?

3. Bearing in mind the apostle's statement in 1 Corinthians 10:4, is there sufficient evidence, or even likelihood, that the references in the following verses in Exodus refer to appearances and activities of the pre-incarnate Christ: 11:4; 12:29; 14:19; 23:20; 32:34; 33:2?[10]

TO THINK ABOUT AND DISCUSS

1. 'Life is difficult.' Is this true for followers of Jesus? If so, in what ways? Read Mark 8:34–35, John 16:33b and Acts 14:22.

2. Thinking about Moses, faced with a seemingly impossible dilemma of the sea ahead and the Egyptian army closing in from behind, why does God sometimes permit us to face problems that seem far too great for us, yet at the same time he supports us? See Judges 7:7; 1 Samuel 7:7–13; Acts 12:5-11, 16.

3. 'Looking upwards.' How easily do you succumb to worry? And how easy or difficult do you find it to obey the Lord's exhortation: 'Do not be anxious ...' (Matthew 6:31–32) or, 'Why are you so afraid?' (Mark 4:35–41).

20 Songs of praise

Exodus 15:1–21

To my shame I confess that, for several decades, when I was re-reading Exodus I skimmed quickly over Moses' song. Christians should be as meticulous as those whose hobby is metal detecting, assiduously covering every square foot of ground with their implements in the search for lost treasure. Grasping a little of the meaning of the Lord's parable of the Kingdom likened to Hidden Treasure (Matt. 13:44), could be at least one legitimate extrapolation of its standard interpretation. Handfuls of hidden riches are to be found when we dig carefully and prayerfully in the 'field' of this chapter.

Have you ever listened to an expert talking about some antique piece of furniture or work of art—a painting by an old master or a piece of Chinese porcelain from the Ming period? I recall seeing an antiques programme in which one of the items was a 17th century, French clock. The expert's explanation was fascinating and I found myself imagining being transported back into that bygone age, when such beautiful things were fashioned to adorn a monarch's palace. But then, when I heard the value of the clock I gasped, because it had become almost priceless, as there were only two known-surviving, similar pieces. To replace it would be, well, nigh impossible.

> The poem we are about to study from Exodus 15 is most probably the oldest surviving poem in the Scriptures.

We all have in our hands just such a priceless work of art. The poem we are about to study from Exodus 15 is most probably the oldest surviving poem in the Scriptures. Unfortunately, I am not an expert who can explain fully its antiquity, for it is very old, going back about 3200 years. However, I will do my best in a sentence or two to point out some of its rarer features. We will handle it with care, the way we would handle a precious Ming vase or a 17th century French clock.

A brief description of some features of the poem

Verse 1 is variously translated. The NIV renders the main verb as 'highly exalted', for literally it means 'risen up like a wave of the sea'. The ESV (from which I am quoting throughout this book) has 'triumphed gloriously'.[1] Both translations are based on the verb which refers to the raging sea. The people had just seen surging waters rushing back to fill the empty seabed, as the wind had suddenly dropped. And the sight of those surging waters is caught up into the poem right at the beginning: the Lord 'has triumphed gloriously'. This is confirmed by the second part of the verse which explains the first line of the couplet: 'The horse and his rider he has thrown into the sea.'

However, at this point we must divert and pause to notice something of interest and significance here. Hebrew poetry is of a literary genre almost unique in ancient literature. Its literary form does not depend on rhyme and rhythm, as does the poetry of most other languages and cultures. One thinks, for example, of the rhyme scheme of sonnets, which follow a distinct and recognizable rhyming format: the first eight lines following the scheme, *a b b a*, followed by *c d d c*, and the final six lines may be *c d e c d e*. Or one thinks of the clever rhythm of John Milton's *L'Allegro*[2] which is intended to create a festive mood:

> Come and trip it as you go,
> on the light fantastic toe.
> In thy right hand bring with thee
> The mountain-nymph, sweet Liberty.

Contrast that, if you are so minded, with a very

different mood, designed to create the feeling of alarming action, as in Byron's poem, *The Destruction of Sennacherib*.[3] In trochaic metre it mimics the thunder of horse's hooves as the cavalry gallops into battle:

The Assyrian came down like the wolf on the fold,
And his cohorts were gleaming in purple and gold;
And the sheen of their spears was like stars on the sea,
When the blue wave rolls nightly on deep Galilee.

Not so, Hebrew poetry. Rather, it employs what has been called 'parallelism': that is, repetition in the meaning of sets of lines, whether in couplets, as here in 15:1 where the same thought is repeated in two different ways, or in a whole series of parallel lines, which together create an expanding description of the chosen theme. An example of this 'cumulative parallelism' is seen in Psalm 19:7–9:

The law of the LORD is perfect—reviving the soul;
the testimony of the LORD is sure—making wise the simple;
the precepts of the LORD are right—rejoicing the heart;
the commandment of the LORD is pure—enlightening the eyes;
the fear of the LORD is clean—enduring for ever;
the rules of the LORD are true, and righteous altogether.

A further point of interest in this parallelistic literary form is that it is only found elsewhere in ancient literature in early Egyptian and Ugaritic poetry, which would suggest that the Hebrew slaves learned it from the Egyptian culture in which they had lived for several generations.[4] However, the children of Israel developed and improved it. A little reflection will bring us to realize that, in the providence of God, they were guided in their adoption of parallelism for their poetry so that, into whatever language the poetry of the Psalms is translated, its poetic form is retained in all its beauty. Had its dependence been on rhyme and rhythm, that would have been well-nigh impossible.[5]

We must return now to the poem in Exodus 15.

In verse 2, the word 'song' is sometimes translated 'defender' or 'might', and is a very old, archaic word; this is the only time it occurs in the whole Bible. Scholars are not absolutely sure what it means, though the Septuagint translates it as 'might'. However, the thought seems to be that because 'The LORD is my strength,' he is therefore also 'my song'. In verse 3, we are told that God is 'a man of war'; this is a similar thought to speaking of him as 'LORD of hosts' and might be compared to the vision Elisha's servant was given of the hills with the Lord's army of horses and chariots of fire (2 Kings 6:15–17).

Some are embarrassed by verse 3 and what they regard as a meaningless and out of date description of God. They opine that Jesus, in his depiction of God as a loving Father whose mercy and compassion is towards all that he has made, refuted and changed this primitive idea of the Almighty. But we must never forget the Lord's burning wrath against all that is evil and perverse. The apostle writes that 'our God is a consuming fire' (Hebrews 12:29). Nor must we neglect the final awesome chapters of the Bible in which we read that God will punish all rebellion against himself and the rejection of his free offer of grace through his beloved Son.

Regarding this, we should bear in mind several other important considerations. In the Old Testament, there is no *explicit* doctrine of hell, for divine judgement is seen as being acted out in the 'here and now', as well as at some future point.[6] However, in the New Testament, it is Jesus himself who introduces the concept of hell; indeed, apart from one use of the word by James, the Lord's brother (James 3:6), the other twelve occurrences of hell (*gehenna*) are from the Saviour's lips.

Furthermore, as we will see more clearly later on in this book, the *exodus* foreshadowed the redemptive work of the Saviour. In Luke 9:30–31 we read, 'And behold, two men were talking with him, Moses and Elijah, who appeared in glory and spoke of his *departure* [lit. 'exodus', see esv marginal reading], which he was about to accomplish at Jerusalem.' But someone may ask what relevance had the crossing of the Red Sea to Christ's death, resurrection and ascension (apart from the apostle's reference to baptism in 1 Corinthians 10:2)? The answer is both sobering and glorious. Because surely the two aspects of God's intervention at the Red Sea on behalf of his people, foreshadowed the awesome events in Revelation 18 regarding the fall and destruction of all defiance against him, while Revelation 21:1–4 and 22:1–5 foreshadow the joy and celebration in Moses' poem. Both the judgement against Pharaoh and the salvation of the fleeing slaves recorded here point down the corridors of time to the final, awesome triumph of Almighty God.

> Both the judgement against Pharaoh and the salvation of the fleeing slaves recorded here point down the corridors of time to the final, awesome triumph of Almighty God.

Now back to the text. In verse 8, we are told that the surging waters were driven back 'at the blast of [God's] nostrils'. As well as being poetry, this is an example of biblical writers' daring anthropomorphism: that is, speaking of God as if he was a human being. The picture is of a furious warrior, snorting in wrath and rushing at his attacker. The metaphorical nature of the whole poem warns us not to take literally the phrase, 'the floods stood up in a pile' (also v. 8).

In verse 9, the Egyptians are depicted as boasting that their 'desire shall have its fill of them'. The NIV translates this as they will 'gorge' themselves on the defenceless slaves. This word is also archaic and depicts an animal devouring the flesh of its prey. Its meaning here, however, is probably that their intention was 'to destroy' or 'to dispossess' them.

In verse 10, we read, 'they sank like lead', literally meaning 'they went gurgling down'. The phrase is onomatopoetic: that is, the sound of the verb echoes the sense. Again, this is an archaic word.

The question posed in verse 11 is significant: 'Who is like you, O LORD, among the gods?' It is rhetorical, for God alone is to be served. Alan Cole comments, 'This is the primitive "monolatry" of early days (the insistence on the service of the Lord alone) which will later lead to the full dogmatic monotheism (the denial of the existence of any other God, apart from the Lord), that we read of in Isaiah 45:5.'[7] The apostle Paul makes the same point in 1 Corinthians 8:5–6: 'For although there may be so-called gods in heaven or on earth—as indeed there are many "gods" and many "lords"—yet for us there is one God, the Father, from whom are all things and for whom we exist, and one Lord, Jesus Christ, through whom are all things and through whom we exist.'

In verse 12 we read, 'the earth swallowed them'. This expression, too, is archaic and means that the earth gulped them down! Here the word 'earth' possibly means the underworld or the grave. Although it had been Moses' hand holding the shepherd's staff that had been stretched out, it was the Lord himself who had acted, for 'You stretched out your right hand,' and then it was that the earth swallowed them up.

Finally, notice that in verse 15, the two words 'chiefs' and 'leaders' are also archaic, and are local clan titles for warrior commanders. A similar kind of phrase is used in the familiar Irish hymn, 'Be thou my vision'[8], where we find the archaic Irish title of the 'High King'. It was used in ancient Ireland to refer to the overlord or the supreme ruler over other smaller, petty rulers, who also referred to themselves as kings. So, the hymn borrows the title 'High King of heaven' for the Lord God.

When we are looking at some old piece of furniture, the expert may point out to us some necessary repairs or possible small alterations. We can see something similar here in this ancient poem. Here is just one example. Although the poem is dated about 1320 BC, the 'inhabitants of Philistia' are mentioned in verse 14, even though it is reckoned that they arrived in Canaan some 200 years later. That may well be a little touch that has been added. But the antiquity of the poem is beyond question, as I have tried to show by indicating there are so many archaic words used in it. Indeed, we have in our hands a most precious work of art, as I have already remarked, possibly the very earliest poem of the whole Bible.

Now we must ask what this poem has to say to us for today.

Our experience of God

I have attempted (perhaps not very successfully) to point out to you the vitality and immediacy of this dramatic poem, used in praise of God after the crossing of the Red Sea. As we read it through, savouring many of its ancient touches and words which are so rare in the Hebrew language, we catch something of the atmosphere of those raging waters, the mighty wind and the awesome destruction of the chariots and their charioteers. It is vital, living and real, terribly and fearfully so. It is the language of eyewitnesses. They are giving testimony to what they saw with their own eyes, heard with their own ears, experienced in their own lives. It is an account by those who were present of something that God really did for them.

And so, this challenge leaps from the poem to meet us: 'How real is our experience of God?'

In the world of art there are always imitations, copies and fakes of the real thing. So, we are dared to ask ourselves whether our Christianity is some reproduction. Is our faith in God something that is a clever copy which, when examined by an expert, is quickly exposed as a fake? Or is our faith just as living

> Is our faith in God something that is a clever copy which, when examined by an expert, is quickly exposed as a fake?

and vibrant as the faith that breathes through every line of Moses' song?

God has arisen in the Hebrew people's experience like a wave of the sea. He has come surging into their lives, like an irresistible breaker crashing and disintegrating on the shore. That is why they are singing: 'I will sing to the Lord, for he has triumphed gloriously'—he has risen up like a wave of the sea .... Read again what the song says in verse 2: 'He has become my salvation; this is my God.'

Incredible as it may seem, these people had lived through the events of the ten plagues, but it appears that many had only seen them as lucky natural disasters. After all, plagues of frogs and flies and gnats were not unknown. So, their hard hearts had still not embraced the Lord as their Lord until now, when the Red Sea had parted for them as God sent that east wind.

Are we today very different? You may attend a lively church. You can have your membership all in order and be doing your little bit in some small way. Yet, like so many down the years, it is possible still to be strangers to Christ: reproductions, imitations, fakes—not the real thing at all. And that is why this question confronts us, and demands from each of us an answer: how real is our experience of God?

God wants to break into all our lives by the breath of his Spirit. He sometimes draws us into the same kind of frightening danger and crisis that these people had faced with the chariots behind them and the Red Sea in front of them. Has the Lord ever brought you into some crisis, perhaps not nearly so terrifying as that, but nonetheless you have felt abandoned and alone? If so, was it that God was waiting to rise up and surge into your life with a gracious deliverance?

Because these people were eyewitnesses and we have their testimony of what they saw and experienced, we still must remember and read about the Exodus and the crossing of the Red Sea. For us, and for the Church of God today, the case is no different, in that the Lord still must have his witnesses. For Christ is on trial before this world. He is arraigned before a judge and jury: that is, before the people with whom you work, or your school, your street, your family. The world has our Saviour on trial. And God is asking for their verdict—*for* Christ, or *against* Christ? And in that trial, we are to act as his witnesses, just as these people were witnesses so long ago. Forty years later, Rahab was to say:

> I know that the LORD has given you the land, and that the fear of you has fallen upon us, and that all the inhabitants of the land melt away before you. 10 For we have heard how the LORD dried up the water of the Red Sea before you when you came out of Egypt, and what you did to the two kings of the Amorites who were beyond the Jordan, to Sihon and Og, whom you

devoted to destruction. 11 And as soon as we heard it, our hearts melted, and there was no spirit left in any man because of you, for the LORD your God, he is God in the heavens above and on the earth beneath (Joshua 2:9–11).

Today, it is you and I who have to bear testimony, so that the likes of Rahab, whose heart the Lord opened, may hear and believe and surrender to our loving Saviour. However, one problem is that the world is expert at uncovering fakes and frauds. We in the churches are not very good at it. We can have a few reproductions and copies, yet we hardly notice. The world is different and does notice, because so many outside of Christ are looking for excuses not to believe, and so they identify the fakes very quickly.

'The LORD is my strength and my song, and he has become my salvation; this is my God, and I will praise him' (v. 2). Is that true of you? Has Christ become your salvation, or are you an elaborate copy of the genuine article? That challenge meets us from this poem.

But notice as well in Moses' song, our exaltation of God.

Our exaltation of God

The people are singing. They have tambourines and they are dancing as they sing. It is a celebration as they tell about God's mighty act for them. I confess that I have never encouraged holy dancing in my congregations;

how would they have reacted if staid Presbyterians started getting up and dancing before the Lord? 'How shocking!' we would say. The Salvation Army, in their early meetings, were often so taken up with the victory of Christ over sin and his gift of the Spirit, that they would seize their flag with its emblem, 'Blood and Fire', and would begin to march around their hall, praising God and his Christ. I like that. If it is genuine and a real spirit of praise has enveloped them, I could not only cope with that, but I could also join in with it.

So, what about our singing of praises to God? Over the years as I have stood in the pulpit and watched the congregation singing, I have thought that some of them looked as solemn as an Aberdonian visiting his bank to withdraw some cash.[9] Some look as if they have just heard their mother-in-law has driven over a cliff in their new car,[10] and they are not sure whether they should be happy or sad. But it is not only Aberdonians who cherish their reputation as being canny, droll and dour. I have ministered in central Scotland as well and some there look as if they are in the dentist's waiting room and are dreading sitting in his chair. Yet others look as if the hymn books in their hands are written in Chinese and they cannot understand anything being sung. It might not be a bad idea for church members occasionally to have a turn of standing up at the front and having a look round the gathering during the praise! So, I ask again: what about our praises to God?

There is a vital clue in this Song about why their singing was so tremendous. It is not the tambourines and dancing, though that must have made a real contribution; singing does need to have some rhythm and lift to it. But no amount of rhythm or lift or dancing or tambourines can make praise real if it does not come from hearts that are throbbing with a living genuine faith.

The clue lies in verse 11. 'Who is like you, O LORD, among the gods? Who is like You, majestic in holiness, awesome in glorious deeds, doing wonders?'

It is doubtful if these people were what we call monotheists: that is, believing in just one God. They probably believed in the gods of Egypt, and the various gods of the different Canaanite tribes as well.[11] But what they had discovered through the events of the past few days and weeks was that their God was the only one to be worshipped and honoured and obeyed. All other gods paled into insignificance beside their God. He alone was worthy to be exalted and magnified and worshipped. This, of course, was part of the cumulative

> No amount of rhythm or lift or dancing or tambourines can make praise real if it does not come from hearts that are throbbing with a living genuine faith.

unfolding of the nature of God, as he used such events as the Exodus to reveal himself as the only genuine God. By the time the inspired poet wrote Psalm 135, Israel had fully embraced monotheism:

> The idols of the nations are silver and gold,
>
> the work of human hands.
>
> They have mouths, but do not speak;
>
> they have eyes, but do not see;
>
> they have ears, but do not hear,
>
> nor is there any breath in their mouths.
>
> Those who make them become like them,
>
> so do all who trust in them.
>
> O house of Israel, bless the LORD!
>
> O house of Aaron, bless the LORD! (vv. 15–19)

We claim not to believe in other gods today, but we do. There are other gods all around us. You see them as you go shopping—retail outlets built like cathedrals or temples, with their stately marble floors, pillars and lofty arches. Rightly so, because they house lots of gods and idols which people worship, love and serve.

We see other gods as we drive along any main road just outside a town. Gently undulating ground, green and pleasant, with little square flat patches where the faithful congregate in turn to perform their liturgies with religious 'crosiers', which have iron or wooden ends to them. Central to their acts of worship are small white balls. And usually near the first smooth, flat patch of green is their temple, where the devotees gather to pour out libations of various kinds; only they usually end up swallowing their libations to the great god of golf. The first day of the week is observed by thousands as their prime day of 'worship'.

Make a list of some of the modern gods. Your inventory will probably fill a full page of writing paper or a screen. And when you have finished, see if you have the honesty to score out the ones you yourself do not worship, and to leave the ones you do worship, perhaps secretly. I assure you that most of us, if we are absolutely honest, will be left with at least a few other gods.

But these people had been drawn by their God to worship him alone. God had so intervened in their lives as to change everything for them. You would have thought that they could never be the same.[12] The night before, they were slaves running away, followed by cruel, ruthless men. The next morning, they had crossed the boundary and were in a new land, their enemies left behind forever. What a dramatic intervention! No wonder they were singing and dancing and praising God. God had been lifted up and exalted in their lives. He was the only One. 'Majestic in holiness, awesome in glorious deeds, doing wonders!' (v. 11).

Every congregation of the Lord's people ought to be doing their best to keep their praise of God fresh and strong. But the real secret of the praise and worship lies in our deepest hearts and souls. The real secret of genuine adoration lies in our attitude to the Lord. We only truly worship when God is enthroned in our hearts, and we cry out: 'Who among the gods is like you, O Lord? Majestic in holiness, awesome in glorious deeds, doing wonders.' That cry resonates when we have heard Christ's own voice, have come before him to bow our knees

> The real secret of genuine adoration lies in our attitude to the Lord.

and surrender ourselves to him completely. Oh, that he would breathe upon his people in our day and send his Spirit to part the metaphorical seas stretching out before us so that we can cross over to the new land and leave our sordid slavery to self and sin behind forever. Then we will praise him. Then the roof of our church buildings will reverberate, echo and resound, because we have seen the majesty of his holiness, the awe of his glory, the wonders of his working!

Our expectation of God

Before the former slaves, stretches out a dreary desert, vast wastes of sands and rolling dunes. They will have sore feet and aching limbs as they journey onwards. But what does that matter? Not a fig, because they are marching to the Promised Land. The final stanza of our precious poem (vv. 13–18) is full of confidence and breathes living faith—a faith that is up to date and relevant. They will face hard trials, a long, long road and grave dangers. But God is with them. That is their expectation, and the pulse-beat of these triumphant lines.

Notice that verse 13 speaks of the 'steadfast love' of God leading them on. The Hebrew word translated, 'steadfast love' (*hesed*), is inextricably bound up in the covenant that God makes with his people, for he makes an agreement with us. This agreement is entirely his, for he initiates it, he draws up the terms, he seals it in the blood of his own Son; 'steadfast love' is used of that covenant.

Then in verse 13 there is also the verb, 'redeemed'. The emphasis here is not so much on the ransom price paid, nor even on the deliverance (although the word does mean 'deliverance at a cost'); rather is it on the close relationship between the Redeemer and the redeemed. The practice was that the next of kin should buy back something or someone that had fallen on hard times (see Ruth 4:1–12). God is his people's next of kin, someone very close to them, who has intervened to buy them back.

And then, also in verse 13, he sings that God will guide (or lead[13]) them to his 'holy abode': that is, to the land he has chosen and promised them, the place where God himself will dwell in their lives. The reference could also be to the location where the Tent of Meeting with the ark of the covenant will be located. For us today, the reference is to his covenant love, signed and sealed in his beloved Son's lifeblood. He condescends to call himself our next of kin, our nearest and dearest, who comes to redeem us. And he provides a dwelling place where he can have his residence in and with us. The apostle Paul anticipates this when he writes that 'we are the temple of the living God; as God said, "I will make my dwelling among them ..."' (2 Corinthians 6:16[14]). This is our expectation of God!

Our Lord Jesus never ever said being a Christian would be a walkover. 'Take up [your] cross and follow me' (Matt. 16:24), he says. But see what he also says: 'My love will never fail you. I have made a covenant with you. It is the New Covenant, memorialized in the cup of blessing. I will stand by my covenant. It will not fail, for I am God and I do not change!' [*words mine*]. Moreover, in his Word, he says to us, 'If anyone ... does not hate ... his own life, he cannot be my disciple' (Luke 14:26–27). But see what he also says in Isaiah 43:1, 'I have redeemed you,' implying that he is our next of kin, our nearest and dearest. In effect, he means that we belong to him now. We have been bought with the costly price of his blood. 'You are mine!'

Neither did our Lord ever say that being a Christian would be a matter of little account. Rather, he promises that 'Whoever follows me will not walk in darkness, but will have the light of life' (John 8:12), for by his great strength he will bring us safely through the hostile wilderness of this world with all its enticements and dangers, to his holy dwelling, where God is light and love, and where 'glory dwells in Emmanuel's land' (Samuel Rutherford, 1600?–1661).

So, what is our expectation of God? I finish with a few of verses of a hymn which we used to sing in our family prayers round the breakfast table when I was a child. They are words which burned like a fire in my soul and I have often recalled down the years:

Begone, unbelief, my Saviour is near,
and for my relief will surely appear;
By prayer let me wrestle, and He will perform,
with Christ in the vessel, I smile at the storm.

His love in time past forbids me to think
He'll leave me at last in trouble to sink;
Each sweet Ebenezer I have in review,
confirms His good pleasure to help me quite through.

Determined to save, He watched o'er my path,
when, Satan's blind slave, I flirted with death:
And can He have taught me to trust in His name,
and thus far have brought me to put me to shame?

John Newton (1725–1807)

For further study ▶

FOR FURTHER STUDY

1. It is significant that the parallelism which characterises Hebrew poetry had its origins in Egypt where, 'Moses was instructed in all the wisdom of the Egyptians and he was mighty in his words and deeds' (Acts 7:22). Assuming that the praise song in Exodus 15:1–8 was composed by Moses along with Psalm 90, we could therefore conclude that, in these earliest poems, Moses laid the foundations for the poetic form of the Psalter as well as for much of the prophetic writings. (N.B. This form of poetry is not altered no matter into which language it is translated.) Here are three types of parallelism (it can take many other forms):

- synonymous parallelism—three stanzas in Psalm 24:1–3, where in three couplet the same thought is restated and re-enforced.
- antithetic parallelism—final stanza in Psalm 1:6, where the 2nd line's contrast enforces the 1st line of the couplet.
- cumulative parallelism—several statements in which six couplets build up understanding of an ever-increasing concept: Psalm 19:7–9

Identify examples of these poetic forms in both Exodus 15 and Psalm 90, as well as in other Psalms.

2. The poem is replete in examples of what we may call 'divine accommodation'—that is, God inspires through his servants' words, concepts and metaphors in which he stoops down to us to accommodate something of infinite divine truths which we fallen daughters and sons of Adam with our finite limitations cannot fully understand. Search for examples of this, beginning, perhaps, with the concept of divine retribution.

3. Bearing in mind that the Book of Psalms was the Jewish Hymn Book, replete as it is with every conceivable spiritual experience of the Lord's people and his fatherly discipline and grace a—veritable 'anatomy of the soul'—to what extent does the music and praise of God

in our congregations measure up to all-embracing theology of the Old Testament Church of God. To put this challenge for further reflection in other words, how much theology are congregations learning from what they sing?

TO THINK ABOUT AND DISCUSS

1. From the first three verses of Exodus 15, make a list of titles that Moses ascribes to the Lord. How relevant are these for us today?

2. From verses 4 to 10, make a list of metaphors through which Moses depicts something of God's just retribution upon a thoroughly evil despot and those who have given him their full allegiance. Compare and contrast this with John's vision both in Revelation 18:1–8 and 20:11–15.

3. Finally, from Exodus 15:11–18, make a list of the metaphors used to describe God's blessings to be showered in everlasting abundance on his people who have put their trust wholly in him. Compare your metaphors from Exodus 15:11–18 with those in Revelation 22:1–5. Discuss how this clear teaching ought to affect our Christian lives in terms of our commitment, our spending, our praying and our outlook on our lives in this dying world.

21 Marah and Elim

Exodus 15:22–27

As long as we seek to serve the Lord in this broken and fallen old world, there will be conflict of one sort or another. After trials from without the people of God, through their oppression, now there come trials from within the company of those chosen by God. Although the starting point must always be a meek and humble spirit, issues that arise and cause criticism, anger and hostility need to be dealt with, through God's gracious help and direction. Yet, it is both comforting and encouraging that, in God's love, the bitterness of Marah is then followed by Elim's springs of water and shade of palm trees.

We began chapter 19 on 'Crossing the Red Sea' with a quotation from the book, *The Road Less Travelled*, by psychiatrist, Scott Peck. I pointed out that the first words were, 'Life is difficult.' You may have gathered that the book is about growing up and attaining maturity.

When he began writing the book, Scott Peck was not a Christian. But, by the time he had completed his book, he had become a Christian. I believe it was one of the most significant books to have been written in the 1980s. Peck's main thesis is that for us to become mature, we need to learn four great secrets of living. I am only going to mention one of those secrets. (If you are so inclined, you can borrow the book from a library and find out something about the other three.)

His first great secret is that we must develop a commitment to the truth and learn to face up to the truth about ourselves.

We should think about that for a moment. When someone criticizes you, what is your reaction? Let me tell you mine. I immediately try and justify myself by proving that I am right. More than six decades ago, in my first year at university, one of my professors was very critical of my work and attitude. I remember the intense feelings of dislike for the man that welled up in me. I found myself loathing him. Why? What I was doing was refusing to accept the truth about myself. I was making excuses for myself. I was trying to justify myself.

Have you ever done that? I think that to some extent we all do. According to Scott Peck, you and I will never grow up to maturity, even though we live to be a hundred, unless and until we become committed to the truth about ourselves and have learned to face it, however difficult it may be.

Perhaps you have already guessed why I am saying this. It is because Scott Peck is absolutely on target. This 'facing of the truth about ourselves' is part and parcel of the gospel. It is part and parcel of Christian growth. And this is one of the lessons from our passage today.[1]

Two moods

In Chapter 20, I only referred in passing to the celebration of God's miraculous deliverance with its singing and rejoicing (15:20). Miriam led them with her tambourine in the victory song and the dancing: 'Sing to the LORD, for he has triumphed gloriously; the horse and his rider he has thrown into the sea' (v. 21). And so, they set out on the next stage of their journey with glad hearts, smiling faces, and Miriam's song on their lips.

The second day, their water supplies were running low. But Moses assured them that they would reach water on the third day. So, they stuck it out. But on the third day their water did run out as the sun reached its zenith in the sky, and the intense desert heat made the going tough as their mouths and tongues became parched. The children became fractious. The sheep bleated, the cattle bellowed their thirst and the people were heard complaining.

At last, late afternoon, they saw the trees and bushes that signalled the oasis. But when they reached the oasis, the water was bitter, and the children spat it out. Then it was, that the mood changed and became ugly and vicious. In the short space of three days, they had gone from an all-time high, to an all-time low. They had gone from elation to despair; from euphoria to anger; from gratitude to glowering rage.

There is a lesson here that is often repeated in the Bible. The change in these people from one mood to such a different mood illustrates the way in which each of us can swing from being high spiritually to sinking really low. One day we are glad and sure in our allegiance to Christ; yet, the next day, we can be ready to turn our backs on him. Some of us might be inclined to explain the change in our mood in psychological terms. I have an acquaintance who invariably attributes this kind of change in mood to some medical condition, treatable with medication!

It could well be that there is a bit of the manic-depressive in many of us; we can have mood swings from highs to lows. It is often self-evident: after we have been on a burn-up, we come down with a bump. However, there is more here. The Scriptures often tell of dramatically changed circumstances, which lead to a complete change in mood. Remember the Lord's baptism. First was a voice from heaven saying, 'This is my beloved Son, with whom I am well pleased.' But then came forty days in the wilderness, and the severe testing of Christ by the devil (Matthew 3:13–4:11).

We can see the same pattern in Elijah's life in his contest with the prophets of Baal on Mount Carmel, and his fervent prevailing prayer for rain so graciously answered. Yet, we then see him running away into the desert and lying down exhausted, wanting to die (1 Kings 18:20–19:18). There is also the incident at the Last Supper of Simon Peter swearing undying loyalty to Jesus, vowing to follow him to prison and to death; but a few hours later he was cursing and swearing and denying he had ever known Jesus of Nazareth (Luke 22:31–34; 54–62).

Whether we think of it in purely psychological terms, or whether we have learned to see it as part of the spiritual battle in which all believers are involved, these mood swings certainly happen. It is common to all Christ's followers. We need to be aware of what is happening so that we can be prepared for it. It cannot be entirely psychological, since circumstances are often involved that are entirely outside of ourselves. In this passage from Exodus 15, it was the transition from the celebration of deliverance to the bitter, brackish waters of Marah.

What we must all learn is that God was leading these people forward. Before them went the pillar of cloud. God knew exactly what the water was like at Marah. It was he who took them there. His purpose was to uncover to them the truth about themselves. They needed to learn something about their fickle natures as they so quickly fell from their euphoric high to their all-time low—the two moods.

The two reactions

I recall vividly how, after the British general election in April 1992, there was great rejoicing that John Major had brought the Conservatives back for a fourth consecutive term of office. He had won over fourteen million votes, albeit a reduced majority in the House of Commons. Some people were even thanking God for his victory! However, six months later those same people were wondering whether John Major was quite as good for the United Kingdom as they had thought, when, on so-called 'Black Wednesday', his government brought us out of the European Exchange Rate Mechanism. The mood among the Tories had swung from a 'high' to a very definite 'low'. Major never again achieved a lead

in the opinion polls. In the next election, in 1997, Tony
Blair won a landslide victory for Labour.

So it was with the Israelites, whom Moses was
leading. The celebration recorded in chapter 15 was
followed by the bitter waters of Marah (meaning
'bitterness'), bringing a bitter spirit. A mere three days
after the jubilation over the crossing of the Red Sea and
destruction of the pursuing Egyptian army, these same
people were cursing and complaining and saying they
wished they had never started out on this mad journey
across the desert to the land of Canaan.

However, notice that the bitterness of Marah's water
was all in God's plan for his people. When you read this
passage in Exodus 15, did you
notice the last four words of
verse 25: '... there he tested
them'? Forty years later,
when they, at length, reached
Canaan, God's Word came to
them again: '... remember the whole way that the Lord
your God has led you ... testing you to know what was
in your heart' (Deuteronomy 8:2). We find the same
thought in Psalm 139, which we know and love so well:
'Search me, O God, and know my heart! Try me and know
my thoughts! And see if there be any grievous way in me
...' (vv. 23–24).

> The bitterness of Marah's water was all in God's plan for his people.

Of course, in one way, there is absolutely no need

for God to test us to discover what is in our hearts. God already knows us perfectly well. But we ourselves often never dream what lurks deep down inside us. And therefore, God searches us and tests us so that we ourselves might make the disturbing discovery as to what we are truly like inside. That is why the Lord actually plans for us some bitterness and even sorrow.

Our reactions respond to our mood, as our mood swings from a high to a low. Some may think this is a chance occurrence because their luck has changed. No. It is part of the journey to the Promised Land, an essential stony pathway of the Christian life. God plans it that way so he can uncover two very different kinds of people.

Firstly, on this occasion, there were the average men and women who moaned, grumbled and complained. Secondly, there was Moses and, I like to think, a few others with him such as Joshua or Caleb. They turned to God and cried to him. I wonder into which group you and I would have come.

When everything seems to go wrong, and our little world collapses like a pack of cards, what do we do then? On which side of the line do we take our place? Are we with the moaners, the grumblers? Perhaps we are well up in the queue with our complaint. Or are we with those who have learned that precious secret of saying nothing, but rather slipping away to find a quiet place where we can be alone to seek God's face, and lay our problem before him?

We may sing away, carried along by the tide of the uplifting enjoyment we find in the words and music of the hymn, 'What a Friend we have in Jesus ...', and we sincerely sing the line, 'Take it to the Lord in prayer ...'.[2] But when the evil day or the trial comes, or when the water we are yearning for turns out to be bitter, so few of us know how to take it to the Lord in prayer. Too often we turn to one person after another before it occurs to us to seek the Lord's face and to pour out our hearts to him.

Has some bitterness come into your life? Perhaps some trial of your faith or maybe some distress or disappointment? Then, how we react reveals to us what is in our hearts. God is bringing us face to face with the truth about ourselves. And he will keep on bringing before us the truth about ourselves until we are willing to face it and, like Saul of Tarsus, to ask, 'Who are you, Lord?' (Acts 9:5); 'What do you want me to do, Lord?'

I know it is not easy. The truth about ourselves is usually the last thing we want to hear. We prefer to blame someone else, or to say that our grumbles and complaints are really because we are concerned for people. We will argue that our reaction is the right reaction, for we are such experts at justifying ourselves. After all, what could be more obvious than to complain about bitter water when everyone is gasping for fresh water? And so, God keeps on leading us down from our highs, down into the lows of his design, all in his loving purpose of persuading us to stand back and look at ourselves, and to accept the truth about ourselves.

Maybe for years, your wife or husband or sister or friend has seen you as you are and has tried to tell you. But in your pride, you have refused to listen. Above all, maybe for years God has been trying to show you the truth about yourself. Is it not time we all looked into our hearts, and let the Lord uncover the arrogance and resentment, the ignorance and self-obsession, the selfishness and self-will?

A little talk with Jesus *won't* make it right, alright, as the trite ditty we sang as children assured us it would. Often it needs the bitterness of Marah, the thirst that kills or the distress that arises when we face possible death. It may need the most drastic measures. Almighty God may have to corner us, pin us down and ground us, until, at length, we are willing to remove our disguise and see the reality of what our hearts are truly like.

Two possible reactions to Marah as God works in our lives to uncover to us the truth about ourselves: complaining and grumbling, or else humble prayer.

Two experiences

The water of Marah was not actually harmful. The water in that same place is said to be still brackish because of the mineral salts it contains. To this day, the Bedouins put the branches and leaves of the barberry bush into the water of this area, for the aromatic flavour of the leaves and bark hide the taste of the minerals and make the water easier to drink.[3]

However, whatever the possible explanation might be, the text is intended to convey to us that there was a miraculous element to this incident. In verse 25 we read, 'The LORD showed him [Moses] a log [or tree], and he threw it into the water, and the water became sweet.' The verb, 'showed', is the root from which the biblical word for 'law' comes. Here, 'showed' means that the Lord instructed or taught Moses. It is also the same root from which 'Torah' comes. Thus, we see that the Bible's meaning of *law* is much richer than our English concept of *law*. For, in Scripture, *Torah* means instruction, showing us the right way, guiding and teaching us. Indeed, ultimately '*Torah*' often has the connation of 'revelation'.

> The Bible's meaning of *law* is much richer than our English concept of *law*.

The old medieval preachers used to spiritualize this story. They said that the piece of wood which God showed to Moses and instructed and guided him to use, was the same wood of the Cross. They allegorized the story, and made the bitterness of the water, our sin, and the sweetness imparted by the wood, the effects of the Cross.

But we have to acknowledge, that kind of spiritualizing of a story in this way is quite inappropriate. Having said that, we must notice something else: the word, '*marah*', is from the same root as the word, 'myrrh'. Myrrh is a resin which drips from the stems of a desert shrub and is prized for its aromatic qualities.

Myrrh was one of the three gifts which was presented by the wise men to the baby Jesus. It was myrrh that was offered to Christ on the Cross as an anodyne to ease his pain. It was also myrrh that was used, along with other perfumes and spices, to prepare his body for the tomb. Therefore, even if the medieval preachers were wrong in spiritualizing this story and making Marah, sin and the wood, Calvary, they were, nonetheless, not all that far off the mark. For this incident is rich in mystical indicators of the law exposing our sin, and the suffering of Christ being the only antidote to the bitterness that sin inflicts on us all.[4]

Very often I have heard the coldest of comforts being offered. I have heard people saying, 'I may be bad, but there are others far worse off than me.' Have you ever heard that kind of comfort? Surely it should be a cause for concern, not comfort, that there are others worse than us! Or I have heard folk say, 'Though trouble has now come my way, I can't really complain because I've had sixty trouble-free years.' Others are born optimists and try to keep their spirits up by saying that everything will turn out all right in the end: 'It always does,' they say. But I am afraid that is also very cold comfort, for the reason that it is not true. Yet others become fatalistic and say, 'Whatever will be, will be'.

We can rest assured that God does not offer us these stern, grey, forlorn comforts. When we turn to the Lord, the first thing he does is to say, 'Listen to me and I will teach you, I will show you, I will instruct you.' And then he goes on to say, 'I know all about Marah and the bitterness you're experiencing. Marah, the myrrh, was given to me at my birth. I tasted it on Calvary, and my body was laid in the tomb anointed with myrrh. I have experienced it, for I have drunk that bitter water to the dregs.'

That is the first experience: Christ coming to us in our trials, instructing us, opening up to us the best of books; unlocking our minds and teaching us about ourselves, but most of all about himself, that he has become one of us, and has shared our grief and carried our sorrow.

The second experience is this: He says, 'I am the LORD, your healer' (v. 26). And the place of healing to which he led them was called Elim; it lies just seven miles south of Marah. It is a lush oasis of twelve springs, where travellers can shelter from the burning heat of the sun under palm trees, and the flocks can graze on the pastures. Take that as a parable for the Lord's people today, as we move on a little way—those seven metaphorical miles beyond our bitterness—and we find, as David so beautifully expressed in the 23rd Psalm, that he leads us beside the still waters to green pastures, which are in truth the paths of righteousness.

Scott Peck is not only right, but his views are in agreement with the Word of God. Basic to maturity, and that includes spiritual maturity as well, is the willingness to admit and face the truth about ourselves and our lives. It is when we are able to accept what God has to teach us about our need of him, and when we are willing to be instructed so that we can change, that God does heal us and take us on to Elim, where we can be at rest and enjoy his refreshment and tender comforts.

> Souls of men! Why will ye scatter like a crowd of frightened sheep?
> Foolish hearts, why will ye wander from a love so true and deep?
> For the love of God is broader than the measure of man's mind;
> And the heart of the eternal is most wonderfully kind.
>
> F. W. Faber (1814–1863)

For further study ▶

FOR FURTHER STUDY

1. Consider instances of 'conflict' in the New Testament churches. See 1 Corinthians 3:1–4; 2 Corinthians 7:2–13; Galatians 2:11–14; Philippians 4:2–3; 2 John 10–11. Which category, if any, did the apostle use in these five different examples: Apology; Avoidance; Confrontation; Active Persuasion; Active Encouragement; Passive Encouragement—or other categories?

2. Have the skills of 'conflict resolution' been given sufficient attention in the preparation of candidates for the Christian ministry? If not, ought there to be in-service training for those with leadership responsibilities? Using your search engine, explore material readily available for biblical teaching on this topic.[5]

TO THINK ABOUT AND DISCUSS

1. Think about mood swings, not only those that are part of everyday living, but also the ones that self-evidently have a spiritual cause. Have you ever discerned a pattern that such mood-swings can occur when you have been involved sacrificially in some Christian work? Might that suggest that the tempter is trying to get back at you?

2. The brackish water at Marah was the cause of the first outbreak of widespread discontent. It was to be repeated several times in the coming months. How should we react when a spirit of grumbling begins to be felt in a congregation and what definite measures does your fellowship have that can be taken to 'nip it in the bud', as we say.

3. Read the following verses: Proverbs 15:18; 16:28; 29:22; Matthew 5:23–24, 25–26; 18:16. Have you ever found yourself being fed unhealthy gossip about anyone in your church fellowship, and if so, how did you react to it. With hindsight, would you react differently now?

4. What are the dangers of division in a Christian fellowship? (2 Corinthians 2:10-11.)

22 The manna

Exodus 16:1–36

The children of Israel had to learn that the journey to the Promised Land needed both trust in and obedience to God. Neither requirement would prove easy. But God would prove to be graciously faithful, even to the extent of his glory being revealed in his infinite mercy of providing a table in the wilderness that was to be a shadow of the Lord's own table today—and this in the midst of his people being on the point of sinning the 'great transgression' (Psalm 19:13c) and turning their backs on their Redeemer.

D o you know these words? 'As I walked through the wilderness of this world, I lighted on a certain place where was a den, and I laid me down in that place to sleep: and as I slept, I dreamed a dream.' That is the first sentence of John Bunyan's great book, *The Pilgrim's*

Progress. 'As I wandered through *the wilderness of this world*...' he wrote. It is a good description of this world, is it not? Spectacular and beautiful though this world is, we live nevertheless in a spiritual wilderness.

Wherever we turn, we find lonely and inhospitable desert wastes stretching into the far distance. No sign of any Utopia. Go to the hot, sandy beaches of Italy, and you are only a stone's throw from Mafia strongholds. Go to the cities of Russia, and you are in the midst of pollution, political chaos and ethnic warfare. Go to the Indian sub-continent, and you are standing close to bitter religious hatred, which the media seldom reports but that simmers close to the surface as hard-line Hindus harass Muslims living among them—and in the northern provinces they often harass Christians also. Go into the Balkans and you become aware of the hostility and war between Serbs, Croats and Bosnians. Go to South America, and in Brazil you are into a country where hundreds of thousands of men are in prisons and where street children in the vast cities live in danger of their young lives.

In the United Kingdom, we now live in cities where just beneath the surface of normal everyday life is an evil trade in immigrants being sold and bought for illegal brothels, and where hi-tech criminals waylay naïve citizens and defraud them of millions of pounds every year. Do you see why John Bunyan began his book with these words, 'As I walked through the wilderness of this world ...'?

Exodus 16 begins with the statement that the people left Elim and came to the 'wilderness of Sin'. The word, 'sin', is not to be confused with our English word, 'sin', for here it means 'clay' or 'mud'. It is an area of the Sinai Peninsula, but its meaning is beyond any doubt. The way forward led through a wilderness of clay— an inhospitable and lonely place, which for us symbolizes this world through which you and I must pass in the few short years of our pilgrimage to the Land of Promise. Therefore, we must turn to consider a little of what soon happened on the journey through the wilderness of this world.

> The way forward led through a wilderness of clay—an inhospitable and lonely place, which for us symbolizes this world.

The quails and manna

Alas, this volatile company of escaped slaves now quickly forget their truly amazing escape from the taskmasters' lashes and their inhuman treatment by the Egyptian ruler. Now, a mood of grumbling spreads among them like a highly infectious disease:

> And the whole congregation of the people of Israel grumbled against Moses and Aaron in the

wilderness, and the people of Israel said to them, 'Would that we had died by the hand of the LORD in the land of Egypt, when we sat by the meat pots and ate bread to the full, for you have brought us out into this wilderness to kill this whole assembly with hunger' (Exodus 16:2–3).

But read on and hear the gracious response of God to their ingratitude and unbelief: 'Then the LORD said to Moses, "Behold, I am about to rain bread from heaven for you ...".' So, we come to the provision of sustenance there in the wilderness for this vast host of people.

We have to begin by asking the question whether the bread from heaven was miraculous, or whether it was purely natural. We are never asked to suspend our rational judgement, so we must briefly consider the manna which appeared every morning (vv. 4–6) and became the staple diet of these people for their forty years in the wilderness, and the quails which appeared in the evening (v. 13).

Firstly, however, a word about the quails. Quails migrate between Southern Europe and Arabia. They pass over this area at that time of the year. They have a low, strong flight but when they are nearing their destination and tired, they fly straight into the nomads' tents, because they have no strength left to rise above them. They are easily caught and make for excellent eating. So much for the quails. No problem there. But what about the manna?

We are given a careful description of the manna. Verse 31: 'It was like coriander seed, white, and the taste of it was like wafers made with honey.' Some have concluded from this description that it was what the Arabs to this day call 'mann', which is a globular exudation of two types of scale insects that live on the twigs of tamarisk bushes in the southwest of Sinai. This substance is chemically composed of natural sugars and pectin. It appears in the spring and continues through the early summer months; that corresponds exactly with the time it first appeared according to the dating given in this chapter. Some, therefore, argue that the miracle of the manna, as with the quails, was only in the timing. Those who consider this 'mann' to have been a naturally occurring substance draw an analogy from Jesus turning water into wine or multiplying fish and bread into a meal for five thousand (John 2:6–11; Mark 6:30–44).

So then, are we to conclude that the manna was this natural substance, similar to honey in origin as well as taste, and indigenous to this area where the Hebrews were at that time? That could well be. But it is not as simple as that. Let me explain what I mean.

Firstly, the manna we know today (called 'mann' by the Arabs, as I have just mentioned) is seasonal, lasting only a few weeks of the spring and early summer, whereas the manna in Exodus was to continue daily for forty years. Secondly, the manna that is found today does not stop on the seventh day, or double its quantity on the sixth day, as did the manna in Exodus (vv. 25–26). Thirdly, the manna we know today does not follow a tribe of nomads across the desert but is limited to one particular area. There is the further consideration that the Israelites did not know what it was, for the name 'manna' comes from their question—in Hebrew, *mān hû?* meaning, 'What is it?' Had it been a natural substance, it is possible that some of their company would have been able to identify it.

There is no middle ground between thinking of this provision as something purely natural on the one hand and accepting it as a miraculous provision from God on the other hand. We do know that God controls and uses the world of nature he has made but, even if we are right in identifying *the bread from heaven* as the secretion of scale insects and chemically composed of sugars and pectin, the Biblical account asks us to accept that this was taken over entirely by God's power and used remarkably to provide a table in the wilderness for his people. That is important, as I hope we will see.

The true bread from heaven

There was a style of teaching on the Old Testament in the 19th century which was known as *typology*. *Typology* tended to use every detail of Old Testament stories as a 'type' or symbol of New Testament teaching. There were occasions when this method was taken to extremes, leading to absurd conclusions. For example, there is a commentary on the book of Exodus which offers fifteen different ways in which the manna was a type of the Bible, and twenty ways in which the manna was a type of Christ.[1]

But, although we have to turn away from that kind of typology which was, at times, taken to unlikely lengths, we must not ignore the Bible's own teaching that the manna was indeed a type of Jesus Christ, who is the true bread from heaven. You may remember the discussion recorded in John 6, which Christ had with the Jews about the bread from heaven that Moses gave them, and the true bread from heaven the Father was now giving them (John 6:22–40). I want to suggest three ways in which the manna speaks to us of the Lord Jesus.

> The manna was indeed a type of Jesus Christ, who is the true bread from heaven.

The first is that the manna was found in the wilderness of clay. The people, you remember, were grumbling about the harshness of the wilderness, its problems and difficulties. They were panicking and were predicting disaster. Looking round for someone to blame, they complained and groused that in Egypt they 'sat by the meat pots and ate bread to the full' (v. 3). They went as far as to say that they would have preferred to die in Egypt rather than to perish of starvation in this desolate desert. They were in the wilderness of clay well and truly, right up to their ankles.

How does God respond to their ingratitude and rebellion? What does he say and do, after they have so quickly forgotten their redemption by the blood of the lamb, and their baptism into Moses in the Red Sea? (1 Corinthians 10:1–2). He could have sent fire from heaven to burn them all up; that would have been no more than they (or any of us) deserved. But instead, God says, 'I am about to rain bread from heaven for you ...' (v. 4), and there was in the morning 'a fine flake-like thing fine as frost on the ground' (v. 14). The desert floor became covered with a source of food.

The picture is plain and speaks to us eloquently of Christ. Here we are, you and I, travelling through the wilderness of this world. It is a hard life. On every side there are heartaches and difficulties. There is illness and weakness. In our own lives, there is sin and failure. When we face problems, we too quickly forget God's promises. We grumble and complain. We behave as if there had been times in the past when the Lord had abandoned us, leaving us alone without help. We react as if God is faithless and uncaring, as if he has forgotten us.

We do not only do that as individuals. We can do it as congregations, as a body of elders or deacons, and in our various committees. We neglect our God again and again, as we turn to various schemes and devices in our attempt to revive his flagging, failing church. As the paraphrase of Psalm 23 has it, 'Perverse and foolish oft I strayed ...' (Henry Williams Baker, 1821–77). And if the holy God was to give to us our just deserts, he would turn away from us forever.

Yet, what is his response to our infidelity and unbelief? He says, 'I am about to rain bread from heaven for you.' And drawing near to us in our foolishness and perversity is the Saviour, who steps right into the wilderness of our humanity of clay. If you think I am stretching the point too far here, listen to Christ's own words:

> Jesus said to them, 'Truly, truly, I say to you, it was not Moses who gave you the bread from heaven, but my Father gives you the true bread from heaven. For the bread of God is he who comes down from heaven and gives life to the world.' They said to him, 'Sir, give us this bread always.' Jesus said to them, 'I am the bread of life; whoever comes to me shall not hunger, and whoever believes in me shall never thirst.' John 6:32–35.

The second way the manna speaks of Christ is that the manna displayed the glory of the Lord. We have the phrase, 'the glory of the LORD', in Exodus 16:7. The remarkable thing is that this is the first time in the Bible this phrase, 'the glory of the LORD', appears. The word, 'glory', has been used twice before: once, in Genesis 31:1 (AKJV), of the great wealth Jacob amassed while working for his uncle Laban; and once in Genesis 45:13 (AKJV), where it refers to the honours heaped on Joseph while he was Prime Minister of Egypt.[2] But here, for the first time, there is this crucial and central theme of the whole Bible, 'the glory of the LORD'.

What does it mean in verse 7? It does not apparently mean some awesome manifestation of God's power which caused the people to fall on their faces. Rather, it refers to the manna, which they would find on the desert floor and which would appear in the darkness of the night while they slept—a sweet and pleasant food to sustain them. That is what is meant by the very first reference in the Bible to the glory of the Lord.

> Are we not all impressed anew with the emphasis that good biblical carols give to the birth of Christ as the glory of God shining down upon this dark world?

Every December, Christians the world over remember and celebrate the birth of Jesus. As we listen to the carols, traditional and modern, are we not all impressed anew with the emphasis that good biblical carols give to the birth of Christ as the glory of God shining down upon this dark world? And yet, is there not a sense in which the glory of the Saviour was then, and still is today, hidden? And is this why, in the book of Revelation (2:17), we read of hidden manna: 'To the one who conquers I will give some of the hidden manna'? The fullness and vision of Christ's glory is yet to be revealed.

There is clearly a tension between the manna as miraculous on the one hand, or purely natural on the other hand, that we thought about earlier in this chapter. And what could be more natural than a new-born baby, lying in a cradle. I suppose a manger of wood lined with hay, with ox and ass in the shadows, makes the Christ Child even more natural; it is all so close to mother earth, so firmly planted in this wilderness of human clay. Nevertheless, there is no middle ground between the natural and the miraculous here either. For his arrival was heralded by angels and a shining star; and the shepherds, kneeling to worship along with eastern astronomer-priests offering their costly gifts, were brought by a divine summons to worship the King who is Lord of all.

Thus, in that little Child was God's glory, planted squarely in the wilderness of clay. As he grew up in the carpenter's shop; as at thirty years old he began to teach and to heal; and as three years later he dragged the heavy cross on his lacerated back and then hung in dying agony, it was glory—the manna on the desert floor (John

17:1). On the first resurrection morning, as he stood in the garden and spoke her name to weeping Mary; as he appeared in the upper room and ate broiled fish and a little honey; and when he said to Peter after breakfast on the seashore, 'Feed My sheep ... feed my lambs ...' (John 21:15–17), it was glory, the glory of the Lord, come down into the wilderness of our humanity. 'The Word became flesh and dwelt among us [literally, 'pitched his tent among us' as the Tent of Meeting was pitched right in the centre of the Israelites' desert encampment], and we have seen his glory, glory as of the only Son from the Father, full of grace and truth' (John 1:14).

The third way in which the manna speaks of Christ is that it was preserved overnight to be eaten on the seventh day (vv. 22–26). This is one of the ways dependence on the purely natural explanation of the manna breaks down. For six days of the week, if the manna was kept overnight, it became fly-blown and rotten. But if it was kept overnight on the sixth day, then when the seventh day of the week dawned, it was not corrupted, but wonderfully preserved.

There is another 'first' in this chapter. Not only is the first occurrence of the phrase, 'the glory of the LORD', here, but we also have the first occurrence of the word, *Sabbath*—the seventh day that was to be holy.[3] To what does the *Sabbath* point? As well as being a divinely appointed day of rest, what else does it speak of? It is the day of Resurrection! It is the day when Christ's body did not see corruption but was preserved and raised in newness of life.

Therefore, in this 16th chapter of Exodus, we have some of the most precious seeds from which the whole of our Christian faith grows. And the resurrection of Christ on the Lord's Day is one of those seeds, planted very early in the story of God's grace towards rebels and sinners. Here we have, therefore, three ways in which the manna of Exodus 16 speaks of the 'true bread from heaven'.

Finally, the work of gathering the manna

Every family had to go out and gather for themselves a supply of manna as their food that would sustain them and keep them alive. It was a daily task to be done. In other words, it was labour. And the Lord refers directly to that necessary work of gathering the manna when he says in John 6:27, 'Do not labour for the food that perishes, but for the food that endures to eternal life, which the Son of Man will give to you.' Can you see the significance of that? It means that we have to work to appropriate daily the spiritual food of Christ. It implies an effort on our part to feed from Christ. The simple 'believism' preached by some evangelists ignores this vital teaching of the Scriptures. The impression has sometimes been conveyed that, once we have surrendered to the Lord and accepted the gratuitous gift of salvation, we then just sit back and fold our arms, because our ticket to heaven has been brought to us on a silver plate, so to speak.

But the Saviour himself does not say that. Rather, he says, 'Strive (the word from the Greek verb, *'agonizō*, literally means 'agonise') to enter through the narrow door' (Luke:13:24). Give everything you have to follow faithfully that pathway that leads to eternal life. Many are travelling along the broad road that leads to destruction. Only a few have truly started out on the narrow way, having passed through the little wicket gate[4] that marks its beginning.

We labour for our living. We toil for the food that is prepared and placed on our tables. We work hard for our clothes and homes and cars. We even work hard for our holidays and leisure time. But what of eternal life? Do we think eternal life is a kind of benign influence that rubs off on us if we attend church occasionally, even regularly? Do we think it is a kind of genetic inheritance passed on to us through our genes from a godly parent?[5] Or do we think it is a bit like the measles—you can contract it if you mix with other people who have it?

No. We have to get up and go out and work for it (Philippians 2:12–13). That means we have to come individually to Jesus Christ and lay hold of him. There has to be a spiritual effort, as we come to Christ and bow before him. We have to reach out our hands and 'knock', open our mouths to 'ask', and be moved in our hearts to 'seek'. These are gospel words, are they not? Seek, ask, knock (Matthew 7:7). Then, have you done that? If you have, then you must recognize and acknowledge that you have done so, and are continuing to do so, only because the Holy Spirit has moved within your life, opening your blind eyes, unstopping your deaf ears, and bending your proud will.

It is the Spirit of God who stirs us to search for that narrow gate to life. It is he who points us to it and moves us to knock, and to beg that it might be opened so that we may enter it. It is by grace that we come to the Lord Jesus, with all the wrestling that involves, and he enables us to toil until we have gathered the true Bread, which is given for

> It is the Spirit of God who stirs us to search for that narrow gate to life.

the life of the world. For indeed, Christ, the very Bread of God, came to the wilderness of our world in humble glory (a glory veiled by his human flesh) to bring eternal life to all who partake and eat of him.

John S. B. Monsell (1811–1875) was an ordained Anglican minister. He was a prolific hymn writer who composed some 300 hymns. Some are still popular today, such as, 'Fight the good fight', and 'Worship the LORD in the beauty of holiness'. He was a friend of

William Gladstone and for five years, from 1870, he was Rector of St Nicolas Church, Guildford; he was also a chaplain to Queen Victoria. A Communion hymn that he wrote is one that I love dearly; it is based on the manna in the wilderness and on the rock from which flowed life-giving water (Exodus 17:6).

I hunger and I thirst;
Jesu, my manna be;
Ye living waters, burst out of the rock for me!

Thou bruised and broken Bread,
My life-long wants supply.
As living souls are fed, so feed me, or I die.

Thou true life-giving Vine,
Let me thy sweetness prove;
Renew my life with thine, refresh my soul with love.

For still the desert lies
My thirsting soul before;
O living waters, rise within me evermore!

FOR FURTHER STUDY

1. Study the arguments for how often we should remember the Lord's death in our services: weekly, monthly or (as in some denominations) quarterly or biannually (can you work out why some celebrate it only biannually?). Also, is there biblical evidence for calling communion, 'a sacrament'—that is, a 'means of grace'—rather than simply a memorial?

2. On Sunday 5 March 2023 during a sermon on Jude 3–5, Alistair Begg, senior pastor of Parkside Church, Ohio, urged that the Lord's Day ought to be regarded as holy in terms of our conversations, pastimes, and meditation, not just during our attendance at worship, but throughout the entire day—that is, from morning until night. To what extent should we regard the fourth commandment as still entirely valid in the New Testament dispensation, bearing in mind the arguments from some highly influential and widely respected, contemporary, evangelical leaders that such an attitude is reprehensible legalism?

TO THINK ABOUT AND DISCUSS

1. The attitude of 'the whole congregation', recorded in Exodus 16:2–3, in essence consisted in the implied threat of turning their backs on God and returning to be part of Egyptian society. Likewise, in the Lord's third temptation (Matt. 4:8–9), Satan was suggesting that Jesus 'swop sides'! Is this a rare/occasional or frequent temptation faced by Christians today? (See Ps. 95:7–8; Heb. 3:7–9; 4:7.) What allurements might the tempter use: money, worldly pleasures, popularity, a new exciting physical relationship, or something else?

2. A retired missionary friend told me that when someone grumbled about the pastor, he asked, 'How much time do you spend in prayer for him?' Note that the account does not say that either Moses or Aaron took the complaints to the Lord, but that God himself took the initiative

(16:4). Does God still hear the grumbles of his people? When we do pray for our pastor, what ought we to be asking for? For God's glory to be revealed? (16:7)

3. Think about communion. Are there any texts from Scripture that you might find helpful to write out and have with you, to read silently to yourself such as Psalm 51:7, 10, 15; Matthew 11:28–30; 1 John 1:9; 2:1–2. Share with each other similar verses to use as you partake. See if you can find texts of thanksgiving as well (e.g., Psalm 16:11).

4. The apostle Paul teaches that communion is a celebration which ought to unite into one body all who partake—that is, into the Body of Christ (1 Corinthians 10:16–17). How ought we to guide the direction of our conversations and fellowship as and if we share a cup of tea or coffee after the service? Do we consciously endeavour to *care* as well as to *share*?

23 Water from the rock

Exodus 17:1–7; John 7:37–39;
1 Corinthians 10:1–10.

The sooner we learn in our Christian pilgrimage that there is no 'ski lift' to the top of the rugged mountain, the better! Spare a thought for Moses and Aaron faced by a baying mob. They took the only possible action in the circumstances: falling on their faces before the Lord (Exodus 17:4; Numbers 20:6). But what of the rioting people?

In this passage from Exodus 17 we have a dramatic picture. The crowd is getting out of control in its anger, brandishing its clubs, sticks and stones. A mob is a terrible beast, and the chosen people of God have become a mob. Moses has resorted to his tent and been on his face before God in desperate prayer. Now God tells him to walk through the rabble, taking with him only the elders. He is to lead them to a nearby area called Horeb,[1] and there he is to use his shepherd's staff to strike a rock that God will show him, and water will flow from the rock.

In my mind's eyes I watch this eighty-year-old man, with his white hair and beard, his flowing Bedouin robes and his staff in his hand, face set having come straight from the presence of God. And I see the crowd falling back when they see the determination on his face, the set jaw, and perhaps even a faint reflection of glory upon him, as he indicates that the elders are to follow him. Going before him is the presence of God, indicated by the cloud. 'I will stand before you there on the rock at Horeb' (v. 6), the Lord has said. We are not told whether the elders saw the symbol of God's presence or if it was given only to Moses. Be that as it may, he knew exactly the rock God meant when he and the elders reached it. Having the assurance that God himself was there with him, he struck the rock and abundant water flowed from it, as promised.

> Having the assurance that God himself was there with him, Moses struck the rock and abundant water flowed from it, as promised.

Repeated ingratitude and unbelief

In chapters 15, 16 and 17, alongside the three human needs of food, water and survival, are three examples of the most atrocious ingratitude. We know how some children have to be told, and told, and told yet again; yet still they disobey.[2] That is what we have here. Three times over, the people rebel, in the face of the most gracious help, provision and guidance of God.

We must remember that they are being led by the pillar of cloud. That is clearly implied in verse 1 by the words, 'All the congregation of the people of Israel moved on ... according to the commandment of the LORD.' They arrive at Rephidim, but do not realize that they are only a short distance from the best grazing area in all Sinai. Here the cloud rests, and so they camp at God's command. They are here because, before they face the next hazard of their journey, they need to be reminded yet again of the power of their God.

We should also notice the timing of the events recorded in this chapter. We are told, in 19:1, that they reached Sinai on the first day of the third lunar month since they departed from Egypt; therefore, we may safely assume that the events recorded in chapter 17 took place sometime towards the end of the second month of their journey through the wilderness. The three miraculous interventions: the manna; the water from the rock; and the defeat of the fierce Amalekites (17:8–13), were, in God's providence, apparently in order that they should accept the Sinaitic covenant in the full knowledge of God as their redeemer and guardian.

But, at the point when the chapter opens, there is no

water! And in the desert, no water is disaster. This time, a different word is used for their grumbling. The ESV translates it, 'the people quarrelled with Moses'. Other versions have, 'the people found fault with Moses' (RSV), or 'the people contended with Moses (NKJV). The modern equivalent could be, 'they wanted to impeach Moses' (along with Aaron, for the verb '*Give* us water' is plural).[3] In other words, they were bringing a charge against them both of gross incompetence and in effect thereby sentencing them to death by stoning. We have that in verse 4. This occurs after all that God has already done for them. Could they not look back and remember? Had they not gathered the manna that very morning? Why do they forget so quickly the column of cloud that hovered on the edge of the camp? And what of their deliverance from slavery and the miracle of crossing the Red Sea, only a few weeks earlier?

I am sure that every Christian can look back and trace the Lord's guiding hand and gracious leading. But when we do look back, are we not also able to remember times when we doubted and questioned God's goodness, occasions when we were unfaithful, and were even ready to doubt and desert our blessed Saviour? Can we not remember that we too forgot our promises, went back on our vows and ignored our best resolutions? We can be every bit as perfidious, ungrateful and blind as these people. We are just as wretched as they were. If we have not yet discovered this about ourselves, then we cannot have gone very far in our walk with God. As one of the Scots reformers sometimes reminded his congregation: 'The devil is never idle and our inner corruption is never barren.'[4]

Some of the more recent Bible commentaries quote an incident from the First World War when a Major C. S. Jarvis was in this same area of Sinai with a company of soldiers. As they were digging in to fortify their camp, a sergeant accidentally struck a rock with his spade, and a spring of water immediately trickled out.[5] Since that happened, research has been done to try and find out if the modern Bedouins have any way of knowing how to locate these potential springs within rock fissures. But no evidence has been uncovered of any Bedouins having water-divining skills. Indeed, it has been estimated that the chances of striking a hidden, hitherto undiscovered, rock-spring by banging the rocks with some heavy implement, would be almost a million to one.

However, God was there, probably unseen by the elders, standing before the very place where the water had risen from its underground reservoir and was ready to burst forth through a fissure, near to the outer surface of the rock.[6] It was God who prompted and guided Moses, for he knew exactly the existence and location of this hitherto undiscovered source of water.[7] So the thirsty people drank. But it was a sacramental rock for, as we shall shortly see, 'the Rock was Christ'. Was this a reason why, after the appearance of this hitherto unknown source of water, the Amalekites are recorded in 17:8 as having decided to attack Israel? I am speculating but it is possible, for a new source of water in the wilderness would be highly sought after and certainly worth fighting for.

God's testing of us and our testing of him

Has God ever left you in some urgent need until you thought it was almost too late? At times he does that quite intentionally. I recall how, on one occasion, I asked God for a sign by a certain date. I even set a day and an hour; it was Friday 21st August 12 noon. I desperately needed guidance as to whether or not I should leave the sphere of ministry I was engaged in at the time and move to an entirely new work. After a full four months of waiting, apparently with total silence from God, the sign I asked for was given exactly three hours before the deadline that I had dared to give to the Lord. All I can say is that for me it bordered on the miraculous, and subsequent events made it abundantly clear that it was God who was acting, confirming the call about which I had been so uncertain—and, if the truth be told, regarding which I was extremely reluctant. I can remember other occasions when God stepped in at the very last moment, seconds before the metaphorical clock struck midnight. Yet, by these seeming delays, the Lord can wonderfully reveal himself to us as our faithful and loving Father. David knew this well, for he wrote:

> The LORD is in his holy temple;
>
> the LORD's throne is in heaven;
>
> his eyes see, his eyelids test the children of man.
>
> The LORD tests the righteous ... (Psalm 11:4–5a)

In verse 7, as well as the word, *Meribah*, meaning 'quarrelling', we also have the word, *Massah*, meaning 'testing'. This is the same word that we find in Genesis 22:1, where we read that 'God tested Abraham'. Both in the Old Testament and in the New Testament, it can be used in either of two very different senses. When God tests us, it is to examine our hearts and souls and to reveal to us the need for full and unquestioning faith in his mysterious purposes. It is used in this sense in God's command to Abraham to take his son Isaac to Mount Moriah, where he was to prepare to sacrifice him as a burnt offering. But, through that severest of tests, God drew Abraham closer to himself.

> When God tests us, it is to examine our hearts and souls and to reveal to us the need for full and unquestioning faith in his mysterious purposes.

The second sense of this same word is when the testing originates not with God but from Satan, working in our perverse and unbelieving hearts. Then, it tends to have its other meaning of 'tempt' or 'temptation'. Thus, the devil tempted Jesus in his endeavour to draw the Son away from total trust in God, and commitment to his heavenly Father's will (Matthew 4:1–11). But, here in Exodus 17:2, 7, the word, 'test', is used of the people who were defying God by requiring him to act according to their demands, instead of trusting his wise and loving providence. In effect, their unbelieving attitude was driving a wedge between God and themselves.

To put it more succinctly, when it is God who tests his people, it is to draw them upwards and ever closer to himself whereas, when we are tempted by Satan, his intention is to draw us downwards and further away from God. James puts it like this: 'Let no one say when he is tempted, "I am being tempted by God," for God cannot be tempted with evil ... But each person is tempted when he is lured and enticed by his own desire. Then desire, when it has conceived gives birth to sin, and sin when it is fully grown brings forth death' (James 1:13–15). The testing referred to, in Exodus 17: 2 and 7, is a 'Siamese twin' along with the temptations of which Matthew and James both write—they are joined at the hip, so to speak.

Back to the first sense of testing, when it is God at work in us. The Lord's testing can be a sore experience and a time of painful refining of our faith while we wait for God to act. But when he does act and fulfil his word, what comfort and encouragement we receive. We see first-hand the evidence of the invisible God. We see him by what he does, in the same manner as we know the wind is blowing strongly by the way the trees bend before its powerful breath. I wonder if any of you who are reading this chapter are waiting for God to answer your hearts' yearning in some way? If so, do not become rebellious. Do not doubt him. He goes and stands before us at the place where the rock is, and from which the water of his life will flow.

The rock is Christ

Paul tells us, in 1 Corinthians 10, that the Rock is Christ (v. 4). In this way, he identifies the water that flowed from the cleft in the rock both with the claim of Jesus in John 7:37–39, and with the cup of blessing in the Lord's Supper. Before we consider Paul's words, we must first notice the promise of Jesus recorded by John: 'If anyone thirsts, let him come to me and drink.'

No one can doubt that there are longings and yearnings in every person's heart. Though originally created in the image and likeness of God, that image has been severely marred, though not entirely obliterated. The remaining faint reflection of our Creator's likeness in each living person is referred to by John when he writes, 'In him was life, and the life was the light of men. The light shines in the darkness, and the darkness has not overcome it' (John 1:4–5). This divine light in our souls is like the tiny pilot light in a gas central heating boiler; that frail glow will never heat the house, for it needs the main burner to be lit and then its powerful flame will do its work and fill the home with comforting warmth.

> The thirst in the human heart turns in many directions and towards many things that can never fully satisfy.

The thirst in the human heart turns in many directions and towards many things that can never fully satisfy. Isaiah pleaded with God's recalcitrant people, asking, 'Why do you spend your money for that which is not bread, and your labour for that which does not satisfy?' Unquestionably, his moving appeal came, unquestionably predicting Christ's appeal, 'Come, everyone who thirsts, come to the waters; and he who has no money, come, buy and eat' (Isaiah 55:1–2). Our fallen human natures yearn for fulfilment, and no one knew that better than Christ, who knows what is in all of our hearts and minds. Therefore, fulfilling Isaiah's prophecy, Jesus stood up and cried out to all who thirst to come and drink from him the water of life. Moreover, at the same time, he identified that water as a symbol of the Holy Spirit, who will make his dwelling in those who respond to his invitation. Thus, just as the water flowed from the Rock at Horeb, rivers of living water will flow from our inner beings as the Spirit of God resides in us.

We must turn to Paul's very relevant words in 1 Corinthians 10:1–5. The apostle wrote, 'They drank from the spiritual Rock that followed them, and the Rock was Christ.' The context of Paul's statement is the solemn warning that came from the water at Horeb, which sacramentally the Israelites drank, tasting the grace and heavenly gift of God. But, having drunk the water and eaten the manna, they turned aside into idolatry, immorality and grumbling. Therefore, 'with most of them God was not pleased, for they were overthrown in the wilderness' (v. 5).[8]

Again from 1 Corinthians 10:4–13, Paul also takes up the theme of Meribah: that is of the testing in which the Israelites engaged, provoking the anger of the God who had been leading them by the cloud that had first appeared at the Red Sea. All the apostle has to say here is based firmly on our passage from Exodus 17. He issues a solemn warning to all who claim to be believers: 'Let anyone who thinks that he stands take heed lest he fall' (v. 12). There can be neither pride, nor self-confidence, nor complacency on the part of anyone who has a place among the professing people of God. Scripture often repeats such warnings. The apostle Peter reminds his readers that their 'adversary the devil prowls around like a roaring lion, seeking someone to devour'. Therefore, they must 'be sober-minded', and 'watchful' (1 Peter 5:8). Martin Luther is reputed to have said that he dared not begin a new day until he had first fed upon God's Word and prayed into his heart and mind the message it had brought him.

However, after his warning, Paul then brings us a word of gracious assurance: 'No temptation has overtaken you that is not common to man. God is faithful, and he will not let you be tempted beyond your ability, but with the temptation he will also provide the way of escape, that you may be able to endure it' (v. 13). There are four points the apostle makes in these inspired words.

Firstly, Paul implies that, in the temptation, we are being pursued, for he says the temptation *overtakes* us. In other words, circumstances can pursue us with a choice between right or wrong; that choice may well have been hot on our heels for some time. On the other hand, temptation might be like some plant in a garden with delicious looking fruit; we know it can be harmful, but it seems so sweet hanging in the sun that we think there would be no harm in tasting it. However, it is toxic and could prove to be lethal.

Secondly, temptation is *common to us all*. Every single living person is tempted in one way or another. No one has a 'get out of jail free' card; no one is exempted (Hebrews 2:18).

Thirdly, before we say Paul has a morbid view of

human nature, see what he says next: 'God is faithful, and he will not let you be tempted beyond your ability' (1 Corinthians 10:13). God knows us better than we know ourselves, and he will not let the tempter push his attack on us too far. The implication is that it is God who is in control. The point when the temptation, which was for our hurt, is unmasked, instead of remaining a temptation, it mutates into being a trial intended by God for our good (1 Peter 1:6–8).

Fourthly, because God is always faithful, he 'will also provide the way of escape, that you may be able to endure it' (1 Corinthians 10:13). It is not that God lays on some trick for us, the way in crime novels the villain cunningly fakes his way out of the trouble he is in. Rather, the Lord uses natural means; maybe the doorbell rings and an 'angel' interrupts our folly. The Spirit will prompt us to stop, to think and to turn our thoughts to Jesus Christ and ask ourselves what he would have us say or do. It is when we obey the Holy Spirit's prompting that we will find 'the way of escape' being offered to us. The Lord is never so gracious as in the dark hour of temptation.

In conclusion, although believers are already clothed with the spotless righteousness of Christ—that is the meaning of our justification—our own personal righteousness is always imperfect in this life.[9] The Spirit's work in our sanctification is in order that the many imperfections in our personal righteousness should be purged or pruned day by day. For, as we journey towards the promised land and the city that has foundations whose designer and builder is God (Hebrews 11:10), we must constantly be cooperating with Christ's Spirit in purifying ourselves, so that when, at length, we arrive in his presence, and see him face to face, we shall be pure, even as he is pure.[10] This must daily be our blessed hope!

FOR FURTHER STUDY

1. See if you consider it feasible to harmonise the two recorded events of water flowing from the rock: firstly, here in Exodus 17:1–8 and secondly, in Numbers 20:1–14a. In the Exodus account, there are three place names: 'Rephidim' meaning 'resting places' (vv. 1 and 8); Massah and Meribah (v. 7). The Numbers account gives two place names: 'Kadesh', meaning 'a holy place' (vv. 1 and 14); 'Meribah' (v. 13). Can you offer a rationale for the two records being of the same event, or else a rationale for the Numbers account referring to a second similar event. (E.g., contrast Matthew 26:34 with Mark 14:30 and with John 18:25–27.)

2. See if you can find other examples in Scripture of the uncanny relationship between Meribah ('quarrelling') and Marah ('testing'). Bear in mind the implication that when people are 'testing' God, their sin can become God's action of 'testing' them.

TO THINK ABOUT AND DISCUSS

1. When Jeremiah was persecuted, beaten and put in the stocks, he remained faithful and courageously delivered God's message to his tormentor (Jeremiah 20:1–6). But then, grieved and depressed, he was angry with God (vv. 7–9 etc.). Have you ever been angry with God because the cross he has laid upon you has seemed too heavy for you to carry? What are your first reactions when you are angry with God? To phone your best friend, or to arrange to see your pastor, or to walk away from God in a huff? Read Numbers 20:2–9, especially verse 6.

2. Contrast Jonah in chapter 4 with Jesus in Luke 13:34–35; 19:41–44. When our anger comes under the control of the Holy Spirit, what effect can it have on our relationship with God (see Hebrews 5:7–10)?

3. The sources of temptation can be either subjective (from *inside* of ourselves) or objective (from circumstances *outside* of ourselves). To

conquer subjective temptations, what counsel does Paul give in 2 Timothy 2:22 (the verse breaks neatly into two parts)? What guidance does Peter give to help believers conquer objective temptations (1 Peter 4:8–9)?

4. If you got the main thrust of the answers to No. 3 above—regarding subjective temptations: 'Run away as fast as you can,' and the answer to objective temptations: 'Resist him; stand your ground,'—what kinds of allurements do you find so attractive that resisting temptation is never easy (e.g., see 1 John 2:15–17)?

24 The foolishness of prayer

Exodus 17:8–16

After God's gracious provision for a grumbling, unfaithful people, the devil tried another tactic on them through the attack of a war-like tribe. At the root, it was a spiritual attack on their very existence as the chosen people and, therefore, it needed a spiritual response—military resistance undergirded by prevailing prayer. And so, a memorial is set up as a reminder of the power of God working through Moses' intercession and the courage of Joshua.

The church and people of God are always called to be distinct from the world. Others looking on must know that we are called to trust in God and live in obedience to him. If we are faithful, we can expect opposition, especially when it comes to matters of morality and ethics. We only have to glance at the church's history to see that.

So it was with the Hebrew slaves, recently delivered

from Egypt. They were heading south through the Sinai desert, making for Mount Sinai where God was going to form them into a commonwealth, seal his covenant with them and reveal his laws to them. That was why the cloud and pillar of fire were leading them south, seemingly away from the Promised Land, instead of northeast towards it.

But just when they thought their troubles and afflictions were all behind them, they found themselves under attack from a war-like tribe—descendants of Esau (Genesis 36:12).[1] We learn from Deuteronomy 25:17–19 that the Amalekites had already cut off the stragglers who were lagging behind, weary and worn out; now they prepared to launch a frontal attack on the main company.

> Just when they thought their troubles and afflictions were all behind them, they found themselves under attack.

In the first part of the chapter, we have already seen how Moses struck the rock and a new abundant supply of water was provided. Water in the desert is always a jealously guarded, precious asset; therefore, I have suggested that the Amalekites wanted this completely new supply for themselves.[2] However, the age-long feud between Jacob and Esau in itself would have been sufficient cause for the attack, even if a newly found spring of fresh water had not come into the equation. And so, we have the account of Moses' prayers and Joshua's defence of the Lord's people.

The foolishness of prayer

Moses drew up a two-fold strategy. There were to be two actions which must be put into effect simultaneously. He would climb a nearby hill, along with Aaron and Hur,[3] and hold aloft his staff, while Joshua[4] would assemble the best fighting force he could muster and seek to repulse the Amalekite assault.

We need to recall what we have already learned about the shepherd's staff which Moses was to hold aloft as he prayed. Why always this staff? He had carried it with him when he met Pharaoh and demanded the slaves be released to worship their God. He had used it as he announced each of the plagues. He had stretched this shepherd's staff over the waters of the Red Sea as Pharaoh's pursuing forces closed in on the fleeing slaves. He had struck the rock at Horeb and the water had flowed from it (Numbers 20:11). And now, in the hour of dire peril, the staff is in his hand again. Why? Why always a shepherd's crook? And why was it always called 'the staff of God'?

We learn in the story of Joseph, several generations earlier, that shepherds and cattlemen were an abomination to the sophisticated Egyptians. Desert nomads did not have the Nile waters to wash in, or the expensive perfumes with which to anoint their bodies. Egyptian men shaved their heads and used cosmetic balms and oils on their skin; whereas, the nomadic shepherds grew long beards and hair, and probably rarely bathed. Apparently, they did not bother too much about body odour or about the strong smell of sheep and cattle on their clothes. So, the shepherd's crook was a sign of a despised people following a despised way of life. And Moses, this Bedouin shepherd, who came with his staff before the mighty Pharaoh, would have appeared to be a despised peasant. The message of the shepherd's staff was to become very clear. As Paul wrote:

> The foolishness of God is wiser than men, and the weakness of God is stronger than men. For consider your calling, [sisters and] brothers: not many of you were wise according to worldly standards, not many were powerful, not many were of noble birth. But God chose what is foolish in the world to shame the wise; God chose what is weak in the world to shame the strong; God chose what is low and despised in the world, even things that are not, to bring to nothing things that are, so that no human being might boast in the presence of God (1 Cor 1:25–29).

This is the foolishness of prayer.[5] In the early days of my ministry in my second congregation, where Robert Murray McCheyne had done his probationary training under John Bonar, older brother of Andrew and Horatius, I raised with some elders the issue of an evening when we would need accommodation for a prayer-meeting as the church halls were already fully booked. One elder mockingly suggested the manse garage; and another elder openly expressed his view that prayer was a waste of time—though he grudgingly conceded it might sometimes have some therapeutic benefit for people who were depressed, 'a bit like yoga', he said.

At that very early stage in the ministry, those men saw prayer in much the same way as the Amalekites would have viewed an old man in his eighties holding aloft a shepherd's staff. This war-like tribe lived by the sword, by robbery, by murder, by plunder. They would have been armed with huge clubs to strike a man dead with a single blow. A shepherd's staff would doubtless have been—as it had probably been at first for the Egyptians—a farcical joke. They could have snapped it in two over their knee! Today's atheists, sceptics and agnostics have much the same view of prayer: whistling in the wind, meaningless mumbo jumbo. As has been said to me often, 'I don't need religion; God helps those who help themselves.'

So, what then are the lessons of prayer here for us all?

1) THE PARADOX OF PRAYER

The paradox of prayer is summed up in the question, 'Why pray when God already knows?' Did not Jesus himself say, '… your Father knows what you need before you ask him' (Matthew 6:8)? Someone might say, 'Surely no one needed to pray about this situation. Hadn't God already delivered his people from slavery? Hadn't he opened up the way through the Red Sea? Hadn't he promised to take them to the land he had covenanted to give to their forefathers? If they truly believed in his word and his mighty acts, all they had to do was to sit back and wait for his deliverance.'

However, repeatedly we meet with this paradox in the Bible. In the Christian Scriptures, there is hardly a historical account of God in action without God's assurance of his deliverance only being activated when his people pray.

So here. Of course, God was going to preserve this ragamuffin band of escaped slaves; his redemptive purposes for the world, that would culminate in the birth of his Son, were to be fulfilled through them. Nevertheless, with God nothing can be taken for granted. Faith (and that implies prayer) and action must firmly clasp hands.

And so, Moses presented his right-hand man, Joshua, with a plan: 'Muster a defence force from among the strongest, fittest men, and go and repulse this attack threatening to annihilate us. Meanwhile, I will go with Aaron and Hur up yonder hill and pray.' It was a twofold strategy: action and prayer. A Puritan wrote this about prayer: 'In vain shall Moses be upon the hill, if Joshua be not in the valley. Prayer without means is a mockery of God.'

The apostle Paul puts it like this: 'For this I toil, struggling[6] with all his energy that he powerfully works within me' (Colossians 1:29). Action and prayer! Human effort plus divine empowerment!

The question as to why we should pray when God already knows what we need and what his purposes are, is one that I am not going to answer at this point. Rather I want to emphasize just now that prayer expresses explicitly our total dependence on God. As Jesus said, 'apart from me you can do nothing' (John 15:5).

> Prayer expresses explicitly our total dependence on God.

There is a verse in the old hymn, 'Stand up, stand up for Jesus', which says, 'Stand up, stand up for Jesus, stand in his strength alone, the arm of flesh will fail you, ye dare not trust your own.'[7]

One of my distinguished predecessors in my second congregation was an aristocrat called Robert Bruce, a direct descendant of Robert the Bruce; the same family today is that of Lord Elgin, whose great-great grandfather purloined the famous Elgin Marbles from Greece. Robert Bruce preached in the Larbert old Kirk from 1625 to 1631; the ruins of the original church buildings are still there in the graveyard. When I ministered in Larbert, I brought his gravestone into the present church foyer to preserve it from further erosion.

On one occasion the gathered congregation waited in vain for him to come from the vestry and so the elders sent the beadle to tell Master Bruce it was past the time for the service to begin. The beadle returned and said that the minister was having a heated argument with someone behind the closed vestry door. When asked what the argument was about, he answered that the minister was refusing to go into the Kirk until that person promised to go with him. Bruce was wrestling in prayer with Christ; he knew the Lord had said, '... apart from me you can do nothing'.[8] That is the paradox of prayer. God waits until we are depending wholly upon him before he visits us with his gracious answer.

2) THE PARTNERSHIP IN PRAYER (VV. 11–12)

Whenever Moses held up his hand, Israel prevailed, and whenever he lowered his hand, Amalek prevailed. But Moses' hands grew weary, so they took a stone and put it under him, and he sat on it, while Aaron and Hur held up his hands, one on one side, and the other on the other side. So his hands were steady until the going down of the sun.

It is a dramatic scene: an old man on a hill overlooking the sprawling Hebrew encampment, from which a small force of primitive men, armed with clubs, staves and maybe a few Egyptian swords they had brought with them, are struggling to drive back the war-like tribe's powerful attack. As long as Moses held aloft the shepherd's staff in his hand,[9] the repulse is winning, but when he takes a break to rest his tired arms, the attack presses back the defenders.

I taught for three years after I first graduated. I was in an English boys' comprehensive school in Guildford, Surrey. The Head Teacher was a most formidable man; he ruled both pupils and staff with a rod of iron and was universally feared. The school engaged a new science graduate, a delightful young fellow, but he could not keep control of any class. The Head Teacher got wind of this, and one day, unexpectedly, he entered the science lab when the boys were virtually rioting. He lined them all up against the classroom wall with their hands up above their heads and stalked up and down for about twenty minutes. As soon as a boy's arms began to flag, he was down on that boy like a ton of bricks, thundering in wrath with his face six inches from the boy's face. After fifteen or twenty minutes, many of the boys were crying with the pain of holding up their hands straight. At last, he allowed them to lower their arms. There was no more trouble from that or any other class, I can tell you![10]

Try it yourself. See how long you can hold your hands up straight above your head without flagging. You will all find after twenty minutes that it is hard going. No wonder then that an eighty-year-old needed a break now and again. But his breaks were proving disastrous for the defenders below in the valley. So, Aaron and Hur rolled a large boulder into position, sat Moses on it and the two of them stood on either side of him supporting his arms. In that way, the prayer continued unabated— for the raised staff was a sacrament of prayer—and the attackers were finally driven off.

> Praying alone is difficult. It is genuinely hard to concentrate long in prayer to God.

Praying alone is difficult. It is genuinely hard to concentrate long in prayer to God. It does help to pray out loud, but you can only do that if you have complete privacy. (I'm not speaking about reading through a long list of missionaries or others you have pledged yourself to pray for; I mean wrestling with God, face to face.) The parable of prayer being enacted here does not necessarily mean that the more people praying, the more effective prayer is. With certain safeguards, that may well be true. Rather, the meaning here for us all is that God intends prayer to be a partnership. In my personal experience, an almost literal application of the lesson of Moses, Aaron and Hur is that of the prayer triplet—three people covenanting to meet together regularly for prayer. But it does not need to be just three;

two, five, eight or ten create a partnership in prayer. It is that unity in prayer that is the point.

So, we learn here that praying alone is not easy. I would like to shake your hand if you can honestly say you find it easy to pray alone for a three- or four-hour stretch. I would love to sit at your feet and learn from you. It is certainly possible but that kind of wrestling with God demands huge commitment and determination. My own mother always rose at 4.30 a.m. to spend two hours in prayer before the thirty-six children she cared for were awakened.

Nevertheless, happy are those who have someone to pray with, because, on account of our human frailty, prayer at times should be a partnership. However willing our spirit, the flesh is weak, as Jesus said to his disciples who were sleeping in Gethsemane when he had asked them to support him in prayer, while he agonized alone, sweating from his brow dark drops of blood in his anguish of soul (Mark 14:32–42).

There is a very sad and tragic sequel to this struggle against the Amalekites. Several months later, after nine of the eleven spies, sent by Moses to reconnoitre the Promised Land, discouraged the people and said they would all be slaughtered if they tried to enter Canaan, some of them said, 'Nonsense, we beat the Amalekites last time and we can do it again.' Moses said, 'Don't try until God gives us the go-ahead.' But they ignored him and went against the Amalekites and were roundly defeated. Many of them were killed (Numbers 14:36–45). They vain-gloriously trusted in themselves, ignoring the Lord who had redeemed them.

What a picture of many of the church's endeavours today, and how often have congregations and individual believers acted with the same presumptuous spirit. If God is not with us in our plans and ventures, however well-intentioned they may be, either they will meet with disastrous results or simply fizzle out! One is tempted to compare some of our attempts with the derisive outcome of the futile endeavours of the sons of Sceva to exorcize an evil spirit (Acts 19:13–16). No doubt casual onlookers at first found the episode hilarious, but in truth it was a most salutary and serious warning. We read that, when the incident became known, 'fear fell upon them all' (Acts 19:17). God forbid that our foolish failures should lead to such a humiliating and chastening lesson.

3) PREVAILING IN PRAYER (VV. 15–16)
And Moses built an altar and called the name of it, The LORD is my banner, saying, 'A hand upon the throne of the LORD!'

An altar in the Old Testament invariably speaks of sacrifice: here, a sacrifice of thanksgiving –giving the glory to God in praise of him because, by his might and his banner, prayer had prevailed and the battle had been won. Thanksgiving made with a sacrifice, implies the thanksgiving was costly in spiritual terms rather than materially. But, as well as being erected for sacrifice, the altar was also built as a memorial. The word used for 'banner' is derived from the Hebrew word for a 'pole', suggesting the pole or banner was used in battle to rally the troops either to the point of defence or attack. But the Lord himself had been the 'banner', rallying the defenders to the conflict.

The ESV translates Moses' terse words literally: 'A hand upon the throne of the LORD'. The NIV's translation tries to give an explanation: 'For hands were lifted up to the throne of the Lord.' However, quite simply, it means that Moses' praying hands were directed towards the throne of grace.

We should also note in passing that the word, 'overwhelmed', in verse 13, simply implies that Amalek's attack was repulsed, not decisively defeated; they would live to see another day and would also continue to be implacable enemies of the Lord's people.

So, what memorials do you have in your life? Sacred reminders of God's grace towards you in your hour of need; reminders of times when you were at the end of your tether, all you cherished seemed about to be reduced to dust and ashes, but God stepped in and raised up his banner and preserved you. Or perhaps you were in a miry pit, the mud up to your knees and you were sinking deeper and deeper; then God heard your cry and lifted you up and set your feet on firm, solid ground, washing you clean and establishing you once again. Have your hands been lifted up in sacrificial, even costly, thanksgiving towards the throne of the Almighty, the merciful and righteous God of justice? Is he not our loving, tender, heavenly Father?

Of course, the greatest memorial of all is what Paul calls 'the thanksgiving' (in Greek, 'the *Eucharist*'), the Lord's Table with bread and wine, enabling us, in partnership and family bonds with each other spiritually, to partake by faith in the body and cleansing blood of the Saviour.

Yes, in the world's eyes prayer is often considered to be foolishness. But the foolishness of God is infinitely wiser than the wisdom of men (1 Corinthians 1:25). And the foolishness of prayer is this: that ignorant, weak, pathetic mortals may cast themselves upon the Lord, may kneel before the throne of the Almighty, at whose right hand is none other than his Son, exalted and Lord of all. Moreover, it is in the name of Jesus that we are invited, even commanded, to lift our hands towards that throne. Paradox, partnership, and thus prevailing prayer: this is the foolishness of the divine wisdom of prayer!

FOR FURTHER STUDY

1. One of the dominant themes of the Book of Daniel is prayer. Outline both the occasion and outcome of Daniel's *partnership* in prayer in Daniel 2; note verses 17–19. Similarly, outline both the occasion and outcome of Daniel's *faithfulness* in prayer in Daniel 6; note verse 10. Do not neglect the qualities of obedience and courage undergirding prayer in the Book of Daniel.

2. Make a list of the various petitions in three of Paul's prayers in Ephesians: firstly, 1:15–22; secondly, 3:14–21; thirdly, 6:16–20. Was the apostle unrealistic and over ambitious in his prayers for the Lord's people, and would it be appropriate for them to become models or templates for our prayers in our congregations today?

3. Is there biblical support for the suggestion that 'static prayer is an absurdity, like a songbird afraid of heights' or 'those who soar on wings like eagles ... like the saints who cut themselves adrift as a will-less piece of wood on the high seas of unfathomable love'?[11]

TO THINK ABOUT AND DISCUSS

1. Do a study of the Lord's Prayer in Matthew 6:9–13. Ask yourselves if can you see how the Trinity undergirds both parts of the Prayer—verses 9–10 and verses 11–13? Why are the pronouns plural: there is no 'me' or 'my' or 'mine', but only 'our' and 'us' and 'we'? What might Jesus have wanted us to be praying for when he used plural pronouns? Discuss the point of each use of a plural pronoun throughout the whole prayer.

2. Moses' prayer needed support because he was physically frail at 81 years old. Does that mean we also need support because of our human frailty? How can it be given? (Matthew 26:38–43; 2 Timothy 4:13a, 21a; Acts 12:12.)

3. As well as Moses needing support, Joshua also needed very direct

support (Exodus 17:11). Can you name any people you know who are engaged in spiritual warfare and who also need prayer support? How do you think we might fail them so that they find the conflict very hard? In what ways can we ourselves receive support, as Moses did, so that we can also support those on 'the front line' of spiritual warfare (Ephesians 6:12)?

4. Do you ever find prayer a lonely, difficult experience? If so, have you tried preaching to yourself a sermon from the Bible passage you have just read, and using your sermon from the Word to stimulate your soul to pray? Discuss how this might help you when you find prayer difficult.

5. Do you have any memorials as reminders of answered prayer? If so, would you feel able to share them with others for their encouragement?

25 Jethro, priest of Midian

Exodus 18

An excellent example of good family relationships is provided in the visit of Jethro to the Israelite encampment in order to unite his son-in-law with his family. Firstly, both men show mutual piety, joining together in an act of worship; secondly, mutual respect is evidenced as Jethro speaks wisely to Moses, who for his part shows wise humility in following the older man's counsel. Consequently, righteous governance of the people of God throughout the ages is foreshadowed in this chapter.

Here is an interesting quotation—words said to have been spoken during an impassioned sermon by a preacher whose fame is stamped indelibly upon European history. I wonder if it strikes a chord in the thinking of some who read it.

The world is passing through troubling times.

> The young people of today think of nothing but themselves. They have no reverence for parents or old age. They are impatient of all restraint. They talk as if they knew everything, and what passes for wisdom with us is foolishness with them. As for the girls, they are forward, immodest and unladylike in speech, behaviour and dress.

It is attributed to Peter the Hermit and so was spoken about one thousand years ago.[1] My point in quoting a medieval preacher is that his sentiments could refer to virtually any generation.

Recently I watched a television documentary on violent children and was distressed to see an eight-year-old boy viciously kicking his mother, spitting at her, beating her and defying her every word. I know that cases like that indicate an extremely disturbed background, and that such behaviour requires specialized care (which of course was the reason for the documentary). Nevertheless, from their early teenage years many boys and girls appear to be increasingly defiant towards their parents. So-called 'peer pressure' is generally held to be a significant factor, along with the invasive influences of the social media.

Compared to the days of Peter the Hermit, in our present generation the problem has been greatly exacerbated through an extremely high percentage of children from the age of ten years upwards possessing smart mobile phones. The former chief rabbi of the United Hebrew Congregations of the Commonwealth, Lord Jonathan Sacks, in his final publication a few months before his death in November 2020, published a major study on western *Morality* (that is the book's title)[2] in which he examines the harmful effect of the abuse of mobile phones. The results of his research make chilling reading. Self-harm, hard porn, social abuse of others, bullying and social isolation of many young teens—these and a multiplicity of other problems have infiltrated society through the apps available on smart phones. Two years after the book was published, I shared some of his statistics with a friend who taught in a Scottish High School. She was quite confident in asserting that already some of his statistics were out of date; for example, she declared that well over 90% of boys had watched hard porn by the time they reached the age of fourteen.

Reverence and respect for family and elders is one of the notable features of this chapter in Exodus. In addition, there is the priestly action of Moses' father-in-law, followed by his wise counsel, which Moses humbly accepted. We take each of these three themes in turn.

Respect for elders (vv. 1–9)

There is a division of opinion as to why and when Moses'
wife and children had been sent to be cared for by Jethro,
Zipporah's father: 'Jethro, Moses' father-in-law, had
taken Zipporah, Moses' wife, after he had sent her
home, along with her two sons' (vv. 2–3a). Probably the
most common view is that his family returned home
immediately after the incident when Moses nearly
died and his wife saved his life by circumcising his son
(Exodus 4:24–26); they were not to be subjected to the
undoubted dangers that would threaten them in Egypt.
Thus, argues this view, they had never been in Egypt,
for Moses was determined to protect them from the
ruthless cruelty of Pharaoh.

Calvin, however, strongly disagrees with this
suggestion, and argues that such an action would have
been both cowardly and deceitful. Why? He insists
that Moses' own family had to experience, along with
himself, the dire conditions inflicted on the Lord's
people in Egypt; more importantly, they also had
to share in the redemption, accomplished when the
destroying angel 'passed over' each home marked by the
blood on the lintels and doorposts.[3]

As to when Zipporah took her sons to visit Jethro,
Calvin writes that Moses had yielded to the desire which
was natural to her as a woman, or, 'induced by his own

feelings of piety, he wished to show respect to an old man so closely connected to him.'[4] I am attracted to Calvin's view, not least on account of the profound respect that Moses exhibits towards Jethro in this chapter.

In our modern world of instant communication between cities and across continents, we might wonder how it was that Jethro, with no internet or mobile telephone, knew that Moses would be 'encamped at the mountain of God' (v. 5). My parents worked as pioneer missionaries during the 1920s and 30s, in the depths of the Ituri forests of north-east Congo, where they never ceased to be amazed at how news rapidly spread from remote village to remote village. There was an unseen 'bush telegraph' so that, within a few hours, word inexplicably spread across the scattered population of a huge, isolated area. Part of the explanation was that it was communicated by drumbeat, but in whatever way it happened, news invariably spread!

One obvious suggestion is that Moses had told Zipporah the Lord's promise to him had been that he would 'worship (serve) God on this mountain' (Sinai, also known as Horeb, Exodus 3:1, 12). But it is also probable that the progress and whereabouts of the escaped slaves would have been well known throughout the Sinai desert, including their arrival at Mount Sinai.

An interesting scenario is implied in verse 6. Having arrived at the outskirts of the widespread Israelite encampment, with its network of criss-crossed pathways between the makeshift tents, Jethro and the little family sat down to rest under one of the booths erected to provide shade from the desert sun. He then sent a message to his son-in-law telling him of their arrival: 'I, your father-in-law Jethro, am coming to you with your wife and her two sons.' The next verse tells us that Moses set out from the centre of the camp to greet and welcome his beloved family.

Of course, Moses would have embraced his wife and two sons. But that was not his purpose or priority in recording this account for us, and eastern modesty would have inhibited him from sharing such details. His subject is Jethro and the lessons to be learned from this figure about whom we know so little. Intentionally emphasized is the profound respect Moses showed to his father-in-law. The AKJV translation that Moses 'did obeisance and kissed him', beautifully expresses the honour he gave to the senior man.

> Intentionally emphasized is the profound respect Moses showed to his father-in-law.

The Lord's command regarding reverence towards our elders is spelled out for us in Leviticus 19:32: 'You shall stand up before the grey head and honour the face of an old man, and you shall fear your God: I am the LORD.' Little attention is paid today to such respectful manners. Far too often the elderly are regarded as now 'past their sell-by date'! And yet, here in the Scriptures, reverence for the elderly is linked directly to reverence for the Lord our God. The clear implication is that those who honour God must likewise honour their elders.

Of course, there is a necessary corollary to this. The apostle Paul points out that, within the family, parents for their part must never be harsh with their children: 'Fathers, do not provoke your children to anger …' (Ephesians 6:4a). Parents must accept God's grace and kindness as the example to be followed: 'God draws us to our duty by showing that he seeks nothing else but our welfare and benefit, in order that we should with a frank heart receive the yoke that he lays upon our shoulders.'[5] Colossians 3:21 has a parallel passage: 'Fathers, do not provoke your children, lest they become discouraged.'

Hendriksen suggests six ways in which parents can provoke their children to anger. Firstly, by over-protection; secondly, by favouritism; thirdly, by discouragement; fourthly, by failure to make allowances that a growing child will develop ideas of their own; fifthly, by neglect; sixthly, by bitter words and actions that can be cruel.[6]

Of course, fondly cherishing our children does not exclude firmness, as the apostle continued in his exhortation to fathers that they should 'bring them up in the discipline and instruction of the Lord' (Ephesians

6:4). We tend to think of discipline as punishment, but it has the same derivation as 'disciple' which means, 'a pupil', or, 'one who is learning'. Disciples give allegiance to the one who is their teacher. So, we should understand discipline to have a positive meaning as well as the often-adopted negative sense of inflicting chastening. (Of course, punishment will often be administered with a view of instructing the pupil.)

In brief, the Old Testament teaching of profound respect and reverence for one's elders is based on the wise, gracious, firm and righteous love that God displays to those whose relationship with him is as his spiritual children.

The priesthood of Jethro (vv. 8–12)

My own view is that Jethro was most probably a 'henotheist',[7] and that he believed in many gods but was prepared to admit that one God was supreme and above them all. It is certain that 'henotheism' was widespread in ancient Israel, for we find the later prophets mocking the idolatry of neighbouring tribes, whose 'idols [gods] are silver and gold ... they have mouths but do not speak; eyes but do not see. They have ears but do not hear; noses but do not smell. They have hands but do not feel; feet but do not walk ...' (Psalm 115:4–7).[8]

Manasseh, for example, while not denying the existence of the Lord God of Israel, was a believer in various other gods and even set up, in Solomon's temple, idols that he had made (2 Chronicles 33:1–9). Nor was he the only offender in idolatrous worship. Israel's tragic story was littered with continuous flirtations and spiritual adultery with pagan deities, all of which brought God's heavy chastening hand upon his unfaithful people.

Nonetheless, Moses recounted to his father-in-law 'all that the Lord had done to Pharaoh and to the Egyptians for Israel's sake ... and how the Lord had delivered them.' The verb 'told', in verse 8, is the same word translated, 'proclaimed', in 9:16. 'And Jethro rejoiced for all the good that the Lord had done to Israel ...' (vv. 8–9). It cannot be doubted that Moses' record of his meeting with Jethro, and the response made to the account of the deliverance from Egypt, was intended to show that the older man had become a firm believer in Israel's God. And so, we have a clear testimony from Jethro, as he blessed the Lord for his gracious deliverance of his people, and his unhesitating affirmation of faith: 'Now I know[9] that the Lord is greater than all gods, because in this affair they dealt arrogantly with the people' (v. 11). Though Jethro's words do not necessarily deny the existence of other gods, nevertheless they convincingly acknowledge their total overthrow by Israel's God.

Generally, in the Christian Scriptures, as the apostle

points out, faith comes through hearing the Word of God (Romans 10:17). [10] But the Lord's work in a person's heart and life cannot be restricted to this general rule. God is able to work in unexpected ways. A parallel example to the account of Jethro's faith is that of Rahab the harlot. She also testified, as Jethro had done, '[now] I know', as she risked her life by protecting the two spies whom Joshua had sent to reconnoitre the defences of Jericho: 'I know

> Generally, faith comes through hearing the Word of God. But the Lord's work in a person's heart and life cannot be restricted to this general rule.

that the LORD has given you the land, and that the fear of you has fallen upon us ... For we have heard how the LORD dried up the water of the Red Sea ...' (Joshua 2:9–10). *I know ... For we have heard!* As far as we are aware, she had not heard of the sacrificial lamb and its shed blood—not as yet anyway. But she had heard of God's mighty acts of deliverance, and what she had heard had been sufficient for the Holy Spirit to create and inspire faith in her heart and soul.

Back then to Jethro, and to the burnt offering and sacrifices that he brought to God (v. 12). The 'burnt offering' was most probably a whole burnt sacrifice when the entire offering was consumed by fire as a thanksgiving to the Lord—nothing being eaten by the worshippers. The 'sacrifices' were most probably for a communal meal, eaten together in the presence of God, as in Exodus 24:11, where we read that the elders 'beheld God and ate and drank', presumably using the peace offerings mentioned in 24:5.[11]

Whatever had been the background and former religious practices of Moses' father-in-law, 'the priest of Midian' (v. 1), we may be assured that on this occasion he offered a sincere and legitimate offering to the God of Israel. Otherwise, Moses, Aaron and the elders would never have taken part in this solemn act of worship, which it is explicitly stated was 'before God'. He would have acted as the priest because he was the elder within his family, in the same way in which Abraham and the patriarchs sacrificed by right of being the elder in their families.[12] The Law had not yet been given and so at this point in time there was liberty both for Jethro to officiate and for the elders to participate. The 'bread' would have been *manna*.

Although we are given only the briefest of details regarding the act of worship that Jethro led and in which Moses, Aaron and the elders shared, we are told that it was done 'before God'. This was the God whose mighty acts were fresh in the hearts and minds of those who participated. Very recently he had provided bread in the wilderness, water from the rock, and mighty victory over a strong enemy hell-bent on what today we would call ethnic cleansing—the eradication of these twelve tribes from the face of the earth. In other words, the God before whom they ate was an awesome God, greatly to be feared, reverenced and obeyed. The hearts of the worshippers would have been brimming over with gratitude.

Believers today should eat and drink with no less a profound solemnity while partaking of our simple meal of bread and wine when we celebrate Christ our Passover who has been sacrificed for us. We too are witnesses of his immense and incomprehensible love in giving himself as our ransom, delivering us from the enemy of our souls and washing away the dark guilt that indelibly stains our souls. We too partake of heavenly manna as we feast on Christ's sacrificial meal 'before God'—our awesome God of burning holiness. Like the priest of Midian, we have heard of and believed the mighty acts of divine justice and love worked out in our redemption. Do our hearts always overflow with tears of gratitude as, like the tax collector, we leave God's house fully justified (declared righteous) in his sight (Luke 18:13–14)?

Jethro's advice (vv. 13–17)

Suggestions have been made that the event recorded in verses 10–27 probably occurred after the Law had been given, by which time the multiplicity of civil regulations had been given. But it should be noted that 'commandments' and 'statutes' had already been referred to earlier in 15:26 when the Israelites had been warned to 'give ear to his commandments and keep all his statutes'. However, the timing is not the issue here; rather it is the focus upon the necessity for pastoral care, along with Jethro's wise counsel to his overworked son-in-law. Although it is clearly stated in verse 13 that Jethro's intervention took place the day after the burnt offering and sacrifices, as I have just suggested, the events recorded in verses 10–12 could well have occurred some days or even weeks after the reunion of Moses with his wife, two sons and father-in-law.

It appears that Moses had to deal with two separate issues every day. The first was instruction to persons or families regarding the will of God for their daily lives; the people constantly were coming to Moses 'to inquire of God' (v. 15). The second issue was adjudicating in disputes that arose. In verse 16, Moses appears to make a distinction between these two: 'When they have a dispute, they come to me and I decide between one person and another'; further, 'I make them know the statutes of God and his laws.' It may not always have been necessary for these two responsibilities to have been part and parcel of a single issue.

To put this another way, sometimes it may have been necessary to give an explanation from God's laws as to the reason for the verdict Moses pronounced upon a dispute. But at other times, enquiries he had to deal with may well simply have been instructions such as how the head of a family ought to act in a particular situation. It is easy to see how, since the Reformation, the office of the eldership in reformed churches has inherited from Moses these two responsibilities—adjudication in disputes and instruction for Christian believers.

Bridging the gap stretching over many centuries from Moses up to the establishment of the New Testament Church of Christ, it has been the responsibility in ancient Israel of priests to undertake these tasks, first entrusted to them through the wise counsel of Jethro. Thus, when Aaron's duties were passed on to him by God, included in them was the role of adjudicator and teacher: firstly, 'You are to distinguish between the holy and the common, and between the unclean and the clean,' and secondly, 'You are to teach the people of Israel all the statutes that the LORD has spoken to them by Moses' (Leviticus 10:10, 11)[13]. Malachi re-iterated this teaching commission: 'For the lips of a priest should guard knowledge, and people should seek instruction from his mouth, for he is the messenger of the LORD of hosts' (Malachi 2:7).

There is a final point that must be made regarding Jethro's advice. It is the humility of Moses as he listened to his father-in-law's criticism of the way in which he took upon himself the full burden of the people's needs for guidance in the various issues that arose every day. 'You and the people with you will certainly wear yourselves out, for the thing is too heavy for you. You are not able to do it alone' (v. 18). There is many a man who would have resented such a direct criticism and would have reacted very differently. After all, was not Moses the great leader who had seen the overthrow of the mighty Pharaoh and brought this great host through desperately dangerous trials?

But no, Moses knew that he was merely an instrument in the Lord's hands. He would have gladly adopted the words of the psalmist many centuries later: 'Not to us, O LORD, not to us, but to your name give glory, for the sake of your steadfast love and faithfulness' (Psalm 115:1).

> Moses knew that he was merely an instrument in the Lord's hands.

Indeed, the trials through which he had passed had repeatedly unveiled to him his own helplessness when faced by a recalcitrant, angry mob, to say nothing of the threat from a greatly superior foe. The past fraught months as God's chosen messenger had made abundantly plain to Moses, not only his own human frailty, but also the 'steadfast love and faithfulness' of the God to whom the psalmist attributed all the glory. And so, meekly, humbly, he accepted Jethro's excellent counsel, and went ahead and set up a structure that became established throughout Israel.

The criteria enunciated by Jethro for those to be appointed to share the burden, points forward to the New Testament church's practice in appointing deacons and elders. They had to be instructed in God's ways; today we would say that they needed to be trained. 'You shall warn them about the statutes and the laws and make them know the way in which they must walk and what they must do' (v. 20). Moreover, they had to be persons of exemplary character: 'Look for able men from all the people, men who fear God, who are trustworthy and hate a bribe ...' (v. 21).

In the early church, the apostles faced a similar situation to Moses, when they found themselves being bogged down by very necessary administrative duties, which were proving to be distractions from their main calling of teaching the Word of God. It is highly likely that it was then that they may well have recalled Jethro's wise counsel to his son-in-law. Be that as it may, they concluded that they must 'pick out ... seven men of good repute, full of the Spirit and of wisdom, whom we will appoint to this duty' (Acts 6:3). The appointment of the seven deacons appears to have been a precedent for Paul's description in 1 Timothy 3:1–13 of 'overseers' or 'elders' in the early church.[14]

The suggestion has been made that the apostle's

first words in 3:1, 'The saying is trustworthy: If anyone aspires to the office of overseer, he desires a noble task,' could well have been prompted by a request from the early churches for Paul to adjudicate on the standards required of elders or overseers. Who could doubt that, knowing the Old Testament Scriptures as he did, what Paul writes was inspired and guided by Jethro's advice in Exodus 18:19–23, as well as by the established practice thereafter in the Old Testament Church of God before Christ's incarnation.

I recall how, several years ago, the chief administrator for ministry in the Church of Scotland stated that seventy per cent of ministers in the Kirk were suffering seriously from burnout—that is, from total spiritual, mental and physical exhaustion. In my own personal experience of the work of ministry, as well as through the task to which I was later assigned, to be a 'pastor to pastors', I can say without fear of contradiction that the problems which overtook Moses have been similar to the problems that have afflicted and weighed down ministers in our day. Far too many have been distracted and discouraged by wearisome duties that ought to be done by others. I suspect that today many young ministers are still being launched into their sacred task without any clear idea of the essential and overriding priorities of Christian ministry.

The second half of this 18th chapter of Exodus is the

place in Scripture to which we must all turn afresh. The lessons that Moses learned all of 3000 years ago are still as relevant today as when they were practised among nomadic Israel during her wilderness wanderings. Our Bibles are always so relevant and up to date, manifestly because human nature has not changed, nor have our problems changed. Yet, we still fail to take sufficiently seriously the lessons that the Holy Spirit has recorded for us. May we learn the same childlike humility of this great servant of God, Moses, the messenger and mediator.

FOR FURTHER STUDY

1. Calvin states: 'These words, *Shepherd, Minister, Bishop, Elder,* are in holy writ taken for all one, that is to say, for them which are called in the Church of God to teach, and to rule his house.' Why does he not include 'deacons' in this list? In 1 Timothy 3, they are mentioned separately to elders (see verse 1 for *episcopes* and 8 for *diakonos*).

2. Comparing and contrasting the duties of Old Testament *priesthood* (self-evidently, there are continuities and discontinuities) with the New Testament *eldership*, draw up a list of responsibilities (in modern parlance, a job description) for both the OT offices and the NT offices in the Church of God.

3. Is burn-out in the Christian ministry still a danger to be guarded against? In what ways ought the leadership team in a congregation undertake to pastor their pastor?

TO THINK ABOUT AND DISCUSS

1. Is there genuinely a difference today between the attitudes and behaviour of young people in the days of Peter the Hermit compared to young people in this third decade of the 21st century? If you think there is indeed a significant difference, give reasons for your opinions.

2. What guidelines could be suggested to Christian parents regarding the use of smart phones by their children? Is there an age limit after which any 'rules' should be put to one side and young people left to manage their own devices? If so, how could parents prepare their children for that stage in life?

3. Read Malachi 2:7. Has there ever been an occasion when you disagreed with your pastor in either his interpretation of a Bible passage or else with his application of it to the daily lives of his congregation? If it is not an insignificant disagreement, but something you felt strongly about, what would be the biblical way of dealing with such a difference of opinion? See 1 Cor. 3:4, 18; Phil. 2: 2–3, 12; 4:2–3; Col. 3:12–15; 1 Thess. 5:12–13.

26 The covenant declaration

Exodus 19:1–8

The foundational terms of the covenant in this passage disclose to us, who are living on the nearside of the cross, the mind and will of God for his chosen people. For, one of the fascinating aspects of Old Testament study is tracing the amazing unfolding of the divine plan as the time slowly draws near for the final unveiling of the Word made flesh. The importance of the Scripture passage for this chapter cannot be over emphasized. For, the terms of the Sovereign God's gracious, but all-embracing, demands on those whom he has redeemed are never rescinded until they are finally fulfilled in the Person and Work of Christ.

The chapter begins by giving precise details as to when and where the covenant was made. Chapter 17 related how, in answer to Moses' prayers with his hands held aloft by Aaron and Hur as he clutched the 'staff of God', the Lord had delivered his people from the fierce attack on them by the Amalekites. That had taken place at Rephidim, possibly the most fertile area in the Sinai desert. We also saw how water from the rock had been graciously provided. Now, a few weeks later, at the beginning of the third month since their departure from Egypt, God was about to make his covenant with them. Therefore, he led them on to encamp at the foot of Mount Sinai. It was at this point that there was unfolded one of the most important events in God's ongoing revelation of his divine grace in their election and redemption.

God has always spoken using words and ideas that are familiar to us. Think of Jesus' parables, and the way in which he often took the most ordinary things of everyday life, such as a lost coin, a lost sheep, a runaway son or a farmer sowing. That is what we have here in Exodus 19. Here is the background.

Mackay puts it like this:

> The law is presented in the context of covenant. Although it does not follow precisely the structure of ancient treaties between an emperor and his subject people, it is modelled after them. The Lord is the Great King, the suzerain, and he tells his people how they can live in a way that pleases him. Their response is not engendered by some slavish fear, but

is to flow from gratitude at all the Lord has done for them.[1]

The structure to which Mackay is referring had four distinct stages, and they are identifiable in these verses. Firstly, the victor was declared and acknowledged. Secondly, the victor then offered a peace settlement. Thirdly, even before the terms were dictated, the conquered side agreed to accept them, and so they pledged their loyalty. Fourthly, for his part, the victor promised his loyalty to the terms he will lay down. These elements are here and they are to be spelled out, enriched and given the fullest meaning that will grow and blossom throughout the whole Bible. Their final fulfilment was to be in the New Covenant sealed in the blood of Christ, our Victor.

The Victor is acknowledged.

'You yourselves have seen what I did to the Egyptians, and how I bore you on eagle's wings and brought you to myself' (v. 4). God is declared to be the Victor. It was not that he had fought against Israel but rather, having fought for Israel, he had delivered them from their oppressors and had brought them out of slavery. The Lord God had

The Lord God had been triumphant, and his people had experienced his glory for themselves.

been triumphant, and his people had experienced his glory for themselves. Moreover, his might and power had been repeatedly confirmed. There had been the crossing of the Red Sea, the bitter water made sweet, the provision of manna and the water from the rock.

At this point, we have to fast forward the tape and proceed straight to Christ, for he is the Person of whom the victory in these earlier chapters of Exodus is constantly speaking. He is the Passover Lamb, the bread from heaven and the water from the rock. The baptism of Israel into Moses at the Red Sea foreshadowed our baptism into the resurrection of the living Lord.

The desert wanderings of the Israelites are a type of our journey through the wilderness of this world, during which the Saviour bears our grief and carries our sorrows. He is the Victor who has defeated death and has been raised triumphant. Thus, as often as believers gather together to praise him and partake of the sacramental bread and wine, they are declaring his victory and acknowledging his Lordship over all. For Jesus Christ is Lord.

The Victor's peace terms must be accepted.

The offer of peace terms, that must be accepted even before they were outlined, was called initiating a covenant. Such a covenant was a mutual agreement that guaranteed peace. The party who offered the covenant had the right to demand acceptance of its terms even before they were disclosed. Here in Exodus, the terms that are going to be given find their focus in the Ten Commandments in chapter 20. Therefore, we read in verse 5: 'If you will indeed obey my voice and keep my covenant ...', followed in verse 8 by, 'All the people answered together and said, "All that the LORD has spoken we will do".'

Christ the Victor offers us peace, but as Conqueror he demands our full obedience and complete surrender. None of us can enjoy or fully enter into the peace of his covenant until we unconditionally render him our obedience. In one way, it might appear that we are risking and gambling our future on terms that we do not yet fully know. In normal everyday life, it would be foolish to sign a contract with some supplier of household goods or services without first carefully reading the terms and conditions. Therefore, at first sight it might seem totally unreasonable that we are asked to pledge obedience to Christ without having had his terms and conditions fully explained to us. Nevertheless, that is how it is, for Jesus Christ says to us, 'Give me your heart, your life and your will. Then when you have given yourself completely to me, I will tell you what I will do for you and what you must do for me.'

However, we must not forget that these seemingly imperious demands are completely reasonable. For, we must remember that not only had God already delivered his people from their slavery but, in apparently impossible circumstances, he had also provided for them in a remarkable way. In other words, he had shown himself to be a God who cared for them with a love that was completely undeserved. They had been given a glimpse into his fatherly provision. It was entirely in the light of their experience of him over these past three months that he was now asking them to put their trust wholly upon him. He was the God who had borne them on eagles' wings and brought them to himself.

The Jesus, whose similar imperious demand is to yield ourselves to his lordship over our lives, is the same Jesus who has suffered and died for us. Why do we then sometimes shrink back from him? Why question him and ask, 'But what are you going to ask me to do, Lord? Tell me first, then I'll decide whether I'll yield to you.' Too easily we forget that we are dealing with the Son of God, the Lord of glory, and we cannot come to him demanding first to know his terms. Many do try first to put before him their personal terms and conditions. That is never the way to a partnership with the Lord of Calvary, the risen and ascended Redeemer.

There are many biographies of godly Christian women and men who have answered Christ's call and unconditionally yielded to him; their stories invariably have proved his faithfulness. One thinks of a man like

C. T. Studd who, in 1913, after service in both China and India, left all at the age of fifty-three to go to the heart of Africa, where he worked until his death in 1931. The year before he died, he had been made a Chevalier of the Royal Order of the Lion by the King of the Belgians. The missionary society he founded remains today one of the largest in the world. However, after Studd had left for Belgian Congo, a scrap of paper was found in the wastepaper basket in his study, on which he had scribbled these words, 'If Jesus Christ be God and died for me, then no sacrifice can be too great for me to make for him.'[2] (These words became a kind of motto for Studd and he loved repeating them.)

The Victor promises faithfulness to his covenant.

Firstly, we should notice in passing that Moses is receiving a further vitally important role in that he is to be the recipient of the Victor's message to the people. In effect, he will be acting as the mediator between God and his chosen people. Secondly, the solemnity of this commission is emphasized by the double designation of the recipients of the message as 'the house of Jacob … and the people of Israel' (v. 3). 'This will be no casual proposal, but the solemnly set out terms of the covenant between the Suzerain and his vassal people. Moses is to act as the royal messenger, bringing the overlord's terms to the people.'[3]

There is a great word that is used scores of times throughout the Bible. In Hebrew it is *hesed*, meaning 'steadfast love'.[4] It refers to the unfailing, faithful love which Christ has for all who have responded to his terms and conditions; without yet having read them they have responded to his summons and cast themselves wholly upon him who gave his life for them, and now lives to be their Lord and Master. Although the word, *hesed*, is not actually used here, verses 4–6 unquestionably exemplify this amazing grace of God towards his undeserving people.

What is the unconditional promise that he makes to those who accept his Word, not yet having read his terms and conditions? It is, 'You shall be my treasured possession.' Although the Victor now controlled the entire land that he had conquered, nevertheless he reserved part of it for his special, personal use. In the same verse 5, God had said, 'all the earth is mine' but you are to be my special possession, my treasure, my delight.

The slaves whom he had delivered had nothing whatsoever to offer God. Indeed, it was the opposite. We have already seen how fickle, faithless and ungrateful they could be. Yet, God had chosen them to be his own treasured possession. The giving was all on God's side. He loved them; why?—because he loved them (Deuteronomy 7:7–8)![5] Indeed, we read later on, in Deuteronomy 9:6–8, Moses' words in this respect:

Know, therefore, that the Lord your God is not giving you this good land to possess because of your righteousness, for you are a stubborn people. Remember and do not forget how you provoked the Lord your God to wrath in the wilderness. From the day you came out of the land of Egypt until you came to this place, you have been rebellious against the Lord. Even at Horeb you provoked the Lord to wrath, and the Lord was so angry with you that he was ready to destroy you.

It is the mystery of our faith that God should choose us to be his special possession, his treasure. God longs to delight in us, to lavish us with his love, to enjoy our friendship and to bless us. His love is unmerited and gratuitous. 'Nothing in my hand I bring, simply to thy cross I cling.'[6]

Yes, his grace and favour are freely and unconditionally bestowed, and can never depend on our human merits, which before God always fall far short of his holy standards. Nevertheless, his subsequent blessing on those whom he has chosen is invariably conditional upon their penitent and humble obedience. Scripture abounds with warnings to the Lord's people not to turn aside from following him, lest his chastening hand should fall heavily upon them.[7] The Psalmist was fully aware of this conditionality of blessing when he wrote, 'If I had cherished iniquity in my heart, the LORD would not have listened' (Psalm 66:18).

A respectful biblical balance must be maintained by Christians today. Taken for granted, God's gratuitous grace can become a snare in which believers may become entangled. They can be lured into a false confidence of thinking that, because the gifts and calling of God are irrevocable, they can do as they please but still retain their salvation. Such behaviour is what Paul called receiving the grace of God in vain: 'We appeal to you not to receive the grace of God in vain' (2 Corinthians 6:1). Indeed, much of the story of the Israelites concerns their grievous sufferings as God severely chastened them because, though they were his chosen elect, they were taking his grace for granted and perversely playing fast and loose with his divine kindness to them.

We must not ignore the explicit implication that being 'my treasured possession among all peoples' and 'a holy nation' means that those who are called and chosen are to be distinct and, in a sense, separate from 'all (other) peoples'. Though believers are never called to become hermits who cut themselves off from the world, nevertheless there must be a visible and genuine difference between those who follow Christ and others who do not. The phrase sometimes used is that 'we are to be in the world, but not of the world'.

Universal priesthood of believers

The important phrase, 'a kingdom of priests' (v. 6), is one of the 'seeds' of the ongoing, cumulative unfolding of God's purposes for his people, which is such a fundamental aspect of the Old Testament's relationship to the New Testament. For example, now that this particular 'seed' had grown and come to fruition through Christ's completed work, Peter picked up all the four phrases in these verses in Exodus 19 when he applied them to believers of all nationalities:

> The important phrase, 'a kingdom of priests', is one of the 'seeds' of the ongoing, cumulative unfolding of God's purposes for his people.

> But you are a *chosen race*, a *royal priesthood*, a *holy nation*, a *people for his own possession*, that you may proclaim the excellencies of him who called you out of darkness into his marvellous light. Once you were not a people [he is writing to Gentiles], but now you are God's people; once you had not received mercy, but now you have received mercy (1 Peter 2:9–10).

But what was the initial meaning of 'a kingdom of priests' and how could it apply to ancient Israel, centuries before Christ had been born? The meaning for the children of Israel was that, surrounded as they would be by idolatrous nations ('if you will indeed obey my voice and keep my covenant'), they were to be conspicuously different, enjoying both priestly and royal dignity—'a kingdom of priests'. They would be *priests* in that they would have a unique access into God's holy presence[8]; they would be *princes* in that they would live as free men and women, and not be subservient to a despot, most of whom in their day were cruel tyrants.

Although the Aaronic priesthood was not yet established, priests apparently already functioned among them (v. 22), and most probably, as with Abraham, the head of the family already had the prerogative of drawing near to God with a sacrifice. But there was another aspect of the priesthood that was to emerge, namely that of setting an example of holiness. The high priest's headdress would bear a golden plate with these words inscribed on it: 'Holy to the LORD' (Exodus 28:36). God's purpose for his redeemed people was that they should be acknowledged as being different from the surrounding nations. They were to be witnesses both to God's moral standards and to his grace and power in blessing them.[9]

The priesthood of believers (Revelation 1:6) today means that we have no need of a human priest to bring us into the Holy of Holies, for we have direct access 'by the blood of Jesus, by the new and living way that he opened for us through the curtain, that is, through his flesh' (Hebrews 10:19–20). Therefore, we are bidden 'with confidence [to] draw near to the throne of grace, that we may receive mercy and find grace to help in time of need' (Hebrews 4:16). The risen, glorified Christ is our great high priest; we have no need of any other mediator to grant us access to our heavenly Father.

FOR FURTHER STUDY

1. Using Mackay's four points of the contemporary covenants agreed by the conqueror with his new Kingdom, can you trace similar elements in 'the new covenant in the blood' of Christ (Luke 22:20), starting with Jeremiah 31:31–34 (Ezekiel 36:22–27), and especially brought out in Hebrews 8 and 9? For what reasons is the New Covenant superior to the Old Covenant?

2. How ought pastors to apply the doctrine of the universal priesthood of believers (Revelation 1:6) within their congregations? What parameters, if any, should be observed in such a pastoral application (1 Corinthians 12:4–31; Ephesians 4:1–16)?

TO THINK ABOUT AND DISCUSS

1. In our daily lives, under the terms of the new covenant in the blood of Christ (1 Corinthians 11:25), in what tangible ways ought we to acknowledge that Jesus is the Conquering Victor? See Philippians 2:9–11.

2. Did you ever find it difficult to accept the Lordship of Christ and promise obedience to him before you fully understood his demands? When you realized what he was asking, how did you cope with that? See, for example, Mark 8:34–38; Luke 14:25–27.

3. The answer to the previous question concerns the issue of our love for Jesus as our Lord. How can we test our love for him and what are the rewards of that love? (John 14:21–23; 15:9–10, 12–14; 21:15–19; see Exodus 19:5.)

4. Exodus 19:6 speaks of the Lord's people becoming 'a kingdom of priests' (see also Revelation 1:6). In the New Testament, the Kingdom of God is seen and experienced in the Church of God. Paul expresses this 'universal priesthood of believers' explicitly in Romans 12:3–8 and 1 Corinthians 12:4–11. Have you been able to identify your particular gift

for 'ministry' (service) in Christ's Church? What is the greatest gift of all and have you ever experienced difficulties in exercising it? (1 Corinthians 12:31b–13:1–13.) Does loving someone necessarily mean you like them, and if not, how do you deal with that?

27 Moses the mediator

Exodus 19:9–25; 33:12–23

'Oh, that I knew where I might find him, that I might come even to his seat!' (Job 23:3). Job's cry has long been echoed down the centuries by people of all creeds, nationalities and cultures. The two passages cited above for this chapter are reaching out to answer this question. For in them the solution is being unfolded for us, beginning with the *need* for the quest—the barrier that separates us from God—and then continuing with the *divine answer* as to the way in which he who is unknown to us has provided, and always will, an intermediary to enable us to 'come even to his seat'.

Ever since our first parents were expelled from the Garden of Eden, there has been a barrier between humanity and the Creator. The barrier, of course, is our sin, which can be defined as 'fall[ing] short of the glory of God' (Romans

3:23). Sin can take different forms; therefore, the Old Testament Scriptures use various words to express its many manifestations. Here are a few examples: 'rebellion' is the act of deliberately defying God's express word; 'transgression' can refer to a particular instance of disobedience; 'trespass' (translated by ESV as 'breaking faith') means stepping across the Lord's explicitly revealed boundary into 'no man's land', as we say; 'iniquity' means perverse or crooked actions that issue from a bent nature; 'unbelief' is another manifestation of sin and means refusing to accept God's Word; 'distrust' is similar to 'unbelief'; 'pride' (sometimes translated by ESV as 'presumption') is yet another form of sin; 'evil' resides in the human heart and is often used as the opposite to 'good'; 'deceit' is yet another manifestation of our fallenness.[1]

Jesus himself gives us a daunting, even frightening, insight into the sin within our hearts:

> And he said, 'What comes out of a person is what defiles him. For from within, out of the heart of man, come evil thoughts, sexual immorality, theft, murder, adultery, coveting, wickedness, deceit, sensuality, envy, slander, pride, foolishness. All these evil things come from within, and they defile a person' (Mark 7:20–23).

It is this multiplicity of sinfulness that comes between humanity and the Lord God, as it forms a barrier that excludes us from his divine presence. For he is 'of purer eyes than to see evil and cannot look at wrong' (Habakkuk 1:13). In the passage we have reached in Exodus 19, this barrier between God and humankind is described as 'a thick cloud' (vv. 9, 16). His burning holiness could not be seen by mortal eyes. An illustration of this might be the power of the midday sun's brightness, that is so dazzling it can permanently damage one's sight unless it is viewed through a pinhole projector or 'eclipse goggles', which are specially made to protect the eyes from the sun's burning brightness. Thus, we read that the Israelites saw the presence of God only as a thick cloud[2] that appeared as dense smoke (v. 18), while his voice sounded to their ears like thunder (v. 19).

Moses appointed as mediator

The imperious demands of the covenant that we learned about in Chapter 26, had been accepted by the people, and Moses had now reported this to God (v. 8). Thereupon, God appointed Moses to a new role as the intermediary between himself and the people (v. 9). 'Behold I am coming to you in a thick cloud ...'; the pronoun, 'you', is singular in the Hebrew,

> God appointed Moses to a new role as the intermediary between himself and the people.

indicating that it is Moses to whom God is specifically and solely referring.

Moreover, the thunderous sound of God's voice would be heard by the people, as the Lord bore public witness that his servant was the chosen recipient and custodian of his word; this would enable them to 'believe you for ever'. At the very least, 'for ever' must have meant for the whole of Moses' lifetime, but it probably was intended to mean that the message he was chosen to mediate would have a permanent place in what we might call 'salvation history', until it found its ultimate, eternal fulfilment in Christ, whose office as Mediator was now being foreshadowed by Moses.

This awesome event would take place over three days. the first two of which were to be days of preparation. There were two important aspects of this period of preparation. Firstly, the people must 'consecrate' themselves over the first two days by washing all their clothes (v. 10). Those who were married also had to abstain from intimate sexual relationships. These outward ceremonial token actions of purification pointed to the need for inner cleansing. The outward aspect of the Christian sacraments is never an end in itself, but always points to an inner, spiritual requirement. Thoughtful Israelites would doubtless have realized this.

The second point regarding the two days of

preparation was that they must not approach the base of Mount Sinai, where God was about to meet with Moses. Any person who left the safety of the encampment and trespassed on the foot of the mountain was to be shot with an arrow, for no one could even step on to the forbidden territory in order to arrest the intruder. This second aspect of the two days of preparation was strictly laid down to bring home to the Israelites the unapproachable holiness of the eternal God.

For you and me today, all this may seem rather strange and primitive. But because Jesus Christ, the great Mediator between the eternal God and us sinful mortals, has opened the way for us to have direct access into our heavenly Father's presence, we no longer are under the severe restraints imposed upon the people of God prior to Christ's coming. However, we can, and often do, take for granted the indescribable privilege that is ours, freely and boldly, to draw near. It was because the Jews, to whom the apostle was writing, had been brought up with an acute awareness of the burning 'otherness' of the Divine Being, that he wrote, 'Let us then with confidence draw near to the throne of grace ...' (Hebrews 4:16).[3]

Approaching the unapproachable

I recall how my wife and I went in 1977 to Forthbank Stadium in Stirling to see a display that hundreds of young people from all the youth organisations in the Central Region of Scotland were putting on in celebration of the Queen's Silver Jubilee. Our twelve-year-old daughter was taking part. The stadium was completely filled a full hour before the Queen's scheduled arrival, but the crowd waited patiently.

Then at last, as the time for her appearance drew near, we began to hear distant cheering: the crowds, lining the streets half a mile away, were greeting the royal cavalcade as it slowly drove past. The anticipation within the stadium began to increase as the cheering grew nearer and nearer, and we could clearly follow the motorcade's progress. At length, the Rolls Royce slowly entered Forthbank, and a mighty cheer arose that echoed across the historic town of Stirling. 'The Queen! The Queen! Long live the Queen!' The greeting arose from thousands of voices as we welcomed Her Majesty. The event is etched in my memory as, quite involuntarily, I thought to myself, 'What will it be like when our Saviour and King returns?'

The third day had now come when the great I AM was to visit his people. In verses 16–20, Moses struggles for words to describe the indescribable. Mount Sinai was enveloped in a thick cloud, and there were 'thunders and lightnings' accompanied by the sound of a loud trumpet blast. There are two ways of understanding these phenomena. Firstly, we can regard them as being similar to the heavy clouds we have all seen at some time or other resting on the summit of a mountain, and the thunder and lightning being much the same as we experience when there is a storm. God has often used the nature he himself has created to serve his purposes, as when an east wind drove back the waters of the Red Sea.

> God has often used the nature he himself has created to serve his purposes.

However, I myself am uncertain about such an explanation. In the account of what we may describe as a momentous event in 'salvation history', these manifestations are second only to the birth, ministry, crucifixion, resurrection and ascension of the Son of God. Therefore, I prefer to regard the words, 'thunder', 'lightnings', 'thick cloud' and 'trumpet blast' as having been used because they were the only verbal options that were available to portray the descent and presence of Almighty God, as the first covenant of grace was about to be mediated to his chosen people through his servant Moses. Children and family pets may be frightened by thunder and lightning, when adults normally take such events in their stride. But this was no normal thunderstorm, for we read that not only 'all the people in the camp trembled', but also that 'the whole mountain trembled' (vv. 16, 18). The approach of the unapproachable is indeed being signified.

The Old Testament writers never forgot this event. It is implicitly recalled, for example, in Psalm 50 where we read of God appearing to judge his people:

Our God comes; he does not keep silence; before him is a devouring fire, around him a mighty tempest. He calls to the heavens above and to the earth, that he may judge his people (vv. 3–4).

I have occasionally cringed as I have heard so-called 'worship leaders' speaking to God as if he was a kind of buddy or mate. Yes, we know that Jesus revealed him as a compassionate and loving Father, like the one who, with tears streaming down his face, ran to meet his returning prodigal son (Luke 15:20). But, in that parable, Jesus' words carry a dignity and profound reverence for the 'waiting Father'. Yes, 'God is love'. Nevertheless, alongside that we must never forget the awesome, burning holiness of our God.

Nor must we forget that, in those hours, when his beloved Son carried on his righteous soul the weight of our sin, there was darkness over the land as the cry of dereliction echoed over Calvary: 'My God, my God, why have you forsaken me?' (Matthew 27:46). Well did Frederick William Faber write, 'O how I fear thee, living God, with deepest, tenderest fears ...' His hymn continues:

No earthly father loves like thee;
No mother e're so mild,

Bears and forbears as thou hast done
    With me, thy sinful child.'[4]

Moses, an imperfect mediator

How flawed are our fallen human natures! Our first parents sinned by neglecting, and then rejecting, the explicit command of God. The question posed by the tempter: 'Did God actually say ...?' (Genesis 3:1), was sufficient to sow the first seeds of unbelief in their minds, leading to their disobedience. Today, we all know what God has said but, perverse as we are, we too question the relevance of his words.

Now we find this holy man, chosen before his birth to be God's messenger and mediator, questioning God's command. In Exodus chapters 3 and 4, he had raised objection after objection to God's commands: 'Who am I that I should go to Pharaoh ...? [When] they ask me, "What is his name?" what shall I say to them? ... they will not believe me or listen to my voice ... I am slow of speech and of tongue ...'.[5] Astonishingly, here he is in the presence of Almighty God, with phenomenal manifestations causing the people and even the mountain to tremble, yet when he is told to go back down the mountain and warn the people not to 'break through to the LORD', lest some of them perish (v. 21), he objects! In effect, he replies to this clear command from God that such a trip back down the mountain to warn the people would be quite unnecessary, for they have already been cautioned to remain within the boundary that had been set.

Graciously, the Lord insists, adding that on his return he must bring Aaron with him. Perhaps God was condescending to Moses' weakness by including Aaron in the instruction, thus giving him a further reason for making the descent and a second gruelling ascent back up. My own personal friends, who have reached the summit of Mount Sinai, have told me that it is a very testing climb. Twice in a day would have stretched the resources of an octogenarian.

There is both a word of warning and a word of encouragement for us in this seemingly minor detail of Moses' reluctance to do as God instructed. When you or I raise objections to what is indisputably his revealed will, we are reacting foolishly and rashly. Unquestioning obedience must always be our response. Notice that I spoke of what is 'indisputably God's revealed will'. I am not referring to impulsive ideas that we at times may imagine to be the divine will; too many sincere believers have mistaken their own thoughts for God's thoughts. If there is any dubiety in our minds we

> When you or I raise objections to what is indisputably God's revealed will, we are reacting foolishly and rashly.

should wait for confirmation from the Lord and perhaps share with wise and godly friends those promptings which we believe are from the Holy Spirit.

The word of encouragement comes from God's response to his servant's objection. Firmly, he repeats the command (v. 24), for he knows only too well the rash arrogance of sinners like us. Moses needed only to reflect on the events of the past three months to recall how faithless and disobedient the chosen people could be. If he had chosen not to remember, he was to be reminded of it later when, after spending many days in God's presence, he descended from Sinai to find the people dancing round a golden calf, imitating the idolatry and fertility rites of surrounding pagan tribes (Exodus 32). Thus, his objection to God's command to warn the people afresh was seen to be ill-judged and quite wrong.

In the divine presence (33:12-23)

We have to wait for Moses to recount to us his experience of the presence of the God who was so awesome in his burning holiness. Chapter 19 closes summarily as the account hastens on into chapter 20 with the record of the Ten Commandments. It is later, in chapter 33 where we have the most significant description of God's chosen mediator meeting with the divine Redeemer.

The context is Moses' confession of his complete

inadequacy to continue with his commission. It would appear that the rebelliousness, obstinacy and unbelief of the majority of those whom he is leading have brought him to a crisis point in his task. Although he himself has witnessed the hand of God acting powerfully again and again on his people's behalf, delivering them, rescuing them and providing for them, he is still not satisfied. Am I going too far when I suggest that he has come to the stage in his relationship with God in which he wants absolutely everything God can give him? We might say that he wants even more of God himself, as much as he can possibly be granted.

And so, he pleads that God will 'show me now your ways, that I may know you ...' (v. 13). His deep yearning is to experience for himself the divine glory: 'Please, show me your glory' (v. 18). Therefore, it came about that God placed him in a cleft of the rock near the summit of Mount Sinai and, passing by him, covered him with his hand. Then as the great I am passed by, Moses glimpsed God's back, for he could not see the divine face and live.

We shall return to this passage in a later chapter to consider its profound implications for the New Covenant but, in the meantime, let us ponder on this holy man's sense of his human inadequacy and his deep desire to know God's presence even more fully. I am reminded of a verse in an old hymn, rarely sung nowadays:

> And none, O Lord, have perfect rest, for none are
> wholly free from sin;
> And they who fain would serve thee best are
> conscious most of wrong within.[6]

I am sure that most, if not all of us, are deeply aware of our inadequacy for the task to which we have been called. But oh, that more of the Lord's people would also share Moses' passion to know God in an even fuller way. When that desire is truly in any believer's heart and soul, the Lord himself will respond and satisfy it in as much measure as our limited capacity can grasp. Indeed, he already has done this through our divine Mediator. For those who have met with Jesus Christ 'have seen his glory, glory as of the only Son from the Father, full of grace and truth'; for, he 'who is at the Father's side ... has made him known' (John 1:14, 18).

For further study ▶

FOR FURTHER STUDY

1. A list of ten words describing our alienation from God is given in the first paragraph of this chapter. In a few sentences, illustrate each of them with a word picture. For example, the word 'sin' could be from the language of archery: The teenage lad with bulging muscles takes the bow, slots an arrow into the string, and sends the shaft flying towards the target some 30 metres away. But the arrow misses and ends up somewhere in bushes, far beyond it. Next to shoot comes a rather nervous teenage girl. She takes aim but her arrow falls short and doesn't come anywhere near the target. That's what God means by sin. He has given us a target to aim at, but when aiming at it, we either miss it completely or fall short of it.

2. Prepare material for a Bible Study on the word, 'mediator'. Useful OT references could be Exodus 20:19; Deuteronomy 5:5, 22–23, 27, 31; useful NT references could be Galatians 3:19–20; 1 Timothy 2:5; Hebrews 8:6; 9:15; 12:24. (NB: In the Galatians passage, the ESV uses the word 'intermediary' as a synonym for 'mediator'.)

TO THINK ABOUT AND DISCUSS

1. Do you think human nature is *always* as bad as the list of words in the first paragraph of this chapter implies? If you do think this list is 'over the top', then what do you think of Jesus' words quoted in Mark 7:20–23? Is Jesus suggesting that we all wear a kind of 'personality disguise' to hide what is often in our hearts and minds?

2. Read Isaiah 53:4–6, 10. What do these verses tell us, firstly, about ourselves (v. 6), secondly, about Jesus (vv. 4a, 5), and thirdly, about God (vv. 4b, 10)?

3. Read 1 Timothy 2:5 and Hebrews 9:15. Using your search engine, look up *'Scotland's favourite painting: Salvador Dali's 'Christ of Saint John of the Cross'*. What do you think is the message that Dali's painting is attempting

to give? Would standing and looking at the painting help someone to become a committed Christian? (See Romans 10:14–17.) Using *words*, how would you explain Dali's *visual* depiction of Jesus?

28 A covenant of grace

Exodus 20:1–2

Once time rolls up like a scroll and the Bride of Christ is swept into the eternity of God's glorious presence when 'face to face' we 'shall know fully, even as [we] have been fully known', then all differences of opinion will be eclipsed forever. However, until then 'we see in a mirror dimly' and only 'know in part' (1 Corinthians 13:12). On the solid rock of Exodus 20:1–2, many a gospel ship has foundered. This issue, of course, is to what extent the Ten Commandments apply today. Are they superseded by 'the law of love'? Or does that same 'law of love' embrace them?

'And God spoke all these words, saying, "I am the LORD your God who brought you out of Egypt, out of the house of slavery".

It is well known that the Church in South Korea has made dramatic progress since the first Christian missionary was martyred there in the 1880s.

Today, every South Korean city has scores of churches which are well attended, generously supported, and still growing fast. Indeed, over the past hundred years, the South Korean Church has doubled every decade.

During a visit to South Korea a few years ago, while I was profoundly impressed by what I saw of the Church, there was something which distressed me. A small movement among certain South Korean believers advocate that the Lord's Day should be regarded the same as any other day, although agreeing that it is a good idea also to meet for worship and fellowship on one special day—presumably the first day of the week.

The commandments today

The argument of this movement's view is simple. When the apostle wrote, in Romans 10:4, 'Christ is the end of the law ...', he meant that the Ten Commandments are now superseded by the only 'Law' that Jesus gave, and so now his followers today are governed by the 'Law of Love'. For we read Christ's words in John 15:12: 'This is my commandment, that you love one another as I have loved you.' This teaching, alas, was initiated into his home country by a South Korean who, while studying theology in London, joined one of the many 'house fellowship churches' there, and then took this interpretation of 'Law', that he had learned in England, back to his own land.

In this book on Moses, I do not intend to provide an exposition of the Ten Commandments in Exodus 20, as I have already made this provision in *And Then There Were Nine*[1], which is still in print and readily available. However, I am re-writing here the first chapter of this book, for there are still commonly held misunderstandings regarding the Ten Commandments and their place today in the New Testament church.

Common confusion

When one is reading the New Testament, especially passages where the Old Testament Law is being discussed, for example in Galatians (2:15–21; 3:1–29), it is easy to be confused by the writer's method. Paul often puts himself into the shoes of the Jew who is objecting to the gospel of grace through faith in Christ, when he speaks of a common Jewish assumption that it had once been possible to attain acceptance with God by fully keeping the Law. But it is important to note that Paul himself never actually says that. Because the Bible nowhere teaches it.

Confusion can also arise unless one understands what Paul means by 'the law'. Some Christians (like the members of the house fellowship church mentioned above) confuse 'the law' with the Ten Commandments. But usually what is meant by 'the law' in our New Testaments is the whole Old Testament system of worship, with its ceremonial washings, sacrifices, categories of what was clean and unclean, along with the priesthood and temple worship, and not least the rite of circumcision. We might even say that by 'the law' Paul means 'the religion of Judaism'. So, the first point that must be made in approaching the Ten Commandments is that they are not to be confused (or even equated) with 'the law' in the New Testament writings. When the apostle is referring to the Ten Commandments, he usually speaks of 'the commandment'.[2] However, that is not to say that Paul did not consider the Commandments an essential part of 'the law', that is, of the Jewish religion.

Distinction made

In the books of Exodus, Leviticus and Deuteronomy, a clear distinction is made on the one hand between the great mass of laws (in the sense of regulations) which they contain, and the Ten Commandments which we find in Exodus 20—and again in Deuteronomy 5. In a very special way, the Ten Commandments are set apart as quite distinct and in a class of their own. They were marked out as different in three ways, for there are three differences between the Ten Commandments and the other laws which go to make up the whole Levitical system of daily life and worship.

1) GOD SPOKE

The first is that the Ten Commandments were spoken by the mouth of God and written by his finger. (As Calvin comments, this writing by God with his finger is clearly expressed as a figure of speech, for God is not a corporeal being.)[3] All the other laws and statutes of the entire Levitical system were given by God through Moses as mediator. But the Ten Commandments came direct from God, as the people heard the thunder of his voice.[4]

2) KEPT IN THE ARK OF THE COVENANT

A second difference is that, of all the many laws given through Moses, it was only the Ten Commandments, written on two tablets of stone, which were kept in the ark of the covenant. The ark itself was in the Holy of Holies, the innermost sanctuary within the Tent of Meeting, into which only the High Priest entered once each year. The Shekinah Glory of God rested on the cover on top of the ark (sometimes translated as, 'the mercy seat', other times as, 'the atonement'[5]), giving both the ark and its precious contents the very highest place in Hebrew thought and worship.

3) APODICTIC ABSOLUTES

'Apodictic' means 'clearly established'. This word explains a third major difference between the Ten Commandments and all other Levitical laws of Judaism. The other laws are what we call *case laws*. But the Ten Commandments are *absolute laws*, clearly established by God, and not open to any kind of change or modification. Moses explicitly states that the first two stone tablets were fashioned by the power of God, and the finger of God had filled *both sides of the tablets*, for there was nothing to be added or taken away. This perfect summary of the revelation of the Lord's will and purpose for his people was complete and definitive.[6]

I once consulted a lawyer over a rather difficult matter, and he began to look up various legal volumes and quote to me court rulings that had been made in the past in similar cases. Much law is established by 'cases'. Glance at Exodus 21 and the following chapters to see that the Levitical laws (regulations) are 'case law'— instructions given for particular situations. But the Ten Commandments are quite different. They are absolutes, 'apodictic absolutes'. They are Commandments spoken by the mouth of God and written by his finger to govern his people's living, whatever the circumstances or conditions of the case may be.

Given these three major differences between the Ten Commandments and Levitical regulations, it is clear why we can neither go along with the bad theology the South Korean took back home with him from London, nor disregard any single one of the Ten Commandments.

Someone may ask what Paul meant when he said, 'Christ is the end[7] of the law'? The answer is that Christ has both fulfilled the law's purpose and aim, and also brought to its termination the Levitical system of sacrificial worship along with the rituals accompanying it—all of which had been pointing prophetically to himself. In fulfilling the law, he has demonstrated clearly that in a very special way it foreshadowed his Person and Work.

> In fulfilling the law, Christ has demonstrated clearly that in a very special way it foreshadowed his Person and Work.

Moreover, in his fulfilment of the Levitical system, he rendered it redundant, for he took upon himself the office of High Priest, though he was himself not only the Priest who offers the sacrifice for sin but was himself that sacrifice. The apostle states that very explicitly: 'how much more will the blood of Christ, who through the eternal Spirit offered himself without blemish to God, purify our conscience from dead works to serve the living God' (Hebrews 9:14).[8]

Further, as Jesus himself said, he did not come to abolish the Law but to fulfil it. 'Whoever relaxes one of the least of these commandments and teaches others to do the same will be called least in the kingdom of heaven, but whoever does them and teaches them will be called great in the kingdom of heaven' (Matthew 5:19).[9]

The grace of law

However, the most important point about the Ten Commandments has still to be made: it is that they are grounded in the mercy and love of God. Why God had chosen this ragamuffin band of fugitives from the concentration camps of Egypt we will never know—except that, inexplicably, he loved them. He does give a reason for his love:

> It was not because you were more in number than any other people that the LORD set his love on you and chose you, for you were the fewest of all peoples, but it is because the LORD loves you and is keeping the oath that he swore to your fathers, that the LORD has brought you out with a mighty hand and redeemed you from the house of slavery, from the hand of Pharaoh king of Egypt (Deuteronomy 7:7–8).

'I love you because I love you!'

REDEMPTION

Moreover, God entered into direct confrontation with possibly the most powerful man in the world at that time in order to free these slaves from their miserable lives of unremitting toil. He ordained the Passover lamb, instructing that its blood be sprinkled on each of his people's doorposts and lintels. He parted the Red Sea by his breath. He satisfied the people's hunger by providing a table in the wilderness and quenched their thirst by water from the rock.

In other words, the Lord was their God. He has loved, redeemed them, provided for them and led them, so they are his people. The Ten Commandments, therefore, are given in grace. That is why the first two verses of Exodus 20 are so important: 'I am the LORD your God, who brought you out of the land of Egypt, out of the house of slavery.' If we disregard this statement or take it away, we are left with only *Law*. Leave these two first verses of the chapter in their place, and we have the *Grace of Law*.

THE WAY OF BLESSING

Properly understood, the Ten Commandments are the pathway of life. 'Do this and you will live,' said Jesus to the lawyer who asked what he must do to inherit eternal life (Luke 10:28). John Ball rightly wrote: 'These words, "Do this and live," must not be interpreted, as if they did promise life upon a condition of perfect obedience ... but they must be expounded evangelically.'[10]

The Lord's words to Moses—'You shall follow my rules and keep my statutes and walk in them. I am the LORD your God. You shall therefore keep my statutes and my rules; if a person does them, he shall live by them: I am the LORD' (Leviticus 18:4–5)[11]—never meant that we can earn God's approval, far less mercy by our obedience. They must be understood as promising blessing to those whom God has redeemed, and who now faithfully walk in his ways. 'Do this and *enjoy* life'— the life I the Lord have gratuitously given to you. Not, 'Do this and *earn* life,' by your own efforts!

This is what the Ten Commandments mean for us today. They are not only the absolute commands of God, but they are also his gracious invitation to us to follow a path that is safe, good and blessed; a path that leads to heaven. It is not that heaven is ever reached because we keep these commands; rather that, having been redeemed by Christ our Passover Lamb, having eaten of him our bread from heaven, and having drunk of him the water of life, our feet are now guided to walk the way of his Commandments. Therefore, they are the path to glory.

HOLINESS

Many of us can remember the first exhilaration we experienced when we found Christ as Saviour. The whole world seemed to be transformed, and indeed was transformed. 'Heaven above is softer blue, earth around is sweeter green, something lives in every hue that Christless eyes have never seen ...'.[12] Our joy knew no bounds. But after some weeks came the realization that the Christian life was more than a vision; it was also a way. A way has to be trodden, and as one walks the straight and narrow way of obedience, feet can become tired, sore and blistered.

I mean that, as young Christians, we had to discover that followers of the Lord must learn obedience to him. Such obedience is often costly. It demands that we say 'No,' to some natural inclinations, even that we die many painful deaths to self—that is, to our fallen natures. Put another way, this obedience to Christ is nothing less than obeying his Commandments. His two great Commandments are actually a summary of the Ten Commandments (Mark 12:29–31). 'Love the LORD your God,' sums up the first four; 'Love your neighbour,' sums up the remaining six.

It is evident, therefore, that to say any single one of the Ten Commandments no longer applies to Christians is quite false. After justification—the divine act whereby we are acquitted at the judgement bar of God and, by his grace, accepted in Christ as children of God—there comes sanctification and the long slow process of holiness that takes a whole lifetime; it consists in our becoming more and more like the Lord Jesus himself. As we obey his Commandments through the help of the Spirit of God, we become like our Lord and enter more deeply into this process of sanctification or holiness.

In other words, obedience and likeness to Jesus Christ cannot be separated from the Commandments of God. The Commandments provide the way of holiness and without holiness no one will see God.

> Obedience and likeness to Jesus Christ cannot be separated from the Commandments of God.

Serving God alone[13]

A final word regarding just one of the Ten Commandments, though of course this will apply to all ten. The second commandment reads:

> You shall not make for yourself a carved image, or any likeness of anything that is in heaven above, or that is in the earth beneath, or that is in the water under the earth. You shall not bow down to them or serve them, for I the Lord your God am a jealous God, visiting the iniquity of the fathers on the children to the third and the fourth generation of those who hate me, but showing steadfast love to thousands of those who love me and keep my commandments (Exodus 20:4–6).

I want you to note particularly one phrase in particular of this second commandment: *You shall not bow down to them or serve them.* These two verbs, 'bow down' and 'serve', are a bit like Siamese twins—*joined at the hip*, as we say. They often occur together in Scripture. The act of 'bowing down' involved kneeling and touching the ground with one's forehead. When Abraham's servant, who had been sent to find a bride for Isaac, found himself guided straight to the right family and young woman, we read that 'The man bowed his head and worshipped the LORD' (Genesis 24:26–27). We are to understand that he prostrated himself before God.

Or consider the incident when the risen Lord met the women coming from the empty tomb. 'Jesus met them and said, 'Greetings!' And they came up and took hold of his feet and worshipped him' (Matthew 28:9). Again, we see this prostration or bowing down. And, as with Abraham's servant, it is accompanied by 'worship' of the Lord.

Some readers may have noticed that, in the translations into English, some versions use the word 'worship' in the second commandment (e.g., NIV), whereas the ESV, which I have just quoted, translates it as 'serve' (v. 5). The Hebrew word used[14] is variously translated throughout the Bible either as 'serve' or 'worship'. Its use along with the verb, 'bow down', indicates that it denotes not merely the offer of profound respect and obeisance,[15] but also the pledge of loyalty and subservience. Therefore, clearly this second commandment means that the covenant people were to give their service, obedience, reverence and loyalty to the God who had redeemed them and brought them out of 'the house of slavery'.

It is both disappointing and surprising that this meaning of 'serve/worship', which is so clear in this second commandment, and its context should have been largely lost to many Christian people in this 21st century. Its meaning has been reduced to singing praise to God. While it is true that genuine 'worship/service' of God is bound to find its expression in thanksgiving and adoration, such praise of God is an effect or outcome of worship, rather than its essence.

Reflect on the third temptation that the devil brought to Jesus in the wilderness:

> Again, the devil took him to a very high mountain and showed him all the kingdoms of the world and their glory. And he said to him, 'All these I will give you, if you will fall down and worship me.' Then Jesus said to him, 'Be gone, Satan! For it is written, "You shall worship the Lord your God and him only shall you serve"' (Matthew 4:8–10).

It is self-evident that Satan was not asking Jesus to sing him a song! Rather, he was demanding that he change 'masters', desert his Father and become the obedient *servant* of the devil. In exchange for such treachery, the devil offered him worldly wealth, power and fame. Jesus in effect replied in the terms of the second commandment, though he was quoting largely from Deuteronomy 6:13.

The apostle Paul frequently called himself a 'servant' of Jesus Christ.[16] He belonged utterly to Christ, who had bought him at an infinitely costly price—his lifeblood poured out in death. Therefore, his life was not his own, it belonged to the one who had purchased him. His service to Christ was his worship, and his worship of Christ was his service, and thus he appealed to the believers in Rome to present their 'bodies as a living sacrifice, holy and acceptable to God, which is your spiritual[17] worship' (Romans 12:1).

> 'Worship/service' means a total and unconditional yielding of ourselves to the God who loves us.

Can we not see how glaringly obvious it is that by 'worship' the Christian Scriptures mean far more than praise and thanksgiving, vitally important though they are? Rather, 'worship/service' means a total and unconditional yielding of ourselves to the God who loves us, has given his beloved Son for our redemption and has implanted his nature in our hearts and souls by his Holy Spirit. The final verse of Isaac Watts' hymn, 'When I survey the wondrous cross' expresses well the true meaning of worship:

Were the whole realm of nature mine,

That were a present far too small;

Love so amazing, so divine,

Demands my soul, my life, my all.

Isaac Watts (1674–1748)

For more than two decades, there has been a flood of contemporary songs of praise and adoration, many of them based on some of the Psalms. Although the tunes to which they are sung have often consisted in a repetitive, unimaginative and often dreary variation of about three notes, the words have at least been faithful to the Scriptures. But, until relatively recently, the so-called 'worship' in many churches has completely neglected the real meaning of 'worship/service'. The biblical theme of God's work of grace reaching into our fallen, struggling natures has been almost entirely ignored. True, the Georgian and Victorian eras of hymnology may appear old-fashioned and out-dated to many. Great hymns such as 'When I survey the wondrous cross'; 'I heard the voice of Jesus say'; 'Rock of ages, cleft for me'; 'Jesus, lover of my soul'; or 'And can it be that I should gain,'[18] are virtually unknown to many thousands of younger believers.

We are grateful that some of the contemporary hymnwriters, such as Graham Kendrick, Stuart Townend, Keith Getty, Michael Saward and others are bequeathing hymns to the church in up-to-date language which answer to our deep spiritual needs by addressing the problems of people's hearts and souls.

Hymns are needed which teach us to appreciate the profound grace and mercy of God over against our faithlessness, fears and fallenness. For the sad truth is that we can sing our heads off without truly offering our whole allegiance and obedience to our Lord and Saviour—and that is what Scripture means by 'worship'.

Thus, we see the abiding relevance of the Ten Commandments, rightly understood in the light of verses 1–2, as the heart of the covenant of grace, along with worship and service of God, as in all the Commandments, but especially spelled out in the second commandment. They can no more change than God himself can change, for they remain the expression of his holy, loving nature. Some readers may find it helpful to learn of the three uses of the Ten Commandments as outlined by John Calvin.

> The first part [of the commandments] is this: while it shows God's righteousness, that is the righteousness alone acceptable to God, it warns, informs, convicts, and lastly condemns, every man of his own unrighteousness. For man, blinded and drunk with self-love, must be compelled to know and confess his own feebleness and impurity.[19]

> The second function of the law [commandments[20]] is this: at least by punishment to restrain certain men who are untouched by any care for what is just and right, unless compelled by hearing the dire threats

of the law. But they are restrained, not because their inner mind is stirred or affected, but because, being bridled, so to speak, they keep their hands from outward activity, and hold inside the depravity that otherwise they would have wantonly indulged.[21]

The third and principal use, which pertains more closely to the proper use of the law, finds its place among believers in whose hearts the Spirit of God already lives and reigns. For even though they have the law written and engraved upon their hearts by the finger of God (Jeremiah 31:33; Heb. 10:16), that is, have been so moved and quickened through the directing of the Spirit that they long to obey God, they still profit by the law in two ways.

Here is the best instrument for them to learn more thoroughly each day the nature of the Lord's will to which they aspire, and confirm them in their understanding of it ...

Again, because we need not only teaching but also exhortation, the servant of God will also avail himself of this benefit of the law: by frequent meditation upon it to be aroused to obedience, be strengthened in it, and be drawn back from the slippery path of transgression. In this way the saints must press on [22]

So may all of us be given the grace and strength of the Holy Spirit to press on towards the prize of the high calling of God in Christ Jesus!

For further study ▶

FOR FURTHER STUDY

1. The view has long been held that the Mosaic law was intended to offer full salvation through perfect observance of it—it was a covenant of works; that was plan A in the divine economy. But because plan A failed, God then launched plan B—a covenant of grace—which involved the incarnation of his Son. Study this interpretation of the Mosaic law to ascertain whether it can be sustained over against the reformed view that both the old and new covenants are of grace.

2. Prepare a study outline for discussion in your congregational house groups on the biblical teaching that the Ten Commandments are not revoked in the New Testament but remain an essential guide to believers in walking before God in holiness.

3. If you hold the theological view of the South Korean movement regarding the fourth commandment, see if you are able to justify from Scripture the view that Sabbath observance is now legalistic.[23]

TO THINK ABOUT AND DISCUSS

1. The suggestion has been made in this chapter that there are three ways in which the Ten Commandments are shown to be distinct from all the Mosaic rituals and regulations. Discuss these three ways and see if you can find any relevance for Christians today.

2. Discuss the 'three uses of the Commandments' and see if you can give practical examples as to how they could work out in daily Christian living.

3. Jesus said the greatest Commandment is to love God and the second greatest commandment is to love our neighbours (Matthew 22:35–40). The first four commandments are about God and the other six are about our neighbours. Is 'love' the right way to keep them?

4. Read Mark 10:17–22. Why do you think Jesus told the rich young man, who thought he had kept all the Commandments from his teenage years,

to sell everything and then follow him? Is the answer found in sayings such as in John 15:9–11, 14?

29 The golden calf

Exodus 32; 33:1–7

Impatience and dissention boil over into rejection of both Moses and God himself and the consequences prove disastrous. The man who had been left in charge weakly buckled under pressure, and so, our blood runs cold as awesome retribution is visited on the leaders of the idolatry and its resulting moral corruption. The divine wrath was followed by Moses' own wrath as the sacred tablets, written by the finger of God, were smashed. And, for a time, God's presence was withdrawn from his chosen people.

The narrative in Exodus 32 follows on from the final words of Exodus 24: 'Moses entered the cloud and went up on the mountain. And Moses was on the mountain forty days and forty nights' (v. 18). We shall consider later the contents of the intervening chapters 25 to 31 but, in the meantime, notice that the instructions recorded there conclude with the statement: 'And he [God] gave to Moses, when he had finished speaking with him on Mount Sinai, the two tablets of the testimony, tablets of stone, written with the finger of God' (31:18). Moses, the Lord's messenger and mediator, for those forty days and nights, had been sustained by God, while the tangible, physical means of grace of the covenant, that were to be provided for the Lord's people, were being communicated to him.

It is important to notice this, for it quickly becomes evident that part of the problem of the golden calf may well have been the absence up to that point of tangible, physical signs of God's requirements of his people. They had heard his covenantal words read to them and given their assent to them: 'All that the LORD has spoken we will do, and we will be obedient' (Exodus 24:7). Although that written and spoken Word of God ought to have been sufficient for them (as it ought to be for all of us), they yearned for some physical, visible object. The reason why Moses had been summoned to spend time on the mountain was that God was condescending to their carnal needs and preparing his servant to bring them just such sacramental signs.

It is, therefore, ironical that they demanded Aaron provide them with a tangible sign. Their impatience and irritation over the length of time Moses had been lost to sight, hidden by the cloud on the mountain summit, is clearly indicated in their coarse words, 'As for this Moses, the man who brought us up out of the land of Egypt, we do not know what has become of him' (Exodus 32:1; NIV's translation brings out something of the angry vehemence the Hebrew is intended to convey: 'As for this fellow Moses ...').

Calvin makes much of the time Moses spent with God and his comment is worth quoting in full.

> God, his Master and Teacher, had been speaking to him out of his own mouth. Wherefore he observed silence for forty days, that he might afterwards freely speak by the authority of God. Thus ought all true pastors of the church to be disciples, so as to teach nothing but what they have received. But although God might have in a moment fully perfected his servant, yet, in order to evince that he advanced nothing which did not proceed from the school of heaven, he was separated for forty days from the human race, so that the Israelites might henceforth look up to him as an angel sent from heaven.[1]

This is a salutary word to all who are called to teach and preach in the church. Too often, a minister's preparation time is squeezed into a spare three quarters of an hour here and there or even into the dying hours of the week on Saturday night, while valuable time has been spent running around at the beck and call of one and another. I have sometimes heard church members commending their minister as they say, 'He's always on the go.' I have been tempted to respond by saying, 'It's good he is diligent in visiting his people, but you ought to make sure that he's not "always on the go" and that his priority is spending time with God.'

Israel's idolatry

All of us know perfectly well that there have been times when, defiantly, we have thrown caution to the wind, taken the bit between our teeth and, ignoring the gentle prompting of the Holy Spirit's voice in our hearts, deliberately have disobeyed the Lord. Worse still, it has not been on one single occasion but repeatedly. Alas, this is the story of fallen human nature. One writer[2] described the demand of the Israelites that Aaron 'make us gods' as 'detestable impiety ... base ingratitude ... monstrous madness, mixed with stupidity'. None of us would want to have such a charge brought against us but, if the hidden truth was known, would we be at times in our desires close to such folly?

The people had apparently surrounded Aaron in the threatening manner that an unruly mob at times does to the unfortunate person who has been chosen to carry the blame for some misfortune. It may be that Aaron, temporarily deprived of Moses' strong presence, weakly attempted to restrain this 'monstrous madness' when he asked the people to 'Take off the rings of gold ...'

which they all wore, for in Egypt men as well as women used earrings. The verb translated 'take off' can mean, 'tear off' or 'break off'. Therefore, he could well have been attempting to cause the people to hesitate—did they really want to part with their valuable jewellery? However, the people were determined, and had Aaron at their mercy.

(Decades later, Gideon was to demand the people donate their golden earrings in return for his help, and the weight of the gold thrown on to a cloak came to 1,700 shekels (Judges 8:24–27).[3] He did not learn from his nation's history, for the artefact he made with their gold 'became a snare to Gideon and his family' (Judges 8:22–27). Idolatry in one form or another was a constant snare that often entrapped the Lord's people.)[4]

We learn later on in the chapter (v. 24) that the gold was melted down in a furnace. The use of the words 'a graving tool' suggests that the image of a calf was engraved upon a large gold plate. The term, 'calf', does not necessarily mean a young animal; the image would have probably been of a bull calf nearing its prime.[5] Such images were common, not only in Egypt, but throughout the ancient east. The strength and power of the deity was intended to be represented

> The strength and power of the deity was intended to be represented by the image.

by the image. When the idol had been fashioned, the people said, 'These are your gods, O Israel, who brought you up out of the land of Egypt' (v. 4). Although both the noun, 'gods', and the verb, 'brought', are plural, it is most likely that the singular is intended, as it would appear that the image was seen as representing the Lord.

In 1893, F. B. Meyer published his book, *Moses, Servant of God*, in which he discusses the nature of the idolatry involved in the fashioning of the golden calf. His comments on idolatry are helpful.

> If we carefully study the question in all its bearings, we shall discover that the idolater does not—in the first instance, at least—look upon his image as God, but as a representation or manifestation of God. It is an attempt on the part of the human spirit, which shrinks from the effort of communion with the unseen and spiritual, to associate God with what it can own and handle; so as to have a constant and evident token of the presence and favour of God.[6]

Mackay agrees: 'If the idol is taken as representing the Lord, then the sin is that of idolatry... the plurals [noun and verb] are deliberate as they elevate the idol to the status of a partner with the Lord.[7]

How long had Moses been on Mount Sinai at this point? Probably about 38 days. Yet, prior to ascending the Mount alone, he had read the 'ten words'[8] to the people and they had pledged their obedience. However, here they were ignoring the second of those ten holy imperatives: 'You shall not make for yourself a carved image, or any likeness of anything that is in heaven above, or that is in the earth beneath, or that is in the water under the earth. You shall not bow down to them or serve them ...' (Exodus 20:4–5). 'Monstrous madness, mixed with stupidity' indeed! It was not that they wanted to renounce God. Rather it was that, like the Egyptians and other nations, they wanted to worship him through the form of the popular contemporary visible appearance of a bull calf, which, as we have just noted, was greatly revered for its strength and power.

We see all around us this craving of the human heart for some visible, tangible object that will bring luck. Often on the television programme, 'University Challenge', we see some members of a team, which certainly comprises of some of the brightest of the nation's minds, with a 'mascot' perched on the podium beside them—a soft toy such as a teddy bear or an adorable little dog, even occasionally a stuffed monkey. Football players run on to the field clutching an amulet hung round their necks. Jewellers do a profitable trade in good luck charm bracelets. The apostle summed up the sinful folly of such attitudes as worshipping 'the creature rather than the Creator, who is blessed for ever! Amen' (Romans 1:25).

I suspect that most, if not all, readers of this book

would always seek to eschew such follies. But our human hearts are deeply flawed. The old nature in us is never wholly eradicated in this life. Even though we seek to mortify what has already been slain in Christ, the remnants of the root of our fallenness are never barren, but constantly sprout with new shoots. That is why, almost without our realizing it, we transfer our allegiance and love to the material things with which our loving Father has endowed us. Was this not the charge that the Lord of the Church brought to the church at Ephesus?

> I know your works, your toil and your patient endurance, and how you cannot bear with those who are evil, but have tested those who call themselves apostles and are not, and found them to be false. I know you are enduring patiently and bearing up for my name's sake, and you have not grown weary. But I have this against you, that you have abandoned the love you had at first. Remember therefore from where you have fallen; repent and do the works you did at first. If not, I will come to you and remove your lampstand from its place (Revelation 2:2–5).

Warm, loving encouragement for, and commendation of, the church, but also the saddest rebuke—their love for the Saviour had waned. To what had their love been diverted? It is a safe guess that the Father's material blessings had taken their eyes off Christ. It behoves us all to take to heart this message to the church at Ephesus.

Moses' anger

We read that, after the image of the golden calf was set up, the people 'burnt offerings and brought peace offerings' (v. 6). The former were sacrifices that were wholly burned up as worship to the Lord but, in this case, worship to their idolatrous representation of him. The latter were sacrifices which provided a feast for the worshippers. What blind naivety! So, after they had eaten their fill, the people 'rose up to play'. There have been various translations of this phrase. For example, the NIV has 'indulge in revelry'. In verse 25, the phrase is explained as 'had broken loose' (RV, ESV), while the NIV has 'were running wild'.[9] There is little doubt that the Hebrew verb implies sexual activity. The same word is used in Genesis 39:14, 17, where Potiphar's wife falsely accuses Joseph of illicit sexual advances towards her.[10]

Joshua had ascended part of Sinai with Moses but had been left behind when Moses entered the cloud. As they descend together (v. 17) they hear roaring and shouting in the encampment. We could be reminded of the sound of football fans as they applaud their team or else volubly disapprove of a decision of the referee. But to Joshua's ears, attuned to the shouts of a military attack (Exodus 17:10), it sounded as if the Israelites were again being threatened by a hostile tribe. Moses, however, knew exactly what they were hearing: it was the sound of drunken singing. As he drew near and 'saw the calf and the dancing, Moses' anger burned hot' (v. 19). He smashed the stone tablets on the rocks at the foot of Horeb, ground the golden image to powder, scattered it on the drinking water and made the mob drink it.

There is a place for anger in the hearts of God's people. After all, was not Jesus also moved with anger as he witnessed the exploitation of sincere worshippers in the temple, where unscrupulous merchants cheated and robbed them? Wielding a whip, he

> There is a place for anger in the hearts of God's people.

drove out both the thieves and bleating animals. Then his disciples recalled Psalm 69:9: 'Zeal for your house will consume me' (John 2:13–17).

'Anger', however, can often be problematic. In Ephesians 4, the apostle warns, 'Be angry and do not sin,' yet a few verses later he writes, 'Let all bitterness and wrath and *anger* and clamour and slander be put away from you' (vv. 26, 31). The tension is palpable. There is much around us to cause us to be angry, similar to the blatant cheating of the merchants and moneychangers in the temple courtyard. Moreover, there are scores of occasions in Scripture where we read of the anger and wrath of God.

But, for us frail mortals, anger can quickly carry us beyond the bounds of wholly righteous emotions into a sinful, carnal reaction of anger that falls far short of the glory of God. Therefore, we must learn carefully to observe the tension in the apostle's warning not to sin in our righteous anger, while in our ongoing daily relationships we must learn to eschew all anger and bitterness. As with anger, so with 'passion'; there can be a holy passion but also an uncontrolled fleshly passion which can lead us into words and actions that we deeply regret.

In his very helpful discussion of the imprecatory psalms, C. S. Lewis makes the point that the absence of vindictiveness in pagan literature is not necessarily a good symptom. He writes:

> This was borne in upon me during a night journey taken early in the Second War in a compartment full of young soldiers. Their conversation made it clear that they totally disbelieved all that they read in the papers about the wholesale cruelties of the Nazi *regime*. They took it for granted, without argument, that this was all lies, put out as propaganda by our government to 'pep up' our troops. And the shattering thing was, that, believing this, they expressed not the slightest anger. That our rulers should attribute to some of their fellow-men the worst of crimes in order to induce other men to

> shed their blood seemed to them a matter of course.
> They weren't even particularly interested. They saw
> nothing wrong in it.[11]

Lewis' argument is that the anger against evil that we find in many psalms is righteous anger and not to experience it is a serious failure for us mortals, indicating how much the image of God in which we are created has been marred in our souls. Robert Bruce, in a sermon on Hebrews 11, says, 'If we come across a religion that practises cruelty, you will know it is from the devil and flows out of hell and human corruption, for it is a godless world that delights in such viciousness.'[12] Part of the point Bruce is making is that believers must always be appalled, grieved and angry when they hear of cruelties inflicted upon their fellow-men by those in power.

Is it a sign of increasing degeneracy in our nation that so much entertainment, both in films and novels, involves violence and murder? The annual incidence of homicide in Scotland since I was a boy has increased from single figures (five or six) to well over seven hundred each year. It cannot be denied that one factor (out of many) in the equation is anger and bitterness in people's hearts. It is too complex an issue for discussion here to explore why there can be such anger. Suffice it to say that human sin will always flourish in society, like some rank growth of toxic weeds spoiling much of the potential beauty and fragrance of a garden. Followers of Christ have to be examples of how to express righteous anger on the one hand, and how to control sinful anger on the other hand.

Moses' intercession

Moses' righteous anger cannot be separated from his impassioned prayer for God's miscreant people. But, at this point in the sacred record, we are confronted by one of those paradoxical statements which can be so baffling to our limited understanding. On account of our darkened minds, the Holy Spirit condescends to use anthropomorphic language[13] in which God is represented as saying, 'I have seen this people, and behold, it is a stiff-necked people. Now therefore let me alone, that my wrath may burn hot against them and I may consume them, in order that I may make a great nation of you' (vv. 9–10). Undoubtedly, the people had acted like a stubborn beast that was refusing to accept the collar over their neck so that, using the attached harness, their master could guide and usefully employ them. Their idolatry warranted the just deserts of the ultimate penalty of the withdrawal from them of the covenantal blessings.

> Moses' righteous anger cannot be separated from his impassioned prayer for God's miscreant people.

But why does God say, 'let me alone'? 'The effect is that God himself leaves the door open for intercession. He allows himself to be persuaded. That is what a mediator is for!'[14] The Lord is declaring 'his high estimation of his servant, to whose prayers he pays such deference as to say they are a hindrance to him.'[15] This is why the Psalmist wrote, 'Therefore he said he would destroy them—had not Moses, his chosen one, stood in the breach before him, to turn away his wrath from destroying them' (106:23).

We should notice three points regarding Moses' role as mediator between God and his people. Firstly, his prayer was selfless: he sought nothing whatsoever for himself. The offer of his descendants being made the heirs of the covenant was ignored. Indeed, at one point he offered himself as a kind of substitute sacrifice on their behalf (v. 32[16]), but no mortal could ever pay the price of sin, only Christ alone. Nevertheless, like Christ after him (Philippians 2:5–8), he sought only the blessings of the covenant for the people whom he had been called to lead and to love. Moses' selfless intercession was indeed Christlike.

Secondly, his deep concern was for the divine glory. Why should the Egyptians attribute to the God of Israel a breach of faith in his declared purposes for those whom he had delivered? The impression of God's apparent breach of his faithfulness to his Word would spread far and wide across the known world. Yet, Moses himself believed and knew from his own experience of God that he was infinitely loving, compassionate and forgiving. How ever could God act as he was now threatening that he would, when his glory was at stake? Moses knew full well that the reputation of the God of Israel was going to be a most striking witness to the watching nations. Rahab would say,

> I know that the LORD has given you the land, and that the fear of you has fallen upon us, and that all the inhabitants of the land melt away before you. For we have heard how the LORD dried up the water of the Red Sea before you when you came out of Egypt, and what you did to the two kings of the Amorites who were beyond the Jordan, to Sihon and Og, whom you devoted to destruction. And as soon as we heard it, our hearts melted, and there was no spirit left in any man because of you, for the LORD your God, he is God in the heavens above and on the earth beneath (Joshua 2:9–11).

Thirdly, Moses pleaded the covenantal promises of God to 'Abraham, Isaac and Israel, your servants, to whom you swore by your own self, and said to them, "I will multiply your offspring as the stars of heaven, and all this land I have promised I will give to your offspring, and they shall inherit it forever"' (vv. 13–14). Commenting on this incident, the psalmist wrote, 'For their sake he remembered his covenant, and relented according to the abundance of his steadfast love' (106:45).

God's Word must always be the foundation of our intercession. We stand on his Word alone—where else can we stand? Too often our prayers arise from flights of fancy, or from our own ideas or from the way we see things. But, when we plead God's clear promises, the Holy Spirit concurring with our requests, these three together—the Word, the Spirit and our prayers—will rise to the throne of God and receive the answer that is pleasing to him and according to his will for us.

Righteous retribution

The immediate outcome of the worship of the golden calf was quite horrendous. It was in three distinct phases. The first phase was the execution by the Levites of those who had indulged in the idolatry and the aftermath of 'breaking loose' into sexual immorality. We need to follow step by step the dreadful stages of this tragic episode.

It began by Moses going and standing at the entrance of the encampment, most probably facing the mountain from which he had just come; it would still have been shrouded in the numinous cloud. The symbolism of his stance would have been clearly understood as he called out, 'Who is on the LORD's side? Come to me'

(v. 26). It was his own fellow tribespeople—for Moses was a Levite—who rallied to his support and came and stood with him, presumably also resolutely identifying themselves with the covenant of God.

Next came the awesome command of God. 'Put your sword on your side each of you, and go to and fro ... and each of you kill his brother [Israelite] and his companion and his neighbour' (v. 27). The approximate proportion of those summarily executed was actually very small, less than 0.001% of the people. Nevertheless, although so small, it was a most severe demonstration of the enormity of the people's sin against the Lord who had redeemed them, had thus far provided for them, and had already made his covenant of grace with them. We should also remember that, before the coming of Christ, there was no explicit teaching of a final judgement after death. Jesus himself was the first to speak about hell. Therefore, in the Old Testament, execution was in effect God's final judgement. For those of us living on the near side of the cross and resurrection, that same final judgement awaits us all after death (Hebrews 9:27).

It has been noted that those who died were a kind of 'installation-sacrifice' for the tribe of Levi to become Israel's priests: 'Today you have been ordained for the service of the LORD, each one at the cost of his son and of his brother, so that he might bestow a blessing upon you this day' (v. 29). When, at length, the various areas of the Land of Canaan were allotted to each tribe as their inheritance, none was given to Levi, 'for the priesthood of the LORD is their inheritance' (Joshua 18:7). They were to be scattered throughout the whole land, acting as priests for each tribe (Deuteronomy 33:8–22).

For us today, Christ's words reflect something of the spiritual meaning of the Levites' sombre and appalling task of executing their fellow-Israelites: 'If anyone comes to me and does not hate his own father and mother and wife and children and brothers and sisters, yes, and even his own life, he cannot be my disciple' (Luke 14:26). The Lord went on to say that what he meant was we must bear the cross and follow him. Discipleship is impossible without whole-hearted devotion to God, and no human bonds must ever compete with, far less displace, our bond with our Master. I am reminded of John Wesley's soul-searching prayer:

> Discipleship is impossible without whole-hearted devotion to God.

Is there a thing beneath the sun
that strives with thee my heart to share?
Ah! tear it thence, and reign alone,
the Lord of every passion there;
then shall my heart from earth be free,
when it hath found repose in thee.[17]

The second phase of the outcome of the worship of the golden calf was the withdrawal from the people of God's presence. In Exodus 33, verses 2 and 3 repeat what has been already stated in 32:34: 'I will send an angel before you ... but I will not go up among you.' The text then goes on to state in 33:7, 'Now Moses used to take the tent[18] and pitch it outside the camp, far off from the camp, and he called it the tent of meeting.' It has been suggested that this signifies the consequence of God's presence being withdrawn from the midst of the encampment.

We meet with this again in our next chapter where I shall deal more fully with it. Briefly, it is most solemn and distressing for the people of God when he withdraws his presence from them.[19] Tragically, there are congregations where the absence of the great King and Head of the Church is not even noticed. But what is noticed is that little by little the spiritual life of that congregation drains away. May the Lord preserve us all from this most severe of his chastisements upon his people when his lordship is replaced by love of other things.

The third phase of the outcome of the incident of the golden calf was a plague that would afflict the camp (32:34b–35). There is no hint as to exactly when this plague would come upon the people: 'Nevertheless, in the day when I visit, I will visit their sin upon them.'

Because there is no mention of a specific pestilence that swept through the camp as it did after the incident of the quails (Numbers 11:33), I am inclined to think that this visitation had the result that none of those who came out of Egypt ever entered the Promised Land, other than Joshua and Caleb. This would connect with the judgement spoken in verse 33: 'Whoever has sinned against me I will blot out of my book.' It may be this to which the apostle referred when he wrote, 'We must not put Christ to the test ... as some of them did and were destroyed by the Destroyer' (1 Corinthians 10:9–10). Therefore, Paul brings these words and this shocking incident right into the New Testament era, and solemnly warns us against receiving the grace of God in vain. For indeed it is still a fearful thing to fall into the hands of the living God.

May God help us all! May we fear the living God with deepest tenderest fears! May we also never forget that our fear of God is not the fear of a cringing dog before a brutal master, but the loving filial fear of those whom he loves and who bow before him in awe and adoration. And, like Joseph so long ago, may we have the grace and strength always to say to the tempter, 'How then can I do this great wickedness and sin against God' (Genesis 39:9).

For further study ▶

FOR FURTHER STUDY

1. We noted three points about Moses' mediatorial intercession:
- Firstly, he asked nothing for himself.
- Secondly, his sole desire was for the glory of God (implied in vv. 12–13).
- Thirdly, his 'leverage' with God was pleading the promises of the divine covenant.
- Can you identify other biblical intercessions which have as their basis any or all of these same points? Can similar points be used in our intercessions today?

2. You may remember that we thought about 'anger' in Chapter 14. Then, it was Moses' anger against Pharaoh's evil obduracy. However, now it is God's anger against a faithless people, which was shared by Moses (vv. 10, 19). Can you find parallels to this anger in Jeremiah 8:4–17, Lamentations 2:1–9 and in Revelation 2:18–29?

3. Notice that, although God did not completely abandon his people, he withdrew his presence from them on account of their faithlessness (33:2–3, 7). What symtoms might we find in a seemingly thriving congregation that would indicate God's presence had departed from them? Unnoticed, he had slipped out from being among them.

TO THINK ABOUT AND DISCUSS

1. F. B. Meyer suggests, '[Idolatry] is an attempt on the part of the human spirit ... to associate God with what it can own and handle.'[20] The reformers taught that there are three specific items God has given us which we can see and touch in our acts of worship: the *baptismal water*, together with the *bread* and the *wine* of the Lord's Supper. Are there any objects used in some churches that are intended to help us to associate God with what we can *touch and see*? For example, what about pictures

of Jesus on stained glass windows or lecterns in the shape of magnificent brass eagles? Should church furnishings always be very simple and plain to avoid deflecting attention away from God? And what about amulets, which some footballers wear round their necks — could they be a form of idolatry?

2. The Ephesian church had lost its love for Christ, albeit the believers were bravely soldiering on in their patient endurance (Revelation 2:2–5). What do you think might have caused them to have 'fallen [from] ... the works you did at first'? What today might rob faithful Christians of their love for the Lord, consequently rendering all their strenuous service unacceptable to God?

3. There was a problem in the Corinthian congregation. Trace what it was by reading in order the following three verses: 2 Corinthians 5:14; 6:1, 12. What do you think was the missing vital ingredient in the believers' lives that Paul says they were 'receiv[ing] the grace of God in vain', and in what ways did this 'restrict' them?

4. Moses' deep concern was for God's reputation (his glory is implied) among the surrounding nations (vv. 12, 13). How does Jesus ask us to make sure God's reputation flourishes among us in our communities (Matthew 5:14–16)? Read John 13:34 and link it with John 17:22 to find out how God's glory should be seen among Jesus' disciples.

30 'Show me your glory.'

Exodus 33; 34:1–9

Moses is faced with a 'disastrous word' regarding the divine reaction to the infidelity of a wicked people on whom God has showered grace after grace. We witness Moses' wrestling with God. Undoubtedly, in his spiritual anguish, the Lord's servant was enabled to win through, being sustained by the One with whom he was struggling. Is this not always the mystery of prayer—the Lord engages in the battle with his servants, striving against them with his left arm while supporting and strengthening them with his right arm?

I do enjoy a game of football on a cold winter's afternoon, but only in the comfort of my living room as I watch television. However, that kind of enjoyment contributes absolutely nothing to the match. The home side slogging it out on the pitch can be greatly encouraged by their supporters who have paid their entrance fee, are braving the cold winter's day and are present there to encourage their team to victory by their vocal support. Indeed, I understand that the fans in the stadium can even influence the outcome of the match as they urge on the players.

So, what has this to do with these passages in Exodus? When we extrapolate the chapter into the present state of the church, we find that, in certain ways, its message is directed to today's leadership teams engaged in the Lord's work. It has a message for ministers as the teaching elder, as well as for the ruling elders and deacons; that is, for all those to whom has been given the awesome responsibility of leading and caring for the people of God. Indeed, it contains some salutary and startling lessons for our church leaders.

However, that does not mean that those who are not ministers, elders or deacons should skip this chapter, assuming it will have no relevance for them. Like the football fans in the stadium, every one of us can have a profound influence on the outcome of the spiritual endeavour with which our churches have been charged. For, every single child of God has a significant role in the ongoing march of the army of God.

We are all called to be soldiers in the conflict against the world, the flesh and the devil. Not all can be captains or lieutenants or sergeants, but every single person who loves the Lord is a foot-soldier. So, if the

Word of God in Exodus 33 and 34 may be understood in its contemporary application as addressing ministers and those who have been ordained to lead the Lord's people, we must realize that we all need to understand the mind of God so that we can think his thoughts, recognize his ways and play our part in his purposes.

> We must realize that we all need to understand the mind of God so that we can think his thoughts, recognize his ways and play our part in his purposes.

Setting the scene

Most nations can look back to their past and recall important events: some battles tragically lost and others gloriously won. For example, the Scottish people remember the Battle of Bannockburn, when Robert the Bruce defeated Edward II in much the same way as the Northern Irish remember the Battle of the Boyne, when William of Orange defeated the Old Pretender, James II. What we in Scotland tend not to want to remember is the Battle of Culloden, near Inverness, in 1746, when the forces of Bonnie Prince Charlie were totally routed by the English. It was the most shameful defeat in Scottish history. The dead lay heaped up on the moors, and the survivors were relentlessly pursued by the victorious army who showed no mercy whenever they overtook exhausted Highlanders trying to escape with their lives. Prince Charlie got away, but never again would he lead the Scots; nor would he ever be their sovereign.

Exodus 33 opens on the same tragic note of that humiliating defeat, except that the situation here is even worse. Moses had been summoned to Mount Sinai to receive the terms of God's covenant with his chosen people, whom he had redeemed and now, through the pillars of cloud and fire, was guiding towards the Promised Land. But, in his absence, the people had rebelled yet again. We have already seen in earlier chapters something of their grumbling and unbelief.

This time, however, they have been guilty of the blasphemy of blatant idolatry, as Aaron weakly bent to their pressure and fashioned for them a golden calf. They then said, 'These are your gods, O Israel, who brought you up out of the land of Egypt' (Exodus 32:4). They were imitating the pagan Canaanites who worshipped the bull calf with disgusting and immoral practices associated with fertility rites.

You will remember how, as Moses came down from the mountain carrying the stone tablets written on by the finger of God, when he saw the golden calf, he smashed the stone tablets into smithereens, and then had the golden calf ground into dust and scattered on to their water, making them drink it. And then came slaughter, followed by a plague (Exodus 32:28, 35), worse than any Battle of Culloden, as the wrath of the holy God descended upon the camp.

I wonder if you have taken in the full import of what has been happening, as we turn now to consider Exodus 33, which is the sequel to the blasphemous worship of the golden calf. Being aware of the events recorded in the previous chapter is essential to understanding what is recorded here. Moses had been in the process of receiving detailed instructions regarding that magnificent tabernacle, or tent of meeting, which was to be the focus of Israel's worship of God for several centuries. (The last time it was mentioned before it was destroyed by the Philistines was when the Lord called the boy Samuel in the night in 1 Samuel 3:3.[1])

However, at this point in the ongoing story, that tent of meeting had not yet been constructed. In the meantime, a small interim tent of meeting was being used as the place where Moses went to meet with God and with which Joshua also was associated (vv. 7–11). We might have assumed that this temporary tent of meeting would have been right in the middle of the Hebrew encampment, as ultimately was the completed tabernacle. If indeed this tent had originally been in the middle of the encampment (as some scholars suggest), after the rebellion against the Lord and the worship of the golden calf, Moses took this structure from the middle of the camp, where it symbolized the presence of God and from which the pillars of cloud and fire appeared, and pitched it outside the camp, separating it off from the idolators.[2] We find that in verse 7.

The verb in verse 7 should be in the pluperfect tense: 'Now Moses *had* taken the tent and pitched it outside the camp.' God had spoken a terrible word of judgement. He had said (vv. 2-3) that, although he would honour his promise to take them to the Promised Land, he would send an angel to lead them safely there; he himself would no longer be among them lest he consumed them for their idolatry. And that *disastrous word* (as the ESV has it in v. 4[3]) had been followed by the physical removal of the temporary tent of meeting to a place far off from the main settlement of the tents, to signify the separation of the presence of God from the people.

Is something of the full horror of all this beginning to dawn on you? It is absolutely awful. Its meaning for us today is this, and I write this in fear and trembling for all the Lord's people: there can come a time when God's presence departs from the Church of God. Significantly, it happened again when the tent of meeting, whose construction is recorded in the rest of the book of Exodus, was finally destroyed with God's judgement on his people in the days of Eli and his two wicked sons. And what was the word that described those tragic events?

Ichabod—'The glory [of the LORD] has departed from Israel' (1 Samuel 4:22).[4]

I want to tell you about a contemporary church, a fine building with the best of craftsmanship, having lovingly gone into its construction. It has a minister and ordained elders. It has a viable congregation: some 250 families with a roll of communicant members numbering some 500. It has provided its pastor with a fine manse. It has an ample reserve fund in case the roof is seriously damaged in a storm. It has PowerPoint screens and a well-equipped office with an efficient secretary. It is situated in a pleasant commuter town. But the one thing missing is the presence of God. The Lord slipped away from that congregation a few years ago and no one really noticed.

Now there is an apathy, a dullness, a heaviness among the worshippers. The praise on a Sunday is tired and flat. Do not get me wrong, there is a reasonable choir who sing very nicely, and there is not only a good pipe organ and organist, but there is also a talented praise band. They sing the best of the old hymns and the best of the new. But the glory of the Lord has departed. So, as the minister preaches, each word seems to have an invisible lead weight attached to it and, as it comes out of his mouth, it falls silently to the floor about a metre away from him. His words do not even reach the people sitting in the front seats, because God withdrew from that church a few years ago. He is no longer there.

Privately, the minister is deeply discouraged. He works at his sermons, but the inspiration he once knew, has imperceptibly melted away. He pores over the Word of God in his study and seeks the Lord's face in prayer. As he leads the worship of the Lord's people, he knows that there is an indefinable blockage somewhere. Some in his congregation blame him. They think the problem with their church is that they have the wrong person in the Manse. Little do they realize that the real cause of the lack of life lies with God because, some time ago, he left using a side door, and no one realized he had slipped out. Now he is no longer present in that congregation.

> The real cause of the lack of life lies with God because, some time ago, he left using a side door, and no one realized he had slipped out.

We must therefore turn to Exodus 33 and see what transpired after God declared that he would no longer be among his people.

The threefold prayer the minister must pray

In the situation I have just outlined, the minister must grasp that the Lord is no longer present among his people. That is the first priority. He has to find somewhere quiet, away from his comatose congregation, which at the moment is on a life-support machine in a spiritual intensive care unit, and he has to meet with God himself alone. He has to go back to his call to the ministry and to his ordination. What he must say to God is found in verse 12: 'You say to me, "Bring up this people", but you have not let me know whom you will send with me.' Moses is there referring to the angel whom (in v. 2) God has said he will put into place as the Intensive Care Unit staff nurse, periodically to check the respiration machine and the glucose drip which is keeping the unconscious body just alive and no more.

I reflect on this with a heavy heart because I know about it. I have been through it twice over in my former congregations. I have lain flat on my face on my study floor before God crying out, 'Lord, you have sent me to this idolatrous people who have a form of godliness but deny and refuse its power! Please, Lord, don't send me alone! I can't take any more of it, Lord.'

Moses' first request

'Please show me now your ways, that I may know you in order to find favour in your sight' (v. 13). In Hebrew the word, 'way', is singular. He is not here asking God to give him directions for godly living or human conduct. Rather, Moses is asking God to unfold to him his divine purpose and the path he, Moses, is being called to tread.

Show me means 'cause me to know'. He realizes that, if God leaves him in the dark about his ultimate plan for this congregation to which God has appointed him as pastor, he will stumble and go astray and take them all down with him. He is pleading before God about the task which God has assigned to him and the responsibility of leading this people forward. So, with holy boldness, he uses as a plea to back up his request: 'Consider too [Lord] that this nation is your people.' This must be every minister's prayer:

'Where are you going to take us, Lord? I must know. The glory of your name is at stake. The increasingly secular and unbelieving community in which we are placed is looking on. They are watching. They see what is happening. They are saying that you must be dead, Lord, and that maybe you never really existed at all. They are saying that the Christian faith is out of date anyway, so what does it matter. Do you want them, Lord, to see your people remaining in a vegetative state until you finally order the life-support machine to be turned off, and there is a last gasp and fevered struggle as a few remaining muscles and sinews twitch and protest about their lovely building being closed down—still not realizing that they are under your judgement, Lord, because of their hypocrisy and worship of this world that has rejected you?'

All this is implied in this first request of Moses: 'Cause me to know your purpose, Lord, for this people.'

God's answer to this humble pleading is: 'My presence will go with you, and I will give you rest' (v. 14). It is actually a very terse reply—in the original Hebrew only four words. The word translated as 'presence' is literally the word, 'face', and is often used to refer to the angel of the Lord (not at all the same angel as in v. 2) when 'the angel of the LORD' means the Lord himself (e.g., Exodus 14:19). God is saying to Moses, 'I have heard your prayer. The pillars of cloud and fire will not be withdrawn. I will stay with you along the way to guide you.' 'I will give you rest', most probably means, 'I will take away your deep anxiety and give inner peace and calm to your troubled mind.'

> Those of the Lord's ministers who seek his face, as Moses did, can be assured that God's appointment of them still stands.

So, those of the Lord's ministers who seek his face, as Moses did, can be assured that God's appointment of them still stands. Their ordination as pastors of the people of God has not been revoked, neither has the Lord deserted them. That is the significance of the first request and the Lord's answer.

Moses' SECOND REQUEST

Now we know that both the first request and the Lord's answer were about his servant's personal relationship with God because, in the second request of that distressed minister to whom we have referred, still lying flat on his face in his manse study, he now prays, 'If your presence will not go with me, do not bring us up from here. For, how shall it be known that I have found favour in your sight, I and your people?' (vv. 15–16.) He added, 'What else will distinguish us from others in our community, other than your presence with us?'

Do you see the difference in this second request? He now brings his congregation into his prayer. At first it was his own appointment as their minister that he prayed about. But now he tells the Lord that he is inseparable from the congregation which has been set in their community to be a testimony to God's grace. And God answers in verse 17, that he will not switch off the life-support machine, as it were, but he will replace the staff nurse in the Intensive Care Unit by taking over the care of the near lifeless body lying there, all wired up himself: 'This very thing that you have spoken I will do, for you have found favour in my sight, and I know you by name' (v. 17).

So, how does the despairing minister react now? Does he get up from lying on his face, go to the bathroom, wash his features—blotched and red with his tears—and use some splash-on lotion so that his dear wife (who has been for some time deeply concerned about him) will not know that he has been weeping before the Lord? Has he finished praying? Not yet, for now as he humbly kneels before the Lord there is a final request to come.

MOSES' THIRD REQUEST

'Please show me your glory' (v. 18). The scholars tell us that the word, 'Please', is actually better than the word, 'Now', which fails to convey the deeply reverential tone of this third request.[5] The word, 'glory', here 'stands for the full unveiling of the splendour and reverence of the Lord'.[6] In part, in chapter 24:10, it had already been revealed to Moses and the elders with the dazzling sapphire blue, causing them to cover their eyes. Something of that glory had been there at our fictional minister's ordination. But now, with Moses, he yearns and cries for more and yet more of God.

(We need to jump ahead a little to chapter 34:1–5 to follow this through, as God tells Moses to climb Mount Sinai once again to be alone with him.)

Try and imagine the scene and the intense heat of the burning sun in the Sinai Desert. At the foot of Mount Sinai, Moses cuts another two tablets of stone with his flint chisel and mallet. Then, in his long Bedouin garments, he first straps the heavy flat stones onto his back with broad bands of calico, and next he gathers up his robes and tucks them into his coarse, camel-leather belt to free his legs as he begins the climb. The people are all in their tents. They have been warned not to come near Mount Sinai, for God is to descend once again on the mountain.

The old man climbs higher and higher, from rock to rock, the perspiration lashing off him, often pausing for breath. Up and up he goes, until at length he enters a thick cloud that has descended upon the mountain, shrouding its heights from public gaze. And there on a small ledge, Moses reaches a fissure in the rock—a deep cleft—and he goes in to rest and shelter from the intense heat. It is wonderfully cool in this cave.[7]

As he rests there, having laid down at the cave's entrance the heavy stone slabs he has carried on his back, the presence of God surrounds him and the glory of the Lord comes upon him. The shadow of a hand slowly covers the entrance to the cave as the dazzling sapphire form passes by. Had that shadow of the divine hand not covered the entrance, no doubt Moses would have been blinded by the brilliance of that clear, crystal sapphire. We must note the word, 'cover', used in 33:22: 'I will put you in a cleft of the rock, and I will cover you with my hand until I have passed by.' It is the same word as is used of the veil that separated the Holy of Holies from the Holy Place in the Tent of Meeting, which Moses would shortly construct according to the pattern God gave to him. Thus, in 40:3 the veil 'screens' the ark in the Holy of Holies. Here, God's hand[8] 'screens' Moses from the blinding brilliance of his full presence.

And so, through that 'covering' hand, God communed with his servant as he declared his sovereignty over all humanity and gave to him the two great words which are at the heart of all that God revealed of himself: 'The

LORD, the LORD, a God merciful and gracious, slow to anger and abounding in *steadfast love* and *faithfulness*' (Exodus 34:6). It is those last two words, 'steadfast love and faithfulness', which we must note particularly. We could accurately translate them as 'grace and truth'. From now on, once the tent of meeting has been completed, the temporary tent will be discarded and the new, glorious tabernacle will be pitched in the very centre of the encampment and the *Shekinah*[9] glory of God will rest upon it and over the ark of the covenant, so that all Israel will know that the Lord's presence has returned and is among his people in grace and truth.

So how do 21st century ministers understand all this? They will turn to the opening chapter of John's Gospel where we read (own translation):

And the Word became flesh and (lit.) pitched his tent right there among us, and we have seen his glory, glory as of the only Son from the Father, full of *grace and truth* ... And from his fulness have we all received, a New Covenant of grace replacing the Old Covenant of grace. For the law [the two stone slabs carried up Mount Sinai] came by Moses; but grace and truth came by Jesus Christ. No one has ever seen God. The only Son who is at the Father's side, he has made him known.

Ministers of today will realize that, in those words from John's Gospel, all the references take us straight back to Exodus 33 and 34. The tent of meeting (the incarnate

Lord) is now pitched right in the middle of the camp at last, and the Shekinah glory shines from the Saviour's face. The glory, which was veiled from Moses, as God covered him with his hand—for no man could ever look upon the unveiled face of God and live—has now shone forth in radiance and infinite love. For the grace of law which was given through Moses has now been fulfilled in the grace and truth of the incarnate Word of God, whose flesh and blood he gave for the life of the world (John 6:51–58, 63).[10]

> The grace of law which was given through Moses has now been fulfilled in the grace and truth of the incarnate Word of God.

So, does our discouraged, dispirited minister rise from his feet with a joyful shout: 'I have seen the glory of the Lord'? I do not think so. Two hours later he is still on his face, but now the tears on his cheeks flow from the adoration of his heart, soul and mind as he has been bathed and filled and saturated by the overwhelming love of Jesus Christ. His study has become a very gateway to heaven and to the shining presence of the throne of God and of the Lamb. And when his wife taps on the door and says, 'Tea is ready, my dear,' and he again washes his face and uses the splash-on lotion, there is a residual glory shining from his features and his loved one can see that her beloved husband has truly been with Jesus.

There is nothing wrong with forming a strategy for your congregation; it is not only okay to build a vision for the congregation's future life and witness, but it could well be part of wise and godly planning. Nor is it wrong to set targets or to discuss the future of your place of worship and what God's will might be for you. But when we have done all these things, and organized missions and other outreach events, our efforts are not enough to warrant turning off the life-support machine, when the congregation has been consigned to that spiritual Intensive Care Unit. The best schemes and strategies in the world will never revive any comatose congregation from its vegetative state.

No. What is needed are the three requests of your pastor, recorded in Exodus 33:

- 'Lord, show me your way, your purpose, your plan.'
- 'Unless you are with us, your face smiling upon us, do not let us take a single step further. How else, Lord, can we be your peculiar people,[11] a clear witness to the people of our parish and district, unless your presence is among us?'
- 'Lord, show us your glory. Bring us to lie at our Redeemer's feet in submission, in total surrender and in adoration, as our love, heart, mind and will are all yielded wholly and utterly to you and possessed by you.'

For just a moment let us go back to the analogy with which we began this chapter of the importance to the football team of their solidly united supporters. The fans cheer louder and louder as their team plays better and better. And the team plays better and better as the fans shout their support louder and louder. Thus, victory becomes increasingly possible as the full-time whistle is getting nearer.

When we, who sit in the pews or in the elders' or deacons' meeting, see our dear pastor's face shining with the reflected glory of the crucified and risen Saviour, the call will be for us, with tears of repentance, to forsake the dust of our golden calves. It is time for us to turn away from all the trash and tinsel that pollutes this beautiful world. So much has absorbed the affection and devotion that rightly belongs to God, causing us to lose our first love for him. Therefore, it is high time that we cry out to God to help us tear down the dearest idols we have known from the throne of God which they have usurped, until, with broken and contrite hearts that God never despises (Psalm 51:17), we unite and join together to adore and worship at the Saviour's feet.

Then will the presence of our crucified and risen Saviour fill his house again. Then will those who have never known or loved the Lord begin truly to seek him. Then will his house be built again and glory be given to our God. That is his promise.

For further study ▶

FOR FURTHER STUDY

1. Find other examples in Scripture of God's presence being withdrawn from his people. You could start with Eli and his two sons: 1 Samuel 2:22–25, 27–34; 3:10–14; 4:4, 11, 16–18, 22. In what way did Eli share in his sons' sin (see 2:29)?

2. Regarding Moses' first request (33:13), what NT passages could define the key role of ministry in God's church for today?

3. Regarding Moses' second request, how can the Lord's presence be recognized by outsiders in our churches today (34:10b)? Explore what the NT has to say about this.

4. Undertake a study comparing Moses' encounter with God on Sinai with John 1:14–18. See if you can explain in a significant sentence the full meaning of John's phrase 'grace upon grace' (v. 16).

5. Note the phrase in 34:9, 'for your inheritance', and explore its meaning in the NT. See Acts 20:32; 26:18; Ephesians 1:11, 14, 18; 5:5; Colossians 1:12; Hebrews 4:1; 9:15; 1 Peter 1:4, etc.

TO THINK ABOUT AND DISCUSS

1. Reduced to its basic meaning, Moses' first request was about God's plan for him. How much have you discovered about his plan for your life and what were the ways in which you felt he revealed this to you?

2. Moses' second request was regarding the way in which God's plan for him would work out among the Lord's people. Discuss how God's purpose for your life will also play a part in your home fellowship's work and witness.

3. Does Moses' third request, 'Please, show me your glory' (33:18), have any meaningful place in your prayers, and if so, how could the Lord answer it (John 1:14.)?

4. The phrase in Exodus 34:6, 'steadfast love and faithfulness', is without

doubt a central and important description of God's relationship with his people. How is this description worked out in our lives as we see it in the birth, ministry, passion, death and resurrection of Jesus? See also Hebrews 2:18.

5. In a poem on 'Prayer', George Herbert has a line describing prayer as, 'Softness, and peace, and joy, and love, and bliss'. He is describing time spent with God entirely to enjoy his presence. Have you discovered this experience of the Lord when you bring no requests or even thanksgiving, but just bow before his throne of grace in the perfect confidence of his love for you?[12]

31 The high priest's garments

Exodus 28; Hebrews 7:23–25

Often when we read the Scriptures, especially the Old Testament, we come across descriptions and metaphors which are instances of God's 'accommodation' of his transcendence to our fallen natures and finite understanding. The elaborate regalia of the High Priest is an example of this gracious accommodation. We must never treat lightly, earthly 'holy places' which were divinely given as 'copies of the heavenly things' (Hebrews 9:1–5, 23). The reality of what is represented by 'copies' here on earth must be far more dazzlingly resplendent than we mortals can ever imagine (2 Corinthians 12:3–4).

Some years ago, I went to Oberammergau in Germany to see the famous Passion Play. It really is quite spectacular—the more so when you consider that there is not a single professional actor in the entire cast of some eight hundred. All on the stage are simply members of the village community of Oberammergau. The costumes of the scribes and Pharisees are magnificent. But the costume of the High Priest, Caiaphas, is quite superb— the flowing high priestly garments, the waist band or sash, and not least the turban.

We come now to the very detailed account of the clothing of the high priest in ancient Israel. 'What a strange subject!' someone says. Nevertheless, we should realize that the Old Testament priesthood is a most important subject. It would take several chapters for a detailed study of the priests and their role in the lives of God's people; it can be sub-divided under many headings such as the sacrificial rituals, the Day of Atonement, the Levitical Festivals, and so on. The priests' office laid upon them the task of intercession for the people as sacrifices were offered, as well as their instruction in the Torah; the priests were the teachers of the Old Testament Church.

However, in this chapter we are only going to take one aspect of the priesthood—the high priest's clothing— which we will look at briefly. Readers will quickly realize that the relevance of all this for a 21st century Christian Church is that the Old Testament priesthood foreshadowed Jesus Christ in his person and work. So really, as we think about the high priest's clothing, we are to be thinking about the Lord Jesus Christ.

One other introductory point before we come to our main subject. Have you ever wondered why the reformed churches do not call their clergy, 'priests', while Roman Catholics and Anglicans do? Of course, not all Anglicans call their ministers, 'priests', as many prefer to call them, 'the vicar' or 'the rector', but many Anglicans do term their clergy, 'priests'. And why do the reformed churches prefer to use the term, 'minister'?

The answer is that one main function of a priest is to offer sacrifices. The reformed churches do not understand the bread and wine of communion to be a sacrifice. We understand the bread and wine are symbols of the body and blood of our Lord Jesus Christ, and communion is *spiritual* communion involving the spiritual presence of our Lord. Roman Catholics and some high Anglicans believe that, in communion, the bread actually becomes the flesh of Christ and the wine actually becomes his blood, so at the mass Christ is sacrificed for sin all over again. The person presiding at that sacrifice is therefore a priest.[1]

> Since the Lord Jesus has died and risen, he alone is our Great High Priest.

This has been a major difference of theology between our reformed tradition and the Roman Catholic tradition. And that is why we have ministers (the word literally means, 'servants'), not priests. The other side to the coin is that since the Lord Jesus has died and risen, he alone is our Great High Priest; that is why nowhere in the New Testament are God's servants, who teach, called, 'priests'. Nevertheless, there is a sense in which all those who have his Spirit are priests to God, for we are called upon to offer the sacrifices of praise, doing good and sharing with others what God has entrusted to us (Revelation 1:6; Hebrews 13:15–16).

We turn now to just one aspect of the Old Testament priesthood as we think about the garments and regalia of the high priest and what they are able to teach us about our Great High Priest, Jesus Christ, who is not only our Priest but is also himself the sacrifice that he offered to God for sin (Hebrews 7:27).

The high priest's garments

There were six main items of clothing:

Firstly, a *tunic and undergarments made of fine linen.* Obviously, they were to cover the body of the high priest, for chaste modesty was an essential in the worship of the holy God.

Secondly, over the tunic was worn *a robe made out of one single piece of blue cloth* and which was put on over the head with a collar woven into the opening for the head; round the hem of the robe were little golden bells alternating with ornamental pomegranates made out of blue, scarlet and purple.

Thirdly, round the high priest's waist was *a sash* to hold the blue robe in place; it was to be skilfully embroidered with an intricate pattern.

Fourthly, the *turban* for the high priest's head was made of fine linen and had a band round it on to which was fixed a golden plate with the words engraved on it in Hebrew, 'Holy To The LORD'.

Fifthly, was a rather mysterious piece of clothing which scholars have not quite figured out: it was called *the ephod* and seems to have been a kind of smock which was worn over the blue robe and tucked into the sash round the high priest's waist.

Sixthly, were two other items which were fixed to the ephod:

- *a pair of gold plates* which went on the ephod's shoulder straps; these gold plates had finely fashioned chains made of twisted gold and into each gold plate was set *an onyx stone* on to which were engraved the names of the twelve tribes—six on one onyx stone and six on the other. So, the ephod's shoulder straps were adorned with these gold plates.
- a *breast piece* (vv. 15–30) which was fixed to the front of the ephod; it was made of golden thread along with blue, purple and scarlet yarn and twisted linen, and into it was set twelve precious stones, one each for the twelve tribes of Israel—

each tribe's name being skilfully engraved on its particular stone. It had a kind of pouch or pocket woven into it in which were kept two other precious stones called the *Urim* and the *Thummim*.

Now, have you followed all that? It can all seem a little complicated the first time we read of it, but it is all here in Exodus 28.

The symbolism of the high priest's clothes

The undergarments (vv. 42–43)

Firstly, *the tunic and undergarments made of fine linen.* Clearly these garments spoke of both modesty and purity in the worship of God. The undergarments were to 'cover their naked flesh'.

I recall, on one trip to Israel, taking a large group of about a hundred people to the Temple Mount in Jerusalem. The Temple Mount, of course, was the original site of Solomon's Temple in Jerusalem. Today, at one end stands the Dome of the Rock—that mosque with the golden dome—and, at the other end, the El Aqsa Mosque, both Muslim holy places. Below the Temple Mount is the famous 'wailing wall', the Jews' most sacred site, for it was built as a retaining wall, and Herod's temple was built above it; only fragments of it remain for, on its original site, stand the two mosques I have just mentioned.

It was a hot day—about 30 C (86 F). Some of the younger

women were wearing very skimpy clothing to say the least—short shorts and bare arms. The Muslim attendants at each mosque were shocked and would not allow such scantily clad women to enter their holy places until they had put on gowns, which the attendants provided, and which completely covered their arms and their legs right down to their ankles. Being rather old-fashioned myself, I saw the point entirely and agreed with the attendants. All the world's great religions have always insisted on modesty being displayed in the worship of a deity. Therefore, there must always be modesty and chastity in the worship of God.

Now, this has a contemporary relevance. Some churches have been introducing dancing into their worship. Young women on a platform at the front will lead the singing with Israeli-type folk dances. I could not object to that for, after the deliverance of the crossing of the Red Sea, 'Miriam the prophetess, the sister of Aaron, took a tambourine in her hand, and all the women went out after her with tambourines and dancing. And Miriam sang to them ...' (Exodus 15:20–21).

However, I have seen video clips of singing at the popular Spring Harvest, with young women dancing on the stage in leotards. 'That's what young people are accustomed to nowadays,' I was told. I would hazard a guess that some readers, like me, would be disturbed by such a practice and find it both offensive and distracting.

On the other hand, some of you might be enthusiastic. Yet, how impossibly hard it must be during the so-called 'worship'[2] for young men watching this display to focus on the glory of the living God.

Nevertheless, very clearly, the message of the high priest's tunic is chaste modesty in all our worship of God. That is quite plain!

> The message of the high priest's tunic is chaste modesty in all our worship of God.

THE BLUE ROBE (VV. 31–35)

Secondly, *a robe made out of one single piece of blue cloth* with the tiny golden bells and pomegranates alternating round the hem.

The blue, priestly robe stood, of course, for the priest's office. In Old Testament days, only the priest could enter the Holy Place and only the high priest could enter the Holy of Holies—the innermost sanctuary where the ark of the covenant was kept—and that was just once each year on the Day of Atonement, *Yom Kippur*. The worshippers in the temple courtyard could not see what was happening. However, as the high priest moved about in the Holy Place, the sound of the golden bells on the hem of the blue robe assured them that he was praying for them and, on *Yom Kippur*, that he was making atonement on their behalf. They could hear his priestly movements.

Not only did the pomegranates symbolize the sweet smell of ripe fruit, but they also stood for healing and well-being.[3] So, taste, smell and sound were all aspects of the high priest's office in the sanctuary.

THE SASH AND TURBAN (VV. 36–40)

Thirdly and fourthly, *the sash and turban*. The sash had to be embroidered intricately: 'You shall make a sash embroidered with needlework' (v. 39). Both these items of the priest's clothes are explicitly stated to give dignity to the high priest's office: 'You shall make them for glory and beauty' (v. 40).

Dignity is not always given in our postmodern culture. The reformers made sure the Bible was carried into church in a simple ceremony intended to give dignity to the Holy Scriptures. The beadle (church officer attending the minister[4]) traditionally opened and shut the pulpit door for the minister as an acknowledgement of the dignity of the office of those ordained to preach the Word and administer the sacraments—note, not ever for the dignity of the ministers themselves. Ministers may differ greatly in their personal dignity. Some ministers can behave foolishly, and adopt a chummy, bantering attitude that detracts from the solemnity of their office and is wholly inappropriate. But, however limited in ability some ordained ministers may be, we still honour the office of the ministry, and even to those who behave and act foolishly we give due respect for the sake of their office.[5]

We must not ignore that on the turban's headband was fixed a golden plate engraved with the words 'Holy To The Lord'. The high priest was God's man and his brow was adorned with a call to, and declaration of, holiness. He had been set apart from all that was unclean and profane and had been dedicated to serve and honour God in all he did.[6]

The ephod (vv. 6–14)

Fifthly, the *ephod* or *smock* worn on top of the priestly robe and bearing the shoulder pieces and the breast piece.

We have noted that the breast piece incorporated a kind of pouch, in which were kept two precious stones called the *Urim* and *Thummim*. Quite how it was done we will never accurately know, but they were used by the priest to find out God's will. That is, they were a means of guidance. God has always promised to guide his people, to lead the way, to block the path if we are on the wrong route, and to assure us of his presence and blessing if we are on the right route. Therefore, the two gems stood for that disclosure of God's will and purpose.

As we have seen, the high priest offered sacrifices for the sins of the people. He, then, prayed for them. Their names[7] engraved on the onyx stones on his shoulders and on individual precious stones on his heart clearly stood for his office, firstly, as the bearer of their burdens before God, and secondly, as the one who in love brought their needs before the Lord, as well as making atonement for all their sins.

Now let us apply all this to our Lord Jesus Christ.

Jesus Christ our great High Priest

MODESTY AND CHASTITY

Christ stands over against us, as the high priest stood over against God's people in Old Testament days. He stands as one in whom there is no sin; on whose tongue there is no deceit; in whose motives there is no malice; whose hands are clean and whose heart is pure love.

Christ stands over against us, as the high priest stood over against God's people in Old Testament days.

But what of you and me? Our self-righteousness is but filthy rags.[8] You throw that kind of waste on the fire. Waste disposal is painless in the Western world, as we use either black bags or wheelie-bins. In India, where I was privileged to minister on several occasions, fires smoulder here and there to burn the filth and refuse, because there are very few rubbish lorries to collect the waste. Much of what goes on in our hearts and minds deserves only the fire of the rubbish dump. There is so much impurity, selfishness and greed within us.

Our total unworthiness and worthlessness before a holy God are not popular themes today. Indeed, quite the contrary! We excuse and explain just about every fault and failing in biological or psychological terms to such an extent that we end up virtually eliminating human responsibility, deliberate wrong choices and innate wickedness. Nevertheless, we remain accountable to our God.

We need a spotlessly pure and holy high priest to plead and act on our behalf. Such is our Lord. And the priest's tunic spoke simply and eloquently of our Lord Jesus Christ in all his modesty and chastity. Sinless and without fault, on our behalf, he enters the presence of the holy God.

THE BLUE ROBE

Some commentators suggest that the colour blue speaks of heaven. I am not sure about such allegorizing. Certainly, the robe is self-evidently symbolic of the priestly office of Christ. We all accept and believe Christ to be the living Word of God; that is, he is God's incarnate Word to us—God's Prophet, so to speak. We know too he is our King, our Head; we are brought into his Kingdom and made citizens of his spiritual realm.

But we often forget that, as well as our Prophet and

our King, he is also our Priest. We have already seen that two of the functions of the priest were to offer sacrifices for sin and to pray for the people. So, the robe reminds us that Christ has offered the one great, effective sacrifice for all our sins—the sacrifice of himself—and that he prays for us.

We sometimes sing, especially at Communion, Thomas Kelly's great hymn:

Inscribed upon the Cross we see, in shining letters, 'God is love';

He bears our sins upon the tree; he brings us mercy from above.

The cross! it takes our guilt away: it holds the fainting spirit up;

It cheers with hope the gloomy day, and sweetens every bitter cup.[9]

Our High Priest has offered the one great sacrifice for sin which alone atones and covers, forever, all our guilt. And now, as our Priest, he prays for us. These mercies of the Lord Jesus Christ are the significance of the blue robe.

The bells and pomegranates on the hem of the robe are the sound and fragrance of this glorious message. It rings out from his life, full of grace and truth. The gospel sounds graciously in our ears! The scent of the breath of our Lord Jesus, as he breathes his Spirit into our spirits, is so sweet, sweeter than pomegranates; it wins our love and our allegiance.

THE SASH AND THE TURBAN WITH ITS GOLDEN PLATE

Dignity! The skilful embroidering conveyed immense dignity in those days of simple, coarse garments. What dignity has our Lord Jesus Christ! He is not, as some evangelists portray him, a beggar at the roadside, pleading for favours from a heedless world. He is the risen, exalted Son of God whose face shines as the midday sun, whose eyes are as a flame of fire, whose tongue is as a two-edged sword, and whose voice is like a thundering waterfall (Revelation 1:12–16).

All honour, majesty, dominion and power are his! Dignity indeed!

'Holy To The LORD' read the Hebrew words, engraved in gold on the headband. We rightly bow before him. He is not the 'Almatey', our 'chum'! He is the Almighty! Let our praise and our songs and psalms always adequately and appropriately reflect his divine dignity!

THE BREAST PIECE WORN ON THE EPHOD

Two stones were kept here to enable the priest to interpret the will of God. But another great High Priest now wears the ephod and shows to his people the will of our heavenly Father. His whole life unfolds the Father's will. Sunday by Sunday[10] the Lord's people gather to hear his Word in order to learn what he is like, and to understand how he wants them to live.

I know that often we are perplexed by life's decisions. But guidance becomes infinitely easier when we are following the Lord Jesus Christ and are obedient to his clear will. When the overall balance and order is right in our lives, then the details will fit into place.

THE PRECIOUS STONES ON THE SHOULDERS AND HEART OF THE HIGH PRIEST
In these gemstones, and the names engraved there, are exemplified words from Hebrews 7:23–25; because Jesus lives forever, he has a permanent priesthood. 'Consequently, he is able to save to the uttermost those who draw near to God through him, since he always lives to make intercession for them.' Our Lord Jesus Christ carries on his shoulders all our burdens and our cares. As the shepherd carries the tired lamb for that last mile of the journey home to the fold, so our Lord carries you and me on his shoulders in all our weakness, weariness and frailty.

But not only the Saviour's strength, exercised for us, is symbolized here; also foreshadowed by these precious stones is his great heart of love. For, the name of each tribe of Israel was carried on the priest's breast. For us today, each family is engraved on a precious stone on the breast of Christ. We must bear in mind all this was in respect not only of his sacrifice for our sins, but also of his prayers for us. He prays for us in our sorrows, our heartaches, our perplexities, our temptations, our fears, our weaknesses.

Robert Murray McCheyne, minister of St Peter's, Dundee, in the mid-19th century, said that as he rose to preach to his congregation, he knew Christ was on his knees in the vestry praying for him.[11] And with sighs too deep for words, understanding our frailty, knowing the sins that beset us, he prays for us. To him we are more precious than topaz, beryl, sapphire, jacinth, amethyst or jasper. Dearer to God are the hearts of the poor! We are his treasured possession—his jewels—says Malachi (Malachi 3:17, NKJV).

> With sighs too deep for words, understanding our frailty, knowing the sins that beset us, Christ prays for us.

This, then, is our great High Priest. Pure, modest, chaste, he is of infinitely more dignity than any mortal man. The glories of his Word sound out more melodiously than any golden bells as he ministers his grace. The aroma of his Person is sweeter and more healing in its properties by far than pomegranates. His guiding hand shows us the pathway of his will in this barren, trackless wilderness of our godless society. He prays for us as he lovingly bears us on his heart and carries us on his shoulders, his strength and love surpassing anything we ever imagine, supporting us in the toil of our earthly lives.

Conclusion

This too brief a study of Exodus 28 challenges each of us: How well do you know and love as your great High Priest, our Lord Jesus Christ? Do you know the Christian life is nothing if it is not spiritual union with him? In all the struggles of our temptations; in all the shame of our failures; in all the arrogance of our pride; in all our crazed stupidity as at times we fly in the face of his clear commandments; how well do we know and love this Saviour who is both the Priest who offers himself as the sacrifice in our place and the High Priest who prays for us?

Because the ascended and glorified Jesus lives forever, he has a permanent priesthood. Therefore, he is able to save completely those who come to God through him, because he always lives to intercede for them. So come to him often; come every day; come many times each day! Accept from his hand God's mercy and his grace to help you, not least in your time of need.

FOR FURTHER STUDY

1. Using the spiritual concepts underlying the seven parts of the high priest's regalia and bearing in mind that believers have been made 'a kingdom, priests to his [the Son's] God and Father' (Revelation 1:6), draw up a job description of the ideal pastor of God's flock, without mentioning by name any one of the seven items of the priestly garments.

2. The priest's four main offices were: leading worship, offering sacrifices, interceding for the people, and asking for God's guidance in important decisions (that includes judgement in disputes). To what extent ought these to be responsibilities of the minister or pastor, or ought some of these tasks to be shared within the fellowship? What New Testament precedencies might guide us in our answers?

TO THINK ABOUT AND DISCUSS

1. When European pilgrims to Israel visit the mosques on the Temple Mount, the Muslim attendants insist on women's arms and legs being completely covered and provide gowns for this before the women are permitted to enter their places of worship. Discuss whether you agree or disagree and give reasons for your opinions. How far do you think this insistence of modesty in dress should apply to worshippers in European countries?

2. Think up words and phrases to describe what each item of the high priest's clothes has to say about the character and qualities of Jesus. To what extent should these same qualities apply to every believer, even though imperfectly?

3. In Hebrews 4:16, the apostle urges believers to 'come boldly (NKJV) to the throne of grace ...'. Bearing in mind that a throne speaks of a king, and the boldness of familiarity would normally be completely inappropriate, how might you reconcile the apparent paradox of 'boldness' (ESV and NIV: 'confidence') before *enthroned royalty*? Do not ignore the splendour of the high priestly regalia which was prophetically symbolic of Jesus our High Priest, nor the description of the throne in heaven, given in Revelation 4.

Appendix 1

'Ordo salutis'[1]

Many (if not most) of the books in the Bible are written with an overall clear plan or purpose. I was first introduced to this when, in my teen years, I abandoned the excellent Scripture Union Notes I had been using and, for my daily readings, took up instead Graham Scroggie's series, *Know your Bible*.[2] Each biblical book is introduced with an analysis of its content, set out in Scroggie's inimitable, alliterative style. However, I was able to get a bird's-eye view of the entire book before beginning to study it chapter by chapter. When I moved on to university, each Sunday afternoon I set myself to study Scroggie's invaluable *Guide to the Gospels*,[3] and again gained enormously from his analytical study of the Gospels. I would go as far as to say that, during those afternoon hours, I was given a knowledge of Jesus Christ that has provided me with a firm foundation for my Christian life these succeeding sixty years.

During my undergraduate days at St Andrews University, each Sunday evening after church, members of the students' Christian Union were invited to the home of one of the academic staff, who was a mature believer. John and Evangeline threw their home open to some twenty or thirty noisy students who were served with supper. Then, John would open the Scriptures to us. I clearly remember some of his helpful insights into the Bible. I will mention two in particular. The first was a bird's-eye view of the book of *Genesis*. Briefly, the life of Abraham exemplified the need for faith. Then, on the other hand, the life of Isaac demonstrates that we are the objects of divine grace, for in every phase of his life Isaac was its object—in his birth, his marriage, his deception by his younger son and so on. Further, the life of Jacob illustrates the need for the Spirit to transform us from 'cheats' to 'princes with God', from 'Jacob' to 'Israel'. Then, Genesis moves on to the novella of Joseph which, so clearly, foreshadows the life of the Father's Beloved One, the obedient son—hated by his brothers, betrayed, unjustly brought low, then lifted up and given a name before which every knee should bow, as he became the Saviour of his people.

This is not to say, of course, that such an overview is all there is to Bible study. Far from it! Why else would I have written the book, *Joseph: his arms were made strong*,[4] or this book on Moses that you have in your hands just now? Rather is it to suggest that our studies, verse by verse and chapter by chapter, can be enriched and informed by approaching the book and its subject with an overview that indicates something of the overall plan and purpose of the inspired author.

This brief introduction brings us to the book of *Exodus*, to those Sunday evenings and to the second insight I vividly recall. And as we sat squashed together in the home of John and Evangeline, I remember being spell-bound as he described this second book of the Bible as a picture book, with large, coloured illustrations, where each picture followed on logically and prophetically. For, they vividly set out the whole story of our salvation in Christ. As only he could do, John turned over metaphorical 'page' after 'page', explaining the accuracy of the sequence of salvation events—what theologians have come to call, 'ordo salutis'. I was totally absorbed, and dwelt on that Sunday evening talk, not for a few days, but for years. And so, the concept that now follows in the first appendix of this book has grown from seeds sown in my heart and mind more than sixty years ago.

The broad panorama

Taken as a whole, the book of Exodus is the ongoing account of God's chosen people. It is the record of the journey from slavery in Egypt to Canaan, the land which was their inheritance, covenanted to Abraham, Isaac and Jacob. That is the wide tapestry on which the story of the Lord's people is woven.

However, the overarching purpose of the book, as well as introducing to us the 'ordo salutis', is to record the ongoing self-revelation of God throughout this journey. That was one reason why Moses was directed to take 'the desert road' (Exodus 13:17–22), because the covenant and the elaborate worship in the Tent of Meeting, with its theologically significant furnishings, had to be revealed before the tribes would be scattered across the Promised Land.

God's unveiling of himself, of course, is the purpose of the entire Bible. It is a gradual process, accomplished through the history of the Israelites, and would involve their patriarchs, judges, kings and prophets, as well as their many vicissitudes. It would be a 'gradual process' because God imparted the knowledge of himself in a manner that was cumulative; that is, a little more of his nature would be unfolded to succeeding generations.

The progression of this divine self-revelation through the Old Testament Scriptures is palpable. We could say that Abraham knew more about God than Noah, that Moses knew more about God than Abraham, that Samuel knew more about God than Moses and that Isaiah knew more about God than Samuel. Yet it was the self-same God, undiminished in any way, that each succeeding generation and their leaders experienced and came to know. The curtain, concealing his mysterious majesty, was being drawn back little by little through God's dealings with, for example, a Joshua, a Deborah, a Solomon or an Ezekiel, and so on.

It goes without saying that, in Scripture, the fullest unveiling of God's awesome splendour and gratuitous mercy came through Jesus Christ, 'through whom he also created the world. He is the radiance of the glory of God and the exact imprint of his nature, and he upholds the universe by the word of his power' (Hebrews 11:2–3). Even then, the final, perfected revelation of the triune God has yet to be revealed, as the last book of the Christian Scriptures, 'The revelation of Jesus Christ' (Revelation 1:1), plainly tells us. Therefore, this unveiling of the divine nature of God was always paradoxically 'already, but not yet'!

Thus, it is within the framework of this panoramic tapestry of God's self-revelation that we find part of its intricate design in Exodus is the foreshadowing of the 'ordo salutis'.

Ordo Salutis

1. SLAVES (TO SIN)[5]

The realization that we are fallen human beings who are slaves to sin is basic to the biblical doctrine of salvation. Knowledge of ourselves and our true condition is surely the first step towards the desire within us to seek God. Indeed, the Hebrew word for 'slavery' represents one of the key foundation stones of the Bible's teaching on redemption.

Therefore, right at the outset of Exodus, we should

note that the chosen people were enslaved (1:13–14): 'So they [the Egyptians] ruthlessly made the people of Israel work as *slaves* and made their lives bitter with hard *service*' (AKJV 'bondage').[6] These words occur repeatedly as the account unfolds and are used to describe the Israelites' doleful condition. The oppressor, of course, is Pharaoh, who refuses to acknowledge God, for the people *serve* him and not some deity whom he claims he does not know.

There is no difficulty in fast-forwarding to the New Testament. (We will be doing this throughout this chapter.) Take, for example, a conversation Jesus had with the Pharisees when he claimed he could impart the truth that would set them free (John 8:31–36). They indignantly replied that, as offspring of Abraham, they 'had never been enslaved to anyone'. The Lord could have cited to them how, through Moses, God had delivered them from bitter slavery, but he chose rather to go straight to the root of our human problem: 'Truly, truly, I say to you, everyone who commits sin is a slave to sin' (v. 34).

Like their fellow Israelites, the Pharisees did their very best by their own efforts to try and attain righteousness—that is, to be acquitted before God of all their sin. Thus, in seeking to establish their own righteousness (Romans 9:31–32), they failed abysmally for, in pursuing 'freedom' in Christ's meaning of the word, they were tragically unsuccessful. They remained enslaved in their sin.

As for Pharaoh, he stands as the arch enemy of God, foreshadowing 'the prince of this world'.[7] Yet, in this despot we are given a hint as to the mystery of the origins of evil. Through Moses, God says to him, 'For this purpose I have raised you up to show you my power, so that my name may be proclaimed in all the earth' (Exodus 9:16). The apostle reiterates this in Romans 9:17.

We have already seen, in Chapter 28 of this book, how Satan had the hellish effrontery to invite the Son of God to *serve* him in exchange for the power and glory of this fallen, broken world! This was the spirit of disobedience and arrogance that held sway in the heart and mind of Pharaoh. Thus, just as enslavement (servitude) of men and women to the Egyptian despot is a major theme in *Exodus*, so similarly in the New Testament is enslavement (servitude) to Satan an ongoing expression of the plight of all humanity.

2. The cry (for deliverance)

If enslavement to Pharaoh was the theme of Exodus chapter 1, in the second chapter we learn that a great cry for deliverance had risen up before the throne of God from the hearts of the slaves: 'Their cry for rescue from slavery came up to God. And God heard their groaning ... God saw the people ... and God knew' (vv. 23–25).

The Christian doctrine foreshadowed is clearly illustrated many times in the New Testament. Three examples will suffice: 'But the tax collector, standing far off, would not even lift up his eyes to heaven, but beat his breast, saying, "God, be merciful to me, a sinner!"' (Luke 18:13). Or the incident of the Philippian jailor: 'And the jailor called for lights and rushed in and trembling with fear he fell down before Paul and Silas. Then he brought them out and said, "Sirs, what must I do to be saved?"' (Acts 16:29–30). Thirdly, 'For everyone who calls on the name of the Lord will be saved' (Romans 10:13; see also Acts 2:21). This basic principle of turning to God is repeatedly asserted throughout the whole of the Old Testament, as well as affirmed in the New Testament.

3. THE PASSOVER AND REDEMPTION (THROUGH CHRIST'S BLOOD)

Before Jesus even began his ministry and immediately prior to his baptism, John bore witness that he was the 'Lamb of God': 'The next day he saw Jesus coming towards him, and said, "Behold the Lamb of God, who takes away the sin of the world"' (John 1:29). John repeated this testimony to Jesus a little later: 'The next day again John was standing with two of his disciples, and he looked at Jesus as he walked by and said, "Behold the Lamb of God"' (John 1:35–36).

The apostle Paul was very specific about declaring Jesus to be the fulfilment of the ancient Passover feast, when a roasted lamb without blemish was eaten in commemoration of the night the lamb's blood was daubed on the doors' lintels and posts: 'For Christ, our Passover lamb, has been sacrificed.' He then went on to urge that the festival (that is, the Passover) be celebrated in an altogether new way 'with the unleavened bread of sincerity and truth' (1 Corinthians 5:7–8).

The three synoptic Gospels all explicitly state that the occasion when the Lord instituted what, from earliest times, was called the Lord's Supper or the Eucharist ('thanksgiving') was the Passover feast (Matthew 26:17; Mark 14:12; Luke 22:7–15). 'The cup of blessing that we bless, is it not participation in the blood of Christ?' wrote Paul (1 Corinthians 10:16). So that, although the lamb's blood smeared on the door lintel was a one-off action, never to be repeated, the wine of the Passover was to be the fulfilment of that sacrificial lamb's blood.

4. Baptism (into Christ)

The crossing through the parted waters of the Red Sea might seem an unlikely foreshadowing of Christian baptism, but the apostle boldly allegorizes this key event in the deliverance of the Lord's people from thraldom to Pharaoh: 'I want you to know, brothers, that our fathers were all under the cloud, and all passed through the sea, and all were baptized into Moses in the cloud and in the sea' (1 Corinthians 10:1-2). The preposition, 'into', is important and implies that the people were baptized into Moses' leadership.[8]

Someone might ask, 'But how can Christian baptism be foreshadowed by 'a cloud' that was given to screen them from their pursuers, or by, in effect, 'a 'dry' baptism' that was only a path and route from one side of the Red Sea to the other side? Both of these were physical manifestations, whereas surely our baptism is a sacramental sign of salvation. The answer is easy, for both the cloud and the pathway through the sea were God's provision for their escape from slavery, and therefore had deep spiritual significance.

Another question arises: 'Why were they baptized *into* Moses?' Again, the answer is easy and obvious. He was God's appointed guide for them (though at every stage he was himself led and guided by God). Furthermore, he was also their teacher (though all he taught them was imparted to him by God who was his Teacher).

Thus we see why Paul easily identified the crossing of the sea under the cloud with the baptism entrusted to the church by Christ. Believers also are baptized 'into Christ' and 'into one body', that is, into 'the body of Christ'.[9] As well as being our Saviour, Christ is also our Guide and our Teacher. Again, it goes without saying that the Scriptures always make it clear that the divine agency in baptism is the Holy Spirit.

5. Bread (from heaven)

The apostle wrote, '... our fathers... all ate the same spiritual food ...' (1 Corinthians 10:1, 3). The Old Testament church clearly understood that there was a profound spiritual significance in the manna, for the Psalmist wrote, 'Man ate of the bread of the angels' (Psalm 78:25). However, the context in the Psalm is that Abraham's descendants were 'a stubborn and rebellious generation ... who sinned still more against him, rebelling against the Most High in the desert ... they did not believe in God and did not trust his saving power' (vv. 8, 17, 22). Nevertheless, this merciful God 'commanded the skies above and opened the doors of heaven, and he rained down on them manna to eat and gave them the grain of heaven' (vv. 23–24). Therefore, the manna was a gratuitous provision from God, their deliverer, and was entirely undeserved. Also, we saw how Moses instructed them to gather it in its six-day cycle, thus reminding them of the Creator God and his Sabbath rest.

Fast-forwarding to the New Testament, the implication in the Lord's teaching contained in John 5 and 6 is that the Jews, 'seeking all the more to kill him, because ... he was even calling God his own Father', were holding up

Moses before Jesus as the true prophet of God. For Jesus responded, 'If you believed Moses, you would believe me; for he wrote of me' (5:18, 46). John, then, goes on to recount the miracle of the five barley loaves and two fish being used to feed the five thousand (6:9–13). The crowd who pursued him clearly saw themselves as disciples of Moses, for Christ referred to Moses again when he said of himself, 'Truly, truly, I say to you, it was not Moses who gave you the bread from heaven, but my Father gives you the true bread from heaven' (6:32).

And so, we read on and hear Jesus saying these crucial gospel words: 'I am the living bread that came down from heaven. If anyone eats of this bread, he will live for ever. And the bread that I will give for the life of the world is my flesh' (6:51). Then, there follows the 'hard saying' when he says, 'unless you eat the flesh of the Son of Man and drink his blood, you have no life in you' (vv. 60, 53). Thus, the spiritual symbolism of the manna in the wilderness pointing forward to Christ, 'the bread of life', is quite undeniable.

The same link, of course, applies to the water from the rock (Exodus 17:6; Numbers 20:10–13). The apostle wrote, '… our fathers … all drank the same spiritual drink. For they drank from the spiritual Rock that followed them, and the Rock was Christ' (1 Corinthians 10:1, 4). There are two slightly different metaphors Jesus uses of this water flowing from him for the thirsty.

First is the one we have just noticed: that is, drinking his blood as well as eating his flesh.

However, there is a second metaphor found in John 7:37–39, where he appears to echo his words to the Samaritan woman that 'the water that I will give ... will become ... a spring of water welling up to eternal life' (4:14). Here, there could be an allusion to Ezekiel 47:1–12 and to the river that issued from the threshold of the temple which steadily increased in its depth and flow until it reached the sea. If Ezekiel's life-giving river is hinted at in Jesus' words in John 7, then it is tempting to follow this through to Revelation 22:1–2, where in heaven there was seen 'the river of the water of life, bright as crystal, flowing from the throne of God and of the Lamb', bringing life and healing for the nations.

6. SPIRITUAL WARFARE (OVERCOMING THROUGH PRAYER)

The events of Exodus 17:8–16, describing the lethal attack upon the Israelites by Amalek, occur after the Passover lamb, baptism into Moses, the bread from heaven and the water from the rock. There is profound significance in this, for it teaches us that, even after God's mighty redemptive acts and provision for his people, they still face conflict from hostile spiritual powers. Believers too easily fail to notice that, when the apostle exhorts us to 'put on the whole armour of God', we are having to take our defensive stand 'against the spiritual forces of evil *in the heavenly places*' (Ephesians 6:11–12). Perhaps unexpectedly, the most dangerous spiritual warfare is where the risen and glorified Christ is now seated *in the heavenly places*; and this is also where, through God's gracious redemptive acts, we also are seated *with him in the heavenly places* (Ephesians 1:20; 2:6).

Most of the armour of God consists of defensive equipment: the belt of truth; the breastplate of righteousness; the strong sandals of the gospel of peace; the shield of faith; and the helmet of salvation. There are only two means of attack: the sword of the Spirit, which is the Word of God, together with 'all prayer and supplication' (Ephesians 6:14–18). Thus, as Moses, in partnership with Aaron and Hur, held up his hands in prayer and supplication, he was taking his spiritual stand upon the covenantal promises of God. I am reminded of the lines in Edward Mote's great hymn, which speaks so eloquently of the beleaguered Christian turning to God in earnest supplication:

> His oath, his covenant, his blood support me in the
> whelming flood;
> When all around my soul gives way, he then is all my hope
> and stay.

> *On Christ, the solid Rock, I stand; all other ground is*
> *sinking sand.*

(Edward Mote, 1797–1874)

7. THE LAW (OF CHRIST)

The Hebrew word, *Torah*, is complex, for it is used in several ways. It sometimes refers to the entire Levitical 'cultus' with its many regulations regarding ceremonial cleanness, sacrifices and offerings, festivals and tabernacle furnishings—and of course the rite of circumcision. *Torah* can also refer to the Pentateuch, the first five books of the Old Testament. In addition, *Torah*, along with *the Prophets* (the Law and the Prophets), is also used to denote the entire Hebrew Scriptures. Finally, *Torah* is used with the meaning of God's self-revelation through the Scriptures.

However, its initial meaning was the Decalogue (the 'ten words')—that is, the Ten Commandments. We must not forget that the stone tablets on which they had been inscribed by the finger of God[10] were kept inside the ark, covered with the 'mercy seat', which was beyond the veil that separated the Holy Place from the Holy of Holies. I admit it is a poor simile, but it is as if the Ten Commandments (the first meaning of *Torah*) were like the proverbial pebble which, when dropped into a pond of still water, causes ever increasing ripples to spread from the epicentre until they reach across the whole stretch of water. So, emanating from the stone tablets are concentric circles which completely embrace the sacred account of God's character and mighty acts across the aeons of human history.[11]

Fast-forwarding yet again to the New Testament, we find a multiplicity of references to the Law. But for our purposes here, we need only to consider a very few of these. The first we should note is the apostle's statement in Romans 10:4 that 'Christ is the end of the law ...'. The Greek word for 'end' is *telos* which means either 'termination' or 'goal'; both meanings are intended by Paul. Here, 'law' means the entire Levitical cultus of washings, sacrifices, festivals, tabernacle ritual and circumcision. Why should this entire system of worship be *terminated*? Because it was all pointing to Christ—he was the *goal* towards which it was directed. Moreover, in his birth, ministry, crucifixion, resurrection and ascension, the law had been perfectly fulfilled.

The second mention of law in the New Testament we should note is from Galatians 3:24–27, where Paul writes:

> So then, the law was our guardian until Christ came, in order that we might be justified by faith. But now that faith has come, we are no longer under a guardian, for in Christ Jesus you are all sons of God, through faith. For as many of you as were baptized into Christ have put on Christ.

In his lengthy comments on these verses, translating the Greek, *paidagōgos*, as either schoolmaster' or 'custodian', Luther wrote:

> A schoolmaster is extremely necessary for a boy

... for without this instruction, good training and discipline, the boy would come to ruin. For it is not the father's intention that his son should be subject to the schoolmaster forever, but that through the instruction and discipline of the schoolmaster, the son may be made fit for accession to his inheritance ... The law was a custodian until Christ comes, the Justifier and Saviour, so that we may be justified through faith in him, not through works.[12]

John Stott wrote:

> The law expresses the will of God for his people, telling us what to do and what not to do, and warns us of the penalties of disobedience. Since we have all disobeyed, we have fallen under its just condemnation .... Like a jailor, it has thrown us into prison; like a *paidagōgos* it rebukes and punishes us for our misdeeds. But, thank God, he never meant this oppression to be permanent for 'the law was our custodian *until Christ came*, that we might be justified by faith'.[13]

What more need I say? The point of the Law's prophetic and preparatory purpose is clearly made by both of these two outstanding theologians!

8. PUBLIC AFFIRMATION (OF FAITH IN CHRIST)

The critical day came when the covenant God made with his people had to be affirmed by them with a public confession of their acceptance of it.[14] The covenant's terms had been recorded and were to be read before the assembled multitude. Both burnt offerings (which must be entirely consumed by the flames) and peace offerings (which were to provide a sacred festive meal for all) were sacrificed on an altar at the foot of Mount Sinai, specially constructed for the purpose; around the altar twelve memorial pillars were raised, representing the twelve tribes. The narrative in Exodus 24 continues:

And Moses took half of the blood and put it in basins, and half of the blood he threw against the altar. Then he took the Book of the Covenant and read it in the hearing of the people. And they said, 'All that the LORD has spoken we will do, and we will be obedient.' And Moses took the blood and threw it on the people and said, 'Behold the blood of the covenant that the LORD has made with you in accordance with all these words' (vv. 6-8).

Once again, it was an easy and obvious step a millennium later for the twelve disciples, as they also partook of the peace offering of the Passover lamb, to hear Jesus saying, as he filled the common cup with the wine, he was sharing with them, 'This cup that is poured out for you is the new covenant in my blood' (Luke 22:20). Personal confession of faith in Christ was to become a prerequisite of participation in the Lord's Supper.

Scholars assure us that, in Philippians 2:5–11, the apostle is quoting the earliest known Christian hymn.[15] It is argued that the Church's first Christian confession and affirmation of faith was simply, 'Jesus is Lord'. His is 'the name that is above every name, so that at the name of Jesus every knee should bow ... and every tongue confess that *Jesus Christ is Lord*, to the glory of God the Father.'

In the Gospels, we read first of John the Baptist making a confession: 'He confessed, and did not deny, but confessed, "I am not the Christ"' (John 1:20). There are seven references in John's Gospel to John the Baptist and, in them all, he is, in effect, saying, 'I am not the Messiah, it is Jesus.'[16] He was always pointing to Jesus. That was his confession.

Paul declares that Christ himself made this same confession before Pilate. The verses are important and deserve quoting in full:

> Fight the good fight of the faith. Take hold of the eternal life to which you were called and about which you made the good confession in the presence of many witnesses. I charge you in the presence of God, who gives life to all things, and of Christ Jesus, who in his testimony before Pontius Pilate made the good confession, to keep the commandment unstained and free from reproach until the appearing of our Lord Jesus Christ, which he will display at the proper

time—he who is the blessed and only Sovereign, the King of kings and Lord of lords, who alone has immortality, who dwells in unapproachable light, whom no one has ever seen or can see. To him be honour and eternal dominion. Amen (1 Timothy 6:12–16).

This public confession of Christ is an important aspect of the teaching recorded in the Gospels. 'Therefore whoever confesses me before men, him I will also confess before my Father' (Matthew 10:32, NKJV).[17] Twice we read of the Jews seeking to dissuade anyone from confessing Jesus as the Christ. The first was with the parents of the man born blind but healed by Jesus: 'His parents said these things because they feared the Jews, for the Jews had already agreed that if anyone should confess Jesus to be the Christ, he was to be put out of the synagogue' (John 9:22). The second time was in John 12:42: 'Nevertheless, many even of the authorities believed in him, but for fear of the Pharisees they did not confess it, so that they would not be put out of the synagogue.'

There is the climactic event when Peter made the great confession. Again, the incident must be quoted in full:

Now when Jesus came into the district of Caesarea Philippi, he asked his disciples, 'Who do people say that the Son of Man is?' And they said, 'Some say John the Baptist, others say Elijah, and others Jeremiah or one of the prophets.' He said to them, 'But who do you say that I am?' Simon Peter replied, 'You are the Christ, the Son of the living God.' And Jesus answered him, 'Blessed are you, Simon Bar-Jonah! For flesh and blood has not revealed this to you, but my Father who is in heaven. And I tell you, you are Peter [*petros*], and on this rock [*petra*] I will build my church, and the gates of hell shall not prevail against it' (Matthew 16:13–18).

I have inserted the Greek words Christ used, for the rock (*petra*) was not the man, Peter (*petros*), but the confession that he had made that Jesus was 'the Christ, the Son of the living God'. Hence the gracious accolade from Jesus that Peter was indeed blessed. It was the Father who had bestowed this revelation upon him of the true identity of the Galilean Teacher.

Paul was equally clear of the central place in the gospel of confession of Christ for salvation: 'For with the heart one believes and is justified, and with the mouth one confesses and is saved' (Romans 10:10). Or again: 'For we will all stand before the judgement seat of God; for it written, "As I live, says the Lord, every knee shall bow to me, and every tongue shall confess to God"' (Romans 14:10–11).

Thus, we see that the book of Exodus has these clear metaphorical pictures of the sequence of salvation in the New Testament. In them are the great principles of God's redeeming work for fallen sinners through the redemption that is in his blessed Son alone:[18]

- slaves to sin
- the cry for deliverance
- the Passover and redemption through Christ's blood
- baptism into Christ
- bread from heaven
- spiritual warfare overcoming through prayer
- he law of Christ
- public affirmation of faith in Christ.

Appendix 2

The order of service for public worship

I have found in recent years that, among some of the younger more progressive (?) ministers, there has been criticism of the 'hymn-prayer-hymn sandwich' which has been traditionally and widely adopted in most Christian congregations for the Order of Service. A number of years ago, I recall feeling uncomfortable as I sat in a congregation (not in the United Kingdom), where I had been invited to preach, while the minister launched the service in a rather radical style. It was clear that he belonged to the bold brigade of younger ministers who had no time for the traditional order of service!

So how did this traditional *order of service* develop? Did it by any chance have its origins in the Bible? If it did, then what are those origins? I want to suggest that the answer is found in the layout and furnishings of the Tent of Meeting, as described in Exodus chapters 25–31 and 35–40; also, in Numbers 2 and 3:38–39, where instructions regarding the arrangements for each encampment of the twelve tribes are given. The twelve tribes were to take up positions on each of the four sides of the Sanctuary, so that the dwelling place of God would be right in the centre; that is, so to speak, God would be in their midst.

1. BEGIN WITH PRAISE

'Enter his gates with thanksgiving, and his courts with praise' (Psalm 100:4). The Tent of meeting (or Tabernacle) was in the centre of the vast encampment of the Israelites. Its entrance faced the sunrise on the east, and encamped there were Judah, Issachar and Zebulun. The various members of the tribe of Levi were divided between all four sides. On these four sides there was to be a clear space between the Levites' much smaller settlements (because this one tribe of priests was spread throughout the entire encampment) and the various other tribes' settlements. However, the families of Moses and Aaron were also on the eastern side, for their particular responsibility was 'guarding the sanctuary itself, to protect the people of Israel' (Numbers 3:38).[1]

Judah, chosen to be the royal tribe (Genesis 49:10), was camped across the entrance to the Tabernacle. Judah's name means 'praise' (Genesis 29:35), hence the Psalmist's exhortation that the worshippers were to 'enter his gates with praise', for they were to pass through Judah to reach the place of worship. This is most probably why our forefathers always began their services looking upwards in praise and thanksgiving to God, for that is how we are to 'enter his gates'. The hymn, 'Praise my soul the king of heaven'[2] is based on Psalm 103, and so is a good example of 'entering his gates with praise'. There are so many praise Psalms such as 8, 24 and 145, as well as a multiplicity of 18th and 19th century hymns in addition to scores of contemporary hymns of adoration.

Therefore, in the era of the New Covenant we are well advised to begin our services by lifting up our hearts and minds to adore, bless and magnify the Lord.

2. CONFESSION OF SIN

On entering the courts of the Tabernacle, the worshipper was at once confronted by the bronze altar (Exodus 27:1–8; 38:1–7). There, the priest awaited him to offer his sacrifice for the atonement of his sins and those of his family. This was the time for worshippers to look inward and acknowledge their need of forgiveness. We are reminded of the tax-collector who 'would not even lift up his eyes to heaven, but beat his breast, saying, "God, be merciful to me a sinner"' (Luke 18:13). Because we are all sinners, there ought always to be prayers of confession, for 'if we confess our sins, he is faithful and just to forgive us our sins and to cleanse us from all unrighteousness' (1 John 1:9).

3. ABSOLUTION

Next, the worshipper would see the bronze basin for Aaron and his four sons to use for washing (Exodus

30:17–21; 38:8). Nothing unclean was to be taken unwittingly into the inner sanctuary. Calvin called the use of the basin the 'washing of expiation'. In his temple Solomon made huge provisions for similar ceremonial washings (1 Kings 7:23–39).

The New Testament makes much of ceremonial or spiritual washing, no doubt taking as an example David's penitential prayer in Psalm 51:2, 7: 'Wash me thoroughly from my iniquity and cleanse me from my sin ... wash me, and I shall be whiter than snow.' So, when Ananias visited Saul, after he had been confronted by the risen Lord, Ananias urged, 'And now why do you wait? Rise and be baptized and wash away your sins, calling on his name' (Acts 22:16). We are not surprised, therefore, that the apostle Paul spoke of the Church as having been cleansed 'by the washing of water with the word' (Ephesians 5:26), and that he declared to Titus that God has saved us 'by the washing of regeneration and renewal of the Holy Spirit' (Titus 3:5).

The writer to the Hebrews relates the spiritual implications of ceremonial washing to the 'full assurance of faith, with our hearts sprinkled clean from an evil conscience and our bodies washed with pure water' (Hebrews 10:22). This is how we are enabled to draw near to God with a clean heart. I do not doubt that the meaning of the (controversial[3]) word 'absolution' is clearly intended here. Prayers of confession should always include the assurance that the Lord 'pardoneth and absolveth all those who truly repent and unfeignedly believe his holy gospel'.[4] In recent years, many reformed ministers have failed to bring this firm, uncompromising affirmation of full pardon to their congregations. (See Footnote 4 below.)

4. FEEDING ON THE BREAD OF LIFE

The next stage of daily worship involved the priest entering the Holy Place, which had certain items of furniture. We consider firstly the table for bread (Exodus 25:23–30; 37:10–16). 'And you shall set the bread of the Presence on the table before me regularly' (25:30). We have already seen, in the previous appendix, how Jesus was the true bread from heaven. Therefore, we must ask how we, who live on the near side of the cross, may feed from Christ.

Beginning with what we have already seen above regarding the 'Bread from heaven' and the obvious reference to the Lord's Supper, we must then extrapolate to feeding from the Word of God. In other words, essential to any Christian service must be preaching and teaching from the Scriptures. Nor should such ministry be arid, purely theoretical or a display of oratorical skill. Rather, it should be the 'bread of the Presence', when the wisdom and ways of Christ are plainly set forth and, through the Holy Spirit's enlightening, directed at the people's minds, wills and hearts.

5. THE ALTAR OF INCENSE

Situated in the Holy Place, immediately in front of the veil, beyond which rested the ark of the covenant, was the altar of incense (Exodus 30:1–10; 37:25–28).[5] The high priest 'shall burn fragrant incense on it. Every morning…' and 'at twilight' (30:7–8). So, both morning and evening of every day of every year the fragrance of the incense, made only for use in the tabernacle worship, must be burned. Its fragrance, therefore, would constantly fill the Holy Place.

The meaning of this fragrant incense is explained to us elsewhere in Scripture, in both Psalms and Revelation. David already understood the spiritual meaning of costly incense being offered during his worship of God: 'Let my prayer be counted as incense before you, and the lifting up of my hands as the evening sacrifice' (Psalm 141:2). In the vision given to John of the glorified Christ standing as a Lamb 'as though it had been slain' (Revelation 5:6) before 'him who was seated on the throne' (5:1). As the living creatures and twenty-four elders worshipped the Lamb, they were holding 'golden bowls full of incense, which are the prayers of the saints' (Revelation 5:8).

Again, we are told that, when the Lamb opened the

seventh seal, after silence in heaven for half an hour, an 'angel ... was given much incense to offer with the prayers of all the saints ... and the smoke of the incense, with the prayers of the saints, rose before God from the hand of the angel' (Revelation 8:3, 4). Amazingly, the effect on earth appears to have been 'peals of thunder, rumblings, flashes of lightning, and an earthquake' (Revelation 8:5). T. F. Torrance comments: 'What are the real master-powers behind the world, and what are the deeper secrets of our destiny? Here is the astonishing answer: the prayers of the saints and the fires of God. That means that more potent, more powerful than all the mighty powers let loose in the world, more powerful than anything else, is the power of prayer set ablaze by the fire of God and cast upon the earth.'[6]

What a challenge to the Church of God today is the altar of incense with its fragrant aroma, rising perpetually day and night before God. Thus, intercessory prayer is a vital component of every service when believers meet together to praise God and feed from his living Word. The vivid imagery of John's vision should stimulate both faithfulness and fervour in our prayers.

6. THE GOLDEN LAMPSTAND

'You shall make a lampstand of pure gold,' was the instruction given to Moses (Exodus 25:31–40; 37:17–24). Known today as the Menorah, pure olive oil was to be the fuel for its seven lamps (Exodus 27:20–21). These lamps were to shed light in the Holy Place, both day and night. Oil in the Old Testament stood for both light (as with the Menorah) and the unction of the Holy Spirit as prophets, priests and kings were all anointed with special grace for their calling.

Its application for the New Testament Church's worship services is plain enough. Without the presence of the Holy Spirit, our service to God is both Christ-less and vain.

> I am the light of the world. Whoever follows me will not walk in darkness, but will have the light of life (John 8:12).
>
> For God, who said, 'Let light shine out of darkness', has shone in our hearts to give the light of the knowledge of the glory of God in the face of Jesus Christ (2 Corinthians 4:6).

7. The Holy of Holies

Beyond the veil, in the Holy Place was the innermost sanctuary, the Holy of Holies (or Most Holy Place), where the ark of the testimony was placed and into which the high priest went only once a year on the Day of Atonement (Exodus 26:32–34; Leviticus 16:15).[7] However, on the cross 'Jesus cried out again with a loud voice and yielded up his spirit. And behold, the curtain (veil) of the temple was torn in two, from top to bottom'

(Matthew 27:50–51). The powerful significance of this is that because Jesus, as a 'forerunner on our behalf' (Hebrews 6:19–20), has entered the inner place behind the curtain (veil), we too may 'with confidence draw near to the throne of grace, that we may receive mercy and find grace to help in time of need' (Hebrews 4:16). In short, through Christ's atoning death, believers may boldly approach the unapproachable.

No one who is familiar with the detailed descriptions of the Levitical regulations regarding the great annual day of atonement, together with the layout and furnishings of the Holy Place and the Most Holy Place, will fail to grasp something of the awesome privilege believers have in drawing near to the Almighty God, who is love and light but also a consuming fire. Thus, while we lift up our hearts and voices to praise the Triune God, nevertheless, we can never do so flippantly or carelessly, but always with joyful reverence.

By way of conclusion, here is one final quotation from 1 Corinthians 3:16–17:

> Do you not know that you are God's temple and that God's Spirit dwells in you? If anyone destroys God's temple, God will destroy him. For God's temple is holy, and you are that temple.

The three prepositions, 'you', are plural while both the nouns, 'temple', are singular. Therefore, the apostle is stressing that the Church is the temple of God, in which he dwells by his Spirit. There are two words in Greek for 'temple': one is *hieron*, which means the entire structure, courtyard and surroundings; the other is *naos*, which is used here and which means the innermost shrine, the dwelling place of God. Thus, as the people of God gather together to worship him in that total yielding of themselves as living sacrifices to him, corporately they do so as the very shrine of the living God. What highest dignity and most awesome privilege, therefore, is ours who, thus, meet in Christ's name!

8. THE OFFERING

See Exodus 25:1–2; 35:4–9, 21, 29. The people gave, 'everyone whose heart stirred him, and everyone whose spirit moved him, and brought the Lord's contribution ...' (35:21). See also 1 Corinthians 16:1–3; 2 Corinthians 8 and 9. The work of God must always be supported by the people of God, 'for God loves a cheerful giver' (2 Corinthians 9:7).

9. THE FINAL BLESSING OR BENEDICTION

See Exodus 39:43; Leviticus 9:22–23.

Summary of the essentials of New Testament 'services of worship'

- Praise
- Looking upwards and outwards towards the Lord our God.
- Prayer

- Looking inwards and confessing our needs.
- The assurance of forgiveness and our adoption.
- The Word of God
- Read with clarity and Holy Spirit enabling.
- Expounded: what it meant then and what it means now.
- Intercessions
- The Offering
- The Blessing

All must be empowered and enlightened by the Holy Spirit so that boldly, yet reverently, we may approach the mercy seat—the throne of grace.

The grace of the Lord Jesus Christ and the love of God and the fellowship of the Holy Spirit be with you all (2 Corinthians 13:14).

Now to him who is able to keep you from stumbling and to present you blameless before the presence of his glory with great joy, to the only God, our Saviour, through Jesus Christ our Lord, be glory, majesty, dominion, and authority, before all time and now and forever. Amen (Jude 24, 25).

Abbreviations and Bibliography

Abbott   Richard Abbott, 'Forked Parallelism in Egyptian, Ugaritic and Hebrew Poetry', (Tyndale Bulletin, 2011).

Baldwin   Joyce Baldwin, *1 & 2 Samuel*, (Nottingham: IVP, 1978).

Binning   Works of Rev. Hugh Binning, (Reprint—Canton, Ohio: Pinnacle Press, 2017), Book Depository Ltd., UK.

Blocher   Henri Blocher, *In the Beginning*, (Leicester: Inter-Varsity Press, 1984).

Bruce, F. F.   F.F. Bruce, *Commentary on the Book of Acts*, (Edinburgh: Marshall, Morgan and Scott, 1965).

Bruce, R.   Robert Bruce, *Preaching Without Fear or Favour,* Sermons on Hebrews 11, *trans.* David Searle (Christian Focus, 2019).

Bunyan   John Bunyan, *The Pilgrim's Progress,* (Edinburgh: Banner of Truth Trust, 1977).

Calvin's Comm.   John Calvin, *The Pentateuch, Calvin's Commentaries, Puritan Series,* (Grand Rapids, Michigan: W.B. Eerdmans, 1960).

Calvin's *Ephesians*   John Calvin, *Commentary on Galatians, Ephesians, Philippians and Colossians,* (Edinburgh: St Andrew's Press, 1965).

Calvin's *Psalms*   John Calvin, *Commentary on the Psalms, abridged by David C. Searle,* (Edinburgh: Banner of Truth, 2009).

Childs, B. S.   B.S. Childs, *Exodus,* (London: SCM, 1974).

Christian Hymns   *Christian Hymns,* (Bridgend: Evangelical Movement of Wales, 1973).

Cole   Alan Cole, *Exodus,* (Leicester: Tyndale, IVP, 1973).

Dennis Lennon   Dennis Lennon, *Turning the Diamond,* (London: SPCK, 2002).

Descartes   René Descartes, *Discourse on the Method of Rightly Conducting One's Reason, Part IV,* (London: J.M. Dent, 1957).

Egypt   Claudio Barocas, *Ancient Monuments of Egypt,* (London: Readers Digest Assoc. Ltd., 1972).

Ellison   H. L. Ellison, *Daily Study Bible: Exodus,* (Edinburgh: St Andrew's Press, 1982).

Fire Lilies	Dr Rhiannon Lloyd, *Fire Lilies: Finding Hope in Unexpected Places,* (Healing the Nations Publishing, 2021).
George Herbert	*The Complete Works of George Herbert 1594–1633,* (London: Pantianos Classics, Paperback reprint of edition first published 1874).
Grimm-Thayer	*Greek–English Lexicon of the New Testament* (Edinburgh: TandT Clark, 1901).
Hastings	James Hastings, *Dictionary of the Bible,* (Edinburgh: TandT Clark, 1919). Article on Myrrh, p. 639.
Hendriksen	William Hendriksen, *Ephesians,* (Edinburgh: Banner of Truth, 1973).
	Colin J., *Miracles of Egypt,* (London: Continuum, 2003).
Humphreys	IBD, *llustrated Bible Dictionary,* 3 Parts, (Leicester: IVP, 1980).
Inst.	Calvin's *Institutes of the Christian Religion,* ed. John T. McNeill, , (Philadelphia: Westminster Press, 1960).
Josephus	Flavius Josephus, *Antiquities of the Jews,* (trans. William Whiston, Routledge, London, 1602).

Letters Revd. Andrew Bonar (Ed.), *Letters of Samuel Rutherford,* (Edinburgh: Oliphants, 1848).

Leupold H.C. Leupold, *Exposition of the Psalms,* (Ada, Michigan: Baker, 1972).

Luther's *Galatians* Martin Luther, *Commentary on Galatians,* (London: James Clark, 1961, 3rd Impression, First published in 1535).

LXX LXX is the Septuagint, a translation by seventy Jewish Scholars of the Hebrew Old Testament into Greek.

Lewis, C. S. C. S. Lewis, *Reflections on the Psalms,* (Glasgow: Collins, 14th Impression, 1979).

Lloyd-Jones Dr D. Martyn Lloyd-Jones, *Prove all Things,* (Eastbourne: Kingsway, 1985).

Lloyd-Jones' Studies Dr D. Martyn Lloyd-Jones, *Studies in the Sermon on the Mount,* (Leicester: IVP, 1972 5th reprint).

Martin Luther Michael A. Mullet, *Martin Luther,* (London: Routledge, 2004).

Mackay John L. Mackay, *Exodus: A Mentor Commentary,* (Fearn: Christian Focus Publications, 2001).

Macnicol Duncan C. Macnicol, *Master Robert Bruce, Minister in the Kirk of Edinburgh,* (Edinburgh: Banner of Truth, reprint 1961).

Martin Ralph P. Martin, *A Hymn of Christ*, (Cambridge University Press, 1967, originally published as *Carmen Christi*). Ralph Martin's study of this passage was originally published in 1967 under the title *Carmen Christi* and then reissued in 1983 as *A Hymn of Christ*.

McCheyne Andrew A. Bonar (Ed.), Memoir and Remains of the Rev Robert Murray McCheyne, (Edinburgh: Oliphant, 1869). Reprint: Banner of Truth, 1960.

Meyer F.B. Meyer, *Moses Servant of God*, (Edinburgh: Marshall, Morgan and Scott, 1953 edition).

Morality Jonathan Sacks, *Morality*, (London: Hodder and Stoughton, 2020).

Mote, Edward A collection of approximately 100 of his hymns was published under the title, *Hymns of Praise, A New Selection of Gospel Hymns, Combining All the Excellencies of our Spiritual Poets, with Many Originals*, (London: John Nichols, 1843).

Morris Leon Morris, *Revelation*, (London: Tyndale Press, 1969).

Noth Martin Noth, *Exodus*, (London: SCM Press, 1962).

Philip

James Philip, *Numbers,* (Waco, Texas: Communicator's Commentary, Word Books, 1987).

Scott Peck

M. Scott Peck, *The Road Less Travelled: A New Psychology of Love, Traditional Values and Spiritual Growth,* (New York: Simon and Schuster, 1978).

Searle

David C Searle, *And Then There Were Nine,* (Fearn: Christian Focus Publications, 1st edition 2000, reprinted 2006).

Sermons

John Calvin, *Sermons on Timothy and Titus,* (Edinburgh: Banner of Truth, 1st pub. 1579, reprint 1983).

Still and Ferguson

William Still and Sinclair Ferguson, *Bringing up Children in Faith not Fear,* (Aberdeen: Didasko Press,). Unfortunately, out of print.

Stott *Acts*

John W.R. Stott, *The Message of Acts,* (Leicester: IVP, 1990).

Stott *Galatians*

John W.R. Stott, *The Message of Galatians,* (London: IVP, 1968).

Strong

Strong's Concordance of the Bible, (London: Hodder and Stoughton, 1890).

Studd, C.T. Norman P. Grubb, *C.T. Studd, Cricketer and Pioneer*, (London: Lutterworth, 15th Impression 1949).

Torrance Thomas F. Torrance, *The Apocalypse Today*, (London: James Clark and Co, 1960).

Wenham Gordon J. Wenham, *Numbers*, (Leicester: IVP, 1981).

Endnotes

Epigraph

1 https://www.poetryfoundation.org/poems/50695/the-windows-56d22df68ff95

Foreword

1 David Searle, *Joseph: His Arms Were Made Strong*, (Edinburgh: Banner of Truth, 2012; 2nd Impression 2023).

Overview

1 Acts 7:22, 'mighty in his words and deeds'.
2 The mystery of divine election is spelled out clearly in Moses' words in Deuteronomy 7:6-8.
3 Look up Exodus 32 and underline the name of Aaron throughout the entire chapter!

Chapter 1

1 See Claudio Barocas, 'Monuments of Civilization: Egypt' (trans. from Italian and pub. *Reader's Digest,* 1972), pp. 57–59, 65.
2 Bruce, F. F., p. 149; see Note 41.
3 Genesis 15:16. 'They shall come back here in the fourth generation, for the iniquity of the Amorites is not yet complete.'

4 Corrie Ten Boom, *The Hiding Place*, (New York: Bantam Books, 1984, first published 1971).
5 Tertullian, *Apologeticus*, L.13. (Originally published in AD 197)

Chapter 2

1 Still and Ferguson.
2 Bruce, F. F. *Commentary on Acts*, p. 390.
3 John Stott, *Commentary on Acts,* p. 307.

Chapter 3

1 Josephus, II, X, 1. It is impossible to determine the accuracy of Josephus' account of Moses' war against the Ethiopians, when he acted as a General of the Egyptian army. However, Stephen's comment, which I quote, may lend some credibility to the account Josephus gives, for Stephen appears to have been referring to Moses' time as a prince of Egypt.
2 Bruce, R., pp. 401–402. Bruce follows Calvin in asserting Moses was acting judiciously.
3 Augustine of Hippo, AD 354–430, renown theologian and philosopher, ultimately became Bishop of Hippo Regius in Numidia, Roman North Africa. His mother Monica died in 388, having

lived to see his dramatic conversion.

4 Dr Helen Roseveare (1925–2016), medical missionary to Belgian Congo, prolific author and international speaker.

5 'Anthropomorphism' is speaking of God as if he were a man; ascription of human form, attributes or personality to God. (*Shorter Oxford Dictionary*, Oxford, 3rd edition 1944, reprint 2009.)

Chapter 4

1 The common expression among the Scots is 'cauld kale het up'.

2 Clearly there are exceptions to this. David was specially chosen, though despised by his older brothers; his brilliant mind is well illustrated in his psalms. Saul of Tarsus was to become God's instrument to write a major part of the inspired Scriptures of the New Testament. But the general point I am making remains valid.

3 See Chapter 3, Note 1.

4 See also Nehemiah 1.

5 The 'God of the Gaps' approach caused Huxley to write: 'Operationally, God is beginning to resemble not a ruler, but the last fading smile of a cosmic Cheshire Cat.' – Julian Huxley, *Religion Without Revelation*, (New York: New American Library, 1956). The image of the disappearing smile of a Cheshire cat originated of course from Lewis Carroll in his children's book, *Alice in Wonderland*.

6 Inst. Book I, Chapter 1, pp. 35–39.

7 Attributed to Bernard of Clairvaux.

8 McCheyne, pp. 241–42. The full quotation includes: 'A holy minister is an awful weapon in the hand of God.'

Chapter 5

1 Leupold argues the case for accepting as valid the Heading: 'A Prayer of Moses, the man of God', p. 641.

2 Samuel Rutherford (1660-61), Minister of the Scots Kirk, lived during tempestuous times when Charles I was attempting to impose episcopacy on the Kirk. Because of his stout resistance to the royal interference, he was banished to Aberdeen where he was confined from 1634 for two years. He called his prison 'Christ's palace' and wrote to a friend, 'I find my prison the sweetest place that ever I was in.' *Letters*, pp. 13, 530.

3 Descartes, Part IV, p. xiv. First published in French, the sentence originally was 'Je

pense, donc je suis.' Those who argue that only the individual who thinks is real and all else exists only in his imagination belong to a branch of metaphysics called solipsism which is based on a philosophy of subjective idealism. Metaphysical solipsists maintain that the self is the only existing reality and that all other realities, including the external world and other persons, are representations of that self, and have no independent existence.

4 The contemporary mountain Jebel Musa is favoured by most scholars as Mt Horeb. At its base stands the Monastery of St Catherine, where Tischendorf discovered the famous 4th century uncial manuscript of the Greek Bible called Codex Sinaiticus of the Greek Bible. St Catherine's library has other ancient manuscripts in Greek, Arabic, Ethiopic and Syriac. (*IBD*, Part 3, pp. 1460–61.)

Chapter 6

1 Calvin's *Comm.*, pp. 490–92.
2 Ibid, p. 476.
3 Calvin's *Psalms*, p. xi.

Chapter 7

1 The Hebrew word, *peh*, usually translated as 'speech' is literally 'mouth' or part of the mouth (*Strong*, 6310); therefore, it is possible the reference is to Moses' lips.

2 Edwards preached his most famous sermon, 'Sinners in the Hands of an Angry God', in Enfield, Connecticut in 1741. Though this sermon has been widely reprinted as an example of 'fire and brimstone' preaching in the colonial revivals, this is not in keeping with Edward's actual preaching style. Edwards did not shout or speak loudly, but talked in a quiet, emotive voice. He moved his audience slowly from point to point, towards an inexorable conclusion. The 'Angry God' sermon has been reprinted many times and is available to purchase on many search engines as an ebook or audio on social media platforms, e.g., https://www.blueletterbible.org/Comm/edwards_jonathan/Sermons/Sinners.cfm

3 The internet has a vast amount of material on the 'Here I stand' speech. A recent contemporary account is given in *Martin Luther* by Michael A Mullet (London: Routledge, 2004). The account of the Diet of Worms is given on pp. 120–28,

with 'the heroic finale, "Here I
stand. I can do no other!"' dealt
with on p. 128.

Chapter 8

1 I can offer no reference for this
   quotation from Spurgeon. Many
   years ago, I heard it during a
   sermon by the Rev. James Philip
   (1922–2009), Holyrood Abbey
   Church, and was so moved by it
   that I wrote it down as soon as I
   returned home.

2 A statute of limitations, known
   in civil law systems as a
   prescriptive period, is a law
   passed by a legislative body to
   set the maximum time after an
   event within which legal
   proceedings may be initiated.
   Once that period of time fixed
   in law has elapsed, no further
   prosecutions can be brought.

3 Lloyd-Jones, pp. 85–86.

4 Lloyd-Jones, p. 79.

5 Isaiah 50:7, spoken
   prophetically of the promised
   Messiah. See also Mark 10:32.

6 Spoken on John Knox's death
   bed, 24 November 1572.

Chapter 9

1 Calvin's *Comm.*, p. 484;
   Mackay, p. 98

2 For an excellent article on the
   overwhelming evidence of the
   benefits of circumcision for
   penile hygiene, see http://

www.circinfo.net/penile_
hygiene.html.

3 The Hebrew noun *sippor*
   means a small bird, and so
   Zipporah can carry the
   meaning of twitterer.

4 We could apply this in a
   general way to non-Christians
   in terms of God's common
   grace to all (in distinction to
   his saving grace to believers).
   In earlier generations it was
   expected that public figures
   and all who aspired to high
   office should be those who
   were of good character and
   reputation. No longer. The
   present fashion is to say that
   one's private life has nothing
   to do with one's public life.

5 Mackay, p. 91: 'We must not
   imagine divine anger is
   identical to ours, because
   human emotions are
   contaminated by sin. On the
   other hand, we must avoid
   reinterpreting divine anger so
   that it is no longer divine
   anger at all! The Lord's anger
   is never unreasonable, nor
   does it get out of control'
   (Exod. 32:10).

Chapter 10

1 Calvin's *Comm.*, p. 485.

2 Incidentally—not that it
   matters—it is likely that it was
   just the first two signs that

were given to them, that is, Moses' staff becoming a serpent, and his leprous hand being made whole. The third sign of the water being rendered undrinkable and taking on the dark colour of blood would later be enacted on the banks of the Nile. However, if some readers are inclined to think the third sign was also given at this time, I would not object.

3 Calvin's *Ephesians*: Calvin's comments on 6:12 (see pp. 218–219) are much more explicit than those of D. M. Lloyd-Jones, referred below in Note 52.

4 If you have access to D. M. Lloyd-Jones' Commentaries on *Ephesians One*, see Ch. 5, 'All Spiritual Blessings in Heavenly Places', pp. 57–80; *Ephesians Two*, see Ch. 9, 'In the Heavenly Places', pp. 126–140; *Ephesians Three*, Ch. 6, 'God's Strange Design', pp. 80–92. Unfortunately, his commentary on Ephesians chapter 6, *The Christian Soldier* omits verse 12 altogether, but his sermon on this verse can be downloaded from https://www.mljtrust.org/sermons.

Chapter 11

1 Indeed, the Republic of Sudan is suffering in a similar way as South Sudan!

2 The dynasty that had been actively seeking to find and execute Moses. See Exodus 4:19.

3 *Egypt*, pp. 140, on Ramesses II's power over Egypt (The New Kingdom, XIX Dynasty, 1320–1200 BC). Dr Ken Kitchen is of the opinion that it would have been Ramesses II who was Pharaoh at this time. *IBD*, pp. 1234–1236.

4 Jeremiah uses a simile of Nebuchadnezzar plundering Egypt 'as a shepherd cleans his cloak of vermin' (43:12).

5 'Myopic' is not an exact synonym for 'short-sightedness' as it can be used with the connotation of 'a lack of intellectual insight'.

6 'Common grace' is the expression used to denote God's kindness and provision for all humanity, irrespective of their creed, for he is their Father in virtue of being their Creator. 'Saving grace' is the expression used to denote those who have been brought into a new living relationship in virtue of their adoption into his family through faith in his Son's atoning sacrifice. (We can add to these two expressions of divine grace a

third category, as when God's 'special grace' is imparted as an anointing for some particular ministry; this is enacted in the OT in the anointing of prophets, priests and kings.)

7 This is not a biblical quotation but rather is an allusion to verses such as Psalm 81:13–16, 147:12–14; etc.

Chapter 12

1 I am aware that not all companies follow this training procedure; however, my illustration is taken from a large papermill in my first parish outside Aberdeen.

2 The rest of verse 3 reads, 'but by my name the LORD I did not make myself known to them'. That does not mean the name LORD was until now unknown. It is used frequently in Genesis. The meaning here is that, although the *sound* of the name LORD was known, its *meaning* had not yet been revealed. See Exodus 3:14.

Chapter 13

1 See article in *IBD*, by Dr K. A. Kitchen, pp. 1234–1236, Part 3. Some readers may be interested to read Colin J. Humphreys treatment of the

first Nine Plagues. Chapter 9, pp. 111–128.

2 A well-known and regularly used colloquial expression without any intended sexist slur whatsoever on (often far cleverer) schoolgirls!

3 The Aswan Dam, or more specifically since the 1960s, the 'Aswan High Dam', is one of the world's largest embankment dams, which was built across the Nile in Aswan, Egypt, between 1960 and 1970. Its significance largely eclipsed the previous Aswan Low Dam, initially completed in 1902.

4 John L. Mackay points out how, in order to undermine the miraculous, some scholars have argued that the plagues were natural disasters. He adds, 'But not all who make the link with natural phenomena in Egypt are trying to undermine the miraculous. Quite the contrary ... the timing of the disasters was clearly dictated by the Lord's command: they started and finished when he laid down, and as he had stated in advance.' *Exodus* (Mentor, Fearn: CFP, 2001), p. 142.

5 See for example, 7:13, 22; 8:15, 19, 32; 9:7, 12, 34–35; 10:20, 27.

6 See for example, 8:19a; 9:20; 11:3.

7 There are three points we should note in this genealogy. Firstly, it is recorded that Amram married his father's sister (6.20); because such marriages were later forbidden in the Law (Lev. 18:12), this detail would confirm the accuracy of the genealogy, as such a relationship would never have been invented had the list been recorded later. (However, the term 'his father's sister' could possibly mean 'a blood relative'.) Secondly, Jochebed is the only name of a person prior to Exodus 3:14 that uses the prefix 'Jo', meaning 'the LORD'; the whole name means 'the LORD is glory'. This confirms that the name LORD was indeed known prior to God's self-revelation to Moses, when the powerful significance of its real meaning was disclosed. Thirdly, only Aaron's family is given here, as he was the elder son; the names of Moses' sons, Gershom and Eliezer, are not recorded until 18:3-4.

8 See also Revelation 2:17, 3:5, 12.

Chapter 14

1 Here, 'redemption' refers to the 'cost', while 'deliverance' refers to 'freedom from slavery'. The two words are not synonymous.

2 We cannot be sure that Ramesses II (1304–1237) wore a golden mask similar to that found in Tutankhamun's tomb (1361–1352). See *National Geographic* magazine, November 2022, for the article on 'Tut's Treasurers'. However, Ramesses' wealth and power would certainly have been marked by imposing and intimidating golden accoutrements. 'It is difficult to find a Pharaonic monument in Egypt today that does not bear [Ramesses II's] mark somewhere. This activity of Ramesses II was an integral part of his intention to make the figure of the Pharaoh the only reference point in the nation's culture. His practice of "usurpation" is typical in this regard.' *Egypt*, p. 180.

3 My memory of the movie is vivid, but I cannot recall either its title or Director! Nor can I vouch for its historical accuracy. However, a very similar scenario also occurs in the film, *Cold Mountain, The Siege of Petersburg*, 2003, Director: Anthony Minghella.

4 Here is a quotation from the first of three sermons by

Binning on 1 John 1:9: 'The current of sin dries not up but runs constantly while we are in this life. It is true, it is much diminished in a believer, and it runs not in such a universal flood over the whole man as it does in the unbeliever. Yet there is a living spring of sin within the godly which is never ceasing to drop out pollution and defilement, either upon their whole persons or at least to intermingle it with their good actions. Now, there is no comfort for this other than that there is another stream of the blood of Jesus Christ that never dries up, is never exhausted, never emptied, but flows as full and as free, as clear and fresh as ever it did. This is so great and of so great virtue that it is able to swallow up the stream of our pollutions and to take away the daily filth of a believer's conversation [daily living].' Binning, Vol. 2, p. 17.

5 In 1835, Robert Murray McCheyne was appointed as assistant minister in Larbert to John Bonar, elder brother of Horatius Bonar the hymn writer; Andrew Bonar, another brother, wrote the well-known Memoir of McCheyne (Reprint: Banner of Truth, 1960).

6 Exodus 21:23–24. 'But if there

is harm, then you shall pay life for life, eye for eye, tooth for tooth, hand for hand, foot for foot.' Some readers may be interested to read Colin J. Humphreys treatment of the Tenth Plague. Chapter 10, pp. 136–146.

7 I am referring to traditional Presbyterian practice that goes back to the Reformation: 'Christ our Passover is sacrificed for us, therefore let us keep the feast.' Book of Common Order, 1979 (St Andrew Press) p. 1.

8 Lewis, C. S., Reflections on the Psalms, Ch. 3, pp. 23–33. Calvin's Psalms.

Chapter 15

1 Note that yeast does not always necessarily stand for pervasive evil; see Matthew 13:33.

2 Calvin in his commentary on this passage does not regard yeast as being symbolic for indwelling sin, but rather says that yeast was not to be used because the bread had to be made in great haste; yeast in the bread would have been too slow in being baked, and the whole tenor of the instructions in the preparation of the meal was that it must be done in haste. Calvin's Comm. p. 642.

3 *Passover Haggadah*, (London: H. Pordes), p. 9.

4 From the hymn, 'When I survey the wondrous cross', Isaac Watts (1674–1748).

5 The term LORD (using small capitals) is used by the translators to indicate that in the Hebrew the word is Yahweh (YHWH), meaning I AM THAT I AM, the name by which God commanded he should be made known to his people. (See the footnote in Exodus 3:14 in the ESV.) Sometimes preachers speak of the 'Angel of Death' passing over Egypt but, in Exodus chapter 12, four times we read that it was the LORD who would pass over. When the LORD himself speaks, he says, 'I will pass over you ... when I strike the land of Egypt' (v. 13).

6 In one of my visits to minister in Rio in Brazil, I had the privilege of spending most of a night with a team of Christian students who were driving down the city's darkest back streets in a campervan with a large urn of hot drinking chocolate, dozens of blankets and fresh bread rolls. They would park and teenagers would come out of the shadows to benefit from this Christian charity. One girl (I would guess 14 or 15 years old) had two small boys with her: one about three years old and the other about two years old; she was clearly expecting another child very soon. The students told me that when the baby was born, the three-year-old child would be left to fend for himself and would join a gang of children of the same age who would live by stealing and pickpocketing. It took a wait of about half an hour before street children would begin to emerge very cautiously from the shadows— cautiously, because big departmental stores employed off-duty policemen to shoot them as they were already expert thieves. That night I also saw a man in his 60s bedding down under sheets of cardboard in an alleyway with a fourteen-year-old girl; the students told me he would have bribed her with a loaf of bread and a few coins to spend the night with him. 'This is where the street children come from,' said the students.

7 From the hymn, 'Beneath the cross of Jesus', by Elizabeth C. Clephane (1830–69).

8 First published in 1766 and now available online as a free eBook. Of course, tens of

thousands of his sermons were published during his lifetime and also his *Explanatory Notes on the New Testament* (Epworth, London, 1954).

9 'The abstinence here recommended must be understood, not as an essential Christian duty, but as a concession to the consciences of others, i.e., of Jewish converts, who still regarded such foods as unlawful and abominable in the sight of God.' Stott, *Acts*, p. 250.

Chapter 16

1 Notice that this act of God was most probably provision being made for the future materials that would be required for the Tent of Meeting. Alas, some of the gold would be tragically abused in the idolatrous fashioning of the golden calf.

2 Elsewhere I have given an explanation as to why the sixth commandment should be translated as in the ESV, rather than the AV's 'Thou shalt not kill.' See David Searle, *And then there were Nine*, (Fearn: Christian Focus Publications, 2000), pp. 98–110.

3 Romans 10:4, 'For Christ is the end of the law for righteousness to everyone who believes.'

4 Calvin's *Comm*. The quotation(s) are an amalgam of several phrases in Calvin's lengthy exposition of the Passover. pp. 640, 641. He deals with the Passover in his commentary as belonging to his exposition of the first commandment.

5 Blocher, p. 120. The fuller quotation may be of interest to some readers: 'The LORD put him in the garden 'to till it and keep it'... We can easily check how far the man's rule differs from that of a self-centered tyrant. In Hebrew 'to till' is literally 'to serve'. Even in his relationship with the soil, mankind must maintain his humility. The use of the verb paves the way for the condemnation of the 'destroyers of the earth' (Rev. 11:18) – those guilty of ecological depredation. Not only will man rule over nature by obeying its laws, but he will do so for the good of creation itself, so that it may fulfil its 'vocation', to glorify the Creator.

6 Romans 1:9; 2 Timothy 1:3, *et al*, always use the Greek verb, *latreuo*, which is the equivalent of the Hebrew, *'abad*. For a further poignant use by Paul of latreuo, see also

Acts 27:23, '…God whose I am, and whom I serve' (AKJV).

7   Joyce Baldwin (1921–95) authored three Tyndale Commentaries, *Daniel*, *Esther* and *Haggai, Zechariah and Malachi*. She also wrote *The Message of Genesis 12–50* (IVP, The Bible Speaks Today series). In Trinity College, Bristol, she worked alongside Alec Motyer and J.I. Packer.

8   Cole, p. 112.

9   See Footnote 87 above.

10 The wider context of this parable is undoubtedly the charge brought against Jesus in Luke 15:2. It appears that someone who had come to know Christ had opened his home and invited 'tax collectors and sinners' to come and share a meal with him so that they could meet and hear Jesus for themselves. He was using his 'very little' to make friends for the Kingdom. Compare with Matthew 9:10–13.

11 Here is a quotation from Os Guiness on contemporary praise hymns: 'Thank God for magnificent exceptions such as the rich, deep hymns of Keith Getty and Stuart Townend, which will join the music of the ages. But much of the run-of-the-mill renewal songs, which are repeated endlessly and constructed more on rhythm than melody, confine Evangelicals within a shallow theology, threadbare worship, fleeting relevance and historical amnesia.' Guinness Os, *Impossible people: Christian courage and the struggle for the soul of civilization* (Downers Grove: InterVarsity Press, 2016), p. 176.

Chapter 17

1   Edith Schaeffer has written extensively on Christian families: *What is a family?* (Revell, 1975); *Ten Things Parents Must Teach their Children* (Baker Books, 1994); *A Celebration of Children* (Raven Ridge, 2000). My reference is from *What is a family?* in Chapter 9, 'A Museum of Memories'.

2   Personally, I deplore children being taken out of the church services after a trivial address to them. A creche for little ones, yes, but from school age children ought to sit with their parents. If the gathering knows anything of the presence of the risen Christ, through the power of the Holy Spirit, the children will be aware of that, even though

some of what is said may not yet be understood.

3 In past theological study and writing there has been a strong aversion against the interpretation of the Hebrew word, *padah*, as meaning, 'payment of a price'. So-called liberal theologians have argued that God could never pay a price to redeem his people and the implications for the doctrine of the atonement are at once evident. But in Exodus 13:13, *padah* explicitly means 'payment of a price'; therefore, its connation is not merely, 'deliver' (as liberal theologians insist), but also, 'ransom', i.e., 'deliver at a cost'.

Chapter 18

1 See the source of this quotation in Question 3 below under 'Time to Think and Discuss'.

2 1 Corinthians 14:40, '[A] things should be done decently and in order.'

3 Galatians 1:15–24. It may be that his total time in obscurity was nearer ten years; see especially verses 10 and 21.

4 Calvin, *Comm.* p. 542.

5 John Bunyan's terminology from *Pilgrim's Progress*.

6 The allusion is to Matthew 7:7–8.

7 See Chapter 4 in this book for Calvin's precise comment on this in his *Institutes*: FOR FURTHER STUDY, No. 1, p. X.

8 These words from 1 Corinthians 13:12, AKJV, are translated by the ESV as 'For now we see in a mirror dimly, but then face to face.'

9 From the hymn 'The sands of time are sinking' by Anne Ross Cousin (1824–1906), based on Samuel Rutherford's writings. The full verse is:
With mercy and with judgement my web of time he wove,
And aye the dews of sorrow were lustred by his love;
I'll bless the hand that guided, I'll bless the heart that planned,
When throned where glory dwelleth in Immanuel's land.

10 Fire Lilies, *Finding Hope in Unexpected Places*, p. 5.

Chapter 19

1 M. Scott Peck, p. 1.

2 I am not using the word, 'beasts', in a pejorative sense, rather it is the normal word used in Scotland for cattle, especially bullocks.

3 The context to which I am referring was that of Newman

(1801–90) leaving the evangelical wing of the Church of England and entering into the Roman Catholic priesthood. The book defending his choice (*Apologia pro Vita Sua*) has run into multiple editions.

4 From a poem based on Exodus 31:20–21, entitled 'The Pillar and the Cloud', by John Henry Newman (1801–1890).

5 Calvin's *Comm.* p.311.

6 You will notice on the Map (p. ?) that the Red Sea divides into two 'fingers', the western one is known as the Gulf of Suez, the eastern one is the Gulf of Aqaba. The actual route taken by Moses has been disputed, but the traditional route clearly indicates that the crossing was at the northern most tip of the Gulf of Suez. We must also bear in mind that the topography of the area will have changed somewhat over the past 3,200 years. The *Yam Suph*, traditionally translated, 'Red Sea', more accurately means 'Reed Sea', after the native vegetation that grew in the marshlands of Egypt at that time. For a Christian scientist's view of the crossing of the Red Sea, see Humphreys, Chapter 16, pp. 244–260.

7 Calvin helpfully comments: 'Moses calls this Being an angel, to which he assigns the name of the eternal God. And with good reason, because our heavenly Father then led the Israelites only by the hand of his only begotten Son. Now, since he is the eternal guardian of his Church, Christ is not less truly present with us now by his power than he was formerly manifest to the Fathers.' Calvin's *Comm.* p. 547.

8 From verse 3 of the hymn, 'My God, how wonderful thou art', by Frederick William Faber (1814–1863).

9 Calvin's *Psalms*, p. xi.

10 See Calvin's comment in Footnote 7 above. For anyone who wants to follow up on this theme of Old Testament 'Theopanies', a useful book is *Christ in the Old Testament*, by James A Borland (Fearn: Christian Focus Publications, 2010, 1st Edition by Moody Press).

Chapter 20

1 '"Triumphed gloriously": better, "has risen up" (like a wave). The word is used both of pride (in a bad sense) and triumph (in a good sense) as here. Ezekiel 47:5 uses the

verb of a river rising in flood.'
Cole, p. 123.

2 https://www.
poetryfoundation.org/
poems/44731/lallegro

3 https://www.
poetryfoundation.org/
poems/43827/
the-destruction-of-
sennacherib

4 Richard Abbott, Forked
Parallelism in Egyptian,
Ugaritic and Hebrew Poetry,
(Tyndale Bulletin, 2011),
pp. 41–64.

5 For an informative outline of
the eight different forms of
parallelism in the Psalms, see
W. Graham Scroggie, *Psalms
Vol. 1* (London: Pickering and
Inglis, 1948), pp. 9–14.

6 Contrast these two verses in
Isaiah 33:14 and 17, and their
immediate contexts.

7 Calvin's *Comm.* p. 124

8 'Be Thou My Vision', Dallan
Forgaill (530–598);
Translator: Mary E. Byrne,
1880–1931

9 This is a common way the
Aberdeen folk often speak
about themselves and their
canny handling of their
finances. They themselves
have a jocular definition of an
Aberdonian as someone 'with
deep pockets and short arms'.

10 Another Aberdonian common

quip that goes with the
proverbial visit to the bank!

11 Henotheism is the worship of a
single, supreme God that does
not deny the possible
existence of other inferior
deities.

12 See, however, Exodus 32, and
the golden calf to be reminded
of the fickleness of human
frailty.

13 The same verb is translated as
'lead' in Psalm 23:2.

14 In 2 Corinthians 6:16, the
Greek word for 'temple' (*naos*)
is used in the LXX of the
innermost sanctuary in the
Tent of Meeting.

Chapter 21

1 Some readers may be
interested to know that in Book
I of Calvin's *Institutes of the
Christian Religion*, the first
chapter heading is 'The
Knowledge of God and That of
ourselves are connected'. In the
first paragraph he says, '[in the
knowledge of ourselves] we
shall learn humility', p. 36. An
editor's footnote (4) comments,
'The close relation between
humility and self-knowledge
constitutes an oft repeated
theme for Calvin.' p. 37.

2 Joseph Medicott Scriven
(1819–86)

3 Cole suggests it could have

been the barberry bush as used by modern Arabs to sweeten the water. p. 129. Mackay comments, 'Modern research has told us about the moringa tree whose crushed seeds provide an environmentally friendly and inexpensive way to purify water.' p. 280.

4 It may be of interest to note that the ancient understanding of myrrh is different in the eastern churches to that of the western churches. The former have traditionally seen myrrh as an agent of healing as well as of anointing as a rite, whereas the latter have regarded it as a symbol of dying and the anointing of the dead body. Also, Eastern Orthodoxy still uses myrrh as an anointing during initiation into the church. Hastings, p. 639; see also website for Myrrh in Eastern Orthodox Church.

5 E.g., www.crosswalk.com/ faith/spiritual-life/how-can-i-resolve-conflict-in-a-biblical-way

Chapter 22

1 I am forbearing from identifying this book for although the author died some time ago, there are relatives who would not be best pleased at having a revered grandfather's publicly work criticized.

2 Genesis 31:1 (KJV—'glory'; ESV—'wealth'); 45:13 (KJV—'glory'; ESV—'wealth'). In both occurrences, the Hebrew word is *kabod*, as in Exodus 16:7, 10; 24:16, 17, etc. However, in Scripture the word for 'glory' is used in two distinctly different ways. The first, when applied to people, *kabod* can mean 'wealth', 'honour' or even 'boasting'; used of God in the OT, *kabod* refers to the unapproachable presence of all his divine attributes, but in the NT it especially refers to Christ's exaltation in his crucifixion, resurrection and ascension, though invariably as accomplished in the unity of the Trinity. (John 13:31–32; 14:13; 17:1–5, 10, 24.)

3 Note that the fourth commandment is the only non-apodictic one (i.e., the other nine are 'You shall/You shall not', whereas the fourth begins, 'Remember ...' clearly pointing back to Genesis 2:2–3). The Sabbath is therefore a creation ordinance.

4 John Bunyan's term in *The Pilgrim's Progress* for a person's

decisive step to follow the Lord.

5   Billy Graham frequently said, in his sermons, that God has no 'grandchildren' — in other words, we cannot inherit from human parents a living relationship with the Lord; however, that is not to deny the immense privilege of being nurtured in a Christian home.

Chapter 23

1   Horeb has already been mentioned in 3:1. The implication is that Horeb is the particular area where God had first spoken to Moses and therefore, they are now in the vicinity of Sinai which will be their next destination when they leave Rephidim (19:2).

2   Alas, not only children!

3   The Hebrew word, '*rib*', translated, 'quarrel', can denote formal legal proceedings; it shares its root with '*Meribah*' (v. 7) which also means 'quarrelling'.

4   Bruce, R., p. 245.

5   Major C. S. Jarvis CMG, OBE, was an expert both in Arabic and in Bedouin customs who, after serving in the Middle East during the First World War, was made governor of Sinai in 1923 on account of his wide experience of the entire area. Quoted by H.L. Ellison, p. 92.

6   My twin brother, John, who worked for many years in some of the most arid desert areas of Malawi, found that below the ground's surface were hitherto unknown vast reservoirs of fresh, pure water. He had shafts drilled and installed a primitive mechanism, invented by the Chinese, to draw up unlimited quantities of water, which has transformed the lives of whole communities. I spoke with John as I wrote this chapter, and he reckons that the underground reservoirs of water he tapped into are now supplying all the needs of up to three million Malawians (see <aquaid lifeline fund>). In his commentary on Psalm 78:15–16, Calvin cites 'the provision from a rock of abundant water as yet further evidence of God's fatherly love and care for his people. Such a flow of water could only have been miraculously brought by divine power from some deep underground reservoir, and not, as some have cavilled, from a fissure near the surface.' Calvin's *Psalms*, p. 373.

7   A New Testament parallel would be the two occasions when Jesus told Simon and the

disciples to cast the net into the water to catch fish. Luke 5:4–6; John 21:6.

8 See also Hebrews 6:4–8

9 Both Robert Bruce and Calvin have helpful comments on the 'imperfect righteousness' of believers. Bruce, R., pp. 529–532. Also, Calvin writes, 'But even when by the leading of the Holy Spirit we walk in the ways of the Lord, to keep us from forgetting ourselves and becoming puffed up, traces of our *imperfection* remain to give us occasion for humility.' *Inst.* III, XIV, 9.

10 The allusion is to 1 John 3:2–3.

Chapter 24

1 The Amalekites had a long-standing association with this area, later known as Kadesh (Genesis 14:7).

2 Mackay suggests that the well-attested springs of water at Rephidim had been fiercely guarded by Amalekite herdsmen, who were probably already using the rich grazing lands of this area. Hence the earlier complaint (17:1) that there had been no water to drink, p. 302.

3 Hur is only mentioned twice in Exodus—here and in 24:14—where he is both sufficiently senior and trustworthy to act along with Aaron as a judge in Moses' temporary absence.

4 This is the first time Joshua appears in Exodus; we next read of him as Moses' 'assistant' (24:13).

5 F.B. Meyer comments, 'Three old men in prayer. Two supporting the third.' Meyer, p. 105.

6 The Greek verb, *agonizomenos*, literally translated would be 'agonising'.

7 George Duffield (1818–88).

8 Macnicol, pp. 191–192.

9 Notice the word, 'hand', is singular here in Hebrew.

10 I have related that incident elsewhere and been told that the dispensing of discipline in that manner would not be permitted in today's more liberal society. My own reaction to the comment was unspoken, but I knew it would be difficult to find a better run Boy's School where good behaviour was constantly a hallmark of every school day.

11 Quotations are from Dennis Lennon, p. 26. His book is an exploration of 'Images of Prayer' in George Herbert's poetry.

Chapter 25

1 Peter the Hermit (AD c.1050–1115) was an influential, if

controversial, figure during the medieval Crusades. He led an army of paupers across Europe to fight against the Muslims who were occupying the Holy Land. On one critical occasion, his powerful preaching aroused and inspired a demoralised, greatly depleted Crusader army to launch a valiant attack against a vastly superior force and so to win a great victory.

2 *Morality*, see Ch. 3, 'Unsocial Media', pp. 49–61.

3 Calvin's *Comm.*, p. 568.

4 *Commentary*, p. 568.

5 Calvin's *Ephesians*, p. 631.

6 Hendriksen, pp. 261–260.

7 Henotheism (from Greek, *henos theou*, meaning 'of one god') is the worship of a single god while not denying the existence or possible existence of other deities.

8 While I was teaching at the Delhi Bible Institute a few years ago, Isaac Shaw, the college principal, told me that Hindu priests argue persuasively against the common Christian view that Hindu idols can neither hear nor speak. Their point is that, after an idol has been fashioned, either from wood, clay or some valuable metal, the priests then invoke a spirit to make the idol its dwelling-place. The answer to that, of course, is that it is not the lifeless lump of wood or clay that is being worshipped, but an alien spirit which invariably is diametrically opposed to Jesus Christ as the divine Lord of all.

9 "Now I know" indicates a freshly acquired insight into the person and work of the Lord ... "Know" is a key word in the development of the Exodus narrative (10:2; 14:4, 18).' Mackay, p. 313.

10 Of course, we must concede that what both Jethro and Rahab heard was indeed the Word of God, but not the 'full gospel', as we might term it, but rather simply an introduction to it.

11 'And he sent young men of the people of Israel, who offered burnt offerings and sacrificed peace offerings of oxen to the LORD' (Exodus 24:5).

12 Genesis 12:8; 15:9–11; 22:2, 13; 26:25; 31:54; 33:20; 35:14.

13 We must not ignore the duty of priests to intercede for the people under their care (see Exodus 28:29); nevertheless the teaching role of the Old Testament priests has tended to be passed over.

14 The titles 'overseers' and

'elders' are used synonymously in Acts 20:17, 28, and in Titus 1:5, 7. The word, 'overseer' (*episkopos*), denotes the office, while the word, 'elder' (*prebuteros*), denotes the person. Calvin comments: '[T]hese words, *Shepherd, Minister, Bishop, Elder,* are in holy writ taken for all one, that is to say, for them which are called in the Church of God to teach, and to rule his house.' *Sermons on Timothy and Titus* (Edinburgh: Banner of Truth, 1st pub. 1579, reprint 1983), p. 237.

Chapter 26

1 Mackay, p. 322.
2 C.T Studd, p. 141.
3 Mackay, p. 325.
4 The word, *hesed*, is normally translated in ESV as 'steadfast love'; as 'lovingkindness' in KJV; but variously as 'love', 'great love', or 'unfailing love' in NIV. It occurs scores of times in the OT, e.g., Psalms 17:7, 26:3, 36:7, 40:10, *et al.* LXX (the Septuagint—the translation of the Hebrew OT into Greek, done in Egypt about 200 BC by seventy Jewish Scholars) translates it as *eleos*, 'mercy'; in the NT, *eleos* is also translated as 'mercy' or 'pity', e.g., Matthew 9:13; Titus 3:5, *et al.*
5 'The LORD set his love upon you ... because the LORD loves you.' His loving compassion, in other words, defies human logic!
6 Quoted from the 3rd verse of the hymn 'Rock of Ages cleft for me' by Augustus Montague Toplady (1740–78).
7 See, e.g., Deuteronomy 6:13–15; 7:12; 11:13–17, 26–28.
8 'Israel is to have the special privilege of priests, to be allowed to "draw near" God, and is to do "service" for all the world; this is the purpose for which Israel has been chosen.' Noth p. 157.
9 Rahab bore significant witness to the two spies of the way in which God's mighty acts had shown the surrounding nations that 'the LORD your God, he is God in the heavens above and on the earth beneath' (Joshua 2:11).

Chapter 27

1 Deuteronomy 31:27; 17:2; 32:51; 32:4; Romans 11:20; Leviticus 26:19; Deuteronomy 1:39; Psalm 36:3.
2 No doubt, Oliver Wendell Holmes (1809–94) had this passage in mind when he wrote, 'All, save the clouds of sin, are thine,' as the fourth line of verse 3 in his once

well-known hymn, 'Lord of all being, throned afar' (Mission Praise 439).

3 AKJV translates it as, 'Let us therefore come boldly ...'. The Greek word *parresia* is used many times in the NT and is often translated as 'openly' as in John 7:4, 13, 26, where it could equally as well have been rendered as 'boldly'.

4 From Frederick William Faber's hymn, 'My God, how wonderful thou art' (1814–1863).

5 Exodus 3:11, 13; 4:1, 10.

6 From the hymn by Henry Twells (1823–1900; written 1868), 'At even, ere the sun was set'.

Chapter 28

1 Searle, *And Then There Were Nine*.

2 Romans 7:7–12; 13:8–10; Ephesians 6:2.

3 Exodus 31:18; Deuteronomy 9:10; Calvin's *Comm*, p.995.

4 Exodus 19:19; 20:1a, 18–26.

5 Exodus 25:17–22: ESV translates as 'mercy seat', NIV as 'atonement'.

6 Exodus 32:15–16. After the original tablets of stone, fashioned by God's hands, were broken, Moses was commanded to prepare two similar tablets for the Ten Commandments to be written on them by God for the second time (Exodus 34:1).

7 The Greek word used in Romans 10:4 and translated as 'end' is *telos*, meaning both 'termination' and 'the end to which things relate, the aim, purpose' (Grimm-Thayer).

8 Also see Hebrews 10:5–14. It is sad to hear some professing Christian teachers bringing the rash and absurd charge against the Father of 'spiritual child abuse' in subjecting his Son to such suffering on Calvary. How very grievously mistaken they are! In the verse I have just cited, Hebrews 9:14, we see the incomprehensible mystery of the holy Trinity acting in perfect, costly harmony for the salvation of 'the many' for whom Christ gave his life as a ransom (Mark 10:45).

9 An excellent exposition of Matthew 5:19 is to be found in Lloyd-Jones, *Studies*, Vol. 1, Chapter 18.

10 John Ball (1585–1640) was an English Puritan divine, born in Cassington, Oxfordshire. After taking his BA degree from St Mary's Hall, Oxford, in 1608, he went into Cheshire to act as tutor to the children of Lady Cholmondeley. See also the

Westminster Confession of Faith, Chapter 19, Paragraphs 2–7.

11 Compare also Deuteronomy 30:11–14.

12 George Wade Robinson, 'Loved with everlasting love', (1838–1877), verse 2, *Mission Praise* 452.

13 In Chapter 16 on 'The Passover', under the sub-heading, 'What do you mean by this service' (12:26), we looked briefly at the meaning of the Hebrew verb, *'abad*– 'to serve' or 'to worship' (see Note 21 below); here we are considering the same theme of 'serve/worship' but in the context of the second commandment.

14 Hebrew, *'abad*, means to work, labour, toil, serve, be in bond-service, be a bondman, be under compulsion.

15 'Obeisance' means offering 'homage'.

16 E.g., Romans 1:1 and Philippians 1:1, where the noun is *doulos*, meaning a bond-slave, or simply a slave.

17 The adjective translated, 'spiritual', is the Greek word, *logikos*, meaning, rational or logical. Thus, the force of what Paul is saying is that these 'mercies of God' ('I appeal to you, therefore, brothers, *by the mercies of God* ...') which he has expounded so fully in the first nine chapters of the letter must logically put every believer under the inescapable obligation of total surrender to the ineffable bounties of love and grace poured out upon them in the gospel.

18 In order, by Isaac Watts, Horatius Bonar, Augustus Montague Toplady and Charles Wesley.

19 *Inst.* II.7.6.

20 In these quotations from Calvin, 'law', means the 'Commandments'.

21 *Inst.* II.7.10.

22 *Inst.* II.7.12.

23 This view is held by certain notable evangelical leaders in our generation. I have heard it said during major evangelical conference addresses that it is fine to leave the church service to go straight to the local supermarket to do the week's shopping. Also, when I was conducting a seminar for pastors on preaching, at a well-known evangelical conference, I was criticized very harshly for asserting that we should 'keep Sunday special': 'You're a legalist,' said a member of the group very harshly with the support of virtually all those taking part.

Chapter 29

1 Calvin's *Comm*, pp. 994–995.
2 Author unknown.
3 1,700 shekels would have weighed nearly 19 kilos, or nearly 3 stones. It was a huge amount of gold. Probably the weight of gold that Aaron received was considerably more than this.
4 For example, Jeremiah 18:13–17.
5 See Psalm 106:20. 'They exchanged the glory of God for the image of an ox that eats grass.'
6 Meyer, p. 187.
7 Mackay, pp. 529–531.
8 Exodus 34:28, where we read of 'the Ten Commandments' (see ESV marginal note: In Hebrew they can be translated as, *the ten words*).
9 Calvin's translation is 'had run naked'; he goes on to say, '... the cause is set forth, whereby he was inflamed so such severity, viz., he saw the people in such a state of nakedness ...' Calvin, *Comm.*, p. 1005.
10 Note the NIV rendering of Genesis 39:14, 17, where the same word is translated as 'make sport of us', followed immediately by, 'He came in to me to lie with me ...'; also see

1 Corinthians 10:7–8, '"The people sat down to eat and drink and rose up to play." We must not indulge in sexual immorality as some of them did ... .'
11 Lewis, C. S., p. 30.
12 Sermon on Hebrews 11:33–37 in: Bruce, R., *Preaching without Fear or Favour*, p. 539.
13 Language which describes in human terms the words and actions of God as if he was a man.
14 Childs, B. S., *Exodus*, p. 567. Quoted by Mackay, p. 534.
15 Calvin, *Comm.* p. 1000.
16 Verse 32: 'But now, if you will forgive their sin — but if not, please blot me out of your book that you have written.'
17 From John Wesley's translation of Gerhardt Tersteengen's hymn, 'Thou hidden love of God, whose height.' (*Christian Hymns* 639).
18 During a lecture in Crieff, Scotland, on the Prologue to John's Gospel, Dr Don A. Carson helpfully suggested that this 'tent' was a temporary makeshift structure used by Moses for prayer before the Tent of Meeting was constructed. (Any reader interested to know more of what he would say about John 1:14–18 should consult *The Gospel According to John (Pillar New Testament Commentary)*,

(Leicester: Apollos, 1991), pp. 126–139.

19 We are reminded of the capture of the ark of the covenant by the Philistines and the name, Ichabod, given by the wife of Phineas to her newborn son. (See 1 Samuel 4, esp. vv. 21–22.)

20 Meyer, p. 128.

Chapter 30

1 1 Samuel 3:3. Commentators suggest there had been repairs and an additional wooden structure added to the tent of meeting, which is why it is called 'the temple of the LORD'. E.g., see Joyce Baldwin, *1 and 2 Samuel*, p. 70.

2 See John L Mackay, *Exodus*, p. 551.

3 NIV has 'distressing words'.

4 We must surmise that the place of worship in Shiloh was available no longer, for when David at length brought the ark of the covenant back to Israel, it was taken to Jerusalem, and not returned to Shiloh (2 Samuel 6:12–15).

5 ESV has, 'Please', but NIV has, 'Now'.

6 John L Mackay, *Exodus*, p. 557.

7 In 1 Kings 19:9, we read that Elijah came to a cave on Mount Horeb. Because in the LXX the definite article is used — '*the* cave' (the Hebrew uses no article) — I have often wondered if the Jewish translators thought this was the self-same cave in which Moses glimpsed the divine glory as God passed by.

8 The expression, 'hand of God', is often used in Scripture but must be understood metaphorically, for God is not corporeal but is Spirit (John 4:24).

9 The Hebrew word, '*shekinah*', does not actually occur in the OT but was introduced by Jewish Rabbis to describe the divine presence settling upon a designated meeting place; it means, 'caused to dwell'.

10 Of course, it is only by faith that the divine glory is seen in Jesus Christ for, during his brief thirty-three years on earth, his Godhead was veiled by his human flesh (Philippians 2:6–11). It is a divine mystery that the fulness of both Father and Son was revealed on Calvary (John 17:1, 5), a mystery indeed 'into which angels long to look' (1 Peter 1:12c).

11 The AKJV has 'peculiar people', but the ESV tends to translate this phrase as a people for God's own 'treasured possession' (Exodus 19:5;

Deuteronomy 14:2). Titus 2:14 has, 'a people for his own possession.'

12 George Herbert, *Prayer* (I) p. 22.

Chapter 31

1 If you question a knowledgeable Roman Catholic as to why their Church regards communion as the re-enactment of Christ's sacrifice for sin, when Scripture plainly states that Christ does not 'offer himself repeatedly... having appeared once for all at the end of the ages to put away sin by the sacrifice of himself' (Hebrews 9:25-26), they will answer that when John was given the vision of the throne of God in heaven, there was 'a Lamb standing as though it had been slain' (Revelation 5:6). Therefore, they will argue that the 'once for all' sacrifice of Christ is an eternal sacrifice, ongoing existentially and temporally. We in the reformed churches have to agree to differ.

2 See comments on 'worship' in Chapter 28, p. XX under the heading 'Serving God alone'.

3 Pomegranates are one of the seven species of fruits enumerated, in Deuteronomy 8:8–9, as special products of the Land of Israel: '... a land of wheat and barley, of vines and fig-trees and pomegranates, a land of olive trees and honey, a land in which you will eat bread without scarcity, in which you will lack nothing ...'. Some Jewish scholars understand them as symbolic of the Land of Promise, and that could well be their significance here. Other Jewish writers go as far as to opine that it was a pomegranate that was the forbidden fruit in the Garden of Eden and, though such a conjecture is extremely unlikely, it indicates the spiritual significance given to this fruit by some of the Jews.

4 An example of this kind of attendant can be found in Luke 4:17 where, when we read, 'And the scroll of the prophet of Isaiah was given to him', it is implied there was an attendant in the synagogue whose task was to select and bring to the rabbi, who would be 'preaching', the appropriate OT text for that day.

5 *Bruce* once made this comment in a sermon: 'The Lord can swiftly prepare an instrument for his use even if the man is a blockhead!' Bruce, R., p. 341.

6 This 'being set apart from others' may be implied by

James when he wrote, 'Not many of you should become teachers, my brothers, for you know that we who teach will be judged with greater strictness' (James 3:1).

7 See Exodus 28:21, 'There shall be twelve stones with their names according to the names of the sons of Israel': Reuben, Simeon, Judah, Dan, Naphtali, Gad, Asher, Issachar, Zebulun, Benjamin, Ephraim, Manasseh; notice that neither Levi nor Joseph were included, as the tribe of Levi were the priests offering the prayers on behalf of the nation, and Joseph's place was taken by his sons Ephraim and Manasseh. This list I have given can be identified from Numbers 2, where the arrangements for the positions of the twelve tribes around the central Tent of Meeting is set out in great detail.

8 Isaiah 64:6: 'We are all as an unclean thing, and all our righteousnesses are as filthy rags' (KJV); 'We have all become like one who is unclean, and all our righteous deeds are like a polluted garment' (literally, 'menstrual cloths'), (ESV).

9 'We sing the praise of him who died', by Thomas Kelly (1769–1855). *Mission Praise* 738.

10 I am disturbed that many followers of Christ today treat the Lord's Day the same as any other day. One day each week that is set apart as the Lord's Sabbath is a creation ordinance. It is the only one of the ten commandments that is not assertoric as are the other nine; that is, they are direct assertions, 'You shall not', or 'You shall'. By contrast the fourth command begins 'Remember ...' for it is directing the minds of God's people back to the seventh day which God blessed and sanctified: 'So God blessed the seventh day and made it holy' (Genesis 2:3).

11 Apologies that I have not a reference for this allusion to McCheyne (it's bound to be in his *Memoirs*), but I can vouch for its authenticity and know it is commonly quoted in his native Scotland.

Appendix 1

1 'Ordo salutis' (Latin) means, 'The order of salvation'. It is a technical term theologians use regarding reformed biblical doctrine to show the consecutive steps of the Holy Spirit's work in believers in their appropriation of salvation.

2 My personal two volume

edition is now out of print, but a one volume edition is easily obtainable on Amazon.uk.

3 *Guide to the Gospels* is also easily available from Amazon.uk.

4 Edinburgh: Banner of Truth, 2012.

5 The parentheses in the eight following headings indicate the NT reality and fulfilment foreshadowed in the OT.

6 The words, 'slaves' and 'service' ('bondage' AKJV), come from the same Hebrew root.

7 English translations tend to use the term, 'the ruler of this world': John 12:31; 14:30; 16:11. However, Ephesians 2:2, (ESV) has 'the prince of the power of the air, the spirit that is now at work in the sons of disobedience.'

8 The Greek preposition Paul uses both here (and in the refs cited in Note 9 below) is not the simple 'εν (in) but 'εις (into).

9 Romans 6:3; 1 Corinthians 12:13, 27.

10 Exodus 31:18. We must bear in mind that only the Ten Commandments were revealed directly by God himself, while the rest of the Levitical cultus was revealed through Moses as mediator.

11 Calvin's treatment of the Decalogue is to set each Commandment in the wider context of the whole 'Levitical cultus'.

12 Luther's *Galatians*, pp 333–334.

13 Stott, *Galatians*, pp. 97–98.

14 The words, 'confession' and 'confess', are used in two different senses or meanings in Scripture. The first use is to confess faith in God and/or in Christ as the Son of God who is Lord of all. The second sense is to confess sin. It is the first meaning that is the subject here. The words, 'testify' or 'witness', generally have a different focus to the word, 'confess': the former tend to mean bearing witness before the world, whereas the latter tends to mean acknowledging before God his (and Christ's) Lordship and authority over us as our Redeemer and Saviour.

15 Martin, *A Hymn of Christ*. Philippians 2:5–11, long cherished and mined for its riches, has shaped the very language and architecture of orthodox Christian confession of Christ. Yet few scriptural texts have generated as much interpretive comment and further study.

16 John 1:6–8, 15, 19–20, 29–31, 32–34, 35–36; 3:27–30.

17 A derivative verb from *homologeo* (confess) is

exhomologeo; it can mean to acknowledge or confess 'freely from the heart, openly or joyfully' (Grimm-Thayer) but, out of its eleven occurrences in the NT, it is only used three times with the meaning 'confess'; mostly it is translated as 'thanks' or 'praise' towards God.

18 Someone might wonder why, in this fairly comprehensive 'ordo salutis', there is no apparent mention of either the judgement of the unrighteous or the reward of the redeemed. However, both of these doctrines are clearly implied in the song Miriam sang, which are dealt with in Chapter 20 of this book (Exodus 15:1–21), under 'To think about and discuss', Questions 2 and 3, p. 361

Appendix 2

1 Numbers 3:38. Helpful discussions of the tribes' placements round the Tabernacle can be found in Wenham, pp. 66–68, 70–71; also in Philip, pp. 38–44, 51–52.

2 Henry Francis Lyte (1793–1847).

3 I am using the word, 'controversial', because Roman Catholic priests pronounce absolution after penance has been done. But that is not what Scripture teaches. The Roman church traditionally has too often replaced biblical repentance with the so-called sacrament of penance.

4 Quotation is from the prayer of absolution in the Anglican *Book of Common Prayer*. http://www.commonprayer.org/offices/absol.cfm

5 For the incense see 30:22–38.

6 Torrance, quoted by Morris, p. 121.

7 Compare with Hebrews 9:7.